Invisible Agents

NEW AFRICAN HISTORIES SERIES

Series editors: Jean Allman and Allen Isaacman

*Books in this series are published with support from
the Ohio University National Resource Center for African Studies.*

Invisible Agents

Spirits in a Central African History

⌐⌐

David M. Gordon

OHIO UNIVERSITY PRESS ⌐ ATHENS

Ohio University Press, Athens, Ohio 45701
ohioswallow.com
© 2012 by Ohio University Press
All rights reserved.

To obtain permission to quote, reprint, or otherwise reproduce or distribute material
from Ohio University Press publications, please contact our rights and permissions
department at (740) 593-1154 or (740) 593-4536 (fax).

20 19 18 17 16 15 14 13 12   5 4 3 2 1

Library of Congress Cataloging-in-Publication Data

Gordon, David M., 1970–
  Invisible agents : spirits in a Central African history / David M. Gordon.
    p. cm. — (New African histories)
  Includes bibliographical references and index.
  ISBN 978-0-8214-2024-9 (pb : alk. paper) — ISBN 978-0-8214-4439-9 (electronic)
  1. Zambia—History—Religious aspects. 2. Zambia—History—Autonomy and
independence movements—Religious aspects. 3. Christianity and culture—
Zambia—History. 4. Religion and politics—Zambia—History. 5. Zambia—Politics
and government—To 1964. 6. Zambia Politics and government—1964–1991.
7. United National Independence Party (Zambia)—History. 8. Lumpa Church—
History. 9. Bemba (African people)—Religion. I. Title. II. Series: New African
histories series.
  BR1446.6.G67 2012
  968.94—dc23

                                                                    2012027989

Contents

Illustrations

Acknowledgments

This book has been supported, sustained, and inspired by many communities. Zambians answered my questions with patience and care. Kampamba Mulenga was a wonderful companion in our journeys across Zambia's Northern Province. I have fond memories of weeks spent with the members of Chinsali's New Jerusalem community who introduced me to the power of their faith. A community of Africanist scholars pushed me to refine many of my ideas. Allen Roberts, Dan Magaziner, Kairn Klieman, Paul S. Landau, Stephen Ellis, Clifton Crais, Tom Spear, Anne Mager, James A. Pritchett, Karen Tranberg Hansen, Parker Shipton, Nancy Jacobs, Megan Vaughan, and Heather Sharkey helped with their insightful discussions and questions following many conference presentations. A community of Zambian scholars, associated with the Network for Historical Research in Zambia, hosted Zambia-focused symposia, which allowed me to fine-tune the details of the book. Marja Hinfelaar, Giacomo Macola, Walima T. Kalusa, Chris Annear, Miles Larmer, Mwelwa C. Musambachime, Jan-Bart Gewald, Bizeck J. Phiri, and several others have all contributed to an invigorated Zambian historiography. Marja Hinfelaar deserves special mention for her work in making available new archival resources that provide the empirical depth to sustain my ambitious arguments. The New African History series editors, Allen Isaacman and Jean Allman, and Ohio University Press's Gillian Berchowitz had confidence in the book, and offered suggestions for improvement.

Bowdoin College provided an unmatched intellectual community. Students, especially in my seminar on Religion and Politics in Africa, inspired me with their enthusiasm and sophisticated thinking about issues unfamiliar to many of them. Discussions with colleagues, over lunch and during faculty forums, helped in conceptualization, writing, and revision. Allen Wells, Rachel Sturman, John Holt, and Elizabeth Pritchard read and provided insightful comments on parts of the book. The interlibrary loan staff, especially Guy Saldanha, persevered in tracking publications obscure to them but essential for my research. Eileen Johnson drew the map. The generous research support and sabbatical leave provided by Bowdoin College contributed to the timely completion of the book.

Academic nourishment alone does not sustain a good book. Arguments about politics and religion with my family, especially my siblings, are frequent; this is yet another stab at a discussion that will always be part of our lively dinner-table conversations. My mother and stepfather are not only supportive but interested in the details of my research. My brother Ryan helped to refine the images. In the ten years that I have been researching and writing this book, my love for my wife, Lesley, has inspired all of my most valuable accomplishments. Love does shape life. While I was nearing the book's completion, my father died. My grief, and my knowledge that he lives on in so many ways, further convinced me of the power of our emotions, our hidden spirits, and our invisible worlds.

Abbreviations

AMU	African Mineworkers Union
ANC	African National Congress
ARC	African Representative Council
BSAC	British South Africa Company
CAF	Central African Federation
CCZ	Council of Churches in Zambia
CfAN	Christ for All Nations
DC	district commissioner
DRC	Democratic Republic of Congo
EFZ	Evangelical Fellowship of Zambia
ICOZ	Independent Church Organization of Zambia
MMD	Movement for Multiparty Democracy
MUZ	Mineworkers Union of Zambia
NRR	Northern Rhodesia Regiment
PC	provincial commissioner
RLI	Rhodes-Livingstone Institute
UCCAR	United Church of Central Africa in Rhodesia
UCZ	United Church of Zambia
UMCB	United Missions of the Copperbelt
UNIP	United National Independence Party
UPP	United Progressive Party
ZANC	Zambia African National Congress
ZCTU	Zambia Congress of Trade Unions
ZEC	Zambia Episcopal Conference

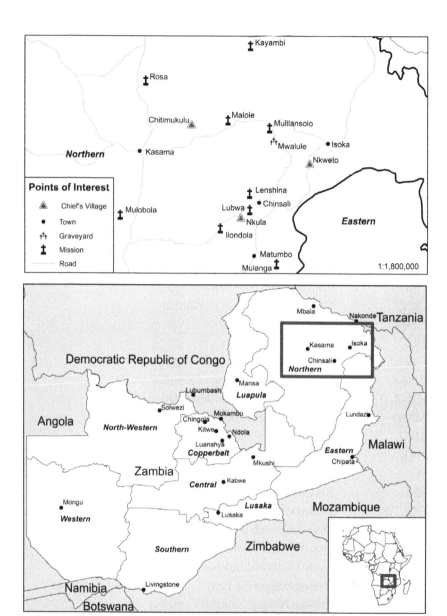

Zambia and Selected Points of Interest. Map drawn by Eileen Johnson.

Seeing Invisible Worlds

INVISIBLE FORCES MOBILIZE US to action. Sometimes they are remote and absolute, such as "freedom" and "fate"; or they are proximate and changing human creations, such as the "state" and its "laws"; or they combine proximity with the personal, as in the emotions of "love" and "hate." Invisible forces are sometimes imagined to be spirits that possess bodies, incarnate the dead, and guide the actions of the living. Yet not all agents of the invisible world are compatible. While we accept the influence of our own invisible worlds, those of others appear implausible forces for change in the visible world. We thus may seek to change, repress, or simply ignore the invisible worlds of others. This book considers various moments of social and political upheaval influenced by conflicting beliefs in invisible agents, including a precolonial ancestral government that claimed to control the spirits responsible for fertility, a prophet's efforts to cleanse the colonial order of witchcraft and evil, and the overthrow of a postcolonial socialist regime thought to be influenced by Satan.

A recent survey, a form of knowledge preferred by secular society, indicates that nearly nine out of ten sub-Saharan Africans consider "religion" to be very important in their lives. But what is meant by "religion"? And in what sense is this set of beliefs and practices termed religion "important"? In this survey, religion and its measure of importance are the spirits that flourish in Africa. For example, the survey indicates that roughly half of the 470 million Christians in sub-Saharan Africa (Christians, we are told, make up 57 percent of the total population) believe that Jesus will return to the visible world within their lifetimes. Slightly more African Christians claim that God will grant prosperity to those with faith.[1] But these beliefs are not part of a removed and detached

1

otherworldliness that many secularists associate with "religion." Even if implausible to some, the spirits of the invisible world—including ancestors, nature spirits, God, the Holy Spirit, Jesus, and Satan—hold implications for realms of human agency. Rather than a history of institutionalized religion, this book is a history of the spirits believed to have influenced this world.

Religious and secular authorities often claim that beliefs in spirits are "superstitions," false beliefs. Spirits have been marginalized by a post-Enlightenment Christianity that guides human actions in this world by focusing attention on the symbolic meanings of religion and on its moral implications. Spirits are distant, appearing only in an afterlife, in heaven and hell, instead of having a direct influence over happenings in the material world and the health and wealth of living beings. Clearly, this is not the position of all Christian believers in the West—now or in the past. Yet this nonspiritual type of religion is found among the mainstream Protestant and Catholic clergy and lay leadership, and has influenced scholarship. Drawing on such post-Enlightenment theological and scholarly abstractions, much scholarship focuses on the distinctions between the otherworldly qualities of sacred spirits and the this-worldly qualities of profane agents.[2] Instead, the history of the entwined visible and invisible worlds that I propose here locates its arguments around the conceptions and sensory perceptions of historical agents who have thought that invisible spirits have exerted power in this world.

Africanist scholarship characterizes such belief in invisible spirits as part of an "African traditional religion" that continues to influence modern life. For philosopher Kwame Anthony Appiah, "most Africans, whether converted to Islam or Christianity or not, *still* share the beliefs of their ancestors in an ontology of invisible beings" (my emphasis).[3] Such accounts draw on a long tradition of anthropological scholarship that describes ancestors as "shades" with a presence in the physical world.[4] Theologians, historians, and other scholars of religion have joined in describing these ancestral religions as such.[5] There is much of value in these accounts. For many people, ancestral and nature spirits have wielded power in this world. And yet the notion of African traditional religion implies a primordial set of beliefs that are static, closed to outside influences, and unengaged with historical changes. If they still exist in modern life, it is because Africans hold on to such beliefs with remarkable tenacity, or so it is argued. However, modernity, in Africa and elsewhere, is neither what it seems nor what it promotes itself to be. Religion is not the past of modernity, but integral to its present logic, the regulation of its rationality, and its modality of power.[6] In this vein, recent scholarship on the African spirit world has shown that it is entwined with modernity rather than being only a residual traditional religion. Stephen Ellis and Gerrie ter Haar identify an invisible world that permeates postcolonial politics across much of Africa;

anthropologists have found "witchcraft" and "magic" to be part of the quotidian experience of modernity.[7] And even at the Western European heart of the supposed secular revolution, the triumph of secularism now appears to have been a mirage, the Enlightenment's publicity stunt.[8]

Invisible Agents develops this line of inquiry. The invisible world discussed here is not a remnant of tradition, but an outcome of and engagement with a particular experience of modernity. My point is not to present Africans steeped in irrational, exotic, or traditional beliefs, but to describe how these rich products of the human imagination inform identities and actions; in other words, to offer an account of historical agency in a world populated with spirits.

THE HISTORIOGRAPHY OF AN INVISIBLE WORLD

Implausible African beliefs have constituted one of the oldest—even foundational—problems for secular Africanist scholars. Nearly four decades ago, Terence O. Ranger published an article that considered connections between millenarian religion and anticolonial nationalism.[9] This approach inspired an effervescence of historical scholarship. Historians found a rich source base in the writings of paranoid colonial administrators who referred incessantly to such connections. Movements that combined ancestral and Christian beliefs in millenarian efforts to rid the visible world of invisible forms of evil were thought pregnant with possibilities for nationalist movements in terms of their forms of organization and their anticolonial ideologies.[10] Ancestral religious ideas, such as rainmaking, could also serve the anticolonial struggle.[11] The recognition that spirits inspired anticolonial agency was a helpful and productive insight, albeit an incomplete and a very particular aspect of spiritual agency. In the emphasis on *connections* between modern politics and primary acts of rebellion, the spiritual beliefs of those who constituted these movements were subordinated to the formal—meaning African nationalist and anticolonial—political role that these movements played. If agency was primarily political and nationalist, spiritual beliefs were but an accident, a colorful detail of human agency.

Scholars have subsequently questioned the supposed evolution of forms of resistance, complicated arguments that religion was simply a cultural component of nationalist struggle, reconsidered the ties between religious organization and civil society, and taken the autonomous claims of faith more seriously. Ranger himself revised his original position in several regards. In a critical survey of the literature, he finds the notion that religious movements constitute "a stage in the evolution of anti-colonial protest" excessively teleological and often inaccurate. Such an approach invariably treats religion as a sort of false consciousness, awaiting an accurate historical consciousness in the form of working-class or nationalist ideas. The explicitly spiritual nature of these movements is ignored by focusing on anticolonial politics.[12] In a more recent literature survey, however, Ranger still seems uneasy with a focus on spirits, especially occult forces, which, he thinks, presents Africans as steeped in strange superstitions.[13]

That spirits are thought to hold power should point to the political importance of religious ideas, not suggest that they are false superstitions. Political scientist Michael Schatzberg has demonstrated the rich analyses that may follow from extending the "parameters of the political," especially to spirits that are thought to exert power in this world.[14] Not only do religious movements appear political in new ways, but conventional political movements engage in often unrecognized forms of spiritual politics.[15] Yet much scholarship on religious movements remains embedded in a secular view of politics. For example, there have been many fruitful inquiries into the public role of Christianity, exploring whether churches are autonomous and promote opposition to the state or are captured by the state and become instruments of patronage politics.[16] Other recent Africanist scholarship focuses on elements of civil society, for example the engagement of women with Christianity.[17] Human agency is still viewed in terms of secular political claims and identities, however. The spiritual component of religion is not what is important; even if religious movements constitute civil society, spiritual beliefs remain a form of false consciousness, sometimes explicitly critiqued, sometimes ignored as irrelevant detail.

A linguistic turn in humanities and social science has helped to point out that the fields of meaning designated by "religion" and "politics" differ across time, societies, and languages. Imposing such labels often reflects interpretative translations of unfamiliar realms of human agency. Scholars sensitive to this problem have shunned "religion" to characterize certain African beliefs and practices. Instead, they often focus on how European missionaries rendered Christian concepts in vernacular linguistic worlds and thereby transformed both Christianity and the meanings of old words, often changing this-worldly political concepts into otherworldly religious concepts.[18] Understanding the transformative power of translation is an important and worthy endeavor. Yet translation itself is not the only key to understanding the implications of spirits for historical agency. In her study of the Lourdes shrine, Ruth Harris expresses unease with the "totalistic way the 'linguistic turn' reduces all human experience to language."[19] Discourses are not closed and contained systems; they engage with sensory, visible, and nonlinguistic worlds that involve work, corporality, violence, and emotions—in other words, those actions, experiences, and interactions that constitute our sensory lives. To understand the agency of spirits, then, is to relate spirits—or spiritual discourses—to this nonlinguistic world.

One way to relate spirits to the nonlinguistic world is to view them as symbols for the sensory, visible world. Indeed, the symbolic form of analysis is a conventional way of reflecting on *religious* discourses. On the other hand, *political* discourses are not usually viewed in this symbolic fashion. But, as pointed out, there is no intrinsic reason for treating discourses that we term religious and political differently. Religious ideas, especially when they refer to this-worldly spirits, are also conscious statements on and about power, rather than subconscious or metaphoric reflections.[20] The bias toward the symbolic study of religion is not evident in all scholarship. Given the clear role of missionary Christian discourses in creating colonial hegemonies, many scholars have discussed them as sources of power. For example, Jean and John L. Comaroff, J. D. Y. Peel, Elizabeth Elbourne, and Paul S. Landau all discuss the influence and African appropriations of colonial Christian missionary discourses, although they generally conceive of power in a Foucauldian disciplinary sense.[21] Efforts to discuss spirits, Christian or otherwise, as sources of power have not been as frequently or as effectively carried out, with a few noteworthy exceptions. Ruth Marshall's study of Pentecostal churches in Nigeria, for example, treats spiritual discourse as a "site of *action* [her emphasis]" rather than being reduced to "its function of signification," in terms of metaphor, metonymy, or symbol.[22]

Most relevant to this book is Karen E. Fields's treatment of religious discourses as sites of power in her pioneering study of Watchtower (Jehovah's Witnesses) during the heyday of indirect rule in colonial Zambia. Fields argues that the colonial state, although purporting to be secular, relied on a range of religious agents, including missionaries and chiefs who claimed spiritual powers. The Watchtower emphasis on a personal relationship with God, through rituals such as speaking in tongues, radically undermined this colonial constellation of power. Political rebellion thus emerged directly from the spiritual claims of Watchtower adherents. By ensuring an independent form of spirit possession and communication, Watchtower members undercut the authority of chiefs and missionaries. While Fields may have proclaimed the end of the chiefs' authority a little too soon—and overestimated Watchtower agency in ending it—her broader point stands; religion was politics. Political struggle invoked spiritual powers that defied and defined authority. Human agency to transform the world emerged directly from these spiritual beliefs. In this sense, spirits were not symbols or stand-ins for political struggles around "real" resources.[23]

Two recent studies of cannibalism and vampirism further illustrate the argument. In the first of these studies, Luise White develops metaphoric and symbolic associations between vampire rumors and the colonial "extractive" economy (even while she suggests that such rumors should not be viewed as "false"). White claims that "vampire accusations were specifically African ways of talking that identified new forms of violence and extraction."[24] She links vampire rumors to a variety of colonial relations, including labor relations, missionary rivalries, anticolonial nationalism, and intrusive medical interventions. The strength of this approach is in its ability to relate belief to historical context; its shortcoming is that the scholarly interpretation of metaphors and symbols may differ from that of historical actors.[25] The relationship of vampires with the extractive colonial economy is an effective and engaging metaphor, but one developed by White, and not by the workers of the Copperbelt. Instead, for the inhabitants of Copperbelt towns, vampire rumors linked the spirit world to the physical world directly. On the central African Copperbelt, people acted on the knowledge that they were empowered or oppressed by invisible forces.

Stephen Ellis, in his *Mask of Anarchy*, also has an account of cannibals, but his cannibals are very real, literally those who eat others to gain power. In Liberia, there were rumors of cannibals similar to those found in central Africa. But for Ellis, the act of eating to gain power was more significant than any imputed metaphoric quality. Belief in cannibals, most importantly the belief that eating people gave rise to forms of power, was not a metaphor for social or political relations, although it probably was a conscious form of metaphor and metonymy employed to acquire power (I really eat people, and thus I "eat" people and exercise power over them).[26] It was not a description of forms of exploitation as if they were like cannibalism, but instead, according to Ellis, people ritually ingested human body parts to gain power over others.[27] The difference in these accounts rests on the emphasis by Ellis on the belief in these practices to acquire power on the one hand, and the emphasis by White on the metaphoric qualities of spiritual beliefs on the other.

If spirits are not metaphors or symbols, however, other ways to explore the relationship between the visible and the invisible worlds, of spirits to the non-linguistic world of senses and experiences, need to be established. For if spiritual beliefs are only discourse, autonomous from an outside reality, they lose their historical relevance beyond the history of a fanciful and disconnected imagination. A critic of Ellis, for example, could claim that cannibalism was no more than a marginal detail of Liberian belief, hardly central to the unfolding of war and politics in Liberia.[28] The actions of bodies and the quotidian interactions between peoples and with their environments become unimportant to the study of belief—or "belief" becomes reified and ahistorical. If spirits are not symbols, historians need to at least find ways of speaking, if not theorizing, about the relationship of spirits to human interactions and environments.

Guidance may be sought in the century-old discussions about the relationship between society and belief among sociologists of religion that cycle through the socioeconomic determinism of Marx's opium of the people, the ethnocentrism of Weber's Protestant ethic, and the functionalism of Durkheim's religion as "social fact." Each approach holds insight and problems, which cannot be revisited here. Durkheim's formulation is the most insistent on the social importance of religion, and yet theoretically cautionary and qualified enough for empirical historians. For Durkheim, the context of religion is central: "If we want to understand that aptitude for living outside the real, which is seemingly so remarkable, all we need to do is relate it to the social conditions upon which it rests." But he also insists that this view is not a "refurbishment of historical materialism":

> Collective consciousness is something other than a mere epiphenomenon of its morphological [social] base. . . . If collective consciousness is to appear, a *sui generis* synthesis of individual consciousness must occur. The product of this synthesis is a whole world of feelings, ideas, and images that follow their own laws once they are born. They mutually attract one another, repel one another, fuse together, subdivide, and proliferate; and none of these combinations is directly commanded and necessitated by the state of the underlying reality. Indeed, the life thus unleashed enjoys such great independence that it sometimes plays about in forms that have no aim or utility of any kind, but only for the pleasure of affirming itself.[29]

For Durkheim, while the forms of belief engage with social functions, they do not simply replicate, represent, or symbolize them. In a similar fashion, historians can recognize that spirits morph to occupy historical landscapes, but are not determined by those landscapes. These spirits, as Luise White emphasizes, are a human dialogue about nonlinguistic worlds. However, even while they can engage with this world, they do not necessarily represent or symbolize it, and sometimes animate the imagination of people in unexpected ways. Spirits can thus mobilize bodies, summon feelings, and transform lives, not unlike charged and fraught discourses about "race," in, say, US society.[30] Their imagined forms (gods, ancestral shades, nature spirits) and qualities (good, evil, indifferent, jealous, or angry) affect how people conceive of and transform their respective realities.

An insistence on the relevance of a this-worldly context for spiritual beliefs thus need not and should not overemphasize social function. The tendency to render the functional aspect of belief is often attributed to British anthropology in the 1930s and 1940s, especially to Branislaw Malinowski, Edward E. Evans-Pritchard, Meyer Fortes, and their students, who sought to demonstrate the rationality of beliefs.[31] The argument against a reductive functionalism seems to be a straw man: even in the 1940s, contemporaries such as Godfrey Wilson critiqued the tendency to dissolve "symbols into a mere reflection of the social structure."[32] Scholarship still explores the social functions of spirits, especially the interconnected "healing" of the body and the body politic. In one example from an excellent book, Neil Kodesh, drawing on much recent scholarship, argues that the idiom of healing was key to the history of political complexity in Buganda.[33] And yet "healing" focuses on consensus-building rather than conflict, revealing only one aspect of the multiple public and private uses and conflicts that mobilized spiritual discourses. As in the insistence of the rationality of African beliefs by the early functionalist anthropologists, this neo-functionalist scholarship is yet another interpretative strategy employed by secularists to render spirits into an explanatory framework with which they are at ease.

A post-Enlightenment discourse that treats spirits as distant, prayer as an ineffective intervention, and miracles and curses as false makes it difficult to understand a world in which people believe that spirits wield influence. The secular mind struggles to appreciate invisible worlds where spirits mobilize bodies to action in a fashion comparable to the invisible forces of their society, such as the state and its laws. Unfortunately, since the burden of the truth about the past weighs heavily on historians, they have had an especially difficult time dealing with worlds invisible and implausible to them. In the classroom, when first confronted with a myth to be used as a historical source, many undergraduates claim that the myth did not "really happen." Professional historians are more nuanced, and yet their visceral reaction is to insist on the language of false consciousness, or at best metaphoric and symbolic beliefs that demonstrate a subconscious rationality, rather than ideas that informed agency. Such scholars imply that spirits delude or obfuscate rather than empower. In the political imagination of many central Africans, spirits wielded power, or gave them or others power. Because spirits needed to be dealt with, they inspired agency. People—in popular movements, religious institutions, and state agencies—mobilized around their spiritual discourses.

THE CENTRAL AFRICAN INVISIBLE WORLD

Since the invisible world is important only insofar as it is a shared collective representation, a way that people talk about the world around them, it has to be appreciated at the level of this collectivity. General claims about the characteristics of the invisible world on a universal, continental, or even regional scale reveal only scholarly abstractions, not those of historical agents. Despite some similarities and pan-regional and transnational connections, Africans do not share an invisible world. Spiritual beliefs break down across nations, ethnicities, and even communities. For that reason, this book engages with a particular central African history, roughly falling within northern Zambia. However, certain general features of the central African region provide a useful backdrop to this particular history.

"Central Africa" is a geographic expression that conventionally refers to the region drained by the vast Congo River. It includes hundreds of ethnic groups, however defined; almost as many languages; kingdoms and decentralized village-based polities; territories colonized by French, Belgians, British, and Portuguese; and nation-states that emerged from these colonies, which range from Cameroon in the northwest to Zambia in the southeast. While the similarities between peoples in this vast region are elusive, commonly related languages that are grouped together as "Bantu" are spoken; in fact, the region constitutes the richest diversity of Bantu languages, indicating the historical depth of settlement by Bantu-speakers, who began to disperse from the Cameroon region more than three thousand years ago. Either through their common ancestry, through pan-regional connections, or through similar experiences (and probably a combination of all these factors), central Africans share certain cultural features and historical trajectories. Scholars have even claimed that there are commonalities to all central African religious movements.[34] While I do not pursue this argument, in the following section some general features of the history of the central African invisible world are related to the particular case study presented in this book.

The central African invisible world has an ancient history. Based on the linguistic spread of religious terms, Christopher Ehret identifies a distinctive and millennia-old set of beliefs in the importance of ancestral spirits alongside the manipulation of evil by witches among central and eastern Bantu speakers.[35] Using linguistic evidence for west-central African societies, Jan Vansina points to the centrality of spirits in forms of government.[36] In the Congo River basin, according to Vansina, "early western Bantu speakers believed that the 'real' world went beyond the apparent world."[37] These early inhabitants of the central African forests acknowledged the religious ideas and even ancestral spirits of their predecessors, the Batwa peoples.[38] Around four hundred years ago, European observers confirmed these spiritual beliefs.[39] Recent ethnographies point to their continuity.[40] In south-central Africa, remnants of Luba and Lunda oral and material cultures describe spiritual interventions in society and politics.[41] Precisely because of shared beliefs, claims to power over people and productive resources were made through the spirit world. Land was unproductive without the spiritual power to make it fertile. At the same time, rival leaders and prophets challenged their opponents' claims to intercede with the spirit world.

An overview of the literature, fieldwork experience, and the historical depth of belief in spirits suggests that spirits in central Africa have become connected to a core aspect of nonlinguistic existence: emotions. Spirits manifested viscerally; they were *felt* by individuals, and heard and seen through emotional phenomena. Dreams, trance states, and glossolalia were all highly emotive manifestations of the spirit world. Jealousy and anger were also related to spiritual forces, and could even cause death.[42] Death separated the spirit from the body; birth brought them back together. Grief and joy gave ancestors their agency. Spirit possession was also gendered and sometimes even sexual. Love was often inspired by spirits (or by witchcraft), and spirits married those they possessed.[43] Like emotions, which sometimes appear without explanation, central African spirits were capricious.

Since emotional actions led to political and social cohesion or transgression, collective imaginations suggested ways to manage emotions. This management or governance of emotions depends on the forces considered to inspire emotions. In Western modernity, social scientists, physicians, and psychologists have theories of emotions and have developed corresponding biomedical, educational, and legal institutions to control emotions, minimize the damage they do, or harness them to acceptable social and cultural ends (from the emotion of love to the institution of monogamous marriage, for example). In central Africa, comparable institutions needed to control the spirits that potentially disrupted or misdirected the stable functioning of society. The management of such spiritual emotions was required at the immediate family and community levels, precisely because of the emotions that familiar intimacy engenders. Across central Africa and beyond, an old form of spiritual government combated "witchcraft," the dangerous spiritual emotions located primarily within the family and local community. That is why witchcraft was the "dark side of kinship," as Peter Geschiere has put it.[44]

The antiquity of the management of spiritual emotions is illustrated in central African oral traditions and charters of governance that join quotidian concerns about witchcraft within the family and the community to stories of powerful conquerors who overcame local witchcraft, especially spiritual emotions such as love and jealousy, or perished while doing so. In such oral traditions, the success of precolonial rulers in calming spiritual emotions indicated their ability to promote fertility and keep in check illness and death. The first chapter of this book describes the dangers and promises of spiritual emotions, and indicates the rituals needed to avert death and to encourage fertility.

Old spiritual beliefs survived even as they morphed to maintain their relevance in modern times. Across the region, the uncertainties of the late nineteenth century, linked to the violent expansion of the slave and ivory trades, ratcheted up the need for spiritual security, especially among the most vulnerable.[45] At first the colonial rulers of central Africa, the British, Belgian, Portuguese, and French alike, relied on the local leaders who had previously mobilized — but did not monopolize — spiritual power. European administrators emphasized the legitimacy of these chosen leaders in terms of their supposed traditional depth and (often paradoxically) in terms of their civilizing potential. The colonial administrations remained at best embarrassed by such leaders' spiritual claims, however, which they tended to discourage. As part of their civilizing mission, colonial regimes implemented legal restrictions on interventions into the spirit world, such as the Witchcraft Ordinance of 1914 in Northern Rhodesia, which expressly prohibited accusations of spirit possession and manipulation, and thereby curtailed old forms of political legitimacy. Movements that dealt with the spirit world became illegal, but remained influential as secretive and occult forms of power. As chapter 2 of this book indicates, when colonial forms of sovereignty disempowered the spiritual agency of chiefs, people sought alternative ways to deal with spiritual malaise and political impotence.

Christian ideas propagated by the mainline Protestant and Catholic missionaries across central Africa worked with the colonial state to disenchant daily life, directing attention toward a spiritual afterlife and away from the presence of spirits in the immediate world. Twentieth-century European Christianity generally focused on spirits that were remote from the world of the living, even if these spirits held moral power and suasion over the living (with the exception of some nineteenth-century Protestant missionaries in South Africa and twentieth-century Pentecostals). European missionaries tried to distance the invisible from the visible worlds and, alongside the colonial administrations, discouraged — or prohibited, in the case of the Belgian Congo — international Christian missions and churches that conformed to existing central African notions of proximate spirits, such as those held by the Pentecostals and Jehovah's Witnesses. These and related Christian movements still prospered and proliferated, but, as chapters 3 and 4 illustrate, outside or on the margins of colonial laws. In the postcolonial period, the mainline churches that emerged out of the European mission societies ignored, or remained inept at dealing with, spirits, especially evil spirits that brought death, sickness, and misfortune.

The failure of European missions and their successor churches to distance the world of spirits from the world of the living does not mean that Christianity was unimportant to the history of the invisible world. Central African Christian beliefs advanced independently of colonial-era missionary doctrines. Even while many formal Christian denominations were established and thrived across central Africa, a particular form and experience of Christianity, replete with distinctive spiritual personae — vampires, ancestors, demons, witches, and prophets — emerged. A colonial (and denominational) focus leads to an incomplete understanding of the way that widespread spiritual beliefs transformed

Christianity.[46] Put another way, Christianity populated the invisible world with new spirits and replaced or eroded the powers of old spirits. International Christian ideas were incorporated into a central African invisible world, and, in turn, this invisible world informed a changing global Christianity.[47]

Central African Christianity thereby came to accept direct spiritual interventions in the visible and physical world. Christian narratives were downloaded into the present. Biblical places were related to the immediate environment and biblical characters were inherited by the living, just as ancestral titles were previously inherited by systems of positional succession.[48] New Jerusalems are now scattered across the region; many a Moses is remembered to have led his people against evil.[49] Even the literate and bureaucratic culture of Western Christianity did not displace the powers of the spirits.[50]

Central Africans recast the moral judgment at the center of European Christian notions of an afterlife in heaven or hell as a struggle against spiritual evil in this world. The spirits of the past, which may have been angry for lack of respect, recognition, or propitiation, became evil spirits. Sin meant the mobilization of these evil forces, and not the transgression of certain church-defined moral codes. On the other hand, the beneficent role of older spirits ceded to the beneficent Holy Spirit. Ancestors gave way to God and Jesus, while all other spirits became demons—regardless of whether such spirits were angry for a justifiable and explicable reason. Christianity thereby contributed to the Manichaean quality of spirits, good and evil, God and the devil, absent in the spirit world before Christianity. As communal ancestors ceded to a universal God, well-being focused on Christian rituals such as baptism, confession, and even exorcism, all of which replaced veneration and propitiation of ancestral and territorial spirits. As a Christian binary morality grafted onto a belief in the presence of spirits in this world, the angels of heaven and demons of hell became part of the immediate world, not just the afterlife. This Manichaean spiritual world became an effective way of characterizing a colonial order that spread hardship and misfortune. Colonialism—with its material forms of exploitation, its assaults on personal dignity, and its racial categorization of the visible world—was an evil to be cleansed by a radical spiritual revolution, an Armageddon.[51]

Even while colonial-era missionaries failed to impose their vision of spiritual belief, they helped to shape secular ideologies and moralities. In alliance with colonial administrators and missionary-educated elites, colonial missionaries set about constructing what they deemed to be a moral civil society. In the postcolonial period this vision of a moral society inspired national philosophies of government, such as the state religion of Zambian humanism with its own civilizing mission that banished spiritual forces to the afterlife. In the Democratic Republic of Congo (DRC), despite the lifting of restrictions on African Christian movements, Mobutu Sese Seko's Authenticité drew on colonial constructions to introduce invented traditions and promoted Mobutu as a heavenly force that descends to govern this world (as in the well-known Zairean state television clip). Nonetheless, both Christian and occult spirits remained a way of conceptualizing power and challenging authority.[52] In fact, precisely because of the inequalities linked to colonial and postcolonial societies, spiritual discourses on power proliferated. In the 1980s, as the final chapter in this book illustrates, Zambian humanism was swept away by a spiritual political theology held by Pentecostal and charismatic churches.

The limitations of secular modes of authority, in particular the late colonial and postcolonial developmentalist state, and an accompanying growth in inexplicable and audacious forms of power, encouraged spiritual discourses. As the state failed to deliver the promised benefits of development, its core mission, justification, and claims to sovereignty were compromised. In the case of Zambia, a prosperous country at the time of independence, Zambians had high "expectations of modernity." The disappointments of the developmentalist state were deeply felt.[53] In other parts of central Africa, such as the DRC, where the developmentalist state gave way to the gatekeeper state, the failure was catastrophic.[54] As the postcolonial state failed in its modernizing mission, or modernity benefited only a few, spirits appeared as a discourse on an unrequited faith in a universal modernity.

The uncertainty of life in central Africa has also contributed to spiritual discourses. Here, another old quality of the spirits has been reaffirmed: that they are capricious. In a similar fashion to Adam Ashforth's argument for the South African city of Soweto, where spirits manifest in a climate of postapartheid uncertainty, in central Africa the uncertainty of life contributed to beliefs in spiritual agency.[55] Economic misfortune, violence, and disease indicated the agency of angry and evil spirits. Without apparent reason, violence afflicted communities or people died of mysterious new diseases. On the other hand, an ordinary person might become extraordinarily wealthy—perhaps even the leader of a new nation. Children could become wealthier than their parents, reversing or rendering chaotic older gerontocratic orders.[56] Such unpredictability in life, inexplicable in terms of hegemonic and secular forms of sovereignty and morality, made the agency of good and evil spirits apparent. The modern Protestant notion that hard work leads to wealth and well-being has not conformed to the lived experiences of most people for whom a discourse on capricious spirits is far more convincing and realistic. Since modernity has been unpredictable, nonlinear, and frequently disappoints, a discourse on spiritual agency is a discourse on the lack of agency by living humans.[57] Central Africans have discussed the capriciousness of spirits as they reflect on the arbitrariness of power and their own inabilities to transform their lives.

Spirits could inspire ideas of revolutionary change. For the European-led missions, conversion to Christianity involved a gradual struggle toward enlightenment, as they inserted the convert into a progressive moral teleology guided by an established church hierarchy. For those who led the nationalist movement, the party would serve the same moral purpose as the mission church. On the other hand, the prophetic spiritual movements examined in this book posed a radical model of conversion that sought to transform the individual as a basis for a spiritual revolution. Conversion in this framework harnessed spirits to local concerns and identities; it critiqued old practices, addressed inequalities, and promoted a utopian future. Since spiritual forces possessed the individual, they allowed for a remarkable and sudden personal transformation. Conversion purified the individual of evil and laid the foundations for a new society. The revolution, often violent, was a cleansing of evil, a personal catharsis or exorcism that led to a reborn individual and nation, and ultimately to heaven on earth.

The connection between violence and beliefs in a spirit world is an understudied aspect of central African history. Violence is often attributed to "big men" who manipulate and indoctrinate credulous and underage soldiers, set about capturing valuable resources, or, in a more sophisticated argument, "rage against the machine" of dysfunctional governance.[58] Such reasonings may explain why people take to arms; they do not explain acts of ritualized brutality and quotidian violence. The belief that people were fighting the devil — or human incarnations of evil spirits — may have inspired violence, or at least represented and made sense of violence. Because of the gendered nature of spirit possession, such violence often targeted women. When nationalist-supporting villagers massacred a community of Lumpa Church members, many of them women, brutalizing and raping them, as described in chapter 6, they considered the members to be incarnations of evil, possessed by demons. For the villagers who committed these acts, killing was not sufficient. The demons needed to be publicly and ritually vilified so that they would fear returning to the land of the living. There is a widely held misconception that Christianity in Africa inspired peace, while colonialism caused trauma and violence. According to this idea, the violence and disruption caused by Christianity and Christian missionaries were due to their role as agents of colonialism; the missionaries were not "true" Christians. To the contrary, as in other periods in the history of Christianity, Christian spiritual beliefs engaged with violent histories, and sometimes inspired violence. Christian spirits could be violent agents. Chapters 5 and 6 of this book point to how Christian beliefs contributed to violence during decolonization. Other examples drawn from the central African region indicate similar histories.[59]

Of course, spirits are not unfamiliar to other parts of Africa and to other parts of the world. In South Africa, spirits formed an important element of political and religious discourse, providing life-giving rain, inspiring struggles against taxation in the nineteenth century, envisaging Zion for the many followers of Isaiah Shembe, revealing apartheid-era witches in the late twentieth century, and contributing to the uncertainties of life in the twenty-first century.[60] The most emotive refrain in the South African national anthem, "Nkosi Sikilel' iAfrica" (God Bless Africa), resounds with a call, "Woza moya," for the Holy Spirit to come down and bless Africa. The proliferation of Pentecostal and charismatic churches in southern Nigeria and Ghana, with their ongoing struggles against evil demons, indicates comparable spiritual agencies.[61] In Liberia, Poro societies provided a parallel power to the state.[62] The Tongnaab deity has offered good fortune in life and commerce to the increasing number of pilgrims who make their way to its shrine in northern Ghana.[63] Spiritual agents can be identified in the history of the African diaspora in the Americas—Haiti, Cuba, North America, and Brazil, for example.[64] Similar conceptions of spiritual power were also found among people with no relationship to Africa, such as in Southeast Asia.[65] On the other hand, spirits have not been as central to religion and to politics in other parts of the African continent. In parts of the African Sahel, for example, even while forms of spirit possession have long prospered, Sharia Islam, with its focus on texts, moral codes, and the afterlife, has repressed spiritual interventions (although Sufi Islam allowed for direct spiritual interventions).[66] Here, the introduction of Christianity engaged with a different set of concerns and politico-religious configurations.[67]

In outlining some of these general features of the central African region, I do not argue that there are unchanging and homogeneous central African traditions, but only point to the importance of proximate and capricious invisible agents in early modern and modern central African history. The exact nature and historical trajectory of this invisible world and its relationship to the visible world diverge in many central African communities. Particular histories were created out of similar experiences, such as the slave-and-ivory trading wars of the nineteenth century, colonial impositions, postcolonial nationalism and socialism, and neoliberalism; and similar changes in the spirit world, including the appearance of an evil Satan, a good God, as well as the diminished role of ancestral shades and nature spirits. This book discusses the role of invisible inspirations in one of these Zambian histories.

METHODOLOGY AND ZAMBIAN HISTORIOGRAPHY

Even while spiritual beliefs are shared, they are private, and thus require the historian to appreciate an internal perspective, a challenge since there are so few written accounts left by believers and since personal beliefs remain hidden from secular authorities. Often the historian reads belief from the accounts of skeptical outsiders. Many of these outside authorities impose categorizations, especially those of "religion" and "politics," onto the experiences and activities of people. To grapple with these methodological quandaries, the contexts that motivated and inspired the writing of the primary and secondary source material have to be appreciated.

This book employs three types of evidence used in Africanist scholarship: fieldwork, oral testimony, and documentary sources. Informal fieldwork for this project began in 1997–1998, when I conducted the research that informed my first book on environment, society, and culture in the Luapula Valley, located adjacent to the Lubemba Plateau, and when I came to appreciate the importance of spirits as a political resource, and began to think about the history explored here.[68] I also developed competency in ChiBemba, the language of the Lubemba Plateau, as well as one of the principal languages of Zambia's urban areas (I studied ChiBemba at Ilondola Mission, one of the Catholic missions discussed in chapter 2). Since then, I have returned to Zambia almost yearly, with significant intervals of fieldwork devoted to this book in 2005 and 2008. My fieldwork involved living in villages and in church compounds, attending services and seminars, and discussing the issues found in this book with the followers and principal clergy of the movements examined. Upon identifying reliable informants, I recorded interviews: in 2005, on popular Christianity (especially the Lumpa movement of Alice Lenshina) and the anticolonial nationalist movement in northern Zambia during the 1950s and 1960s; in 2008, on the Pentecostal and charismatic churches that have proliferated across Zambia since the 1980s. Like all historical sources, memory represses, disguises, and reveals selectively. Yet fieldwork and interviews open up local perspectives, even in the interpretation of documentary sources.

The documentary sources, including unpublished archival material but also publications such as newspapers, memoirs, and government publications, that inform this book are found in libraries and archives in Zambia, the United Kingdom, South Africa, and the United States. Each repository holds secrets that yield only after lengthy investigation and interpretation. Crucial to the interpretation of documents is an appreciation of the contexts of their writing: What was emphasized? What was left out? And why? Any one document emerges from multiple perspectives, prejudices, experiences, informants, and other documents. In an archive, the enterprising historian can identify the paper trail, the many revealing documents, often hidden in obscurely titled files and boxes, that lie behind a single published government report or commission of inquiry. Historical investigation is an engagement with archives to understand this multilayered construction of documents, a sort of fieldwork in the archives, which in turn relies on understanding the historical contexts in which the documents were written.

An effective appreciation of local history and historiography is thus crucial to the interpretation of documents. The writing of Zambian history began in the encounter between Zambian oral historians and outsiders, including missionaries, colonial officials, and anthropologists. The first accounts of the precolonial Zambian past, generally the migration of Luba and Lunda royals into a land inhabited by much earlier settlements of Bantu-speakers, appeared in the district notebooks of colonial officials and the publications of mission societies. Certain missionaries or mission societies took special interest in collecting these stories. The Catholic mission society, the White Fathers, for example, undertook extensive surveys of all aspects of culture, history, and religion in the areas where they proselytized. This represented the beginnings of a long tradition of Catholic missionary scholarship that stretches from Edouard Labrecque, whom Giacomo Macola describes as an "indefatigable organizer of culture throughout northeastern Zambia," to Hugo F. Hinfelaar's insightful work on Bemba women's engagement with Christianity.[69] (While Protestant missionaries also collected histories, their emphasis on a progressive civilizing mission meant that they were less interested in historical traditions than were the Catholics.) Many of these missionaries spent decades in the field, were fluent in local languages, and were avid collectors of culture and history.

Missionaries believed that there was only one religion, even while each group could possess a different secular history. Thus, non-Christian narratives deemed religious were problematic, while those narratives that were viewed as historical were acceptable. Christian stories had to replace ostensibly religious narratives, but ostensibly secular histories were permitted, and could even be promoted. Missionary publications thus separated the religious from the historical; the former were beliefs that had to give way to Christianity; the latter could be kept as markers of distinct human communities. In mission-recorded oral traditions, the agency of living beings replaced the agency of spirits. Stories about the spirit that the missionaries would call God (*Lesa*) and the origins of humankind, for example, were unacceptable in the published missionary scholarship. Much subsequent historical scholarship is based on these sanitized missionary publications. Fortunately, the missionary researchers left a paper trail: the original unpublished writings and research notes are now available in mission archives. These notes were the product of careful research: the missionaries considered knowledge of customs repugnant to them as a weapon in efforts to combat them. "Morally speaking, many customs are directly opposed to the Christian code," a White Father, Louis Etienne, wrote. But he also noted that "as long as the missionary does not acquire a thorough knowledge of these customs, he will be unable to remedy them; he will be able to impart only a superficial culture, a semblance of Christianity, which will always be merely a thin veneer superimposed upon paganism, fatally lacking in depth, and certain to crumble under any serious trial."[70] Accounts of such customs and histories thus exist in many missionary documents, although they rarely found their way to missionary publications. If possible and necessary, I have made use of these unsanitized research notes.

In the late nineteenth century, the British government awarded a charter to Cecil John Rhodes's British South Africa Company (BSAC) to rule a vast territory, which included present-day Zambia and Zimbabwe. The BSAC recruited colonial officials who were responsible for the implementation of a variety of colonial exactions, such as taxation and the recruitment and organization of labor for the incipient mining industry. Since they struggled to govern their vast districts, colonial administrators turned to existing elites in their efforts to maintain control. In order to determine the "legitimate" rulers of any particular area, they collected histories, which were reproduced in many district notebooks, now found in the National Archives of Zambia (NAZ). The tendency to research and write down local histories and traditions increased after the British government declined to renew the BSAC's charter in 1923 and took over the administration of Northern Rhodesia in 1924, formally introducing indirect rule during the 1930s. Officials responsible for the implementation of indirect rule, such as W. Vernon Brelsford, produced several monographs and articles from their collection of local knowledge, first written as appendices to their many "tour reports," which are also found in the NAZ.

Like the missionaries, these local colonial officials were interested in particular narratives. Mirroring a concept of royalty and aristocracy in their own societies, colonial officials focused on lineage and on the strength of inherited traditions. Thus, despite the fact that many of the colonial officials spent several years in an area and developed fluency in local languages, their accounts of the basis of political power were partial and culled to their particular interests. However, these officials also viewed it as their duty to repress "false" beliefs. Thus, in their battle against the spirits, they left valuable archival traces that can be employed by the historian. At times, such archives represent the prejudices of a secular mind, identifying an exotic and irrational "other." And yet, like the missionaries, colonial officials knew that success in their struggle against beliefs they considered false depended on the accuracy of their data.

The third productive encounter between Zambians and outsiders occurred with the arrival of the anthropologist. In northern Zambia, Audrey I. Richards, Bronislaw Malinowski's student, was a pioneer of colonial anthropology. Her work on the northern Zambian kingdom and people termed the "Bemba" began in the 1930s and drew on a long collaboration with Paul B. Mushindo, an elder of the Church of Scotland's mission in northern Zambia, as well as the support of various liberal settlers and colonial officials such as Stewart Gore-Brown and Thomas Fox-Pitt. Richards's work, characterized as functionalism, sought to appreciate the totality of cultural and religious forms that informed sociopolitical arrangements. A major concern of her initial analysis was with the forces of change that she perceived as having disrupted the cohesive functioning of tribal society.[71] Richards continued to publish about Bemba society and visited occasionally up until the late 1960s. Her many articles, which drew on copious field research notes, detail Bemba sociopolitical organization and their religious expressions.[72]

Richards's functionalism gave way to an embrace of change by a progressive school of colonial-era anthropologists centered at the Rhodes-Livingstone Institute (RLI). They, too, benefited from a dialogue with local interpreters and ethnographers.[73] There was great diversity in their scholarship, which included the sociological studies of Godfrey Wilson and Monica H. Wilson (close collaborators and friends of Richards), the symbolic cultural ethnographies of Victor Turner, the structural functionalism of Max Gluckman, the detailed longitudinal field investigations of Elizabeth Colson, and the liberal historical accounts of Lewis H. Gann. Many of them wrote about what they presumed to be single ethnic groups (the Lozi, Lunda, Tonga, etc.). But instead of fearing change and "detribalization" with increased urbanization and the growth of the copper-mining economy, a preoccupation of functionalist scholarship, the RLI anthropologists were fascinated by the new cultural forms emerging in the towns. They sought to represent African societies of Northern Rhodesia in the midst of a great transformation from village to urban life. To a certain extent, their progressive politics may have led them to overestimate the permanence and the linearity of such changes. Their "expectations of modernity," as James Ferguson's more recent ethnography puts it, shared by the growing literate and cosmopolitan urban Zambian population, would not materialize in the postcolonial period.[74]

As with the colonial missionaries and administrators, there was much that was repressed by these anthropologists. Richards imagined an ordered tribal society where power devolved from the paramount; that which did not fit in this view was left out (or represented as anomalous signs of tribal breakdown). The RLI anthropologists struggled to relate spirits to society. Often influenced by Marxism, they ignored the richest components of their data (e.g., for Godfrey Wilson), or they focused on ritual (Gluckman) or symbol (Turner) rather than spiritual agency.[75] Fortunately, as with the missionaries and colonial officials, these anthropologists left detailed field notes in various archives, and, when carefully examined, they, too, provide richer source material than the final published accounts. This book has especially benefited from a careful reading of Richards's research notes.

As independence approached, rival political and religious movements fought over followers and over the implications of the end of European colonialism. The conflict between popular nationalism and other prophetic movements around the time of Zambian independence left rich archival traces, underappreciated by other studies. For example, this is the first book to employ the detailed archival sources on the battles between the United National Independence Party (UNIP) and prophetic movements such as Watchtower and Alice Lenshina's Lumpa Church. Readers who want to appreciate the multiple perspective and documents that lie behind a widely cited official report, the *Report of the Commission of Enquiry into the Lumpa Church*, the long-established authoritative text on the Lumpa Church, should consider the archival documents referenced in chapter 6.[76]

In the heady days after independence, as Kenneth Kaunda and the UNIP took over the control of the colonial state and a booming copper economy, Zambians and foreign scholars expressed high hopes for the nation. A nationalist historiography celebrated the emergence of this new order. Some looked to the precolonial period to identify indigenous forms of statecraft. Andrew Roberts charted the political history of the rise and fall of the Bemba polity, demonstrating the secular logic of precolonial forms of political organization, and culling religious and mythological aspects from his history.[77] Robert I. Rotberg rendered the rise of African nationalism in central Africa as the growth of a liberal secular modernity against an authoritarian and anachronistic colonial state.[78] Henry S. Meebelo looked to the early colonial period to identify how acts of resistance against the colonial state eventually manifested as the rise of a nationalist movement. Millenarian or "religious"-based agency was imagined to give way to secular nationalism.[79] This intellectual project engaged with a political project, the creation of the state religion of Zambian humanism, which is documented in the United National Independence Party archives, a valuable resource for understanding the postcolonial state's response to spiritual beliefs.

When Kaunda's rule failed to meet the expectation of party activists and the one-party state was declared, the nationalist historiography appeared Whiggish and dated. But even as Zambians became disillusioned and critical of Kaunda's regime, scholarship remained muted, at least compared to the far more critical and analytical scholarship about, say, Mobutu's Zaire. In part this was because under Kaunda, Zambia hosted southern African liberation movements, and hence was a sympathetic home to some of the radical historians and social theorists of southern Africa.[80] The critical tradition of scholarship that did emerge during the 1970s and 1980s generally emphasized structural forces rather than historical agency. Scholars, drawing on a Marxist dependency theory then in vogue, wrote about the structural "roots of rural poverty," a legacy that the postcolonial Zambian regime found difficult to counteract.[81] Marxists were also interested in religion. In one example particularly pertinent to this book, Wim M. J. van Binsbergen placed religious practices within their socioeconomic contexts; or, in his language, he linked a distinctive religious superstructure to underlying transformations in the mode of production. Even while his descriptions were far more subtle than the determinism of his analytical model, van Binsbergen stressed class forces instead of treating the content of religious ideas as statements of power. Marxist abstractions replaced spiritual assertions. His chapter on the Christian Lumpa movement of Alice Lenshina, a central concern of this book, stands out in this regard. He argued that Lenshina's movement was constituted by peasants who radically rejected state control and the petty bourgeois leadership of the nationalists, an analysis that he could only sustain with little reference to the concepts held by Lenshina's followers.[82]

By the 1990s Zambian historiography began to look beyond the blinkers of theoretical Marxism and view the heterodox struggles of ordinary people. Samuel N. Chipungu edited an important collection on the experiences of Zambians under colonialism.[83] A new generation of anthropologists offered alternative views to the paradigms of tribal change developed by their predecessors, the RLI anthropologists.[84] Karen Tranberg Hansen published ethnographies about marginalized groups, servants, women, small-scale traders, and youth.[85] James A. Pritchett's long period of fieldwork informed his analysis of alternative forms of corporate organization.[86] Megan Vaughan and Henrietta L. Moore questioned Richards's contention of a stable and traditional Bemba tribal society where practices such as *chitemene* (a form of slash-and-burn agriculture) were engrained in culture and would collapse under the stresses of modernity.[87]

At the end of the 1990s, a post-nationalist historiography emerged. A seminal moment in the dissemination of this historiography was the convening of a conference in Lusaka in August 2005 and the publication of a selection of its proceedings, *One Zambia, Many Histories*. This was, in the words of the editors, a decisive attempt to "place at the centre of the analysis the counter-hegemonic political and religious histories and projects that stubbornly refused to be silenced in the name of national unity."[88] Some examples from the volume stand out in their relevance for this book. Giacomo Macola demonstrates the intolerant and exclusionary nature of UNIP's nationalism, which allowed little opportunity for political dissent.[89] Miles Larmer discusses the political opposition that was forced underground after the banning of the United Progressive Party (UPP) in 1972. Even the once-powerful trade union movement increasingly succumbed to—even as it resisted—co-option and incorporation into UNIP.[90] The church, as Marja Hinfelaar points out, proved to be one of the few spheres of civil society that remained autonomous from UNIP and able to critique its leadership and practices.[91] Their weekly newspaper, the *National Mirror*, thus provides an important source for independent voices in the postcolonial period, and is employed extensively in the final chapters of this book.

My post-secular argument is related to this latest post-nationalist and in some senses postmodern trend. It questions some of the central tenets of nationalist history alongside modernization theory, with its assumptions of secular agencies and its progressive teleology. This focus on the multifarious and unexpected narratives and epistemologies, the centrality of spirits in Zambian history, may upset those who seek solace in their secular worlds. The methodological approach promoted here attempts to extend the vistas of my predecessors—the missionaries, colonial administrators, anthropologists, and progressive activists—and make visible the rich, complex, and dynamic worlds that they ignored, repressed, or rendered invisible.

AN OVERVIEW

This history of a world populated with spirits begins with the oral tradition of the Bemba Crocodile Clan royals that recalls their migration to northern Zambia, their battle with the "owners of the land," and their death and burial in a sacred grove, indicating the ability of the royal ancestors to calm dangerous emotions and to ensure fertility and fecundity. The first chapter, "The Passion of Chitimukulu," ends in the late nineteenth century, when the slave trade and warfare impinged on south-central Africa to an unprecedented degree, and local prophets challenged the hegemony and efficacy of these Crocodile Clan spiritual claims and interventions.

Chapter 2, "Christian Witches," turns to the early twentieth century, when the Bemba royals were incorporated into the colonial state. Even as the Bemba rulers were empowered as indirect rulers by the colonial district commissioners (DCs), they were disempowered as mediators with their ancestral spirits. In addition, new Christian spirits challenged or replaced the ancestors. And yet evil proliferated, in part because Christian moralities and notions of sin became associated with angry spirits and even witchcraft. But ideas of evil spiritual agents also spread because they provided an effective way to describe the colonial order. Movements such as the Bamuchape witchcraft cleansers harnessed new Christian spirits to cleanse the evil that the missionaries stubbornly refused to recognize.

The newly established copper-mining towns of the 1920s and 1930s, where a number of Bemba men and women sought employment and opportunities, form the backdrop to the third chapter, "Satan in the City." Here a new type of Christian movement, free from European missionaries, the

"Watchtower," took guidance from the international Jehovah's Witnesses pamphlets that associated the authorities of this world with Satan. For the Watchtower movement on the Copperbelt, the colonial authorities and mining companies were Satan's agents. In the name of the Armageddon and a new heaven on earth, Watchtower fomented opposition among workers dislocated from rural environs and liberated from indirect rule. In a series of strikes, they confronted the colonial authorities, missionaries, European-educated African elites, and the secular urban civil society that these elites were in the process of creating.

Chapter 4, "A New Jerusalem," returns to the rural Bemba heartland by considering the rise of a revolutionary church led by the Queen, "Regina" or "Lenshina" in the ChiBemba language, who sought to replace old beneficent spirits with new spirits, God and Jesus, in order to eradicate the influence of evil witchcraft. Not only did Lenshina innovate the ideas of the Bamuchape witchfinders and Watchtower to challenge the Christianity of the missionaries and the political sovereignty of the colonial state, but her spiritual quest addressed the afflictions of the most marginalized of groups, rural women, burdened by a patriarchal colonial order.

Popular nationalism spread in the same areas as the popular Christian movements. Chapter 5, "The Dawn," considers the rise of a nationalist movement that brought Christian spiritual notions into the struggle for a popular sovereignty, leading to an explosive, Manichaean, and sometimes violent movement that demanded faithful adherence to the mass movement. Popular nationalism had such a close resemblance to millenarian religious movements that elite attempts to contain expectations through a program of secular moral reform were challenged.

By the early 1960s, the followers of Alice Lenshina and the nationalist movement fought for influence, resulting in a brutal civil war in northern Zambia. We witness in chapter 6, "Devils of War," striking examples of spiritual agency during this civil war, as enemies became devils, bullets turned to water, and brave fighters were described as Christian heroes.

The war ended when Kaunda sent in colonial troops to forcefully disperse Lenshina's followers' villages. The victory of Kaunda's nationalists and their seizure of the colonial state apparatus in 1964 promised to inaugurate an era of secular socialism, guided by Kaunda's state religion, humanism. Chapter 7, "God in Heaven, Kaunda on Earth," argues that humanism was never a convincing philosophy for Zambians. They turned instead to spiritual mediators, such as the Archbishop of Lusaka, Emmanuel Milingo, who exorcized the evil spirits that afflicted Zambians who were losing faith in the nationalist vision.

Chapter 8, "A Nation Reborn," explores the agency of the neoliberal Holy Spirit, which promised wealth and advancement in a post-socialist era. In

1991, Christians led the way in challenging Kaunda and his humanist state religion, contributing to the downfall of Kaunda in 1991. Zambia's second president, Frederick Chiluba, declared that Zambia, blessed by the Holy Spirit, would be reborn and prosper as a Christian nation. Pentecostal-inspired spirits framed the challenges and opportunities of a neoliberal order.

1 ⇔ The Passion of Chitimukulu

THE HISTORY OF THE BEMBA kingdom's rise prior to the nineteenth century remains vague. In Bemba renditions, the military conquest of the region by the Luba-related Crocodile Clan was entwined with stories of autochthonous magical powers, especially those of women, and the passion of the Crocodile Clan's leader, Chitimukulu, "the Great Tree." Objects such as the staff of rule, depicted below in figure 1.1 and on the cover, evoked memories of similar conquests across south-central Africa. Similar figurines could have represented a number of different iconic heroines praised in many of the savanna's most renowned stories of conquest: Luweji of the Lunda, Bulanda of the Luba, or Nachituti of the Kazembe kingdom. For the Bemba it would have been of Chilimbulu, the woman with beautiful scarifications who seduced the roaming Bemba hero, Chitimukulu. Her half-closed eyes, sculpted ears, and enlarged navel and genitalia indicated paths of connection to the powers of the spirits. She held her breasts, perhaps containing secrets to human fertility and agricultural fecundity.[1] The conquering king ruled by harnessing her powers; his failure to possess her, to contain and control the dangerous spiritual emotions that she invoked, would, men claimed, lead to the collapse of an order that underpinned their patriarchal civilization.

The objects and stories that tell of the Crocodile Clan's powers built on older conceptions of the relationships between people, the land upon which they relied, and the dead; they reconciled the spiritual powers of the autochthons with claims to rule by conquerors. Politics, then, was also religion, and religion was politics; the competition over ideas with which people could comprehend their past and apprehend their future. New politico-religious constellations could not be imposed in a foreign vocabulary, for they would lose

Figure 1.1. Luba staff of rule. Such staffs were probably sculpted near the central Luba polities in Katanga, DRC, and either distributed to indicate political affiliations or traded throughout the region. This staff is similar to one possessed by the Bemba Crocodile Clan lord, Mwamba. On Mwamba's staff the figurine was said to have been of the autochthon, Chilimbulu, whose scarifications seduced Chiti and were used as a fertility relic. Reproduced with permission of Museum aan de Stroom, Antwerp.

the powers that rendered them useful. Yet they could equally not celebrate the past, as they would then not provide legitimacy for the new rulers. The Crocodile Clan conquerors thus offered innovations within the existing collective political imagination. They claimed to intervene with the spiritual forces crucial for social and economic well-being, linking their ancestral spirits and their relics of rule to the most vital aspects of ordinary existence—the fertility of people and the fecundity of agriculture. The Bemba expected the Crocodile Clan's government to ensure that ancestral and nature spirits were placated, and that the living prospered free from spiritual malaise and witchcraft.

The ideas of this Bemba politico-religious edifice were not written down: religion was not restricted to the dogmas of scriptures; politics was not subject to the laws of constitutions. No document would allow the future scholar to easily reconstruct the basis of rule. Surviving objects, such as the staff of rule described above, and various other relics, including stools, bow stands, and other objects, provide some clues. But the most important fragments of evidence are praises, proverbs, and stories, which would eventually be written down and come to be known collectively under the general rubric of "oral tradition." At first glance, the oral tradition appears to be a historical representation. But, like all history, the oral tradition established its importance, relevance, and appeal not because it rendered past events correctly, but because it gave an account of the correct relationships among people, the world that sustained them, and the dead. Historical discourse, as V. Y. Mudimbe has established, was also religious discourse.[2]

Historians preoccupied with change in a narrowly conceived secular political realm have focused on struggles around physical forms of wealth such as people and land. Detailed histories of competing lords and polities leave out the language, idioms, and terms in which political struggle took place. The most significant study of precolonial Bemba political history, for example, argues that much in the Bemba political charter, their oral tradition of genesis, should be relegated to the "student of myth and social structure rather than the historian."[3] It would seem ludicrous in other contexts to exclude the central ideas and objectives of politics from a political history. As J. Matthew Schoffeleers demonstrates, such mythical elements point to the ideological basis of precolonial polities.[4] The objectives of political struggle were the spiritual powers that allowed the people to reproduce and the land to produce.

There have, of course, been many accounts of "Bemba religion." But in these accounts religion appears as superstition or, at best, a timeless tribal dogma that is a partial revelation of a true religion. Concerned to spread their religion, missionaries separated history from religion and focused on the relationships of local spiritual beliefs with Christian dogma.[5] Anthropologists, too, discussed religion as if it somehow belonged to individual tribes. Audrey I. Richards's seminal study conceived of religion as a functionalist legitimizing device for Bemba chieftaincy, "sacralising the political structure on which the tribe depend[s]."[6] Hugo F. Hinfelaar's more recent study combines missionary and anthropological approaches with a progressive concern for women's agency. Here, Richards's emphasis on Bemba chieftaincy is substituted with a Bemba religious dogma located among commoners and women.[7] Religion was not dogma or tribal trait, however; it was history, a description of past relationships between peoples and spirits that held ongoing implications for the identities of the living.

Emotions are at the narrative center of Bemba historical discourse. The oral tradition moves forward through passionate actions linked to love, seduction, jealousy, and death. "Story is at the heart of the way humans see themselves, experience themselves within the context of their worlds," according to renowned scholar of southern African oral traditions Harold Scheub. "And emotions are the soul of storytelling."[8] In his fieldwork notes on the nearby Nyakyusa, Godfrey Wilson noticed that "the ordinary intense feelings of men are often felt to have in themselves a directly religious quality. Sexual excitement, grief and fear bring into communion with ultimate realities."[9] Precisely because of their centrality to livelihood and their visceral manifestations, emotions were expressed spiritually. The Bemba oral tradition is a history of attempts to govern these spiritual emotions. The appeal and importance of the Bemba oral tradition emerged from these spiritual emotions. Audrey I. Richards thought that Bemba religion both sacralized political authorities and ritualized individual emotions.[10] Yet, instead of these being discrete foci of Bemba religion (sacralizing the political structure on the one hand and ritualizing individual emotions on the other, as Richards claimed), they were one and the same. The Bemba oral tradition reminded people of the love that sustained life and the jealousy that threatened it. In the narrative, the Crocodile Clan of Chitimukulu promised control over the spiritual emotions that gave life, fertility, and fecundity, but which could also lead to death. Only through harnessing such individual passions was the political authority of the Crocodile Clan sacralized. Passion individualizes, as Emile Durkheim argued, but it also enslaves.[11]

During the late nineteenth century, global economic forces began to impinge on the Bemba kingdom in an unprecedented fashion. As a result of internal dissent stemming from the spread of the kingdom and the subjugation of people such as the Bisa and external challenges from the Ngoni and an intensified slave trade, the Bemba kingdom faced new challenges. The instabilities of the nineteenth century ratcheted up the stakes in battles over political power. The Crocodile Clan rulers made a concerted effort to harness and control spiritual emotions. Only through the Crocodile Clan, the rulers claimed, would people fall in love, fertility and fecundity flourish, jealous and angry spirits be placated, and hunters and soldiers be imbued with the bravery to capture their prey and defeat their enemies. Even while the Crocodile Clan sponsored rituals and ceremonies that enhanced their access to the spirits, prophets also offered alternative spiritual interventions. This violent turmoil of people, spirits, and emotions led to the proliferation of invisible agents that began to be perceived as evil.

DESIRE AND DEATH

The Bemba politico-religious constellation rested on a frightening, magical, and dangerous story of desire and death. The characters existed in the liminality of human experience and had access to a world that was beyond the ordinary.[12] We do not know the narrative's exact performance and articulation prior to the nineteenth century; indeed, it might not have been rendered as a single story, but performed on many different occasions with different emphases. If the bare outline of the founding story refers to "historical facts," they probably took place in the seventeenth century.[13] But the oral tradition was likely influenced by the wars of the nineteenth century. The Roman Catholic White Father missionary Edouard Labrecque wrote down the most complete version of the oral tradition in the early twentieth century. Through the twentieth century, several successive attempts to write down the oral tradition in its entirety display differences in both form and content. Instead of attempting to write down a more authentic version—since there is no urtext—I have culled and summarized sequences from several sources that are most important for this discussion.[14]

On one level, the oral tradition is a fairly typical story of the strife between fathers and sons and the restoration of ties between sisters and brothers found within charters of the ChiBemba-speaking Lala, Lamba, and Aushi matrilineal clans that surround the central Bemba polity.[15] Thereby, the narrative introduces many familiar elements, necessary and convincing fragments and clichés that joined it to other stories—and places the Crocodile Clan's polity within a vast network of matrilineal cultures. But unlike many of the more ordinary and widespread clan-based narratives, the Bemba oral tradition makes a claim for the divine origins of the Crocodile Clan. The first sequence of the story establishes these grandiose origins through their link with a celestial mother. The joining of sky and earth, a basic principle of sacred Luba politico-religious kings—and a refrain to which the Bemba oral tradition returns repeatedly—was thereby achieved:

> A lord, Mukulumpe, was hunting in a forest when he met a beautiful woman with large ears like an elephant. She said that her name was Mumbi Mukasa, she had come from the sky, and she belonged to the Crocodile Clan. Mukulumpe and Mumbi Mukasa married and had three sons, Nkole, Chiti, Katongo, and one daughter, Chilufya (or Bwalya Chabala).

The Crocodile Clan

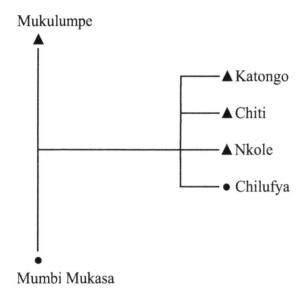

Mukulumpe

▲

┌──── ▲ Katongo

├──── ▲ Chiti

├──── ▲ Nkole

└──── ● Chilufya

●

Mumbi Mukasa

The Autochthons

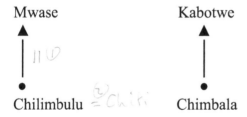

Mwase   Kabotwe

▲   ▲

●   ●

Chilimbulu = Chiti   Chimbala

Figure 1.2. Diagram of the Crocodile Clan. As indicated in the oral tradition of the arrival of the Crocodile Clan rulers on the Lubemba Plateau.

The marriage between the hunter and the celestial woman, Mumbi Mukasa, establishes the possibilities for a royal family, as illustrated in figure 1.2, and for the spread of Luba and Lunda political institutions. But in family there was also jealousy and discord. The sons display their maternal devotion by building a tower to their mother's home, but after it collapses and causes destruction, they have to flee the wrath of their father. They rescue their sister, however, restoring their most affectionate matrilineal affiliations:

The royal sons tried to build a tower to their mother's home in the sky. But it collapsed and killed many people. Their angry father, Mukulumpe, banished their mother to the sky and imprisoned their sister, Chilufya. He blinded one son, Katongo, who managed to send a warning with the talking drum to his brothers, Nkole and Chiti, of a trap set by their father. The brothers fled eastward, led by a white magician, Luchele Ng'anga. After they crossed the Luapula River, Chiti sent five men to rescue his sister, Chilufya. She joined her brothers, carrying seeds for Bemba agriculture in her hair (in some versions, Nkole carried the seeds in his hair).[16]

The white magician, Luchele Ng'anga, was the first of a line of famous migrant prophets who ignited the political imagination of northeastern Zambians over the next two centuries. Perhaps, as the anthropologist Luc de Heusch claims, Luchele Ng'anga was a solar hero, representing the dawn of the new era, the rays of the rising sun that led the Crocodile Clan eastward.[17]

While the potential symbolic interpretations are further discussed below, here I want to draw attention to the quotidian aspects of the story, the basic emotional principles upon which the mythical grandeur was built. The falling in love, the establishment of family, the emotional ties between mothers and sons and brothers and sisters, all of which move our story forward, and lead to the eastward migration of the Crocodile Clan. Upon arriving in the new land, there is a second love affair: a married woman, Chilimbulu, the Bemba heroine depicted on the staff of rule, seduces the most admirable of the migrating sons, Chiti, with her beautiful tattoo. The jealousy that this act of passion ignites leads to Chiti's death. But his death, and the consequent revenge killing, provides the sacred principles upon which the Bemba kingdom comes to rest. In his death, Chiti became the ancestor who ruled over the land, Chiti the Great, Chitimukulu, the title of the Bemba paramount, and a position inherited by succeeding Crocodile Clan patriarchs:

> Chilimbulu was the wife of the hunter Mwase. With her attractive scarifications, she seduced Chiti. But Mwase caught them while they were having sex. They fought over Chilimbulu, and Mwase killed Chiti with a poisoned arrow. Nkole then avenged the death of his brother Chiti. He killed Mwase and Chilimbulu and cut up their bodies, but carefully preserved Chilimbulu's attractive scarified skin. In future, the skin would be kept as a royal relic, a *babenye*. A "virgin" (or guardian of the relic) would wear the skin of Chilimbulu when it was time to plant the first seeds.[18]

The celestial ancestry of the Crocodile Clan could not overcome the local magic of the earth; the dangerous desires that a woman inspires. Such desires had to be appropriated and made productive: the skin of Chilimbulu became the *chibyalilo* object of power used to bless the seeds when it was time to plant.[19] While the paramount Chitimukulu kept Chilimbulu's skin, subordinate Crocodile Clan rulers received a staff of rule with designs that traced out Chilimbulu's scarified skin and represented her body as a means to communicate with the spirit world.[20]

Chiti's brother Nkole then found a place to bury Chiti. The graveyard also had to be cleansed by an act of passion:

> Nkole then searched for a graveyard to bury his brother Chiti. He found an unmarried Luba woman of the Sorghum Clan, Chimbala. She offered a beautiful forested grove for Chiti's grave. Nkole requested that she cleanse the burial party. But cleansing could only be performed by a woman after she had had sex with her husband. So her slave Kabotwe had sex with her. Kabotwe (or Chimbala) would then become the caretaker of the graveyard, Mwalule, the father of "Mwalule," "Shimwalule."[21]

Chiti was buried, bringing the spiritual power of the celestial Crocodile Clan down to earth. Nkole arranged the burial and then joined his brother:

> Nkole carefully preserved the corpse of Chiti by soaking it, drying it in the sun, and wrapping it in a cow's hide. He burned the remains of Mwase and Chilimbulu, so that they could be buried with Chiti. But the smoke from the fire also killed Nkole. They then prepared the body of Nkole in the same way. As the elder brother he was buried above Chiti. They were both buried beneath a termite mound, with their heads facing east.

The graveyard, termed "Mwalule," became the spiritual center of human and agricultural fertility. The burial of Chiti and Nkole is the end of the charter tradition of genesis, although the oral tradition of the Crocodile Clan continues to narrate significant episodes of their rule, mostly during the nineteenth century.

EMOTIONAL POWERS

There are various ways to interpret this first portion of the oral tradition. In typical Luba stories of the founding of the sacred kings (*mulopwe*), the migrating royal marries the local earth priest.[22] This marriage has been interpreted to indicate the unification of local ancestors with Luba sacred royalty, creating a new form of leadership, the *mfumu* (usually translated as "chief").[23] Such a secular political interpretation has been developed by Andrew Roberts, who wrote the still-unrivaled account of the precolonial history of the Bemba, and discusses the oral tradition as a founding political charter that establishes a relationship of dominance of the migrating Crocodile Clan over the autochthons. The story has no greater historical relevance for Roberts. However, that it remained a political charter through the nineteenth century, was so popular, and took on such a generic form, so similar to the many narratives of the south-central African interior, indicates the centrality of the story to Bemba consciousness during this time period.

The Bemba oral tradition is distinctive from the generic Luba oral tradition in one important way. The Luba genesis narrative features Nkongolo as the uncivilized king who is overcome by the foreigners (the hunter Mbidi Kiluwe and his sons) who bring sacred kingship. The Bemba oral tradition, by contrast, places emphasis on autochthonous spiritual powers by claiming that sacred governance was present in the form of the sacred *mulopwe* kings before the arrival of Chitimukulu.[24] The claims of divine kingship were thus not sufficient to legitimize Chitimukulu's rule; he had to join the sacred principles of kingship with the powers of the local owners of the land. He did this by first having sex with a local woman, then being killed by her husband, and finally being buried in the earth. In his burial, the king became part of the land and a local ancestral spirit. Even while they killed the autochthons, the Crocodile Clan royals died at their hands. For they could then claim to have conquered and succumbed, both of which were necessary to become the ancestors, the *mipashi* (sing. *mupashi*) of the land.

Throughout the Bemba oral tradition, there is reference to powers of the sky and the earth, along with attempts to bring about a new dawn by joining the sky with the earth. Perhaps, like a millenarian Christian movement, these represented efforts to create heaven on earth. For Luc de Heusch, this aspect of the oral tradition explores structural oppositions between sun and earth, civilization and savagery, which informed Bemba cosmology. The dangerous but necessary attempts to join the spirits above and below, the sky and the earth, as in the liminal moments of dawn, are indeed evident throughout the oral tradition: from the Crocodile Clan's failed adolescent attempts to reach their celestial mother's homeland to their migration led by the solar hero Luchele Ng'anga toward the rising sun in the east, and finally their death and burial, in which the Crocodile Clan established their celestial connections through being dried by the sun's rays and thus bringing the sun down to earth.[25] Documentary evidence from the nineteenth century provides some support for this ambitious symbolic interpretation. In 1868, Livingstone was told that the Bemba believe in "Reza above [Lesa, or "God"], who kills people, and Reza below, who carries them away after death."[26] Bemba cosmology associated ancestral spirits, *mipashi*, with the earth below, *panshi*, where the ancestors are buried (even while the etymology of *–pashi* and *panshi* may be distinct). Nature spirits, *ngulu*, by contrast, refer to the sky above (*–ulu*).[27] The opposition of spiritual forces from above and below may have ancient roots in Bantu-speaking societies: objects of power, such as *minkisi* from the western Bantu-speaking Kongo, were also known to come from above or below.[28]

The symbolism needs to be supplemented with the more mundane and emotional aspects that made the story all the more gripping and significant for listeners. Sex, jealousy, and death are all age-old sources of fascination for storytellers and their listeners. The narrative is an emotional tragedy that describes a family feud, the fleeing of sons, exile, an illicit desire, and an adulterous relationship that leads to death and revenge and—more death. What is interesting—and constrasts with secular emotional tragedies that unfold due to the mysterious and fatalistic qualities of "love"—is how linked emotions are to spiritual forces: love and seduction to the spiritual and ritual forces that promote fertility; jealousy and anger to the witchcraft that kills Chiti and Nkole. Chilimbulu seduces (and perhaps bewitches) Chiti with her scarified skin. This same magical and beguiling skin was then used to bless the land. The skin relic brings about fertility, a mysterious power that referred to the water monitor (*mbulu*), a secretive and strange creature.[29] Mwase, the jealous husband, fights with Chiti over Chilimbulu, and kills him with his magic. Even in death, his witchcraft kills Nkole. Such is the power of love and of jealousy—it inspires fertility and it inspires death. Only through rituals were such passions contained and made productive for health and wealth. Like Jesus Christ, Chiti died for his people. However, his passion, unlike Christ's, was anything but ascetic. It was ignited by the body of Chilimbulu and had to be controlled by the Crocodile Clan ancestors.

In this oral tradition, then, we have some early evidence of the governance of spiritual emotions, which lead to reproduction and fertility or to death. Rulers needed to channel and deal with such dangerous emotions, and if death resulted, they had to know proper mortuary rites, so as to prevent the unruly behavior by dissatisfied ancestors (hence the detailed focus on the way Chiti and Nkole were buried).[30] The political charter legitimized the Crocodile Clan patriarchs' claims to harness the spiritual emotions: if emotions were calmed and directed, they could lead to fertility and reproduction; jealousy, on the other hand, led to death, the consequences of which could be dealt with only through prescribed rituals.

ROYAL ANCESTRAL SPIRITS
AND LOCAL NATURE SPIRITS

The division between *ngulu* nature spirits and *mipashi* ancestral spirits further illustrates the ways that the Crocodile Clan governed spiritual emotions. *Ngulu* were old spirits that were said to exist prior to the rise of the Bemba polity.[31] They were independent of people, sometimes manifest in wild animals or natural sites. Throughout the region, such *ngulu* inspired spiritual emotions. When they possessed people, they had very physical effects, including emission of rhythmic whimpers (*ukusemuka*), as well as a form of glossolalia or prophecy (*ukusesema*). At times they inspired those possessed to dance.[32]

Mipashi, by contrast, were the ancestral spirits of the dead, freed from their corporeal form. *Mipashi* could control phenomena in the natural world, and at times they inspired people to act in certain ways. It was most important that an ancestral *mupashi* return to its original clan. A newborn baby cried until an ancestral *mipashi* had possessed and given the baby a name. However, after a death of one partner in marriage, the most intimate of emotional relationships, something of the dead remained in the grieving spouse: that something was the *mupashi* spirit. It had to return to the original clan, and that was why a partner had to be "married" (or cleansed by sex) with a member of the dead spouse's clan.[33]

Within the Bemba polity, as well as the related eastern Lunda, royal clans claimed that their ancestral *mipashi* replaced the emotional *ngulu* spirit possession of commoners. The ancestors of humans achieved dominance over the spirits of nature. At least in the political heartland of the Bemba, non-chiefly ancestors and *ngulu* spirits became relatively marginal. The Crocodile Clan could not be possessed by *ngulu* and directed veneration toward their ancestors instead.[34] The ancestral *mipashi* of royalty calmed people, displacing the turbulence that *ngulu* inspired.

Among non–Crocodile Clan commoners, however, alternative spiritual formulations proliferated. Spiritual emotions were dealt with primarily at the local level. The head of a family, clan, or village had personal shrines, *mfuba*, either in the individual houses, at the foot of a bed, where their personal ancestors resided, or in or near sacred points in the village in miniature hut shrines. In 1868 Livingstone found such shrines in villages across the northern plateau. Places of veneration were also found in old burial grounds.[35] Termite mounds were the most sacred of burial sites, the "church of the ancestors."[36] The Crocodile Clan attempted to appropriate and innovate this local spiritual governance. By being buried under a termite mound, Nkole and Chiti could become the ancestral archetype. The politico-religious Crocodile Clan constellation oriented itself around these existing quotidian spiritual forms by offering a centralized polity that dealt with the emotional turmoil of family and collective economic ventures such as hunting and agriculture.

In addition to local ancestral shrines, people made use of the supernatural agency of objects to combat and to harness spiritual emotions. If used in the right fashion, many objects had the potential to affect nature and people. *Bwanga*, commonly translated as "magic," more accurately refers to the power of objects used for a required purpose, ranging from bravery and success on a hunting expedition to love and fertility. A feather, a leaf, a root, or part of an animal or person could be used, as long as it was understood and manipulated in the correct way, often through metaphor and metonymy. For example, the *chibyalilo* planting ceremony (from the verb *ukubyalo*, "to sow"), which was performed to ensure that a seed grew into a plant, required objects that grew and expanded, such as bark from a tree that became swollen when wet, the skin of a type of animal that grew in size when wounded, or the soil from a termite mound that rose from the earth. All people could use *bwanga*; it was part of everyday life. But individuals who faced difficult circumstances employed specialists, men and women of knowledge who were adept in knowing the powers of objects, *shinganga* (literally, the father of the art of *bwanga*).[37]

At the center of the Bemba polity, the presence of *shinganga* and the use of *bwanga* were discouraged. The Bemba royals claimed that they were immune from *bwanga* and that they were personally responsible for the welfare of the people and the land. The *bwanga* used in the *chibyalilo* agricultural ceremony, for example, were linked directly to Chitimukulu. In his village, the wife of the relic (*muka benya*) wore a belt made from Chilimbulu's scarified skin and planted the first seeds. People could then plant their own gardens and be sure of prosperity. The crops would grow, like the termite mound under which the first Crocodile Clan royals were buried. Nevertheless, while the royal clan tried to control the use and proliferation of *bwanga*, it remained an autonomous invisible agent used in quotidian life.[38]

During times of war, sickness, and death, when emotions afflicted all, government intervention in the invisible world was most urgently required. If Chitimukulu should fall ill and fail to perform the appropriate ancestral rites, the land would spoil, no rain would fall, crops would not grow, and general misfortune would abound. During such times leaders needed to demonstrate their spiritual agency. Rites of passion, which involved a leader having sex with his head wife ("the wife of the land"), ensured the fertility of the land and blessed the most significant tools of agriculture, the ax and the seed. During and after such acts, when the king was most closely linked to the land, both good and bad fortune could result.[39] Such rites affirmed and acted out aspects of the original charter, especially the dangerous sexual relations between the migrant Chiti and the autochthon Chilimbulu.

The graveyard where the kings were buried became the spiritual center of the Bemba polity, the place where the ancestral kings remained. It combined the ancestral graves and shrines of the Crocodile Clan with their particular *bwanga*, their chiefly *babenye* relics. Many of Chitimukulu's sacred *babenye* relics, such as the skin of Chilimbulu, were kept in a shrine hut at Mwalule, allegedly built by the prophet Luchele Ng'anga. These relics were the keys to the land, and their possession indicated ownership over the land. A usurper had to capture the relics before conquering the land. Three elderly women, the "wives of the relics" (*bamukabenye*), were their protectors. About once a month Chitimukulu's chief councilors, the *bakabilo*, came to Mwalule to make sure the relics were well kept and to perform ceremonies appropriate to agricultural, hunting, or military affairs.[40] The territory around the graveyard was known as Chilinda (the place that is guarded). The actual graveyard fell under the control of the autochthon Kabotwe's descendants, who retained the title of the father of the graveyard, Shimwalule.[41] That Chitimukulu's grave-yard, Mwalule, would be cared for by a former "slave" indicated the sacred power of subordinates and dependents. The story established a social hierar-chy, but recognized the spiritual agencies of those at the bottom of the hierar-chy, illustrating the acts of negotiation involved in developing the consensus between conquerors and autochthons necessary to consolidate a polity.

The Mwalule graveyard and its *babenye* shrine center joined other local rul-ers and places, with their distinctive stories, to the royal court. The Chishimba Falls, for example, where the Chambeshi River cascades in a series of magnifi-cent waterfalls, were long associated with the suicides of a father, Chishimba, and his daughter and her suitor, after a failed marriage. Chitimukulu took the lamp used to illuminate the marital hut and kept it as *bwanga*, one of his *babe-nye* relics, at the Mwalule shrine. At Chishimba, a goat was given to the *ngulu* spirit, and left in a cave behind the waterfall. The royal clan appropriated or at least associated older stories of love, familial strife, and serene natural wonders with their spiritual center. A story and a relic attached an ancestor, such as Chishimba, to Chitimukulu's court. The ancestor's name became the title of a local ruler or a *bakabilo* councilor to the king.[42]

A few abstract nature spirits escaped the focused politico-religious atten-tion of the Crocodile Clan rulers. The most general of such nonancestral spirits was *Lesa*, an omnipresent but remote spirit. Lesa was prevalent across the region from at least the late eighteenth century and probably much ear-lier; in 1799 Father Pinto, of José Maria de Lacerda's expedition, reported belief in "the existence of a sovereign creator of the world . . . 'Reza' [Lesa] . . . a tyrant that permits his creatures' death."[43] The linguistic spread of the term and of proverbs regarding Lesa suggests an even older presence.[44] Oral testimony indicates that Lesa might have replaced older ancestral cults of the earth or bush, especially those linked to Shakapanga (the father of the bush) or Mushili Mfumu (the earth chief). There is some evidence of Lesa as a feminine owner of the earth, a "mother-earth" spirit that "gives birth to crops as a mother brings forth children."[45] However, many names related to Lesa indicate an association with thunder and with the sky, which contrast with the spirits of the earth below.[46] The earliest recorded stories about Lesa tell of it giving a man and a woman the choice between food and eternal life; the couple chose food, and hence humans became mortal, returning from the sky to the earth below.[47] Of course, this story may have been influenced by biblical Eden narratives that could have spread across the region from the eighteenth century, if not earlier. Indeed, since so many proverbs and narratives have been influenced by the Christian missionary translation of Lesa as the Christian God, a precise precolonial definition of Lesa is elusive.[48] Nevertheless, while Lesa may have been thought of as the original spirit, omnipresent and allowing life and death, it was marginal compared to the ancestral and nature spirits who intervened directly in the affairs of family and in the immediate bounties of nature, or who were agents in causing illness and death.

Lesa or similar spirits were favorable and benevolent spirits, an indication of emotional well-being, the way relationships between people and nature should be in the absence of turmoil. Yet times of death and upheaval led to a proliferation of angry and jealous spirits, almost evil, that disrupted normal life. *Chiwa* and *chibanda* were the bad living dead, those who died with a grudge, from suicide, or who were wrongly accused by their relatives.[49] Or they were roaming ancestors, unable to find their people and have their names restored to newborn babies.[50] Stories of capture and consumption by such angry spirits were frequent. Specialists dealt with this type of spirits; if the disruption was connected with the dead, they dug up the bones of the dead and burned them, so that they could no longer haunt the living. In other cases, disembodied *chiwa* evil, almost an evil wind (*umuze uwipe*), inspired people to do harmful acts, such as killing a neighbor or relative.[51] Sometimes harm originated from savage mythical figures, such as Mwansakabinga or Kanama, who kidnapped and carried away young children.[52] Such angry forces inspired antisocial actions in men; agency lay in what the missionary Edouard Labrecque termed "occult" forces, rather than living people. A murderer, for example, was one who was "seized" by such magic (*Bamwikata bwanga*).[53]

Jealous people mobilized occult forces and were perhaps even initiated into associations of witches (*baloshi*). They accessed spiritual power to harm others and were also experts in the use of poison. Among the Luba, witches were detected by the use of potions or horns with powder inside, objects that gave people the power to see the invisible. If caught, the accused persons could be subjected to the *mwavi* poison ordeal. Those who were guilty would die instead of vomiting the poison. The killing of a witch was dangerous, as unless certain ritual prescriptions were followed, the spirit of the witch returned to cause havoc in the community. People cut up and burned witches in a ritual that resembled the burning of the original jealous husband, Mwase, so that they could no longer employ their witchcraft.[54] At the center of the Bemba polity, the Crocodile Clan claimed to deal with such dangerous individuals, obviating the need for other *shinganga*.

Good fortune could also "fall upon" (*ukuwilwa*) people. When possession was good, it meant a step on the path toward recovery from sickness, misfortune, or even anger and jealousy. A benevolent *ngulu* spirit spoke through the possessed and often entranced person, who prophesized (*ukusesema*), revealed unknown things, including the name of the *ngulu* protective spirit. Henceforth, the person would belong to that spirit, they would become *bangulu*, and through their possession they would help others to understand the spiritual forces behind possession.[55] An early twentieth-century description points to women as especially potent victims and agents of possession:

> These women assert that they are possessed by the spirit of some dead chief, and when they feel the "divine afflatus," whiten their faces to attract attention, and anoint themselves with flour which has a religious and sanctifying potency. One of their number beats a drum, and the others dance, at the same time singing a weird song, with curious intervals. Finally when they have arrived at the requisite pitch of religious exaltation the possessed fall to the ground, and burst forth into a low and almost inarticulate chant, which has a most uncanny effect. All at once are silent and the b'asing'anga [*Bashinganga*] gather round to interpret the voice of the spirit.[56]

Women were especially prone to such emotional possession, perhaps because they were closer to the spirit realm of the bush (*mpanga*) or that of the earth or bush spirits of Lesa and Shakapanga.[57] But these explanations are the intellectual reasonings of Western scholars. Perhaps women *felt* the spirits, and because of this ability, women were prophets, but also victims of possession and agents of witchcraft who met in the most secret of associations.[58] They were most closely linked to the spirit world, with its opportunities and dangers — in other words, its powers.

Crocodile Clan attempts to harness and control the spiritual power of women is further illustrated in their relationship to the *chisungu* ceremonies that introduced girls after puberty into womanhood and prepared them for marriage and childbirth. The consistency of *chisungu* instruction was maintained by the molding of clay figurines, *mbusa* — a lion, a tree, a bracelet, a stupid husband, a snake—which were associated with songs and dances that taught of the duties and relationships between husband and wife. A "mother" of the *mbusa* relics, *nachimbusa*, organized the ceremonies and was responsible for teaching songs and dances along with their meanings to the girls. In addition to being paid to oversee ceremonies, she attained a special status and could wear a feathered headdress reserved for royalty. The ceremonies, which lasted for several months, culminated in a celebration at the transition to womanhood and marriage.[59] Even in this rite, the Crocodile Clan's influence became evident. The Chilimbulu design painted on the huts used for the *chisungu* rites reminded initiates of Chilimbulu's scarified skin that had seduced Chiti and led to his death.[60] Around the Crocodile *mbusa*, women sang: "Take the girl to the crocodile," meaning the initiate should be put under the authority of the Crocodile Clan.[61] Twentieth-century accounts of the ceremony associate its history with the oral tradition of the Crocodile Clan and claim that the migrants, Chiti, Nkole, and Chilufya, brought it with them— even while its widespread prevalence indicates an older and autochthonous presence.[62] According to Hinfelaar, in the nineteenth century the royal clan began to appoint *nachimbusa*, and the ceremony prepared women to be submissive wives of royals rather than emphasize their autonomy and religious importance.[63] Yet evidence for the depth of this transformation in the precolonial period is spotty; one of the earliest twentieth-century observers reported neither crocodile *mbusa* nor the imposition of the authority of the Crocodile Clan on the ceremonial rites.[64] Outside the Bemba political center, *chisungu* rites remained autonomous of Crocodile Clan influence.

The Crocodile Clan royalty incorporated local spheres of politico-religious experience by replicating their ancestral shrines in the villages that they conquered and over which they claimed authority, thus replacing shrines to local ancestral and nature spirits with ones to their own ancestors. They claimed responsibility for overcoming and harnessing spiritual emotions and for getting rid of witches. Their personal *bwanga*, the *babenye* relics, ensured prosperity. All termite mounds represented the graves in which the titleholder Shimwalule buried Chiti and Nkole. Such sacred sites became conduits for the spread of the Crocodile Clan's power. Like the colonial administrative centers, the Bomas, which later spread the constellations of power of indirect rule, the authority of the Bemba court spread to outlying villages through its sacred sites.

These sacred sites were not only about legitimizing the Crocodile Clan, however; locals viewed them as an opportunity to indicate their own agency in the Crocodile Clan government.[65] This was particularly the case in oral traditions for which there were no authoritative texts that established and fixed their meanings, no dogma. Individuals could retell and refine stories in substantially different ways, appealing to different interpretations. Shimwalule, the caretaker of the graveyard, told a different version of the story, for example. He was not a slave of Chimbala (the original owner of the Crocodile Clan graveyard) but her lover, and he married her upon the request of Nkole. In exchange for the land and for taking care of the graveyard, Chitimukulu was to send a portion of his wealth to Shimwalule.[66] For such leaders, the reciprocity between conqueror and conquered formed the basic political principle of the Bemba polity. The royal court might choose to underemphasize this reciprocity, but the story told by Shimwalule reminded them of their promises. Shimwalule, as guardian of the royal graveyard and the spiritual center of the Bemba polity, was an especially powerful local agent, for he looked after the living dead. "Chitimukulu, Nkula and Mwamba always send me big presents because they know that I am their father," Shimwalule told a burial party in the 1930s. "If I am doing my work wrong here as Shimwalule the spirits of the dead chiefs will be angry with me and punish me."[67] A former slave or subject was the interface between the living kings and their ancestors; he took care of the dead so that their anger would not intervene in the world. He alone was responsible for ensuring that the Crocodile Clan's ancestral spirits would facilitate fecundity and fertility, bringing the sun down to warm the wet earth and allow the crops to germinate and grow.

The Crocodile Clan genesis story, then, opens up and attempts to reconcile through Chitimukulu's death, the conflicting orientations of the Bemba political imagination: that of the sky and the earth, the royal court and the village, and men and women. The state was linked to the migration of the Crocodile Clan patriarchs who descended from a celestial mother, and were led by the prophet of dawn, Luchele Ng'anga. Then there was the earth, the spiritual powers of autochthonous women who held the secrets of production and reproduction. In death and burial, the Crocodile Clan patriarchs became enveloped in the earth, bringing heaven down to earth and offering a new polity to the people of the Bemba plateau. They created a state that harnessed the spiritual powers of women and overcame the turmoil and witchcraft of village, clan, and family. While the Crocodile Clan claimed that their ancestral spirits governed the land and displaced local ancestors and nature spirits, the polity still rested on an old expectation that government would play a role in the invisible world that ensured prosperity and protected from harm.

EVIL AFFLICTIONS

The Crocodile Clan's ability to deal with jealousy, witches, and angry spirits was not always convincing. Ancestral and nature spirits proved ineffective in explaining the war and upheaval linked to the growing trade in slaves. The quotidian hardships and afflictions of the mid- to late nineteenth century could be explained only by a generalized evil that seemed to afflict the land

and the people, an evil that would increase with the European colonial and missionary occupation.

From the 1860s to the 1880s, the Bemba polity attained its greatest degree of centralization and geographic reach under the leadership of Chitapankwa (reigned from the 1860s to 1883; d. 1883), who became Chitimukulu after capturing the *babenye* relics from his sick mother's brother, Bwembya.[68] The expansion of the central Bemba polity under Chitapankwa was a reaction to the military challenge posed by the Ngoni of Mpezeni to the north and east. Chitapankwa strengthened Bemba military outposts, such as the Ichinga (the defensive fortress) province of Nkula, by appointing his closest matrilineal relatives as overlords who could defend the political heartland of Lubemba and the spiritual center, Mwalule. In addition to standing in a relationship of perpetual kinship to Chitimukulu, these relatives were in a position to succeed the king. The Crocodile Clan rulers also employed ambitious sons as lords, whose positions relied on their loyalty to their fathers as they were excluded from the usual opportunities of advancement available to the Crocodile Clan matrilineage. The Crocodile Clan and their direct dependents benefited from the growing trade in ivory and slaves with the East African Swahili and Nyamwezi. The process contributed to the militarization of the Bemba polity.[69]

There were internal challenges as well, especially in the areas where the Bemba established new military outposts. The class cleavages that had developed due to the imposition of Bemba rule and the opportunities for accumulating wealth were striking. In 1867, south of the Chambeshi, presumably in the area ruled by Nkula, Livingstone reported on "poor dependents on Bemba, or rather their slaves, who cultivate little, and then only in the rounded patches . . . so as to prevent their conquerors from taking away more than a small share. The subjects are Babisa—a miserable lying lot of serfs."[70] The rulers, protected by stockades adorned with skulls, had access to so much Katangan copper that they were "obliged to walk in a stately style, from the weight."[71] Fifteen years later, Victor Giraud reported that the Bemba royals were large and fat, from beer. Nkula was dressed in imported cloth with chains of large red glass beads and surrounded by a hundred men armed with bows and arrows and flintlocks.[72]

In addition to the growth of wealth and military power from the late nineteenth century, a close examination of the ritual, ceremonial, and religious roles of Chitimukulu and the Bemba royals during the late nineteenth century suggests an attempted expansion (or at least a consolidation) of such roles. Chitimukulu Chitapankwa's praise name was *Mukungula mfuba* (he who sweeps away the personal ancestral shrines), suggesting less of an increase in secular authority (as Andrew Roberts claims) than an attempt to enhance Chitimukulu's spiritual powers by attacking older ancestral and nature shrines.[73]

Chitimukulu Chitapankwa was like the colonial and postcolonial prophets who eradicated the witchcraft of old and purified the people and the land. Under his reign, the Crocodile Clan's ancestral welfare became tied to the welfare of the land and the people. When locusts and wild animals, lions and crocodiles, afflicted Lubemba and Ichinga, Chitimukulu Chitapankwa constructed a shrine to his uncle Bwembya (whom Chitapankwa had deposed) and sent offerings to Shimwalule at the royal graveyard.[74] In war against the Ngoni, Chitimukulu Chitapankwa, after being purified by the *babenye* relics, invoked a patriotic ancestral appeal:

> Oh my ancestors who were kings before me, lead me on this expedition to attack the *Muchime* [the stabbers, the Ngoni], who have come from afar to take the land from us without cause. . . . The land is ours, all our ancestors are buried in it, and we must save it, and drive our enemies away. Oh spirits of the ancestors, pray to God for us that we may be able to overcome the *Muchime*.[75]

The increasing demand for slaves to trade for guns and cloth ratcheted up the stakes in the Bemba royals' claims to judicial authority. Compensation for crimes, including murder, adultery, poisoning, and witchcraft, was increasingly paid for in slaves and imported cloth (in turn purchased with slaves) instead of goats, hoes, and axes. While the victim of a crime received some compensation, the lord who had adjudicated the dispute also received payments. Those acquired through judicial services marched in Swahili, Ovimbundu, Nyamwezi, or Chikunda caravans toward an uncertain future in the Indian Ocean and Atlantic worlds.[76] The demand for slaves widened notions of criminal liability and increased the Bemba royals' claims of judicial importance by emphasizing the Crocodile Clan's ancestral ties to the land and their autonomy from the everyday forms of witchcraft that afflicted commoners. Only the Crocodile Clan could deal with the danger of witches. It was no surprise that Chitimukulu Chitapankwa swept away the shrines of lesser men, ancestors, and spirits. The intensification of the slave trade increased the stakes in claims to spiritual power as well as the greed, jealousy, and uncertainty that indicated the agency of angry and even evil spirits.

During Chitimukulu Chitapankwa's reign, the spiritual powers of the Crocodile Clan came to be represented, enacted, and performed in royal ceremonies and dances, with abundant beer, the grandeur of which impressed and appealed to many. Consumption, patronage, and the possibilities and promises of wealth became part of these grand gatherings. Chitimukulu was the host, the *mwine lupepo*, the owner of the ceremony, secure in his political authority and demonstrative of his generosity. But most of all, such ceremonies venerated ancestral ties and imbued Chitimukulu with spiritual power.[77] While few remain, it is also likely that in this period ancestral power objects, such as the Chilimbulu staff, either commissioned or traded from Luba artists, celebrated the sacred royalty of the Crocodile Clan.[78]

The burial of the chief was the most dangerous of times, when emotional turmoil could become spiritual and political turmoil unless ritual prescriptions were followed. The death of Chitimukulu Chitapankwa in 1883 probably established the "traditional" model for such ritual prescriptions. After his death, Chitimukulu was embalmed in the fashion referred to by the oral tradition. Only upon the ripening of the royal millet crop that was planted when he died could the king be buried. The close councilors (*bakabilo*) of the king and those who dealt with his death (*bafingo*) then embarked on a journey that lasted up to a week, a type of funeral procession from Lubemba to the Mwalule graveyard, with stops at several sacred sites. The journey itself was perilous. The pallbearers fought with the embalmers to release the body and with the men of Shimwalule. A death in such ritual battles signaled good fortune. Slaves, dependents, and the three head wives of the dead paramount accompanied the procession. At the Mwalule graveyard, the *bafingo* struck them with a club on the bridge of the nose. If they lived, the dead paramount had "forgiven" them, "vomited them out" (*mfumu ya muluka*).[79] Those who died were buried with Chitimukulu and those who lived became personal slaves of the gravekeepers. The paramount was laid to rest on top of the head wife, another wife supported his head, and another his feet. The burial, referencing and reinforcing the oral tradition of Chiti and Nkole, was a period of great terror that demonstrated the spiritual agency of the dead royals and their ties to the land. Their return to the earth below (*–panshi*) and conversion into ancestors, *mipashi*, claimed to secure the well-being of the kingdom and provided a model ritual for the correct ways of dealing with death.[80]

The occasional outburst of ceremony, grandeur, and terror did not legitimize the Bemba royals without contestation. The farther from the political center that Bemba authority spread, the less convincing the reach of the Crocodile Clan ancestral cult and the greater the profusion of alternative spiritual agents. Rulers who had only a shallow genealogy of local ancestors could not claim the same spiritual authority over the land as those who ruled at the same place as several generations of their ancestors. To the east, Chitimukulu's perpetual nephew Nkula ruled the defensive fortress of Ichinga; to the north, Nkhweto watched over Chilinda (the place that is guarded); and to the south, Mwamba conquered the Bisa. In all of these border territories, many of them conquered by the Bemba only in the late nineteenth century, the Bemba faced invasion by the Ngoni and frequent challenges from exploited subjects, especially the Bisa. Here the ancestral cult of the Crocodile Clan was fractured by alternative spiritual agents. Among the Bisa, for example, agricultural *tulubi* shrines associated with *ngulu* were evident.[81] To the south and west, *mikishi* (sing. *mukishi*), spiritual forces held in objects that were representative of communal cults, replaced the relics of the Crocodile Clan chiefs.[82] One of the most famous of such communal or clan *mikishi* was Makumba of the Bena Ngulube (the Pig Clan) of the Aushi of Lake Bangweulu. Makumba was an object, perhaps a meteorite, dressed in python and human skin and adorned with feathers. It blessed the seed before planting, and was generally responsible for rites surrounding agriculture, in the same fashion as the skin of Chilimbulu.[83]

Independent hunting associations also dealt with spirits. The hunt was an emotionally intense time: the danger of the bush required bravery; killing and the conquest of nature needed the support of the *ngulu*. The *Butwa* association, for example, most prevalent east of the Bemba polity, especially around the Bangweulu and Luapula swamps, recognized the spiritual authority of the original inhabitants of the land, the "Batwa." The associations had organized leaders, *Shingulu* (the father of *ngulu*), public gatherings, and sacred *mulumbi* houses.[84] They had their own identity marks, scarification patterns that ran in a V-shape from the head to the chest. Figurines, sometimes representations of men, such as that depicted in figure 1.3 below, had copper eyes that viewed the spirits through trance, wide-open mouths that talked to spirits, and feet that traversed the visible and invisible worlds.[85] Perhaps initiated by groups of hunters seeking good fortune before they ventured into the bush, the associations were territorial cults, "concerned with man's role as a transformer and recipient from his natural environment."[86] They were probably linked to a more extensive system of Bulumbu possession and divination that stretched from Kasai to the southern edge of Lake Tanganyika.[87]

Bemba military expansion in the late nineteenth century to secure trade routes, guns, and slaves took the Crocodile Clan lords to areas where their spiritual powers were unknown and not respected. For example, when the Bemba royal Mwamba extended the reach of his authority over the Bisa, challenges to his rule were recalled in stories about the powers of Bisa prophets and spirits. In one such story, Mwamba tested the power of the Bisa prophets by challenging them to summon a lion to devour one of his wives while she drew water. She was caught and killed by a lion. An angry Mwamba had the prophets thrown into a bonfire, but they survived and were found sitting in the ashes of the fire the following morning. The prophets then summoned lions to chase Mwamba from their land.[88] He fled, but a successor returned a few years later, and the conflict-ridden history continued. In 1888, just prior to the European colonial period, Mwamba captured Bisa subjects and sold them to Swahili slave traders.[89] Farther south, the Bisa rebelled against the Bemba lord

Figure 1.3. Butwa figurine. Associated with the Tabwa to the north of the Bemba polity. The figure would have been used invoke the forces of the invisible world. Note the emphasis on body parts that access the invisible world such as the feet, the genitalia, the navel, and the eyes. Reproduced with permission of the Menil Collection, Houston.

Chikwanda and killed him, exacting the revenge of Chitimukulu, which led to greater Bisa subjugation and exile.[90]

Warfare inspired emotions that gave reign to spirits. In accounts of warfare, the efficacy of both Bisa and Crocodile Clan magic looms large. The Bisa were especially renowned for their war magic, including the *ilamfya*, a horn or drum treated with various *bwanga*, most potently the blood of captives.[91] Upon defeating their enemies, Bemba warriors cut up and burned their bodies, so that they could not become angry *chiwa* spirits and disturb the peace of the land.[92] (The practice once again referenced Nkole's treatment of Mwase's body in the Bemba oral tradition.) They brought the heads of the slain opponents to the Crocodile Clan lords, where they adorned village stockades and suggested the powers that the royals had over living and dead.[93] The Bemba also developed *ilamfya* to deal with the magic of their opponents and employed specialists, *Bachamanga*, to ensure success in war and to cleanse the warriors who might be haunted by those they had killed.[94] Chitimukulu and his appointed chiefs claimed exclusive rights over the use of these *ilamfya* and war specialists.[95] The murder of another person, perhaps the most emotional of all human actions, required special spiritual controls and governance.

New prophets claimed to mediate with ancient ancestors, the chiefs of old (*mfumu sha kale*) who evaded attempts at appropriation by the Bemba political authorities. The old chiefs were not even embodied by living kin; they appeared in dreams or possessed people or offered guidance on rituals concerning hunting and agriculture. No stories affiliated them with the Bemba royals. Such ancestors became spirits independent of narratives even as they were linked to nature.[96] People found them in places of beauty and serenity — waterfalls, the sources of rivers, and in large trees — inscribed in the natural features of landscape.[97] They also took the form of animals. When a hunter encountered a python, lion, or crocodile, he had to treat it with respect and wish it good health, lest it be the spirit of an old ancestor that had become an *ngulu*.[98]

At the center of the polity, Bemba politico-religious life attempted to marginalize other forms of spiritual power, such as territorial cults linked to *ngulu* veneration. The Crocodile Clan court organized a structured ritual and ceremonial life that replaced the localized system of *ngulu* appreciation and *bwanga* manipulation, even as it built on their spiritual conceptions. The most powerful Bemba ruler boasted that he "swept away" the ancestral shrines of others. He alone could control the spiritual emotions that gave rise to and threatened fertility and fecundity. Yet in the areas surrounding the Bemba villages, prophets mobilized alternative forms of spiritual power by claiming to be mediators with ancient ancestors and nature spirits more powerful than those of the Crocodile Clan. And even in the Crocodile Clan villages, the royals struggled to contain the use of *bwanga* and the spiritual agency of new prophets.

⤸

The Crocodile Clan posed a solution to a political imagination preoccupied with the spiritual power needed to ensure human reproduction and agricultural productivity. They claimed that their celestial origins catalyzed the power that led to the germination of crops and the reproduction of people. From the spiritual center at the Mwalule graveyard, their ancestors would intervene in the forces of nature. They appropriated sacred sites, incorporated old stories into their charter, and molded their *babenye* relics from the debris of conquest and the *bwanga* of old. The secrets to prosperity and reproduction lay with the spiritual emotions evoked by local women; the Crocodile Clan offered a government that controlled and harnessed these spiritual emotions. The scarified skin of Chilimbulu that had seduced Chitimukulu became the most sacred of royal relics, promising fertility and prosperity. The jealous husband, Mwase, could kill but would be contained by Crocodile Clan rule; and even the worst outcome of spiritual agency, death, could be dealt with through the mortuary rites introduced by the Crocodile Clan.

While the Crocodile Clan narrative of migration, sex, and death became a convincing politico-religious charter for well over a century, it remained vulnerable to alternative conceptions of spiritual agency. The Crocodile Clan's spiritual power was drawn from many past stories and principles; they innovated existing politico-religious ideas rather than revolutionizing them. In an increasingly desperate effort to maintain their authority in the face of external and internal challenges during the late nineteenth century, royals became unjust and cruel toward their subjects. People must have wondered whether angry spirits had possessed their rulers; perhaps they thought that elites had become witches and were employing spirits to gain unprecedented power. In the midst of this scramble for power, the Crocodile Clan's hegemony became precarious. Preoccupied with fertility and fecundity, their narrative offered no response to the injustice and harm that arose out of the wealth of new elites and the deepening subjugation, exploitation, and even sale into slavery of their dependents.

People needed to explain misfortune; they grasped for concepts that dealt with the global violence that challenged old relationships between people and the land. Destructive emotions of jealousy and anger were not sufficient to explain changes in the visible world. A new concept of evil became a convincing way to view the world; such evil had made people cruel and unjust. The Crocodile Clan could not control this roaming anger-cum-evil, in the wind, in wild animals, in slave traders, in disturbed ancestral shades, and in themselves. Many, even at times the Crocodile Clan (especially during war), turned to local specialists, such as the *shinganga*'s manipulation of *bwanga*. These specialists helped and healed, but, like the Crocodile Clan, they did not offer any lasting solutions to the scale of destructive change. People searched for collective ways to solve the problem of evil; they looked for the solar hero, Luchele Ng'anga, to lead them to a new dawn. And they became intrigued by the stories of a few strangers who roamed across Bembaland and spoke of eternal deliverance from the sin of witchcraft and the evil of Satan.

2 ⇆ Christian Witches

IN THE EARLY 1930S, the Roman Catholic missionary society of the White Fathers applied to open a mission in the Crocodile Clan chief Nkula's area, around twelve miles from the already established Protestant mission of the Presbyterian Church of Scotland at Lubwa. Since the land was designated "Native Trust," Nkula had to approve the White Fathers' application before the colonial administration would agree to the mission. Nkula refused. He did not want the Catholics to open a mission in his chieftaincy, and especially not near his own village. At first glance, Nkula's denial of permission for the White Fathers to build a mission seems strange. The White Fathers founding Bembaland missionary, Bishop Joseph Dupont, had boasted of his good relationship with the Crocodile Clan chiefs and had tried to cultivate a "Christian Kingdom" among the Bemba, at one point even claiming to inherit the Crocodile Clan royal title, Mwamba. Six missions had already been established near the Bemba heartland and another four on the periphery. The sacraments of the White Father held broad appeal; a significant proportion of the Bemba had been baptized. Nkula was quite accustomed to Catholics in his community. He was not a Christian and held no particular loyalty toward the nearby Presbyterian Lubwa Mission, a rival of the Catholics. Surely, the mission would bring employment, education, and medical resources, even if Nkula was not affiliated with the church. Yet Nkula was insistent in his refusal to allow the White Fathers mission. Then, quite suddenly, he changed his mind and agreed to the mission. If his initial refusal seems strange, his change of mind appears even more inexplicable.

Nkula's decisions took place in the midst of a changing spiritual politics. Christian missionaries and prophets advocated doctrines that talked about the pervasiveness of "sin," and questioned the power of nature and ancestral spirits even as they spoke of new invisible agents, God and Satan. The Christian missionaries were also divided and fiercely competitive with one other, and spoke of false religious doctrines. Social and economic changes affected this spiritual history. Men departed for work opportunities on the central African Copperbelt and in Tanganyika. The absence of these men in addition to colonial tax demands increased quotidian burdens for those left behind. As the colonial order became more demanding, an emergent cosmology of evil became entwined with angry ancestors, economic conditions, missionary doctrines and rivalries, and political authorities.

Colonial indirect rule promoted the rule of Crocodile Clan lords, making Chitimukulu a "paramount chief," and his closest clan members "chiefs," each with their distinctive territories. At the same time, however, the Crocodile Clan was increasingly unable to intervene in the spiritual landscape. Indirect rule curtailed their ability to rid the land of witches and to promote fertility and prosperity with their *babenye* relics. Karen E. Fields argues that during colonialism, the notion of "customary rule" became entrenched as the chiefs' secular power declined and new ways of justifying their authority became necessary. In her understanding, the "supernatural" aspect to chiefly rule was largely a product of the machinations of indirect rule and the writings of colonial anthropologists, especially the most famous ethnographer of the Bemba, Audrey I. Richards, who conducted her fieldwork in the 1930s at the height of indirect rule.[1] In this regard, Fields overstates the influence of indirect rule. Chapter 1 demonstrated that aspirations for spiritual power were a significant aspect of the precolonial political struggle, even if such aspirations did not always legitimize the rule of chiefs, as Richards claimed. In fact, even at the height of indirect rule in the 1930s, there were tendencies by colonial administrators to de-emphasize the sacred powers of chiefs in favor of a notion of secular custom and tradition. The chiefs were prevented from performing their spiritual duties and encouraged to perform bureaucratic and administrative tasks instead. Thus, even as their colonial authority grew, chiefs were profoundly disempowered.

Those chiefs who dwelled on the past and carefully guarded their ancestral *babenye* relics remained invested in a narrow and anachronistic conception of ancestral power, relegated to a realm of tradition and unable to combat new forms of evil. The most influential new spiritual resources of the early colonial period were the Christian narratives of a god, his son, and a devil, the rituals offered by the Catholic missionaries (especially the sacrament of baptism), and books offered by the Protestants. The Bemba adoption and adaptation of these spiritual resources was part of a long-standing tradition in seeking out ways to access the invisible world. But the new spiritual concepts also applied to new colonial relationships: a Manichaean spiritual discourse engaged with a Manichaean colonial order. Christianity introduced a spiritual vocabulary that helped to engage with the colonial order.

Many Bemba interpreted one of the core missionary ideas—the pervasiveness of sin and the influence of Satan—as evidence of the pervasiveness of witches. But while the missionaries proclaimed the pervasiveness of sin, they, along with the colonial administration, denied people the ability to eradicate witches. People thought of these Christians not only as prophets but as witches, who could manipulate the invisible world for good and for evil. Christianity created witches and an unprecedented demand for their eradication, even as old forms of witchcraft eradication were prohibited by the colonial authorities. This disempowerment could be remedied only through prophetic movements that engaged with old and new invisible agents.

THE MISSIONARIES

By the late nineteenth century, rumors of the return of the heroic magician, Luchele Ng'anga, spread across the Bemba highlands. European missionaries who wandered across the land were quick to claim that such rumors referred to them. David Livingstone had crossed the Bemba lands, circling around the marshlands of the Luapula and Bangweulu, before he died there in 1873. He babbled about a new god and his son, and promised a salvation for the living and the dead—but his words seemed too strange and his powers too insignificant to be taken seriously. Some twenty years later a man in white robes with a flowing white beard and fierce eyes appeared. He called himself Bishop Dupont, a Roman Catholic White Father missionary, and he told the Bemba that he was intent on making a home in their land, to spread the word of his god. Because of the ferocity of his expression and his temper, people called him *Moto Moto*, "the Fire." At the same time, new men were coming from the east, black men; some of them spoke ChiBemba and had been sold only a few years prior as slaves. Now, they also spoke the white man's language. They asked about David Livingstone, told people of the new civilization promised to Africans, and of the schools that people should attend if they wanted to become part of this civilization. They spoke of Satan, who had possessed the rulers of the Bemba and caused them to act in evil ways. One of these black missionaries, David Kaunda, settled in Nkula's area, near the Boma outpost established by the white men and called Chinsali.

The Roman Catholic White Fathers first set up a mission among the Mambwe, a small and politically marginal group north of the Bemba, in 1891. But they soon began to make overtures to the Bemba. In keeping with the policy of their founder, Bishop Lavigerie, who encouraged the conversion of kings instead of ordinary folk, the White Fathers imagined that the conversion of such a powerful kingdom would be the most effective way to spread their religion.[2] At first Chitimukulu had warned the missionaries not to enter his kingdom. So instead, Moto Moto approached Makasa, Chitimukulu's perpetual son and oftentimes rival. In 1895, Makasa invited Dupont to establish a mission station and then withdrew the invitation, apparently fearing the retaliation of his subjects or of Chitimukulu himself.[3] Dupont persisted, and Makasa agreed eventually to the building of a mission on Kayambi hill. From there, Dupont went on tours, enticing Crocodile Clan royals with gifts, and promising British South Africa Company (BSAC) officials that he would help to end the Bemba slave trade with the Swahili. Through his diplomacy, Dupont hoped to make a claim for the White Fathers across the Bemba lands. Three years after his mission was established at Kayambi, an ailing Crocodile Clan lord, Mwamba, called for Dupont and allegedly named him as his successor before he died. While the BSAC dismissed Dupont's claim to chieftaincy, Dupont was able to secure a second Bemba mission at Chilubula, and the BSAC recognized the White Fathers' influence over a large part of Bemba highlands.[4]

The districts of Chinsali, as well as those to the north and south of the Catholic influence, fell under the control of the Presbyterian Livingstonia Mission.[5] By the end of the century, the Livingstonia Mission had established the Mwenzo Mission (1894) and the Overtoun Institute to train teachers and craftsmen. They did not have the resources to open their own missions among the Bemba and observed the Catholic advance with frustration. But they did have a growing corps of trained African teachers and evangelists whom they could send westward to stall the Catholic advance. They thought the situation was desperate: "a veritable slumland—a seething mass of sinful humanity beyond all remedy save the 'all-remedy,' of the great physician. Jesus the Great Physician—His never-failing medicine for sin-sick souls—His accessibility."[6] In 1904, fifty students at the teacher training institute accompanied a European missionary to the Bemba area. They included David Kaunda and two Christian Bemba who had been rescued from a slave caravan. Upon their return, the group reported that "these Bemba are very ready to receive Christ as their King."[7] Livingstonia decided to open a mission at Chinsali. At first, there was no European available, and so in 1905, they instructed David Kaunda and his wife, Helen Nyirenda Kaunda, to open a school and to start mission work.

In contrast to the White Fathers' emphasis on kings, Kaunda and the teachers encouraged the conversion of ordinary people; after all, many of the teachers were former slaves. The Presbyterian emphasis on egalitarianism and individual achievement cut against the hierarchical tendencies of both the Catholic Church and the Crocodile Clan rulers. Kaunda roamed the area, selecting young men whom he encouraged to come to his school. He reported that there was a great desire for education. By 1907, Kaunda had established a network of schools and a congregation of several hundred who gathered in churches and sang approximately fifty different hymns that Kaunda had translated into ChiBemba from the ChiNyanja and ChiNyamwanga languages. (Despite their proliferation, the Christian schools were clearly opposed by some—there was at least one instance of a chief of ancestors, *mfumu ya mipashi*, instructing girls to desist from going to school.)[8] Helen Kaunda also attracted a following of enthusiastic women who advocated against beer drinking. Eight years later, in 1913, Rev. Robert D. MacMinn and his wife, Josephine Haarhoff, joined this small but growing community of young men and women.[9]

While Catholic and Protestant missionaries wanted to ensure that the converted were well-versed in their particular doctrines, they also wanted to ensure that their competitors did not gain a foothold in the villages. Thus, mission rivalries led to two distinct emphases in their ongoing efforts to create Christians: on the one hand, there was a vanguard of evangelists who were converted and trained; and on the other, a populace trained in turn by these evangelists who had only a loose affiliation to the mission and their doctrines.

The character of this evangelical vanguard depended on the mission. By 1904, the Catholic Kayambi Mission had expanded the recruitment of adult men to become a cohort of paid catechists. They were required to undertake schooling at the mission and annual retreats to ensure loyalty and discipline.[10] Their long period of official instruction was not a broad education and hardly touched on secular matters. Instruction was paternalistic and autonomous activities were discouraged.[11] The Protestants, by contrast, relied on paid teachers who were literate and had received a broader education than their Catholic counterparts. Early Protestant educational efforts should not be exaggerated, however: James Chisholm, one of the first missionaries at Mwenzo, wrote to his superiors that "many of the natives are born teachers, and do not need to know much till they are fit to impart their knowledge."[12] Nevertheless, education was seen to be part of evangelization and "the most potent barrier against the inroads of Catholicism and Islamism."[13] In addition to secular school instruction, the teachers also offered church classes and Sunday school. In keeping with the vision of the Livingstonia Mission's Presbyterian Kirk emphasis on self-governing and self-supporting churches, the teachers, the most faithful cohort of church followers, were granted greater autonomy than the Catholic catechists.[14]

The Catholic missionaries desired a break with "paganism" and, in return, promised the introduction of new rituals, such as communal prayer and the administration of sacraments of baptism, confession, and marriage. Candidates for baptism had to abstain from older practices, ranging from sacred dances to polygamy. They then had to memorize catechism in daily sessions during a three-week intensive training course, even if they could not understand the catechism. (Dupont's *Catéchisme en Kibemba*, published in 1900, was, according to later missionaries, "full of nonsense and contradictions.")[15] The most popular aspects of Catholic conversion were the sacraments of confession and communion, perceived by the Bemba as a path to purification.[16] As a result, the Catholics counted the large number of baptized Africans as their successful "converts": in 1913, when the Bembaland mission separated from Nyasaland, there were 6,000 baptized Christians; in 1946 the number was about 180,000 of an approximate 500,000 total people in Northern Province.[17]

The White Fathers did not share the Protestant concern with a "civilizing mission." They placed less emphasis on transformations in the domestic realm (with the exception of prohibiting polygamy), less emphasis on transformation in the moral order of society, and less emphasis on broader education and literacy. They did not seek to impose new temporal work regimens, such as those described by Jean Comaroff and John L. Comaroff in their study of Protestant missionaries among the Tswana.[18] For the Protestants, education was key since conversion entailed the individual's ability to approach and understand the scriptures. By contrast, prior to the 1920s, especially under the influence of Bishop Dupont, the White Fathers discouraged education that would lead to acculturation—they sought conversion without the "destructive" influences of "civilization."[19] There was more than a philosophical and theological difference: few of the White Fathers knew English, the colonial language, and hence the capacity for secular instruction was limited. Since services were still in Latin, there was also less of a religious need to learn English. Their pupils and catechists were thus at a marked disadvantage regarding secular education compared to those taught by predominantly English and Scottish Protestants, and at least a few Bemba abandoned Catholic schools for Protestant schools. Thus, while the Catholics counted the number of baptized Christians as evidence of their success, the Protestants counted the number of teachers and schools established. By 1925, Lubwa Mission had established 99 schools where 141 teachers taught 4,218 students (2,457 male and 1,761 female).[20] In 1927, the Northern Rhodesian government decided to differentiate between real schools and what they termed "sub-schools." The Church of Scotland managed 204 schools and 1,463 sub-schools, while the White Fathers had only 17 schools and 530 sub-schools. In other words, Catholic schools were fewer and inferior.[21]

African teachers and catechists carried the Christian message into villages, where, away from the direct influence of the mission, a far looser interpretation of mission doctrines prevailed. The missions accepted that for many instructed by the catechists and teachers, conversion would be partial and subject to "backsliding." The ability to implement their vision in the villages and outside the immediate orbit of the mission was limited. Despite Catholic baptism, older rites and forms of veneration continued. Breaking with "paganism" was at best partial: *mfuba* shrines were relocated to outside the villages; *chisungu* inititation rites and *ukupyana* marital succession practices became secretive. Similarly, even while the Protestants may have attempted to spread their civilization, they were frustrated by what they witnessed in the villages. But the emphasis on Presbyterian Church autonomy meant that the Livingstonia Mission possessed even fewer coercive mechanisms than the Catholics in their attempts to implement the more ambitious aspects of their civilizing mission.

Much of the intellectual work in grafting the Christian invisible world onto the ancestral one involved translation. During one of his first tours of Chinsali with David Kaunda, Reverend MacMinn claimed, "Everywhere the cry was 'books, books.' It is pitiful to see a class of some twenty with a single tattered book between them."[22] The Protestants, MacMinn especially, set about to meet this demand. For the next two decades, together with mission collaborators, especially Paul B. Mushindo, MacMinn began translating portions of the Bible and popular Christian texts.[23] The Presbyterians had an evolutionary theory of African religion, believing that it was tending toward monotheism and all they had to do was reinforce such tendencies.[24] They thus searched for terms that could be appropriated and developed in a Christian direction, choosing the popular nature spirit, *Lesa*, as God; and the ancestral shades, *mipashi* (sing. *mupashi*), as the Holy Spirit.[25] No local term was given for Satan: presumably because he had a name, and the old demons and angry ancestors, *chiwa* and *chibanda*, were not absolutely evil. Thus, Satan became "Satani" or ("Shetâni").[26] The construction of a new Christian vocabulary was preferred by the Catholics, who feared syncretism with a pagan past.

The spread of literacy and the distribution of Protestant printed books and pamphlets in ChiBemba proved decisive, even in the more remote villages. By the late 1920s, there were twenty-six ChiBemba titles in circulation, five of which concerned secular education, two moral stories for children, and the remainder religious texts: *The Pilgrim's Progress*, translations of portions of the Bible, devotional services, catechisms, and notes for preachers.[27] A full ChiBemba version of the Bible, however, was completed only in 1956, by Lubwa clergy Paul B. Mushindo and Reverend MacMinn.[28] The Protestants thereby established the basic framework for a ChiBemba Christian vocabulary.

One of the most important Christian terms was "sin," along with the Christian morality it implied. Catholics and Protestants viewed sin as a moral problem; they spoke of its pervasiveness in an attempt to spread the notion of guilt and Christian law. This was not how it was understood. Even the translation indicated confusion: *lubembu*, the word chosen for "sin," originally meant adultery—the most immoral and antisocial action, which would supposedly bring about guilt. But such antisocial behavior was thought to be inspired by bewitchment: if, for example, a person sinned, he was most certainly a witch.[29]

Some African Christians at the time preferred the term *bupondo* when referring to sin, a direct reference to antisocial behavior that led to murder; in other words, the actions of witches.[30] The appropriate course of action was to find the *bwanga* witchcraft and confess as a witch, not ask for forgiveness. The missionaries expressed great frustration at the lack of appreciation of their moral notion of sin and the lack of repentance. For example, the Catholic missionary Louis Etienne wrote:

> Christian morality . . . is completely falsified and out of focus. To quote but one example: adultery is not an offence against God—this concept does not even enter into the native mind. . . . The idea of transgressing God's commandments, and of incurring guilt, would never occur to anyone. The consequences can thus be well imagined.[31]

The Protestants had similar thoughts: after hearing of a mother's drowning of a baby thought to be possessed by an evil spirit, Reverend MacMinn complained of the enormity of their religious task.[32] But this did not mean that the Bemba lacked morality and thereby acted in an antisocial fashion. It meant that antisocial behavior, what the missionaries termed "sin," was perceived as evidence of witchcraft. And the white missionaries were often guilty of such antisocial behavior. Villagers must have noted the double entendre when the missionaries declared that Satan is the enemy, *mulwani*, another term for the white foreigners (in addition to the less confrontational *basungu*).

Missionary translations would have had little effect if not for the historical context in which they occurred. In addition to the transformation due to the onset of colonial capitalism, people witnessed the emergence of fierce competition between those who claimed access to these new invisible agents. Following the favorable reports of the Phelps-Stokes commissioners on missionary schools, the colonial government offered inducements for missions to expand their educational facilities. The White Fathers realized that if they did not change their orientation and expand schooling, they would lose both funding and evangelical opportunities to the Protestants. They increased the number of schools, set up a teacher training center at Rosa Mission in 1926, and looked for opportunities to establish new missions.[33] They also realized that through their early translation and publishing efforts the Protestants were gaining a monopoly over Bemba books, and thus the White Fathers began to be involved in translation work and the publication of vernacular instructional books. From the 1930s, the Catholics matched Protestant efforts in the publication of influential ChiBemba texts. Between 1929 and 1932, Fr. Van Sambeek, who pioneered the expansion of secular Catholic schools and the teacher training school, edited three Bemba readers, *Ifyabukaya*, written by his trainee teachers. *Ifyabukaya* was used as a school reader across Bembaland, and it quickly became the standard version of Bemba history. Compared to the Protestant texts, the Catholics focused more on traditional life and tribal histories and less on didactic works about Christian moral improvement. The first Catholic translations of portions of the Bible began to appear in 1953.[34]

The Lubwa missionaries, perceiving themselves as holding out against Catholic intrusion, responded with alarm when they learned of Catholic efforts to compete for government funds to open more schools and missions in their immediate vicinity.[35] When the White Fathers established the Ilondola Mission barely ten miles from Lubwa in 1934, the Lubwa missionary David Brown complained: "The Roman Catholics invaded this year a district hitherto cared for by our Mission alone. They are said to have boasted that in a few years they alone will hold the field. . . . Though we endeavor to avoid friction, and have instructed our Native helpers to that effect, we do not propose giving way to Rome."[36] Soon afterward, Catholic missions were established at Chalabesa (1934), Mulobola (1935), Mulanga (1936), and Mulilansolo (1936), almost encircling the Protestant Lubwa Mission and the Chinsali District (see the map on p.xii.[37]

Competition between the missions seemed to be a holdover from old European rivalries. It had, however, a very local dimension that would echo previous Bemba struggles over spiritual power. Rumors of the evil and corrupt practices of the competing missionaries circulated within the missions and among the villages that had loose and tenuous affiliations to either the Catholics or the Protestants. A Lubwa missionary accused the Catholics of "shady and reprehensible means of proselytizing and thrusting [themselves] on the people. Bribing chiefs and headmen is one of these means. . . . One chief . . . seized and handcuffed one of our teachers and compelled him to sit through a Romanist service."[38] Complaints went well beyond the formal reports to the mission authorities, and led to vociferous campaigns across the Bemba highlands. For example, Protestant attempts to counter Catholic influence led to the distribution of ChiBemba-language anti-Catholic documents, such as "Fifty Reasons Why I Have Not Joined the Church of Rome," which was also the subject of an essay competition among Lubwa's teachers.[39] The Catholics adopted similar tactics by increasing the role of the lay apostolate in promoting Catholic loyalty and doctrine. Fervent Christians organized in "Catholic Action" cells that supervised and monitored the Christian behavior of the villagers. Catholic Action adopted the "Legion of Mary" handbook, pioneered in Ireland in the 1920s, with its distinctive military tenor and emphasis on aggressive evangelism.[40]

The missionaries' attempts to convince the Bemba of the truth of their respective doctrines, and the misguided, even evil, beliefs of their competitors, introduced an aggressive tone to spiritual politics. Attempts to combat the advance of rivals became fervent, with the lay leaders focusing on the spiritual power of their particular brand of Christianity. The angry ancestors and devils of the past became associated with competing Christian doctrines. Evil had a new face, no longer a force of the jealous spirits, but of beliefs and doctrines, sometimes even inspired by Satan. The point was not that such beliefs were false, and thus spiritually impotent, but that they were evil and manipulated the spirit world for personal power. Rivalries gave greater force to claims that missionaries were witches or hid witches within their churches and communities.

By the 1930s, an educated class of Bemba teachers and catechists had emerged, influenced by missionary ideas, although not controlled by the missionaries in all regards. The distribution and dissemination of books and baptism, the new spiritual resources offered by the missionaries, did not remain under the control of the missions, their catechists, or educated teachers. As ordinary people became more involved in rivalries over doctrines and forms of salvation, the use of such spiritual resources expanded. Good and evil took on new qualities, referring not only to ancestors and spirits, but also to the beliefs and institutions of the living, their writings and their doctrines.

THE CLEANSERS

The Christian missionaries spread a vocabulary of sin and evil even as they denied the existence of witchcraft, the way in which such sin and evil were manifest. The refusal of Christian missionaries to acknowledge witches only meant that witches were able to hide within the new Christian churches. One young woman possessed by the *ngulu* spirits of old told her audience, "Christians said it was a sin to do as I do, but I see Christians full of sins."[41] The missionaries were alternately called witches (*baloshi*), enemies (*balwani*), or vampires (*banyama*); at the very least they harbored witches who fled to the missions to escape witchcraft accusations and trials.[42] At the White Fathers' Chilubula Mission, there was a tree that the White Fathers only had to shake, causing a leaf to fall; a person would die for each leaf that fell. "There are more Christian *baloshi* [witches] than any other kind," an informant told Audrey I. Richards.[43] Christianity concealed witches; and the colonial prohibition on witchcraft accusations, the Witchcraft Ordinance of 1914, left people vulnerable to witches:

> At first there were only a few deaths, but the doctors burned the sorcerers. Then the Europeans came and told us not to burn sorcerers . . . and the doctors ceased. . . . This meant there was no one to cure people and no one to tell them what their illnesses were. . . . Those who could straighten things in the old way said, "We can do this only to go straight

into gaol." So the sick people went to the Europeans to be cured but some diseases were beyond the Europeans, so the sick people died.[44]

Ngulu nature spirits could have protected people from witches. But the colonial authorities made sure that those possessed were not "tempted into becoming a witchfinder." Chinsali's district commissioner diligently reported, "I personally make a point of interviewing all ngulu [or *bangulu*, those possessed by *ngulu*], thus letting them know that I am aware of their activities and trusting this knowledge will keep them off dangerous ground."[45] Witches started to afflict people in an unprecedented fashion. "Chinsali has a reputation for possessing more than the usual number of witches," complained the same DC, even as he denied people the ability to eradicate them.[46] Measures to combat the witches became more desperate. An old man was banished from the village after he caused a child to fall mysteriously into a fire. An old woman dreamed that a girl told her she was not a witch. Nevertheless, for the villagers this proved her witchcraft. She was banished and her home burned down when she refused to leave. A Lubwa schoolteacher was accused of rape and witchcraft. He passed a "boiling water test" to prove his innocence, apparently helped along by his knowledge of some "medicine" (*muti*). Nevertheless, the missionaries dismissed him from his teaching post at Lubwa for participating in the ordeal.[47]

The missionary claim that they were liberating people from the belief in witchcraft only contributed to the spread of witchcraft and rumors of occult evil. Audrey I. Richards argued that this surge in witchcraft was "inevitable as a product of violent changes in tribal organization and belief."[48] This was part of the story. But Richards, in a surprisingly shortsighted observation that could only have come about from a relentless focus on the breakdown of tribal institutions instead of the broader historical context, contrasted such violent changes with peaceful missionary teachings. The missionaries, like Richards, believed that fear was the source of witchcraft accusations, and that they, together with a progressive colonial state, needed to root out such fear. Referring to the witchfinders, the presbytery of Livingstonia appealed to the colonial government "to curb the sinister activities of these deceivers and robbers of their fellow Africans." They called on "all Christian people, within and without its bounds, who have themselves liberated from belief in Witchcraft, and from fear of its imaginary powers, to strive continually by prayer, by example and by persuasion to free from this terrible bondage of fear all their fellow Africans."[49] For many Bemba, however, claims that Christians did not practice witchcraft were further evidence that they did. After all, the missionaries had proclaimed the pervasiveness of sin, a manifestation of witchcraft. And rivalry between the missionaries had introduced new fears and new notions of evil.

Sin and witchcraft became associated with certain denominations. The evil that Catholics proclaimed of Protestants and vice versa became a popular discourse on spiritual others.

A new opportunity to get rid of witches and witchcraft came about in the early 1930s through traveling groups of young men who claimed to have a medicine that eradicated witchcraft. They called themselves *Bamuchape*, "the people who cleanse." They promoted a purification that would rid the world of witchcraft and evil that emanated from the discontented dead. The Bamuchape heralded from colonial Malawi, where a mythical founder, Kamwende, was said to have died and been resurrected, with a vision to rid the world of *buloshi* witchcraft. The Bamuchape traveled from one village to the next, until they had cleansed much of northern Zambia. They used a mirror to identify witches, who were then forced to drink a soapy potion made out of a brownish-red powder that was said to come from the crushed roots of a tree found in Malanje, Malawi. If they should dare to perform witchcraft in the future, the potion would make them swell up and die. If witches tried to hide, the Bamuchape would reveal them—Kamwende himself could expose them. For three to six pence, the Bamuchape offered medicine to combat future acts of witchcraft or perhaps even make people immune to the demands of the colonial district officials.[50]

The local precedents for Bamuchape witchcraft cleansing were the *mwavi* ordeals, in the past administered by chiefs with the help of *nganga* doctors. Indirect rule and the Witchcraft Ordinance prevented chiefs from administering the *mwavi* ordeal, and the Bamuchape administered a form of the ordeal instead. Since they had no position of authority in the administration, the colonial administration allowed the Bamuchape to do their work, as long as they dealt with the witches without direct accusations and violence to them. Rather than direct accusations, their medicine (or "magic," *bwanga*) worked by persuading people that they were witches. The consequences of admitting to being a witch were relatively minor, little more than confessing sins; witches only had to drink medicine to prevent them from performing witchcraft in the future. The medicine would do no harm; in fact, it could also protect from other witchcraft and from the attacks of wild animals such as lions and snakes (the protective medicine was sometimes different and offered at extra cost to the medicine that purified witches). In some cases, there was local pressure and a temptation to accuse people directly, which could result in physical violence against witches. A few of these instances came to the attention of the colonial authorities and prosecutions resulted in fines, canings, and imprisonment that ranged from a few months to several years of hard labor. For that reason, the Bamuchape were careful to secure the permission of the district officials, who were instructed by their superiors to allow the Bamuchape to work but not to give them any official written permission for fear that it would be treated as official sanction. Such official sanction did come from the chiefs who welcomed the Bamuchape and often insisted that all their people gather for purification.[51] People welcomed the permission granted by the colonial authorities and the support of the chiefs: "This is the best thing the Bwanas have ever done for us," Richards was told. "Now at last they are allowing us to free our country from witchcraft."[52] Indeed, perceiving that witchcraft was integral to local religious beliefs and not a violent aberration, the colonial state in Northern Rhodesia became somewhat more tolerant, focusing on witchcraft accusations (not the belief in witchcraft itself), and reducing the punishment for accusations.[53] A solution to witchcraft seemed to be at hand, and the Bamuchape were enthusiastically received.

The Bamuchape deployed techniques and concepts introduced by the missionaries. As if they were delivering a church sermon, the Bamuchape lined people up and instructed them. They claimed to spread the word and power of God, *Lesa*, who would eradicate the witches. "God has sent the Muchapi with a strong remedy, much stronger than European drugs, because it is a cure for the country, it will kill all sorcerers and put an end to sorcery in the entire world," declared one Muchape in 1935.[54] Unlike *mwavi*, which was used to identify and administer justice to witches after they had performed witchcraft, the Bamuchape offered a purification that cleansed the witchcraft of past, present, and future. It was a salvation. Their *mwavi* ordeal thus resembled baptism, a Christian spiritual resource adapted to protect from witchcraft. In August 1933, in the Ufipa District, slightly north of the Zambian border with Tanzania, the head of the Bamuchape preached to a gathering of nearly two thousand people:

> Your Missionaries came to the country some 50 years ago; they tried with all their best to save the people and teach you not to kill one another yet without success. But we feel sympathy for you have lost dear friends, some of you standing here, not because God took them away—but by being poisoned by these witchcraft, whom you will see today. We follow God's law that "Thou shalt not kill." This commandment is being observed and fulfilled by us [more] than any religion. For they all fail to save people—but we do. . . . I know that some of your Christians argue, but I tell you some of your native ministers of religion have been found in possession of a skull of a European Lady. I do not know where they killed this lady, and took her skull. So you must not trust the Christians, they are the people who are hiding in this religion, and are the great witchcrafts more than any one else.[55]

The Bamuchape, then, acted against sin (thou shall not kill) by combating witchcraft. They promoted the salvation that the Christians promised but were unable to deliver because they harbored their own witchcraft. Conflicts with the missionaries, especially the Catholics who prohibited their followers from being cleansed, became more pronounced, and gave even more substance to the rumors that the White Fathers were witches or harbored witches within their church.

Despite their rivalries, the missionaries and Bamuchape were similar in many regards, most of all in their insistence on a transformation, a "conversion" that rejected old practices. For the Bamuchape, while there was no permanent salvation, no heaven or hell, and no millenarian vision attached to purification, there was the promise of a new identity through the eradication of evil witchcraft and thereby the promotion of good in the individual and the community. This new identity would be achieved by cleansing old forms of sin and magic. The most fervent Christian missionaries and their local agents had burned the shrines and other "idolatrous" objects; or, at the very least, they insisted that such shrines be situated well away from the villages that they visited.[56] Eternal life in heaven would thereby be achieved, the missionaries claimed. However, by insisting that they were combating the evil spirits that afflicted this world, the Bamuchape were far more successful than the missionaries in the purification of such objects. Emptied of their spiritual power, they were discarded. Outside the villages, "charms" that the missionaries had tried to eradicate for decades, mostly horns (*nsengo*) containing potent medicine (*muti*), piled up.

THE CHIEFS

Like the missionaries, the Bamuchape attacked the evil of the past. In fact, they went beyond the missionaries in confronting the ancestral religions oriented around *mfuba* spirit shrines and even the relics of clans and chiefs. Much to Audrey I. Richards's amazement (and perhaps disappointment), the Bamuchape identified sacred objects, including protective magic and even the *babenye* relics of chiefs, as potential magic *bwanga*, and insisted that they also be given up and purified. In her persistent focus on a systematic "Bemba religion," Richards thought these were the actions of "quacks," exploiting the ignorance of the young as tribal institutions collapsed. These were not acts of charlatans preying on ignorance, however, but popular attempts to associate the spiritual resources of the past, including those of the chiefs, with witchcraft. Chiefs not only had their spiritual roles sidelined by indirect rule; popular movements attacked the basis of their spiritual authority. In doing so, the Bamuchape were only partially successful; a more thorough attack on the spiritual agency of chiefs would have to wait another twenty years.

Why, then, did chiefs collaborate with the Bamuchape? Chitimukulu, for example, welcomed the Bamuchape in the hope that they would "take away all the *buloshi* witches in the country."[57] One reason was that the strictures of indirect rule had changed the nature of chieftaincy by basing their political power on their ties to the colonial state instead of their spiritual mediations.[58] Progressive colonial officials, such as the one-time district commissioner and amateur ethnographer W. Vernon Brelsford, perhaps in an unconscious reflection about the nature of European colonial rule, went as far as arguing that the spiritual authority of the Crocodile Clan was never as important as their authority by right of physical conquest.[59] The missions and their Christian followers further questioned the spiritual power of the chiefs by denying the validity of ancestral claims over the fertility of the land and the people. Yet people still expected chiefs to deal with the spirit world, eradicate witches, ensure fertility, and bring good fortune. There were rumors that the chiefs had actually been bribed to permit witches and vampires in their areas or were themselves vampires.[60] To maintain legitimacy, chiefs had to find new ways to respond to these challenges and mobilize the appropriate spiritual resources. Their subjects forced them to work with prophets, who in many ways challenged their authority and legitimacy. South of the Bemba heartland, the Lala chief Shaiwila collaborated with the son of God (*Mwana Lesa*), Tom Nyirenda, to kill the witches that plagued his people.[61] Similarly, the Crocodile Clan chiefs worked with the Bamuchape to rid the country of witchcraft.

The best example of the transformation of chieftaincy was the most sacred of Bemba rulers, Shimwalule, who cared for the ancestral spirits of the Crocodile Clan at the Mwalule graveyard, the spiritual center of the Bemba polity and the place where the first Chitimukulu and his brother Nkole were buried after being killed by the magician, Mwase. In precolonial times, after Shimwalule had buried the Chitimukulu, he abdicated in favor of his brother (or his sister's son), who would kill him, or so it was claimed. Colonial administrators did their best to adapt to such rules; at first, for example, they accepted the principle that the position would be succeeded after the burial of a Chitimukulu. Nevertheless, when the first BSAC official at Chinsali, Robert Young, heard that Shimwalule had administered the *mwavi* ordeal, he had him removed from his position and replaced by his rival brother.[62] Still, the pressures to eradicate witches remained, and his successor worked to eradicate witches in 1918.[63] In 1924, a former Shimwalule titleholder, Chandamali, angrily rebuked the "Bwanas" for disallowing the *shinganga* to perform their work, for allowing witchcraft, and for preventing ritual purification, all of which could have led to the death of a government messenger.[64] With the onset of a formal policy of indirect rule in the 1930s, the position of Shimwalule was again to be thrown into question. The DC complained of the tendency for Nkhweto and Shimwalule to take their "religious duties more seriously than their administrative ones."[65] Brelsford wrote at length about Shimwalule and advocated an

end to his chieftaincy: "He is an undertaker and a priest rather than a chief."
Most of all, Brelsford complained about the ritual prohibitions on leaving the
Mwalule graveyard that prevented Shimwalule from attending district meetings of chiefs, especially those that concerned the institutional development of
indirect rule, such as the Native Treasury.[66] Both the provincial commissioner
and the secretary for native affairs feared that such changes would interfere in
"tribal structure," but they were willing to consider the possibility of splitting
Shimwalule's position into two, one a permanent chief and one a paid priest.[67]
In 1940, Brelsford discussed the possibility of incorporating Shimwalule's area
into that of the Crocodile Clan chief Nkhweto.[68] Brelsford went on to publish
an account of Shimwalule, where he argued that "as priest and undertaker he
[Shimwalule] cannot be integrated in the present system, so he should relin-
quish his administrative functions to another and himself retain undimmed
his ancient religious prestige."[69] By 1948, the Shimwalule chieftaincy had
been incorporated into Nkhweto's area, an arrangement that satisfied nobody.
Shimwalule refused to recognize Nkhweto's rule; and the new DC, complaining of Nkhweto's insobriety and unreliability, sought to have his entire area
incorporated into the more progressive chieftaincy of Nkula.[70]

Indirect rule and the missionaries also devalued the *babenye* relics as the
basis for a chief's political power. Previously, a usurper or a new chief had
to capture the *babenye*, which served as a spiritual technology to rule over
a portion of land and make it fertile. The *babenye* were the ultimate source
of power: to succeed the chieftaincy meant taking possession of the *babenye*
relics. Some missionaries confronted the spiritual power of the *babenye* relics
and insisted they be done away with. More insidious, though, was the replacement of the relics with the agency of God, *Lesa*. The Presbyterians introduced a harvest ceremony where Lesa blessed the seeds.[71] Responsibility for
the well-being of the harvest began to shift from the *babenye* of Chilimbulu's
skin to Christian blessing. A White Fathers textbook claimed that the shrine
at the spiritual center of the Mwalule graveyard, reputed to have been built
by Luchele Ng'anga, was actually built by roaming Jesuits.[72] The White Fathers even gave the statue of a Catholic saint to Chitimukulu for him to place
among his other relics.[73] For the Catholics, Christian artifacts could replace
Chitimukulu's old "pagan" *babenye* relics! By the 1930s, the relics were still
part of ceremonial and ritual succession, but the ultimate source of authority
and power began to lie with Christian spiritual agents.

NKULA'S CHANGE OF MIND

In the midst of these swirling and contradictory changes, as the Catholics set
out to expand their missionary presence in the Bemba heartland, Nkula's initial opposition to the White Fathers' mission at Ilondola, and his subsequent

change of mind, can be better understood. He was confronted by challenges on several overlapping fronts: tendencies of indirect rule to compromise his ability to get rid of witches; the devaluation of his *babenye* relics as the most potent spiritual resources of the land; and the emergence of alternative Christian spirits, Lesa and Satani, along with new spiritual resources, baptism and books, over which Nkula had little control. The growing community of Christians even questioned his right to settle divorce cases in his court.[74] Furthermore, the White Fathers were themselves witches and vampires: allowing them to establish a mission went against Nkula's most important duty — keeping the land free from witches. "It is known to be extremely unwise for a native to quarrel with a White Father. They are credited with all the powers of the witches and wizards," the DC wrote to Audrey I. Richards. "No Chief would willingly agree to the opening of a White Father's Mission in his country."[75] There may have been an even deeper reason for Nkula's refusal. The area that the Catholics had requested had previously been a *mfuba* shrine and sacred grove where *ngulu* were found. It was called *Kamateshi*, "the place of the high trees that were not allowed to be cut down."[76]

In the midst of the struggle over the mission, Nkula fell ill. This was surely proof of Catholic bewitchment. Nkula reckoned that perhaps if he agreed to the mission, they would stop bewitching him. In desperation he agreed, but many claim that his concession had come too late to placate the Catholics, for when he died shortly after, they still blamed Catholic bewitchment.[77] After his death, a White Father visited the DC, where, with the "most awful leer that would have put him on the wrong side of the Witchcraft Ordinance if he had made it to a native," asked him: "Is it true that the Government refused the new mission because the Chief refused? Nkula refused and now he is dead."[78] Whatever their motivation, the colonial administration then agreed to the new mission. The White Fathers acquired rights of occupancy on thirty acres of Native Trust land and named the new mission Ilondola, literally, "the land that was recovered," perhaps from paganism, but probably from the Protestants who had undermined the White Fathers' ambitions to establish Bembaland as a Catholic Christian kingdom.[79] Nevertheless, it remained a feared place, even for the educated elite. Many years later, when the then Zambian president Kenneth Kaunda, son of the Protestant missionary David Kaunda, visited Ilondola, he was reported to be especially "nervous," despite having visited many other Catholic churches.[80]

It took three years for the burial rites and succession of the new chief Nkula, witnessed and reported on by the DC, Brelsford. In the installation ceremony of 1937, the *bakabilo* councilors handed the old *babenye*, including two stools of his ancestral predecessors and a bow, to Nkula (a few stools had already been destroyed thirty years prior). The dances were innovations: the popular

Mbeni dances of the Copperbelt and even "pseudo-European dances now beginning to come into vogue with some of the more sophisticated." The first speech of the new Nkula to his councilors and priests referenced the ultimate authority of the colonial administration and hardly made mention of his ancestral relics. "Please remember to say what your hearts want to say, because any complaint you make in the future will not be accepted. . . . If among you there are some who want these people [referring to a rival house] as their chiefs say now in the presence of the District Commissioner. . . . I know that these people who regard themselves as chiefs in this country always go to Bwanas and tell them lies."[81] A year later, at the ceremony to establish the chief's village, Nkula told his audience that the tribes (*mikowa*) of the land included not only the Bemba and the Bisa of old, but also the white people who had conquered the land and now "belonged to the country."[82] But to refer to the "white people" Nkula used the term *babuta*, "the sacred white," instead of the conventional *basungu*. Perhaps he was acknowledging that the spiritual power of the white conquerors would complement that of the Crocodile Clan. The whites' spiritual resources were needed to ensure the welfare of the land and the people. In 1944, Chitimukulu placed a copy of the biography of Moto Moto, Bishop Dupont, among his *babenye* relics.[83] The White Fathers became known for their ability to make rain; although such powers could be attained only through the manipulation of the invisible world—the most important spiritual resources used to make rain were the body parts of captives.[84]

↜

The Catholics and the Protestants introduced important and novel spiritual resources. The Catholics popularized new rituals, especially baptism, as a path to purification; the Protestants introduced a Christian Bemba vocabulary, along with literacy and books as a path to a progressive and moral Christian civilization. Mission rivalries introduced the idea of false Christian doctrines as sources of evil, a concept that found a keen audience in the colonial environment. The agency of Satan in promoting false doctrines, along with the pervasiveness of sin, made efforts to combat witchcraft ever more urgent. The Bamuchape responded to these spiritual insecurities, even while they also fomented greater turmoil and spiritual uncertainty. Since the Catholics prohibited the Bamuchape from visiting villages where Catholics held sway, Catholics gained the reputation of being witches, or hiding witches, a reputation that at least some of the White Fathers cultivated to enhance their power and authority, and perhaps to acquire one of their most significant missions, Ilondola. Mission Christianity thereby contributed to the perceived presence of witches and the need to eradicate them.

The colonial administration proclaimed chiefs as indirect rulers, while at the same time removing from them their most important political function, their interventions into an invisible world that ensured fertility and fecundity. The Crocodile Clan chiefs thereby lost a significant element of their political power: they could no longer claim to keep their lands prosperous and free from witchcraft. God was replacing their *babenye* relics as the source of prosperity and spiritual protection. The chiefs had to collaborate with and rely on new intermediaries with the invisible world such as the Bamuchape.

By the late 1930s, rivalries between the three movements that dealt with spirits—Protestants, Catholics, and Bamuchape—combined with other colonial transformations and led to feelings of disempowerment and insecurity. New sources of spiritual power such as books and baptism were tapped to combat the witches that appeared during this time of uncertainty. But people wanted a more convincing resolution, more forward-looking and permanent than that offered by the Bamuchape. In the midst of the spiritual afflictions of this world, they were not satisfied with the Protestant and Catholic missionary focus on the next world. They wanted innovators who were able to utilize these spiritual strategies to combat witches, to purify, to destroy chiefly relics, to find new places for the ancestors, but also to create a new heaven on earth. They wanted a process of conversion and transformation that was focused on spiritual afflictions of this world and that went beyond the transient purification of the Bamuchape to offer a lasting resolution to the problem of evil.

Three different movements responded to the call to end evil and to forge a heaven on earth: Watchtower, Lenshina's church, and the popular Zambia movement. Like their missionary predecessors, however, these movements promoted rivalries that created evil even as they sought to end it.

3 ☙ Satan in the City

IN APRIL 1935, a note signed by "G. Loveway" was posted outside the work-ers' compound at the Nkana mine on the Copperbelt of colonial Zambia. It complained of persecution, increased taxation, and stagnant wages. "Listen to this all of you who live in the country," the note began. "Know how they cause us to suffer, they cheat us for money, they arrest us for loafing, they persecute us and put us in gaol for tax. . . . He who cannot read should tell his companion that on 29th April not to go to work." This was no ordinary call for the growing number of Zambian copper miners to strike. "God will be with us," Loveway proclaimed. "These words do not come from here, they come from the wisers who are far away and enable to encourage us."[1] Over the next month, more notes appeared, warning of strikes and declaring that the miners should not fear death. By the end of May, without a formal trade union move-ment, miners at Nkana, Luanshya, and Mufulira went on strike. They shouted angrily at the mine managers, "taxation" and "money," their grievances. They attacked the mine compounds and threatened those who dared to go to work. For almost a week, three of the most productive mines on the Copperbelt shut down. The situation quickly escalated beyond the control of the local police force, leading to the mobilization of police reinforcements from Southern Rhodesia and the soldiers of the Northern Rhodesia Regiment. The most se-rious incident emerged when an alleged "1,000 Bemba" miners surrounded and stoned the Luanshya mine compound offices. Nervous police killed six and injured twenty-two strikers before colonial troops arrived and managed to force the miners to withdraw.[2]

Since the mid-1920s, when the European exploitation of the Zambian Copperbelt mines began, the area had changed from a rural backwater to a series of interconnected and growing towns. African men and women from the surrounding areas, especially those of the ChiBemba-speaking regions of northeastern Zambia who constituted about half the new employees of the Copperbelt, settled here, either working in mines or supplying the towns with goods and services.[3] Colonial efforts to control African subjects in the towns quickly came against the limits of indirect rule. Colonial chiefs could not extend their authority to the diverse peoples of the Copperbelt, since they did not have the mechanisms of control equivalent to those in the villages. People who settled on the Copperbelt sought alternative ways to organize communities and promote urban identities. Dance societies brought men and women from similar cultural and linguistic backgrounds together. The Kalela dance, a variation on the Mbeni dance of East Africa, mimicked European colonial rituals and structures, especially those of the military and colonial bureaucracies.[4] New ethnic affiliations emerged out of the broad ethno-linguistic regions of origin of the newly urbanized. Village political rituals, such as the jokes told between rival clans, became ways to identify ethnic identity and difference. The Ngoni and Bemba, for example, became "tribal cousins," as rivalries and conflict gave way to necessary and tenuous forms of cooperation.[5]

Urbanites also began to find new ways to cleanse evil found in the social, political, and economic conditions of the Copperbelt. Witchfinding associations, such as the Bamuchape witchcraft cleansers, were common in the early years of Copperbelt settlement. But evil no longer emerged only from angry ancestors and village relatives in this cosmopolitan new world. Chiefs no longer mediated exclusive access to ancestral power—and, in any event, the powers of the ancestors had declined. Whites, with their industrial technologies and printed texts, possessed spiritual powers different from and perhaps more powerful than the ancestors' and nature spirits'. The spiritual potentials of the new religion, Christianity, needed to be explored and appropriated. But the hierarchical nature of the European mission churches allowed few opportunities for African prophets to access this spiritual power. The pamphlets of the Watch Tower Bible and Tract Society offered a way to harness spirits to deal with the struggles of the Copperbelt.

The ethnography of the Copperbelt has underrepresented the spiritual history of urbanization. Despite being a major site for the study of African urbanization, religious experience has not been a major area of analysis in the historiography of African urbanization in a fashion similar to Wallace D. Best's history of African American migrant religious experiences in Chicago.[6] This absence dates back to the first ethnographies of the Copperbelt by Rhodes-Livingstone Institute scholars, who discussed economics and new identities in the urban areas, and focused on spirits only in accounts of the ancestral religions of rural tribes.[7] More recent ethnographies of the Copperbelt, as if to compensate for the primordial focus of their academic ancestors, have found it problematic to treat the spiritual claims of their interlocutors seriously. In one recent example, James Ferguson's influential book hardly mentions Christianity and tends to conflate spiritual forces with evil magic, which, he seems to argue, attain significance not because of their supernatural qualities, but because they may refer to "real" acts of poisoning.[8] The problem with this interpretation is that to believers, witchcraft (or even poisoning) has supernatural and spiritual qualities. Even Luise White's history of vampires and labor relations on the Copperbelt treats such supernatural agents as rumors with metaphoric implications rather than as spiritual forces.[9] By contrast, Walima T. Kalusa's recent work on Christian missionary efforts to transform African approaches to the dead, especially to invisible ancestors, blazes a new line of inquiry, further explored in this chapter.[10]

The earliest publications that focused on religion in the urban areas evaluated missionary efforts to cater to African moral and social needs. In 1932 the British-based International Missionary Society sponsored a commission of inquiry into the role of the church on the Copperbelt. The published findings, titled *Modern Industry and the African*, laid the groundwork for a series of studies that informed the policies and practices of the Copperbelt missions.[11] The reformist advocacy of such missionary scholars, however, viewed the spiritual claims of urban Africans as superstitions that would be done away with through modern missionary efforts and better adaptations to urban life.

Much of the existing literature on Watchtower, one of the most significant urban African movements on the Copperbelt, concentrates on its early manifestations in the rural areas. In an influential article, Terence O. Ranger analyzed the most notorious episode in the history of early Watchtower, that of Tom Nyirenda, or Mwana Lesa (the son of God), who drowned as many as 191 witches before colonial authorities arrested and executed him. Ranger argues that the Mwana Lesa movement combined the Christianity of Livingstonia's Protestants and Watchtower with long-standing Lala millennial beliefs in the eradication of witchcraft.[12] In a sophisticated study of Watchtower during the colonial period, Karen E. Fields views the movement as a challenge to colonial relationships of authority, offering "shock after shock to the fundamental relationships of indirect rule."[13] This was accomplished primarily by transferring the customary power to eradicate witches from the chiefs to the Watchtower preachers and assemblies, thus removing much of the religious—and hence political—basis for chieftaincy. The replacement of chiefly sacred authority was indeed one aspect of Watchtower, along with a range of religious movements, from the precolonial territorial cults, such as Butwa, to Bamuchape and mission Christianity. Like Ranger, Fields's argument applies most strikingly to early Watchtower such as the Mwana Lesa movement.

But from the 1930s, Watchtower had its most powerful following and political impacts in the urban areas. Here the colonial state continued to view Watchtower as a challenge to "customary authority"; by doing so, they fundamentally misunderstood the basis of its social, political, and spiritual interventions in the urban areas (in turn, misleading a generation of scholars). Customary rule was not a political force on the mines; Watchtower members did not need to offer resistance to customary rulers. Instead, they had to engage new forms of spiritual power. They had to confront Satan in the city.

Part of the confusion about the nature and impact of the Watchtower movement, then, is that its name refers to several distinctive movements, with different leaders and situated in different historical moments. Tendencies to conflate the different movements and show connections between them influenced both the colonial response and scholarship. In colonial Zambia alone, there were at least five socially and historically distinct Watchtower movements. First were the eastern and southern movements, led by Hanoc Sindano and Elliot Kamwana, that spread from the mission bases in Cape Town and the mines of Southern Rhodesia. Then there was the radical baptism and witchcraft eradication movement of Mwana Lesa, Tom Nyirenda, who insisted that all who were not baptized by him would be killed by God and went on to drown those he alleged were witches. At the same time, Jeremiah Gondwe led a more conciliatory and longer-lasting movement. A millenarian urban and peri-urban Watchtower, led by Joseph Sibakwe, among others, began in the 1930s (a closely related workers' movement also emerged in the Copperbelt towns of Katanga). And finally, the transformation of urban and peri-urban millenarian Watchtower into the formal Jehovah's Witnesses was realized, with active involvement—never supervision—by European missionaries in the late 1930s and 1940s. Even while connections between these movements existed in the minds of both the colonials and the adherents, formal links were tenuous and unclear. The doctrinal relationship rested on the appreciation of pamphlets published by the Watch Tower Bible and Tract Society. Yet the interpretation of Watchtower literature, as well as its relationship to vernacular ideas and political struggles, and the character of local leadership, differed substantially across time and place.[14] This chapter is most concerned with the latter two movements, the radical and politicized urban Watchtower in the early 1930s and its transformation into the Jehovah's Witnesses after 1935 through engagements with elite educated Africans, the colonial state, and international missionaries.

The core message of the international Watch Tower Bible and Tract Society was that Satan was found on earth and had to be defeated in the battle of Armageddon, which would lead to a new order. It was a view of the invisible world that held meaning for the colonial order. Unlike the early rural manifestations of Watchtower, the struggle in the mining towns was not against evil witches or against colonial chiefs, but against the agency of Satan in the colonial urban order. This was a striking innovation in political thought. Watchtower members did not fight against colonialism in support of old rulers, but because the colonists were, as the Watchtower pamphlets proclaimed, agents of Satan. An end to colonialism would bring about heaven on earth, not because the colonists had been defeated, but because Satan had been defeated. Freedom from colonialism meant freedom from Satan. Thereby, Watchtower joined a spiritual struggle with an anticolonial struggle, transforming Christianity into an uncompromising and confrontational anti-colonial movement.

The anticolonial content of Watchtower and similar movements has been noticed by several scholars. John Higginson, for example, explored Watch-tower as an early manifestation of working-class consciousness in Katanga in the Belgian Congo.[15] With greater freedom to organize on the Northern Rho-desian Copperbelt than in the Belgian Congo, the Watchtower movement has been mentioned in several historical accounts of the growth of the working class and the rise of opposition to the Northern Rhodesian colonial order.[16] The targeted anticolonial nature of such movements was only one aspect of their politics, however. By the 1940s, some of Watchtower's main opponents were found not in the colonial state, but in the native welfare associations and incipient nationalist movement. No study has explored the genesis of the tension between the nationalist movement and Watchtower, which emerged following the promotion of a secular African politics by the colonial state, mis-sionaries, and the elite African welfare societies following the radical activism of Watchtower in the 1930s. This secular sphere introduced political concepts that broke decisively with concerns to engage agents of the invisible world. Yet this secular politics was neither secure nor hegemonic. A millenarian and apocalyptic spirituality remained a feature of a tamed Watchtower, even as it seemed to be safely relegated to the sphere of religion. For Watchtower follow-ers, freedom still meant defeating Satan, but, unlike the millenarian activism of the 1930s, it meant renouncing the influence of Satan rather than combat-ing his agents in this world. The trade unions and the new nationalist move-ment would take on the struggles of this world instead. Nevertheless, within this ostensibly secular anticolonial movement, the spiritual millenarianism of Watchtower continued to influence ideas of and strategies for liberation.

SATAN AND THE COLONIAL ORDER

A massive social transformation on the central African Copperbelt began in the initial decades of the twentieth century. At first copper mines exploited the rich deposits in the Katangan Province of the Belgian Congo. By the 1920s,

mines began opening in colonial Zambia, with the most rapid growth taking place between 1925 and 1929.[17] Mining companies recruited African labor
from across the subregion, especially from the ChiBemba-speaking northeast;
by September 1930, Africans working in all the mines and concessions in colonial Zambia totaled 31,941, a nearly fourfold increase from the approximate
8,000 workers three years prior.[18] A railway line that transported men to the
mines and copper from the mines connected the administrative capital, Livingstone, with the future capital, Lusaka, and the growing Copperbelt towns.

The Copperbelt quickly became a new ChiBemba-speaking center that
escaped the control of the Crocodile Clan chiefs. Here, political and religious
leaders mobilized support by claiming to represent a cosmopolitan modernity,
just as chiefs had begun to appeal to tradition. To be modern meant engagement with the world of books, with new technologies, with the politics of the
world, and with new forms of bureaucratic organization, all driven by a sense
of progress and civilization.

The first agency of this modern sentiment was the Native Welfare Society.
Unashamedly elitist, the welfare society sought to improve Africans through
close collaboration with progressive elements within the colonial state and
with the missionaries.[19] Between 1930 and 1932, welfare associations sprang up
across the major towns of colonial Zambia, most notably in Livingstone, Lusaka, Kabwe, and Ndola. In Livingstone, the first capital of colonial Zambia,
about 350 people elected the officials at the first meeting of the association on
April 19, 1932. The speeches promised an "uplift" of the people, a deliverance
of "European civilization" to Africans, while at the same time criticizing the
colonial administration for not adhering to their civilizing mission. In Kabwe,
the site of some of the earliest mines in Zambia (established in 1916), the association had about two hundred members. In Ndola, Ernest Muwamba, the
Livingstonia-educated cousin of Clements Kadalie, the leader of the South
African Industrial and Commercial Workers Union, held fortnightly meetings
that campaigned around issues affecting urban Africans. His brother, Isaac
Muwamba, a senior clerk at the provincial commissioner's Lusaka office,
headed the Lusaka Native Welfare Society. He was considered the most educated and influential African in Lusaka, with a personal following of workers
and teachers who consulted him on all matters.[20]

The welfare societies did little to deal with the spiritual life of the towns.
By the 1930s, salaried Africans sought new ways to approach the spirit world.
They wanted to spread the gospel of Christ, of literacy and the Bible, and of
civilization—for them, all were linked together. The Watchtower of the 1930s
provided an outlet for these new salaried moderns. The movement morphed
from its antiwitchcraft focus of the previous decade into a movement that
sought to eradicate the evil that possessed those in charge of the colonial

order, not only because of "injustice" or "oppression," but because colonial rulers were agents of Satan.

Joseph Sibakwe led the urban and peri-urban Watchtower movement that emerged in the early 1930s. He had been part of Watchtower in his home district of Fife, an area that had been vulnerable to Bemba and Swahili raids before colonialism, marginalized by the more powerful chiefs during colonial rule, and most recently under the influence of the Mwenzo Welfare Association. The colonial authorities deemed Sibakwe to be "the biggest Watch Tower man in Northern Rhodesia today." He was reported to have been in communication with the Watch Tower Bible and Tract Society regional headquarters in Cape Town.[21] Sibakwe began by touring the villages around Lusaka, Kabwe, and the Copperbelt that were situated near the new railway line that snaked into the interior, bringing laboring men to the mines, goods to the countryside, and ideas back and forth.

Sibakwe did not search for witches, as the Bamuchape and rural Watchtower preachers were doing at the same time. His preaching, baptizing, and church-planting along the line of rail motivated a new political project that emerged out of the Watch Tower Bible and Tract Society publications, especially the pamphlet literature written by Judge Rutherford that had become increasingly fervent and fiery after World War I. According to Rutherford, World War I was supposed to have been Armageddon, with the victory of the armies of Jesus Christ against Satan. Yet, in 1918–1919, just as Christ's forces were about to proclaim victory, Satan infiltrated the governments of the United States of America and Great Britain. Since then the imperial Anglo-American system had been in the hands of Satan. Together with the leaders of big business, the politicians "hired" the preachers to protect them from the "detestable" classes—that is, the true followers of Christ who would inherit the earth after the final battle. Big business, the leaders of empire, and the established clergy were the essential elements of Satan's organization.[22]

It took no great leap of the imagination to apply these writings to the colonial order in which Sibakwe and his followers found themselves. Sibakwe told followers that King George was not a real king, but a representative of Satan who stole the people's taxes. In the coming war, all would die except for Watchtower members who bore a mark on their foreheads that would protect them from harm. In the new order, the formerly condemned would judge their oppressors. King George's government would soon end and be replaced by a new one led by Americans and Watchtower members. In this government, the Africans, and not Europeans, would be the magistrates. The established churches were tools of Satan. He called for a collection of money to help bring this new order into existence, and claimed that Nimrod (the grandson of biblical Ham) would be the first African to collect taxes to be used for the benefit of all the people and not for King George.[23] "European agents at work in Africa are depicted as being all of abomination and uncleanness, the open enemies of Jehovah and His witnesses," wrote a Luapula-based missionary who witnessed Watchtower in the 1930s. "Jehovah will vindicate the righteous and destroy those who oppose His rule," the Watchtower claimed. The "Watchman on the Wall," which adorned the churches and sites of assembly, symbolized the hope for a new order in which the exploited and wronged would judge their former rulers.[24]

The emphasis on ridding the world of Satan included combating colonial forms of oppression. By 1932, employers on the Copperbelt heard their workers murmuring "Merik," those whom they imagined to be American Watchtower adherents who would rescue them from exploitation and bring about an end to Satan's rule.[25] A Watchtower branch in Luanshya, led by Lefati Mwambula, took up issues relating to the workers and attempted to make representations to the governor on their behalf.[26] Missionaries of the mainline churches on the Copperbelt claimed that "whole districts" became Watchtower. A Watchtower preacher would attract a crowd by shouting a version of the scriptural teaching "The first shall be last and the last shall be first." Those who wanted to know more were taken into the bush where they allegedly learned that "the white man who is first, shall be last, and the native, who is last, shall be first."[27]

The leaders of the Watchtower movement came from the literate working-class elite, generally employed by the colonial administration or the missionaries. In Lusaka, a former teacher called Siwani, who worked as a cook in the government hostel, was in charge of Watchtower in the local township. Peter Mufukwa, a clerk at the Lusaka hospital, took charge of the northern Lusaka suburbs and ordered Watchtower pamphlets; while Kapesa, a worker at the farmers' Cooperative Society, preached in the old town compound.[28] Watchtower meetings were held in European stores managed by Africans, in the compounds, outside places of employ such as the Lusaka hospital, and in workers' homes. A decade earlier, such leaders would have organized similar meetings of welfare societies. Indeed, as urban Watchtower increased in popularity across Lusaka until an estimated 75 percent of urban residents attended Watchtower meetings or had some sort of affiliation, the welfare society declined. In Kabwe, the founders of the welfare association, Abiner Kazunga and George Nyirenda, became Watchtower preachers instead. By 1932, Isaac Muwamba's Lusaka Welfare Society had lost its entire membership to Sibakwe's Watchtower. Muwamba was so embittered over the loss of his status and supporters that he agreed to spy on Watchtower on behalf of the colonial administration.[29]

Watchtower did not critique the colonial regime for their betrayal of the civilizing mission in the same fashion as the welfare societies. They sought to appropriate the objects of civilization that had spiritual power. The supernatural and religious claims of Watchtower were an intrinsic part of its comment on modes of colonial authority, not a metaphor or coded critique. Political agency was tied to these spiritual claims. In what can be described as an industrial animism, Sibakwe claimed that technology was imbued with spirits that would empower the oppressed. Upon completion of the railway, all Europeans would depart, leaving Africans in charge. Indeed, all machinery, which, according to Watch Tower Bible and Tract Society doctrine Christ had given power when he invisibly returned to earth in 1874, would be handed over to Africans.[30]

In their battle against Satan, Watchtower sought to appropriate and disseminate the education that had been denied Africans. Sibakwe revealed the books that the Europeans had hidden from Africans, and which, he claimed, had real spiritual power. One book had a lock and a key engraved on the cover—a Watch Tower Bible and Tract Society symbol for opening the door of knowledge that the established clergy had hidden from people. Sibakwe claimed it meant that previously whites had locked the doors of knowledge from Africans, but he had found them and would open the doors.[31] He allegedly used a book with "equality written down in it," to make himself invisible and evade arrest by the district commissioner.[32] The books themselves held sacred and divinatory power: one had an illustration that showed Satan "typing a record" of the 1914–1918 war.[33] The Watchtower books were not only symbols of the new power of literacy or a comment on colonial modes of authority; they were thought to have real spiritual power.

Sibakwe emphasized his prophetic role. He warned his followers of rivals who challenged his exclusive access to the power of education, telling them that they should not join the welfare association, which was "fooling them." They needed to listen to him instead, since even the African clerks, who held the highest position attainable in the colonial state, were on his side.[34] Sibakwe's colleague, Peter Mufukwa, carefully controlled access and viewing of Watch Tower Bible and Tract Society pamphlets, a few of which were translated into ChiNyanja. Mufukwa boasted that he had a book so powerful that it could instantly make him more educated than the head of the welfare society, Isaac Muwamba.[35] The power of other authorities—European colonial officials, chiefs, or educated elites—was marginal compared to the spiritual power of the Watchtower prophets and their books.[36]

In addition to books of sacred knowledge, there was the power of documents, especially the certificate of authorization. According to the Native Schools Ordinance legislation, formulated after the Mwana Lesa movement, all African preachers had to have certificates of authorization from the local district commissioner. While they may have preached without them,

Watchtower preachers actively sought out colonial certificates that disseminated and made available the invisible powers of writing.[37]

Sibakwe's career came to an abrupt end in 1932. In part due to the influence of the Native Welfare Society leader Isaac Muwamba and his informers, Sibakwe was arrested, sentenced to six months hard labor, and deported to his village.[38] Watchtower did not disappear, however. The struggle over the politics of modernity and urban life that positioned Sibakwe and his followers against Isaac Muwamba and his welfare society elite continued. Together, the welfare societies and Watchtower both contributed to an explosive rebellion in 1935, and ultimately to the rise of new forms of social and political organization on the Copperbelt.

A SECULAR POLITICS

The prosecution and persecution of Sibakwe drove the urban Watchtower movement beneath the radar of the colonial administration at least until 1935. There are few reports of Watchtower activities until the strike of 1935. The strike revolved around colonial attempts to increase taxation for urban workers and thereby to discourage migration to the urban areas, since in the midst of the Great Depression the Copperbelt mines had little need for labor. Watchtower's opposition to the payment of tax to the agents of Satan proved a popular way to mobilize around these economic complaints. The Russell Commission of Inquiry that investigated the strike found that that Watchtower had encouraged antagonism toward colonial authority and was a factor in leading workers to strike.[39] Scholarship on the strike agrees on the centrality of Watchtower ideology. Charles Perrings found that Watchtower provided "a vehicle for the critique of industrial conditions and colonial society generally"; for Sholto Cross, it "generated ideas of confrontation, and a vocabulary of protest."[40]

The Watchtower movement had little to do with the direct organization of the strike, however. By 1935, the leaders of the formal movement, such as Lefati Mwambula, the head of Watchtower at Luanshya, attempted to distance themselves from what they viewed as the primitive and untutored Watchtower of the previous decade. To do so, they worked in close collaboration with Cape Town headquarters of the Watch Tower Bible and Tract Society, and especially their local representative, Petrus Johannes de Jager. Following the international trend, they named themselves Jehovah's Witnesses, instead of Watchtower, even while "Watchtower" was still used in ordinary parlance. After the strike, these Watchtower leaders insisted that they had nothing to do with the strike. Nevertheless, the colonial authorities identified Mwambula as one of the chief culprits behind the strike: He had been one of the chief organizers of a Watchtower meeting in Lusaka in the prior month, and had been in Luanshya only a day before miners refused to go work. Immediately after the strike police detained him and confiscated fifty pounds of Watchtower literature in his possession. Still, Mwambula vehemently denied his involvement to both the commission and to the Cape Town Watch Tower headquarters. Colonial authorities could find no direct evidence implicating him or any other Watchtower leader in the strike.[41] Instead of Watchtower, one of the men who beat the war drums to gather and encourage the strikers was a Roman Catholic compound elder, the type of leader in whom the colonial authorities and mine management had vested their trust.[42]

The problem for colonial authorities and the commission of inquiry was that even while it was fairly clear that Watchtower did not organize the strike, signs of Watchtower discourse were everywhere, in the notices posted outside the compounds, the letters sent to the miners, the willingness to die for their cause, and the angry cries of the miners. Through the energetic preaching and sale of the popular pamphlets, Watchtower ideas spread far beyond the formal organization. For three pence in English and four pence in ChiNyanja, urbanites could read of the great battle to come, between Satan and his empire and those who would inherit the earth. The danger of Watchtower, then, was in its pamphlet literature, which extended its ideas far beyond its members. Watchtower resembled a social movement, not a church.

Quotidian struggles against working conditions, salary stagnation, taxes, and other forms of material injustice were only tangential to Watchtower politics: its pamphlets and preachers told of a revolutionary and millenarian supernatural intervention that would transform the nature of the world, delivering it to righteous followers. "We teach our people to be quiet and peaceful and not quarrelsome," claimed Mwambula. "At present they must go from door to door preaching the gospel of Christ, and they must know that in time to come Armageddon will come."[43] "The wrath of God . . . is coming," Anna Nkulukusa, a Kabwe-based preacher, told the commission of inquiry, "and it is not coming upon one particular person but everyone who is a wicked person."[44] The supernatural aspect to Watchtower millenarianism contributed to its uncompromising political stance. The insistence that humans could remove Satan and his evil influence from the world made Watchtower so politically threatening.

Immediately after the strike of 1935, the colonial authorities embarked on a campaign to undermine the broader influence of Watchtower. Instead of banning the movement outright, as they had with Mwana Lesa and the Belgians had with Watchtower in the Congo, Northern Rhodesian colonial officials sought to tame Watchtower. The central aspect in this strategy would be to make sure that Africans no longer believed in Satan's spiritual interventions into the visible world. They would thus respect a divide between what the colonists and the missionaries viewed as the religious realm and the political realm. There was a degree of hypocrisy here: the colonial state still relied heavily on Christian missionaries as well as the chiefs, and the missionaries relied on the colonial state. However, even in the 1930s, the colonial administration sought to emphasize the secular roles of such religious agents—the educational and moral role of the missions and the traditional role of the chiefs. Religion was thought to be about the preparation for an afterlife, which effectively directed moral actions in the world, and not about the active involvement of the spirits in this world. Most missionaries agreed with this vision of religious life and confronted African insistence on spiritual intervention. By the 1940s, the colonial authorities had begun to introduce the notion of a secular state and civil society, distinct from religious associations. This idea, fervently followed by the Protestant-rooted welfare societies, proved to be a significant innovation in African political organization and ideology.

A first step in the taming of Watchtower was to bring it under the control of Europeans, who, colonial officials reckoned, understood the divide between secular and religious authorities. Instead of an acephalous social movement, Watchtower would thereby become a typical European-controlled mission church. Yet spiritual interventions in the visible world were a central tenet of the international Watch Tower Bible and Tract Society. Immediately after the strike, the international Watch Tower Bible and Tract Society complained that they had been blamed unfairly by the Russell Commission for the strike. The secretary of the South African branch wrote a confrontational letter to the governor of Northern Rhodesia that contested the arrest of Watchtower members after the strike. He accused the established Protestant and Catholic churches of spreading false rumors about the Jehovah's Witnesses, maintaining both their innocence and their right to organize according to the principle of religious freedom.[45] Petrus Johannes de Jager told the 1935 Commission of Inquiry that Watchtower in Northern Rhodesia had to defend themselves in front of "the highest authorities of the seventh world power of the Devil's organization." He appealed to "British public opinion to see to it that British imperialism is forced to give us a square deal."[46] Despite their complaints, the Jehovah's Witnesses did agree to send a representative to Northern Rhodesia to "supervise" African preachers. Much to the disappointment of the colonial authorities, however, they chose the confrontational de Jager.[47] Far from reforming Watchtower, de Jager immediately set out to defend the African community of believers. He wrote to the governor and to the Northern Rhodesian advertiser, denying Watchtower involvement in the strikes, which he claimed were caused by Bemba Catholics instead. He also protested the banning of Watchtower literature.[48] By the end of September, following complaints from chiefs and labor supervisors across the Copperbelt, the colonial government placed restrictions on de Jager and informed the Watch Tower Bible and Tract Society headquarters that he was not a suitable representative.[49] Despite the protests of de Jager and the Cape Town Watch Tower Bible and Tract Society, de Jager left Northern Rhodesia and the society sent another representative, Llewen V. Phillips, to oversee operations there.[50] Still, as de Jager had, Phillips resolutely opposed attempts to dilute the message of the Watch Tower Bible and Tract Society, and encouraged the flouting of rituals of authority, including the bowing down to representatives of political authority such as chiefs.[51]

The second avenue of colonial efforts to tame Watchtower revolved around efforts to control the distribution of documents. Watch Tower Bible and Tract Society publications, especially those that linked the Anglo-American Empire to Satan, were prohibited.[52] The secretary for native affairs termed the Watchtower literature "blasphemous and seditious" and suggested to the governor that in addition to prohibition, they should be dealt with "at the source."[53] After some negotiation, the Watch Tower Bible and Tract Society agreed that all literature would be imported through its representatives and submitted to the local colonial official for approval.[54] This arrangement prevailed until 1940, when the Watch Tower Bible and Tract Society publications were once again banned because of their claims that World War II was the Armageddon (the appearance of a ChiBemba Watchtower pamphlet *Armageddoni* had the colonial authorities especially perturbed).[55] Simultaneously, the colonial government sought to encourage and even sponsor what they deemed to be acceptable and moderate publications of the established churches. The administration began to publish its own vernacular newspaper, *Mutende*, in 1936. They also established the Native (later, African) Literature Committee, consisting of two missionaries, a senior administrative official, the superintendent for native education, and one African member, to publish material suitable for African audiences, preferably in the Zambian vernaculars.[56] The Catholics also published a monthly periodical for Bemba-speaking Christians on the Copperbelt.[57] Watchtower leaders still sought ways to circumvent colonial restrictions by introducing new, popular techniques of dissemination. For example, they distributed gramophone recordings of Judge Rutherford.[58] Nevertheless, as more written tracts spread across the Copperbelt towns, the colonial administration did manage to dilute the power of the Watch Tower Bible and Tract Society publications. Books and pamphlets remained popular, but they were increasingly seen to be products of this world, authored by ordinary people, and not representative of extraordinary supernatural agency.

The 1935 strike also gave impetus to mission efforts to organize a coordinated response to the Watchtower movement. In 1931, the influential report *Modern Industry and the African* had suggested the promotion of a united Protestant Copperbelt missionary society to cater to urban Africans.[59] In the following years, the London Missionary Society and the Church of Scotland promoted their activities on the Copperbelt and made tentative moves toward amalgamation. The strike of 1935 brought matters to a head. Only a fortnight after the strike, missionaries gathered and decried the lack of educational and religious instruction on the Copperbelt, which they argued had led to the strike. Discussions over the following year led the principal Protestant missions to establish the United Missions of the Copperbelt (UMCB)—a precedent for the later formation of several united Protestant bodies, most significantly the Church of Central Africa in Rhodesia (CCAR) in 1945, and the United Church of Central Africa in Rhodesia (UCCAR) in 1958, which was reconstituted as the United Church of Zambia (UCZ) in 1965.[60] A central aspect of their mission on the Copperbelt was the transformation of spiritual beliefs toward the dead.[61] The Catholic White Fathers called a meeting where, mimicking the widespread colonial identity registration, they proposed to issue workers Christian identity cards, which would act as "passports" to moral living and Catholic sacramental practices while on the Copperbelt.[62] With an emphasis on welfare work, missionaries hoped that such efforts would serve the educational, moral, and spiritual needs of urban Africans, thereby diminishing the appeal of Watchtower and lessening the chances of radical political actions.

The final, and in the long run, the most decisive aspect of the effort to separate religious from political spheres lay in the promotion of progressive secular political parties and civil society. The roots of this secular civil society were already present in the welfare societies that had opposed Sibakwe's Watchtower in the early 1930s. Immediately after the strike, the welfare societies once again asserted themselves against Watchtower. D. S. Rain of the Ndola Welfare Society wrote to the Northern Rhodesia advertiser, complaining of the "imported religion from Europe controlled by heathen Africans without any proper leader." The "seditious" Watchtower literature, Rain continued, needed to be banned and the enlightened activities of the welfare societies encouraged instead.[63]

Through the 1930s, the colonial authorities were still reluctant to vest too much authority in autonomous secular African organizations, preferring the combination of tribal elders to control workers and beer hall meetings to cater to their social needs. The strike of 1935 only confirmed the colonial perception of the need to shore up support for the system of tribal administration of the mines by setting up a more formal system of "tribal elders." Yet, as the demand for labor once again grew in the late 1930s and the mining companies encouraged a "stabilized" workforce, the system of tribal administration further eroded, becoming unwieldy and anachronistic. In March 1940, following directly upon a European strike, African miners went on strike again, with the worst consequences at the Nkana mine, where troops killed seventeen miners and injured sixty-five.[64] The 1940 strike made clear the inadequacy of the system of worker supervision and representation. The official commission of inquiry still favored the strengthening of indirect rule and chiefly authority on the mines through tribal elders. Nevertheless, they acknowledged the prospect of a more progressive approach to labor relations.[65] Indeed, another influential report deemed the existing system of tribal representation unsatisfactory and encouraged the formation of new "groups, societies or other bodies for the purpose of discussing public affairs."[66]

Historians view the 1940 strike as a decisive moment in the "continuing development of worker consciousness among the African miners."[67] Notwithstanding the teleological aspects of the argument, educated elites, progressive missionaries, and elements within the colonial regime did begin to advocate for more autonomous and more moderate African-led organizations.[68] "Had there been at Nkana recognized representatives of the Bantu workers, or had their appointment even been suggested during the strike," wrote the progressive young missionary Reginald J. B. Moore, "serious consequences might have been averted."[69] Protestant missionaries began to publicly criticize aspects of the urban colonial order, such as the "Colour Bar," which restricted opportunities for African economic and political progress.[70] For the missionaries, the strike once again revealed the "vast spiritual and moral needs" of the African workers that their missions needed to serve. Now, even more than in 1935, they thought it crucial to develop African civil bodies—and they had the support of many members of the colonial administration.[71] Moreover, through the 1940s African welfare societies once again proliferated and joined with African urban advisory councils to campaign on a broad range of issues affecting urban life.[72]

The combination of native welfare societies and progressive thinkers in the colonial and missionary establishment began to lay the groundwork for African representative bodies in the industrial and political spheres. To be sure, many in the colonial administration and mine management were reluctant reformers at best, and had to be prodded constantly by these progressive elements. Nevertheless, by the 1940s, the economic and political authorities on the Copperbelt became increasingly convinced of the need for some form of African representation. It became all the more important for this representation to be cast in a modern and secular form that conformed to colonial expectations and fell within colonial modes of control.

By the late 1940s, two forms of representation had emerged. Under pressure from the Northern Rhodesian Legislative Council members, the Colonial Office sent a trade union specialist, William Comrie, to organize an African workers' union. Comrie encouraged a group he termed the "Disciples," who would spread the "gospel of trade unionism about the Copperbelt."[73] In part due to the potential threat of African workers becoming involved in more radical forms of trade unionism, the Colonial Office agreed to rapid unionization. Helping to organize one of Comrie's first meetings was Kenneth Kaunda, an employee in the welfare department at the Nchanga mine and the son of David Kaunda, one of the founders of the Mwenzo Welfare Association and a Bembaland missionary. A combination of elite workers committees and welfare society members launched the Shop Assistants Union in January 1948. In February 1948, workers elected Lawrence Katilungu, a recruiting clerk and one of the leaders of the 1940 strike, as union president at Nkana. By March 1949, several local mine unions had amalgamated into the African Mineworkers Union (AMU).[74] According to Comrie, the most fervent opponents of unionization were members of the Watchtower movement. In fact, union campaigns for closed shop agreements were aimed principally at Watchtower members.[75]

The second secular agency was African representation in government. After World War II, the colonial state, egged on by the increasingly dissatisfied African elite, began to support limited forms of African representation. In 1945 local advisory bodies, such as the urban advisory councils and the provincial councils, were supplemented by a colony-wide African Representative Council (ARC) of twenty-nine members. The elite members of the welfare societies took their places in the ARC, which was only an advisory body and had no formal political power. Nevertheless, it was symbolic and representative of the possibilities of a broader African political representation. By 1948 the ARC could select two of its members as "unofficial" members of the Northern Rhodesia legislative body. For the first time, representatives of Africans were being replaced by African representatives.[76] Within the towns of the Copperbelt, the provincial commissioner became increasingly aware of the danger of a dissatisfied African intelligentsia alongside the inadequate forms of tribal representation and marginalization by European urban councils. He followed the district commissioner's suggestion in proposing elected urban African councils, with real financial and legislative responsibilities, along with reforms that would encourage a self-employed African middle class.[77]

Inspired by the radicalization of the nationalist movement to the south and west of the continent, elite Africans organized their own progressive nationalist movement in 1948, named the Federation of African Societies, effectively an amalgamation of the most important welfare societies. In 1951, the organization became the African National Congress (ANC), and members elected Harry Nkumbula as its president. It grew into the most widespread and respected organization that campaigned for African political rights and against segregation and the industrial "Colour Bar." By the early 1950s, as chapter 5 details, the ANC conducted its first campaign that mobilized a broader base of African society against the onset of the Central African Federation.[78]

The transformation of African political organizations and trade unions from the millenarian radicalism of the 1930s to moderate trade unions, representative councils, and a national congress seems to represent the rise of a secular political and civil society. It conforms to the post-1945 liberal developmentalist colonial project and to a progressive nationalist narrative. By the early 1950s, liberal elements of the colonial state and their progressive allies appear to have succeeded in the creation of a secular African political and civil society distinct from African religious movements. Spirits no longer seemed to inform political struggle. In 1948, colonial officials considered Watchtower harmless enough to unban its monthly publication, *Crisis*. A survey of twenty district commissioners in the late 1950s confirmed that Watchtower was no longer thought to be involved in politics. "Nowadays," one DC wrote, "whenever there is trouble of a political nature, the Watchtower members . . . actively take the side of authority."[79] Rather than inspiring strike action, Watchtower members were vocally opposed to it. They turned up for work when the African Railway Workers Union went on strike in 1952 and the African Mineworkers Union went on strike in 1955.[80] Watchtower members refused to become involved in the campaign against the Central African Federation in 1953.[81] In addition, Watchtower discourse was less prevalent in worker grievances and strike actions. The colonial state's creation of a secular political and civil realm where Africans gained some representation seemed to have marginalized Watchtower's radical influence.

The narrative of political development and secularization, however, elides the fact that Watchtower continued to grow even faster than it had previously, remaining more popular than the organizations of secular civil society or even the nationalist movement. By 1959, the Jehovah's Witnesses had 28,000 active preachers, up from 15,000 in 1952.[82] At the Roan Antelope mine in Luanshya, Watchtower had a higher proportion of adult allegiance than any other denomination.[83] At one Copperbelt assembly in 1959, 30,800 gathered; at another in the densely populated Luapula Province, a hinterland of the Copperbelt, 17,000 to 19,000 people congregated over three days.[84] Watchtower had changed, but it maintained its appeal among urban Africans. It was not the case, as claimed by Sholto Cross, that "the ideological accommodation to the new industrial culture which was the basis of much of Watch Tower movement's appeal had by and large taken place."[85] Watchtower remained a popular way to confront the spiritual issues that faced people in the mining towns.

The secularization narrative also misses that fact that Watchtower millenarianism would permeate popular politics as nationalism transformed from an elite to a mass movement. The nationalist elite, while inheriting the modernist project with secular claims, broke decisively with the colonial state after settler interests prevailed in the creation of the Central African Federation in 1953. They insisted on the sovereignty of the "people"—albeit that the people were led by them—instead of the sovereignty of the Colonial Office and the district commissioners. But even as the "people" accepted and celebrated the elite nationalist leadership, they recast the terms of the struggle from the attainment of secular civilization to the sacred millenarian revolution of Watchtower. Political millenarianism informed by Watchtower became pervasive as the nationalist organization changed from an association of elites to a popular movement.

Watchtower also remained involved in politics, just not the politics visible to the colonial state or to secular historians. Their refusal to be involved in the affairs of the colonial state did not indicate that they respected a divide between secular politics and religion. Quite the opposite: since Satan ruled the politicians of the world, they refused to have anything to do with them. Only through removing oneself from the influence of Satan would Armageddon come about. Spiritual agencies still had to be dealt with, but the tactics had changed from direct confrontation to an evasion of the state, which, with the spread of Watchtower, would ensure that Satan had no more followers. The political battle thus became the search for new converts, people who would no longer allow themselves to be controlled by Satan.

By the 1950s, the missionary scholars John V. Taylor and Dorothea A. Lehmann were surprised by the lack of Watchtower interest in social reform, given their prior turbulent political involvements.[86] Indeed, Watchtower no longer did battle on the immediate and quotidian issues facing urban Africans, such as taxation, salaries, political representation, and segregation. In part, as many Watchtower scholars and practitioners emphasize, there is a distinction between the earlier Watchtower and later Jehovah's Witnesses. Yet such a distinction ignores the most significant aspect of continuity, the belief in the presence of Satan. Watchtower followers still knew that Satan was in the world, and that injustice was proof of his presence. Their activism was thus directed at people who could be saved, not at the agents of Satan. After all, why struggle for social and political reform today when the route to true justice was through the eradication of Satan's influence in the world? "Armageddon is surely coming," a Watchtower preacher proclaimed in 1950. "That is what we are here to concentrate on and so there is no point in being interested in worldly things."[87] Lehmann and Taylor witnessed remarkable enthusiasm and organization in planning meetings to convert people in preparation for the Armageddon.[88] In fact, much as it had for revolutionary Marxists, the lack of justice in this world proved to Watchtower that change was coming. The difference was that unlike Marxists, Watchtower activists believed that revolutionary change would come from the sacred world and be helped along by prayer and individual faith, not by the inevitable progress of dialectical materialism.

Sacred millenarianism did not decrease; it was submerged, hidden by the modernizing projects of the developmentalist colonial state and the emergent African nationalist associations. Watchtower members had not given up on their struggle against evil. They had, rather, accepted that freedom from evil comes from harnessing spiritual power to fight Satan in this world, not from confronting those who were but Satan's agents. Change required a spiritual revolution. But this struggle against evil did not mean rendering unto Caesar the things that were Caesar's; it meant, instead, to continue the struggle against evil by an evasion of the state and its agents, a complete rejection of the power exercised by the state, the agents of Satan. In the many elaborate constructions that housed Watchtower assemblies from towns to villages, the power of spiritual interventions still remained an influential force. In other words, while the colonial state and progressive educated elite had helped to create a secular civil society, the spiritual realm as a source of power remained a popular concept. On the central African Copperbelt, Watchtower was—and still today remains—one of its most influential expressions.[89]

The secularization of politics has appealed to the sentiments of a generation of historians who viewed such change as the almost inevitable development of African politics. For the liberals, African welfare societies were the seeds of democratic nationalism; for the Marxists, African trade unions were the origins of working-class consciousness.[90] In both cases, a universal modernism was seen to have superseded the millenarianism of Watchtower. Even those historians sympathetic to the acts of resistance by Watchtower members explained them in terms of their opposition to chiefs and colonial authorities, or their capacity to organize the working class. Historians never took the sacred politics of Watchtower seriously, nor the claim that Watchtower made repeatedly: that freedom involved ridding the world of evil, and such change would come about when people renounced Satan. Only then would the world be changed. When nationalist movements appeared, historians tended to focus on them instead of on those movements that advocated change through such spiritual agency. The choice to follow the path of secular politics and organization has led to a history of the political imagination that conforms to a colonial vision of politics.

As Watchtower became a "religious" organization, it battled Satan by depriving him of followers. Instead of Watchtower, the welfare associations, nationalists, and trade unions struggled against the colonial state and the mining companies over the grievances that Watchtower had first identified as evidence of Satan's presence: taxation, paltry wages, and the general exploitation of colonial subjects. But this secular politics drew on earlier Watchtower ideas: the colonial state and its agents were not simply oppressive, racist, and exploitative—they were evil. On the other hand, while the colonial administration did not agree with the elite nationalists, they thought that they shared a common understanding about the nature of politics. In alliance with the missionaries and progressive Africans, the administration carved out a secular sphere distinct from a religious millenarianism. As the following chapters demonstrate, the uprisings of the 1950s would prove that their efforts failed. Popular notions of spiritual evil infiltrated reformist secular politics. Spirits still guided agency, even in those secular realms from which they appeared to have been banished.

4 ⇜ A New Jerusalem

MULENGA LUBUSHA NGANDU was born in the Chinsali District in the early 1920s. Her mother and her father, a village policeman who fought for the British during World War I, were members of the royal Crocodile Clan. She married Gipson Nkwale soon after puberty and had a child with him. After the death of Gipson, she was "cleansed" and "inherited" (*ukupyana*) by his cousin Petros Chintankwa, with whom she had five children.[1] As with most mothers, she was named BanaKangwa (the mother of Kangwa) in honor of her first child. In all these respects she lived a life typical of a Bemba woman in the first half of the twentieth century. But in early September 1953, she fell ill, probably with cerebral malaria, and her life took an extraordinary turn. The events of the next few days are unclear, revealed in many myth-like stories. Most of them narrate how BanaKangwa died, and then the next day came back to life. While dead, she met Jesus:

> I found myself in the middle of an ocean. I held onto a rock and nearly drowned. Only my head remained above the water. Then three people who wore bright white clothes came to me and said you are not supposed to cross to the other side to the place of the righteous. I heard a voice of our lord Jesus. He told the angels that they should throw a rope onto the water and immediately the rope came and it touched the rock to which I held. From the other side of the river, they sang:
>
> | Posa ulusale paBemba | [Throw the rope on the ocean |
> | Noushikonke fyakwalesa | Those who don't follow God's command |
> | Taka buke nakalya | Shall not cross at all] |

Then the angels said: "Now cross and go to the place of the righteous."
"How will I cross?" I asked.
They said: "You will cross on the rope."
"I will drown," I replied.
They said: "If you have faith, you will cross and reach the other side."
I took hold of the rope and started walking on it quickly. I reached the other side of the ocean where there was a big and beautiful city. This *musumba* [city/mission/palace] does not exist on earth, there is no comparison on earth in its beauty, size, and splendor.[2]

While in the beautiful city on the other side of the ocean, BanaKangwa met two angels, who found that her name was not written in the book. She had to return to the living and ensure that her name was written in the book before she died. The angels taught her hymns, and instructed her to save her people by making sure they also had "passports to heaven." This would be accomplished by abolishing the sin of witchcraft.[3] Her vision rejected the heavenly afterlife promised by the missionaries in favor of a spiritual quest in the physical world.

When BanaKangwa woke up, she went into the bush, where she sat under a large tree and received two books from God, one for black people and one for white people. Another woman, BanaMutupa, approached her, thinking that perhaps she was possessed by an *ngulu* spirit. BanaKangwa told her to go away and to leave her alone, since BanaMutupa was not a baptized Christian. She called for baptized Christians to come to her instead, in particular her husband, Petros, and a Christian leader, Leah Kasomo. But it was too late — the book for black people was swallowed up by the earth before the baptized Christians arrived.[4] The ancestors from below had taken the book from the sky.

BanaKangwa wrapped the second book, the Book of Life (*ibuku lya Mweo*), in white cloth. Together with her husband and two young girls, she walked to the Presbyterian Lubwa Mission, with which she was affiliated, to tell them of her visions and gift. There, on 18 September 1953, she met with the Scottish missionary Fergus Macpherson. According to Macpherson, BanaKangwa arrived at the mission in midafternoon, asking to see him. Through his clerk, Macpherson instructed BanaKangwa and her followers to attend afternoon prayers. After the service, Macpherson noticed her "sitting against the wall, on one of the pews, looking very ill and weak." She told Macpherson that she had died and that Jesus had sent her back across the river, since her time had not yet come. While she was at the river, Jesus had taught her some hymns, "songs of a very simple evangelical theme," a few of which she sang for Macpherson. He did not write them down, but remembered one phrase, "Tatwakabuke umumane, kano imitima yasambwa" (We shall not cross the river unless our hearts are washed).[5]

Those who were close to BanaKangwa claim that the meeting with Macpherson was the beginning of the divisions between her and the Lubwa Mission. Macpherson allegedly took the Book of Life from BanaKangwa and hid it under his shirt while they prayed with their eyes closed.[6] Other accounts claim that BanaKangwa told Macpherson she had been instructed by Jesus to preach the word of God, but Macpherson refused to allow her, since she was a woman. He certainly did not allow her to preach in the Lubwa chapel.[7] Many people remember BanaKangwa meeting with the influential Lubwa reverend Paul B. Mushindo before Macpherson, although Mushindo claimed that he was away on a journey at the time and met her only after she had talked to Macpherson.[8] Perhaps Mushindo baptized BanaKangwa as "Alice," the European name by which she came to be referred by many followers and by the missionaries.[9] Oral accounts could have emphasized the meeting with Mushindo to highlight the future tensions between her followers and the African teachers who were closely associated with the mission.[10] The notion that Macpherson stole the book and took it to Europe was reinforced when Macpherson took overseas leave at the end of 1954. In Macpherson's absence, relations between BanaKangwa and the Lubwa Mission deteriorated. Kenneth Mackenzie, Macpherson's replacement, and Mushindo sent a letter to BanaKangwa, warning her to desist from baptizing people. They also informed their congregants not to be baptized again.[11] The district commissioner recorded a meeting with "Alice" at the beginning of 1955, when she told him that she would establish her own church since she attained the right to baptize from God directly, and not from the Lubwa Mission.[12] At the end of 1955, the Lubwa church elders expelled BanaKangwa and her twenty-six closest followers from the Presbyterian mission.[13]

Freed from the constraints of the Lubwa Mission, with its hierarchical structure and male dominance, BanaKangwa established the influential and autonomous "Lumpa Church," the church that "went beyond" other churches and hastened all to salvation here on earth.[14] She became known as the Queen, "Regina," or "Lenshina." Stories of Lenshina's resurrection and her communications with God spread across the Bemba heartland, eastward to Malawi, and south and west to the Copperbelt. Upon hearing the good news, many made the pilgrimage to the striking church that Lenshina's followers were building at Zion, "Sione," next to Kasomo Village. Numerous mission reports complained that the majority of their members had been baptized by Lenshina and her husband, Petros, during 1955 and 1956.[15] By 1958, between 60,000 and 100,000 people claimed some sort of affiliation to the Lumpa Church, far more than the combined membership of the Catholic and Protestant missions, and nearly 90 percent of Nkula's chieftaincy in the Chinsali District, where Lenshina had her Sione headquarters.[16] The most faithful and generous followers were given names from heaven (*ishina lya mulu*) and became choir leaders who disseminated the distinctive and beautiful hymns that Lenshina had learned while in heaven.

At first Lenshina's church drew some notice from missionaries, anthropologists, and colonial officials concerned with African "Ethiopian" churches or millenarian movements. Based on reports of those close to the movement and limited fieldwork, the missionary scholars John V. Taylor and Dorothea A. Lehmann wrote a sensitive account of Lenshina's syncretic practices.[17] Yet it was only after the violent conflagrations of 1962–1964, discussed in chapter 6, that Lenshina's church drew sustained attention and led to an official government commission of inquiry, which has subsequently been widely cited as the principal historical source on the church.[18] The commission's *Report* was well researched and as balanced as could be expected, given the tumultuous political context. Yet the precise terms of reference of the commission precluded a scholarly appreciation of the Lumpa movement. It also focused on the events of the 1960s, instead of giving a full account of the movement in the 1950s, which was when Lenshina's movement was at its strength.

In an influential article, Andrew Roberts argued that the Lumpa Church combined two movements that had swept across south-central Africa since the early twentieth century: witchcraft cleansing cults and African independent churches.[19] While Roberts also acknowledged *connections* between the Lumpa Church and nationalist politics, he argued that the Lumpa Church "was not, except accidentally, an organ of political protest."[20] If only looked at on one level, Roberts is correct: the Lumpa Church was an African Christian attempt to eradicate witchcraft and distanced itself from politics, with its first commandment insisting explicitly that "the Lumpa Church is a church in which God and His Son Jesus Christ are to be praised. It is not a political organization." A careful examination of the early ChiBemba versions of this commandment, however, indicates an interesting slippage in translation; instead of having nothing to do with "politics," "the church did not seek to quarrel or to govern" (Te cilonganino ca fikansa ne ca buteko, iyoo).[21] This was an evasion of the state, rather than a claim that the movement had nothing to do with the arrangements of power in this world.

As Wim M. J. van Binsbergen points out, it is problematic to restrict an analysis of politics to a sphere "defined by the political elite themselves, as its exclusive frame of reference."[22] For van Binsbergen, the struggles surrounding the Lumpa Church were part of an attempt to incorporate the peasantry into this formal political sphere. The Lumpa Church was a peasant movement that "radically rejected state control."[23] In his Marxist analysis, then, the Lumpa Church was explicitly political by leading a movement that attempted to evade incorporation into a state increasingly dominated by the urban and bourgeois leadership of the nationalist movement.

Two White Fathers have offered the most-nuanced attempts to explore the ideas that informed Lenshina's movement by examining Lumpa hymns. Jean Loup Calmettes, in his unpublished thesis, argues that van Binsbergen overestimated the revolutionary nature of this peasant movement; instead, Calmettes claims that Lenshina resurrected a neo-traditional system based on the model of Bemba chieftainship.[24] With a similar body of evidence but with an emphasis on symbolism, Hugo F. Hinfelaar focused on the Lumpa promotion of matrilineal and matriarchal ideals found within what he terms "Bemba religious dogma."[25] These revealing interpretations rely on a selection of Lumpa hymns, which were indeed important sources and statements of Lumpa ideas. Yet the hymns emerged at different times and had different emphases. To accurately understand the historical development of the Lumpa movement, we need to appreciate who sang the hymns, when, and where. Moreover, Hinfelaar's symbolic approach introduces another layer of problems. How does the scholar interpret apparent symbols without imposing meaning on them? In my many interviews, Lumpa Church adherents did not agree with Hinfelaar's interpretation of Lumpa symbols. As Kwame Anthony Appiah points out, such a symbolic approach may stem from a tendency for modern Christian intellectuals to "treat doctrines that were once taken literally as metaphorical or . . . symbolic."[26] For Lenshina's followers, the spirit world was real, not symbolic.

Lenshina and her followers employed the spirit world to transform their historical circumstances. In her analysis of the Watchtower movement, Karen E. Fields points to how conventionally religious acts, such as "speaking in tongues," challenged the sacred basis of political authority.[27] In a similar fashion, the Lumpa pioneered forms of political agency that sought to bring about a new order through spiritual interventions. The movement did not adopt the revolutionary slogans of Marxist theorists or the symbolism of Catholic intellectuals. The Lumpa spiritual revolution had to emerge out of familiar ideas, change out of continuity. Lenshina's church was a politically revolutionary effort that challenged the spiritual basis upon which political authority had previously rested, offering a new invisible world dominated by a Christian God and Jesus.

A long tradition of Africanist scholarship has identified the political role of prophetic movements in their connections with secular movements. The teleological and evolutionary nature of accounts of the transition from so-called "primitive" and "proto-nationalist" forms of rebellion to nationalist uprising has already been pointed out. That is not the concern here. On one level there were connections—although not linear and one-directional—between the Lumpa movement and Zambian nationalism: there were activists who were part of the Lumpa Church and the African National Congress (ANC), later the Zambia African National Congress (ZANC), and the United National Independence Party (UNIP). Robert Kaunda, ANC activist and the elder brother of the future president of Zambia, Kenneth Kaunda, was secretary of the church, and one of the mission-educated leaders who claimed the Lumpa as an African church, explicitly highlighting its nationalist role. The argument here, however, is that the political role of the Lumpa Church has to be evaluated in terms of what secular discourse defines as its religious claims. Lenshina employed the spiritual technologies of the missionaries, books, and baptism, to destroy the remnants of the chiefs' spiritual powers and to cleanse witchcraft and sin. After her movement had swept across northern Zambia, the Christian God appeared to be the ultimate source of authority.

BEGINNINGS

In the early 1950s an array of unsettling social, economic, and political forces affected the highlands of northern Zambia. Conflict over the advent of the European-dominated federation of Northern Rhodesia, Nyasaland, and Southern Rhodesia in 1953, further explained in the next chapter, led to suspicions of a settler landgrab, even while the coronation of the "Regina," Queen Elizabeth, was "celebrated" across the colony. The Catholics had embarked on an aggressive program of proselytizing in the name of the Legion of Mary, their own "Regina." There was an outbreak of smallpox that spread across the region in 1955 and 1956, with unusual severity and a high mortality rate.[28] And the village economy was under continued economic strain and change brought about by the migration of predominantly male labor to urban areas. The burdens of the most vulnerable, in particular the women of the villages, had become heavier as this agrarian society encountered colonial capitalism.[29] These political, social, and economic factors all explain why people felt the presence of spirits acutely. None of them, however, explain the form that Lenshina's movement took.

The Queen's church was patterned on an expansion of south-central African political systems comparable to Luba sacred kingship. It contained a vision by a founder, in this case a brave heroine, who traversed the land of the dead and was sent back with a set of spiritual teachings, rituals, and sacred objects. She established an extensive bureaucracy based on the telling of her oral tradition and the diffusion of her sacred objects. On occasion, her followers even used the title of a Luba sacred king, "mulopwe," to address Lenshina. Another popular title was *lubuto lwa chalo*, "the light of the world"; or even *lubuto mulopwe*, "the light king," perhaps a reference to the dawn and the solar hero, Luchele Ng'anga.[30] She drew on a maternal political idiom common to matrilineal clan oral traditions of genesis. Even the Bemba royalty were descendant from the celestial mother, Mukulumpe. A letter written or dictated by Lenshina to the governor of Northern Rhodesia addressed him as "mother of the whole territory of Northern Rhodesia." She went on to complain, "Am I suffering in doing the work of God because I am a woman? . . . That is why I am begging you the mother of all of us, if you can see how I am suffering because of being a woman, and because of my words which I have been sent to warn people so that they may know, and stop doing all the evil things on this earth . . ."[31]

By the 1950s, the dissemination of Christian doctrines about the afterlife, about a new god with an old name, *Lesa,* and about the separation of the land of the dead from the living, had disturbed the authority of royal and village ancestors. The ancestral authority of the Crocodile Clan was more precarious than ever before. The everyday and ordinary use of magical objects, *bwanga,* was frowned upon, or feared, in this environment of spiritual insecurity. For those influenced by mission ideas, all *bwanga* became associated with sin and witchcraft. And even while the missionaries proclaimed the pervasiveness of sin, they failed to cleanse the land of such sinful witchcraft—a spiritual and political vacuum that Lenshina's movement would fill. Lenshina sought to eradicate such evil spiritual forces by instructing her followers to obey certain ritual and moral practices, which would lead to spiritual interventions or at least control over spiritual forces that caused harm. Her relationship with Jesus Christ, the ultimate ancestor, ensured that she was the vehicle through which these spiritual interventions could occur, but only if her rules were obeyed.

Lenshina built on Catholic, Protestant, Watchtower, and Bamuchape attempts to attain and spread spiritual power; she innovated within a changing collective imagination. Like the missionaries, she insisted on doing away with the evil ways of the past. Her practices of purification held some similarity to Catholic confession, communion, and baptism, and her name, "Regina," appeared in Catholic Latin liturgies.[32] Her emphasis on a new moral order and the transferal of the morality of heaven to earth resembled Protestant conversion, especially of the more radical evangelicals. She also received revelations in a fashion similar to the Bamuchape leaders, but, like the Watchtower, she attached these revelations to the doctrines found in the books and pamphlets. The story of her own revelation and resurrection closely mirrored the Protestant text *The Pilgrim's Progress,* of which at least two ChiBemba versions had been in circulation since the late 1920s.[33] Lenshina appropriated and subverted the narratives of such texts. Instead of remaining in heaven, as the characters in *Pilgrim's Progress* did, she returned to the land of the living to cleanse people of witchcraft. Lenshina wanted to create a new community of Christians, not only in preparation for the afterlife, but to create heaven on earth. She also differed from the Bamuchape, who sought to placate the angry ancestors. In fact, the more radical followers of Lenshina cared little for the ancestors; they were most concerned with witches, who were agents of Satan. Lenshina sought salvation here on earth by eradicating the sin of witchcraft.

Lenshina and her followers offered an effective way of dealing with sinful witches. The chiefs' mediations with spirits were superseded by the Queen's relationship with Jesus and God, "Tata" Lesa. Those who invoked older forms of ancestral protection became witches who refused to acknowledge the supremacy of God and the New Jerusalem:

> You witches, be on your guard
> You will face the creator
> Because of the charms you prepare. . . .
>
> You shall get into trouble
> You, leader of the wicked
> You who teach your friends how to bewitch
> You shall suffer, as you cause them to suffer
> See for yourself, wicked person.[34]

Salvation and freedom began with a pilgrimage to Lenshina's temple, where people surrendered objects of witchcraft, *bwanga*. As they did so, Lenshina and her deacons wished them health but sought to ensure that they had brought all of their bad magic:

> Good health to you, all my children
> Even as I greet you, I am reticent
> Because you may have left your bad things behind.[35]

Lenshina's political objective was the eradication of the evil in people's hearts and the evil stored in bad things, *fyabubi*.

The center of Lenshina's movement was the temple, *tempile*, situated in a grass enclosure next to the area under the *museshi* tree where Lenshina had her first visions and received the Book of Life. Upon visiting the *tempile*, Lenshina, or at least her agents, distributed medicines and remedies that ensured good health, fertility, and a prosperous harvest.[36] In the *tempile*, Lenshina and her husband, Petros, baptized and purified the pilgrims, freeing them from the sin of witchcraft. A small hut to one side was reserved for marriage ceremonies.[37] Young women carried the *fyabubi* that spread misfortune, and deposited them outside the grass enclosure of the *tempile*. Here they were rendered

Figure 4.1. Remnants of the tree under which Lenshina had her visions; and the *tempile*, where people came to surrender the *bwanga* witchcraft. Photo by author, 2005.

harmless.[38] Many of these bad things were part of an older ceremonial life that had previously ensured fertility and good harvests: "horns [*nsengo*], beads, lion claws, medicine pouches . . . ceremonial battle axes (*mbafi*) and ceremonial hoes (*tulonde*)."[39] (See fig. 4.1 and 4.2 below.)

The struggle against evil witchcraft involved pragmatic spiritual interventions as opposed to the moral interventions emphasized by the missionaries. Take, for example, a church service held in Mukuni Village in 1956. Inside an impressive village structure, sign-posted "Lumpa, the Great Meeting Place of African People," a young woman gave a sermon that drew from the Old Testament story of the burning bush. It had particular resonance to local Christians since the burning bush was the insignia of the Church of Scotland (the church under which the Lubwa Mission fell). But for the Bemba, who relied on the burning of the bush to fertilize their fields—the *chitemene* style of agriculture that sustained the Bemba in the sandy soils of the northern plateau—the miracle was that the bush *did* burn and created life. The young woman told the congregants that God had sent the Catholics to burn the bush, but they did not burn it and only stole the treasure. Then God sent the Watchtower and the Protestants. They failed to burn the bush. *Then God*

Figure 4.2. *Bwanga* surrendered to Lenshina outside the *tempile*. Photo by author, 2005.

sent his sister Lenshina, and she burned the bush.[40] A biblical fragment was adapted and made to speak directly to Bemba farming practices, the burning of the bush to prepare the *chitemene* fields. Previously, the Bemba royal Crocodile Clan ensured the prosperity of the land. Now Lenshina mediated over the forces of nature that ensured the economic viability and prosperity of the village. Instead of ceremonies that revolved around the Crocodile Clan's use of *bwanga*, in particular Chilimbulu's scarified skin, or the blessings of the mission churches, Lenshina provided the spiritual power to turn seeds into crops and food.[41] One of her hymns named her church the "house of seed."[42]

Beyond agriculture, the movement developed new forms of social morality that advocated for women and for familial stability. Lenshina relished her position as a young and attractive mother (see fig. 4.3, below). Audrey I. Richards described her as "round, fat and cheery in a dark blue frock with a bulging breast stuck out to a spoilt fractious, unpleasant little girl."[43] Her seven children remember her maternal role fondly.[44] Even after her resurrection, she maintained her affectionate term of address as "Mama." Many of her church's moral codes supported mothers and motherhood. By 1957, Lenshina had developed twelve rules (or "commandments") that instructed people to refrain from bad actions, such as insults, lying, cursing, and selfishness. But her most demanding rules centered on the role of women in families. She prohibited polygamy and insisted that a widow must be allowed to remarry, presumably without the *ukupyana* widow cleansing to which she had been subjected. Drinking alcohol and smoking, habits of men that wasted the resources of women, were banned, initially in church but increasingly in the presence of any Lumpa adherent.[45] While she advocated against the *chisungu* initiation ceremonies for girls, her narrations and hymns drew upon *chisungu* principles of personal transformation. Take, for example, the song of the initiate crossing the river, a possible inspiration for Lenshina's dream and her conversion narrative of crossing the water:

> I, the paddler of a canoe
> I want someone else to paddle me across.
> Me, poor creature.
> You will get me to the other side.[46]

Instead of the mother of the initiation ceremony, the *nachimbusa*, carrying the girl across the water to adulthood, in Lenshina's narrative and hymns, Christ carried the converts to the other side of the water, where they would become Christians. This was not a movement that dealt with the supernatural spirits in the afterlife of the Christian missionaries. Introducing such gendered rituals and moral codes involved the spirits in the pressing concerns and struggles of women's everyday existence. By bringing together the concepts of witchcraft and sin, Lenshina related spiritual interventions to pragmatic concerns.

As in the European mission churches, Lenshina's church consisted of different types of followers. Several leadership positions were established. Those closest to Lenshina, often relatives, were the "deacons" (*badikoni*). By 1958,

Figure 4.3. Alice Lenshina, n.d. (1950s). Reproduced with permission of Ministry of Information, Zambia.

there were 106 churches in the Northern Province, led by ten deacons.[47] Under the deacons, there were the preachers, known by their old Bemba name, *shimapepo*. The mission-educated, often responsible for writing letters of instruction, were the teachers (*kafundisha*). Church elders were referred to as judges (those who heard and disciplined; *bakumfwa*); and then there were choir members. All of the church leaders had visited Lenshina headquarters, learned the stories of her resurrection, and heard the beautiful hymns that God had taught her while she was dead. Lenshina and her husband, Petros, instructed these church leaders, who were similar to the Protestant teachers and Catholic catechists. A church bureaucracy was established.[48]

While its strength always remained in the rural Bemba plateau, Lenshina's deacons began to follow the Bemba migrants who traveled to the burgeoning urban areas. Men wearing long white robes, calling themselves the twelve disciples of Lenshina, arrived on the Copperbelt in early 1956, preparing for visits by Lenshina, which she made in greater frequency from then on. On the Copperbelt the church took on a different character. Fewer women were involved, and disillusioned ex–mission teachers, who were drawn predominantly from the Lubwa Mission, which had stopped paying a number of teachers a few years prior, dominated the leadership.[49] Sandy Rain, a former Lubwa teacher and welfare society member, and Robert Kaunda, who was the elder son of the founding Lubwa missionary David Kaunda (and who was dismissively insulted by a European Lubwa missionary as "a uncontrolled moody pain"), pioneered the movement on the Copperbelt.[50] When Lenshina visited the Copperbelt and Lusaka at the end of 1956 to raise funds for the building of her church, the colonial authorities reported that the vast majority of the church's leaders were members of the ANC. At a Kabwe meeting, the treasurer claimed that "this church is for Africans only, as Congress is for Africans too, and that this country is for Lenshina and all who follow her."[51] Yet even here the movement was not simply an arm for secular nationalist politics. Sandy Rain, one of the most urban and politicized Lumpa members, insisted that Lenshina is "no false prophet, she is a true minister. God our Father does not want his children to perish, therefore again and again he sends a sentinel to warn us of impending danger."[52] The church was most popular in the Copperbelt towns of Kitwe and Luanshya, with regular prayer meetings of sixty to seventy people. Combined membership figures with the other Copperbelt towns of Ndola, Mufulira, and Chingola totaled thirty-five hundred; an estimate for all of the urban Copperbelt and Lusaka would be almost double that number, organized in at least sixteen churches and led by about the same number of deacons.[53]

Hymns contributed to Lenshina's popularity. The *shimapepo* preacher was also a choirmaster who directed local choirs in more-remote villages, mostly consisting of young girls (the cohorts of young girls found in Lenshina's choirs were another indication of the links between the *chisungu* initiation groups and Lenshina's church). As mentioned, the White Father scholars Calmettes and Hinfelaar have closely analyzed the content of such hymns and indicate some of the core values of the Lumpa Church. Yet one must be cautious in generalizing such ideas across time and space. After all, we do not really know who composed the hymns and when.[54] Robert Kaunda, a man known to have significant musical talents, for example, wrote down many of the hymns and may have been involved in their composition; yet, in many ways he was marginal to the rural base of Lenshina's followers.[55] Any of the principal ten choirmasters at Sione, Lenshina's headquarters, could have composed hymns, not to mention the fifty other choirmasters who directed choirs across the country.[56] Except for a few very popular hymns, the significance of any one hymn to the entire movement is unclear. Understanding their symbolic meanings is even more difficult.

Regardless of the hymns' meanings, for several weeks of each year the choirs made a pilgrimage to Lenshina's headquarters where they would learn new hymns. En route, they sang, attracting the attention of many villagers, missionaries, and colonial officials.[57] "Passionate dirge like melodies expressing an intense devotion in a wholly African idiom," according to one missionary. "This is the music a man sings when his heart is nearly mad with sorrow," commented another man upon hearing the hymns.[58] Perhaps the literal or symbolic meaning of any one hymn was less important than their collective beauty, than the emotions that all of the hymns conjured in those who heard them, and which gave them spiritual significance.

The urban connections of the church provided opportunities for the financing of rural projects. Colonial and missionary accounts emphasize that church finances were provided by the giving of one penny for baptism and the surrender of witchcraft by "ignorant" villagers. Donations were always central to Lenshina's vision, and even incorporated into versions of her oral tradition, when, upon her return from heaven, Petros had to give Lenshina a sixpence.[59] Yet these funds were minor in comparison to the giving by those in urban areas, where people were charged at least double for the same services. The church also embarked on business opportunities. By 1958, the church had at least two five-ton trucks, which were loaded with rural produce, especially delicious dried caterpillars, for transport and sale on the Copperbelt.[60] As the funds accumulated, the church grew into a major business. Thereby the urban wages of men were effectively remitted to the rural economy.

The most important rural project financed by these funds was the building of the Kamutola Church at Sione, next to Kasomo Village. Kamutola was modeled on the White Fathers' Ilondola Mission, except it was one foot longer (although the Lumpa claim that the design was not a copy, but divine

Figure 4.4. Exterior of Zion church, n.d. (1964?). Photo by Fergus Macpherson. Original held by Jack Thompson.

inspiration). The Lumpa offered their labor; they remember their efforts with great pride. Its completion was meant to inaugurate the age of a New Jerusalem, a utopia. The church itself was striking, its size and design unprecedented for a church financed and built by rural Africans (see fig. 4.4 and 4.5, below). Inscribed above the door was "Uluse Kamutola," a reference to Matthew 11:28: "Come to me, all you who are weary and burdened, and I will give you rest." On the exterior foundation stone was inscribed Lenshina's story of death and resurrection and her instructions to perform God's work on earth, as indicated in figure 4.6. Inside the church, a nave with a series of arches on either side led to a raised pulpit. Thousands gathered when it opened in November 1958, expecting that Jesus would deliver the first service.[61]

After the opening of Kamutola Church in 1958, the character of the Lumpa Church began to change. Many more people arrived to see the magnificent church. The village was transitioning into a town, with people gathered from across the region, remaining not only for baptism but to forge a permanent community of believers. A structured Sunday church service began. But most of all, what began as a movement to cleanse the sin of witchcraft took on a millenarian quality. The Kamutola Church was meant to bring about a New

Figure 4.5. Interior of Zion church, n.d. (1964?). Photo by Fergus Macpherson. Original held by Jack Thompson.

Jerusalem. On one level it did; Lenshina had created a community of faithful Christians who advocated and lived with a new morality. Yet on another level it was disappointing. Jesus did not arrive and, outside of Sione, evil prevailed. No remarkable spiritual interventions were evident. Sinners and witches were to blame. The Lumpa became even more determined to cleanse them.

MISSIONARY RIVALS

In addition to the use of missionary spiritual resources and ideas, Lenshina's movement became enmeshed in the bitter rivalries between the Catholic and the Protestant mission churches. The Lumpa adapted the language of religious conflict to their particular concerns with witchcraft. At first, the Lubwa Protestants encouraged Lenshina's criticism of the Catholic mission.[62] But Lenshina and her followers went further than the Protestants in claiming that the Catholics spread evil and were witches; it was, after all, the "Romans" who had killed Jesus. They had probably done so through their witchcraft. Catholic rosaries, crosses, and medals were objects of witchcraft—in a fashion similar to the *babenye* relics of chiefs and *chisungu mbusa* of young girls. Lenshina had to purify all such objects.[63] Her followers stole *bwanga* objects from the

Figure 4.6. Foundation stone of Zion church. The stone reads "Lenshina M[ulenga] 25 October, 1953 Died; 26 October Rose from Death; 27 Met Jesus who gave her the work. Our Father Builds on the Rock." Photo by Fergus Macpherson, n.d. (1964?). Original held by Jack Thompson.

missions. At Kayambi, missionaries found "rosaries torn, crosses and medals thrown in the fire."[64] Catholic converts who went to be baptized by Lenshina had their crosses and rosaries torn off.[65] "Indeed for Lenshina people," complained a White Father, "the rosary is the charm invented by the Romans to throw people in Hell."[66] Prayers that missionaries offered were thought to be curses.[67] When the White Fathers appeared in the villages, the Lumpa cried, "Mulwani aisa ee utufunya kuli tata" (The enemy is coming to chase us from our father).[68] If the White Fathers still attempted to pray in the villages, Lenshina's followers would drown them out with hymns and drums.[69]

The White Fathers viewed such acts as provocation and antagonism rather than an attempt to purify Catholic witchcraft. They could not accept that Lenshina sought to cleanse them, to get rid of their evil, as the Catholics sought to cleanse the Bemba of their sins. The White Fathers crusaded against Lenshina in a far more aggressive fashion than the Protestants. They produced a pamphlet, *Mwitina bena itempele* (Do not fear the people of the temple), and undertook "Rosary Campaigns."[70] Catholic action programs, a new youth movement, and Corpus Christi processions were organized.[71] "Fight is often good," wrote a Kayambi White Father missionary.[72] Another White Father referred to Lenshina as a devil (*diablesse*).[73] The Ilondola Catholic mission sent spies to report on Lumpa activities. By the end of 1956, they boasted of their faithful Christians who were "growing more fervent, more generous and stronger against the enemies of the Church."[74] Chalabesa Mission cited "heroic examples" of Christians who "attacked the regina-sect messengers, forbade them to delay and preach in their villages and beat their own children who followed the crowds to Kasomo [Lenshina's headquarters]."[75] Only in 1957 did the Catholics temper their response: a circular letter called on the missionaries to "calm down in our direct attacks . . . we should be less negative and more positive."[76]

At first, the Protestant missionaries at Lubwa embarked upon a campaign to ensure that Lenshina and her followers clarified their relationship to the mission.[77] By the end of 1955, as mentioned, they had expelled Lenshina and her closest followers due to their competing baptismal practices.[78] A few Lubwa missionaries developed a respect for Lenshina, however. Fergus Macpherson and Vernon Stone accepted her "spiritual gifts." Nearly all of them commented on her beautiful hymns, which challenged the commonly held missionary perception that the Bemba could not sing (they realized it was less about the quality of Bemba singing than the quality of their Protestant hymns!).[79] The Lubwa missionaries were convinced that the problem was not with Lenshina directly, but with their own Christian converts, who, in the "absence of deep conviction based on personal spiritual experience and adequate Bible teaching," deserted the Lubwa Mission for Lenshina's church.[80] By 1956, they had sent letters to Lenshina and her leaders, complaining that they had split the Lubwa Protestants, and suspended their church membership. However, they decided not to confront Lenshina's followers directly and instead launched a campaign to convince people of the importance of the scriptures and that "no true Christian should be made to subscribe to teaching about medicine for growing gardens and for guarding people from dangers, oracles speaking with the voice of God, or to the attacks made on the Word of God and the Church of Jesus Christ."[81] Near Lubwa, they had decided to limit any large-scale campaign, since it "seems to increase ill-feeling."[82] Here, their most decisive impact, they felt, would be to spread education and literacy.

Rather than the foreign missionaries, the most fervent conflict was between the Lumpa and the loyal African followers of both the Catholic and the Protestant missions. Lumpa members began to explicitly confront the literate teachers and the hold they had over the interpretation of the Bible. As the first copies of the Protestant translation of the Bible arrived at Lubwa Mission in 1956, Lenshina's followers declared it *chibolya*, a deserted village.[83]

The significance of the Bible was subordinated to the hymns that God had taught Lenshina directly and the Book of Life that she had received from God directly (which was stolen by the missionaries). Lenshina distributed written documents, "passports to heaven," circumventing the spiritual authority of the teachers and missionaries' access to heaven. The Lumpa withdrew their children from mission schools.[84] An early opponent of Lenshina, Lubwa reverend Paul B. Mushindo became a target of witchcraft accusations.[85] By 1958 Lumpa Church members even accused the former teachers who had joined them, especially Robert Kaunda, of embezzling church funds and ostracized them. Enmity with the loyal mission communities ratcheted up the degree of polarization and the radicalism of Lenshina's followers.

The African educated elite attached to the Catholic missions responded most aggressively. In May 1956, a Lumpa adherent, Joseph Mumba, accused a Bemba White Father, Pascal Kakokota, of witchcraft. Kakokota was not prepared to take the matter as lightly as his European colleagues—in any event, the consequences for him were more serious. Kakokota took the complaint to Nkula's Native Authority court. Nkula, not powerful enough to adjudicate a dispute between a White Father and Lenshina, referred the case to the colonial Boma, who found Kakokota's accuser, Mumba, guilty under the Witchcraft Ordinance and imprisoned him for one month. In response, about five hundred Lumpa followers launched a protest outside the colonial Boma at Chinsali. The protest lasted nearly ten days, until it was finally broken up and sixty-four people arrested, including Lenshina's husband, Petros. Under pressure from the colonial administration, Chitimukulu imprisoned twenty men and twelve women in hard labor, fined seven men and fourteen women, and had eight juveniles caned. Lenshina's husband was sentenced to six months of hard labor for refusing to obey Chitimukulu's orders and a further two years for proposing violence to the assembly. This was the first open conflict between the Lumpa and the colonial administration.[86] But the colonial administration also acted against aggressive Catholics, at least one of whom was imprisoned for six months for "provoking" people at Lenshina's Sione headquarters.[87]

The missionaries had trained a community of converts who were paid to evangelize, to spread the influence of the missions, and to gradually bring about a Christian modernity under their leadership. For them, the problem of sin was pervasive, but would be dealt with through social reform encouraged by the promise of heaven and the threat of hell. For Lenshina, conversion entailed a break from the past and the creation of a new society, purified of the evil spirits of this world, and freed from the missions and their hierarchical modernity. This was a program radically different from the emphasis on salvation, confession, and membership of a church hierarchy found in Protestant and Catholic missionary discourses and practices. Lubwa missionary Vernon Stone perceived the difference:

> It would be a sin to deny that our orthodox Christianity has not produced wonderful fruit and is still producing it . . . all that a *Christian layman* can be. . . . He takes his full part in the Courts of the Church, where time and again his lead is more spiritual, more Christian than that of us Ministers; he imbues the school with his spirit. . . . Introduced to white man's knowledge and religion . . . they become leaders in all parts of life. . . . A school like Lubwa lays the Christian foundations on which we hope and pray that the *incipient African middle class* will build its ethos in the next generation. . . .
>
> But when we look at *people proper*, the *ordinary villager*, a very different picture presents itself. They belong to a *People Movement*, but it is not the Church. They have with their own hands erected simple Churches in nearly every village, they gather enthusiastically three times a week at worship. . . . Alice has succeeded in bringing into being a People's Movement . . . her success marks our failure. . . . It leaves one with the feeling that nowhere has the missionary succeeded in really integrating Christianity in the daily life of the people. (emphasis in original)[88]

In addition to offering a Christianity for ordinary people and integrating it into the concerns of everyday life, Lenshina's "people's movement" was a revolutionary and uncompromising political intervention. It identified the kingdom and, as indicated in this popular Lumpa hymn, offered a choice between being saved or lost:

> Believe, all of you, the owner is coming
> Come together and praise
> There is no king who surpasses me
> Come together and praise
>
> The unfortunate one
> Who fails to come to the Kingdom of God
> When you have failed
> Where will you go?[89]

THE DEATH OF THE ANCESTORS

Lenshina's followers not only eradicated witchcraft and confronted missionaries. The most successful battle that her followers waged was against the most powerful edifice of indirect rule and the rulers of the past—Chitimukulu's Crocodile Clan, or, more precisely, the spiritual power of the Crocodile Clan's ancestors. Lenshina's spiritual authority usurped that of the chiefs. By 1953, mission Christianity alongside the bureaucratic pressures of indirect rule and the agency of prophetic movements such as Watchtower and Bamuchape had already rendered such spiritual authority vulnerable; nevertheless, unlike the urban mining towns, chiefs in rural areas still had power. Lenshina's movement was a blow to the Crocodile Clan's authority, which increasingly relied on the colonial state and the claims of tradition. The Crocodile Clan's *babenye* relics were emptied of their spiritual powers.

At first chiefs acknowledged Lenshina as an intermediary between the world of spirits and the physical world. In the same fashion that the Crocodile Clan chiefs had used Bamuchape to clear their lands of witches, chiefs began to use Lenshina. After all, Lenshina was a member of the Crocodile Clan and she had a convincing and remarkable story of her resurrection from the dead. In the midst of the challenges faced by the erosion of their spiritual authority and the concomitant demands of their subjects who insisted that chiefs eradicate witches, they gave their support to her, in spite of the misgivings of the colonial administration. In 1955 Chitimukulu called on the colonial administration to allow and even to encourage Lenshina's movement.[90] Chiefs Makasa, Mukungule, and Nkolemfu soon followed.[91] The Bemba chiefs viewed Lenshina's movement as an opportunity for a collaboration that would support their diminishing ability to keep their country free from witchcraft.

In the wake of the Mau Mau uprisings in Kenya, the upper echelons of the colonial administration expressed concern about Lenshina. However, local administrators dismissed such concerns. One of the first substantial reports reckoned that "Lenshina's appeal is to a very low mental level and it is doubtful her adherents have the capacity to keep to themselves anything in the nature of a secret oath." There seemed little danger of another Mau Mau among Chinsali's villages, with their "ignorant female majorities."[92] The report advised that for the meanwhile at least, the colonial administration should "leave Alice in her peculiar but profitable Wonderland."[93] Protestant missionaries claimed that the colonial administration was behind the alienation of the Lumpa. In particular, Fergus Macpherson claimed that the Lumpa began to distrust the colonial administration after the district commissioner interrogated Lenshina about her supposed encounter with Jesus, asking her what Jesus looked like, and warning her not to disturb peaceful villages.[94] Macpherson probably overstated the significance of this meeting. While the encounter with the district commissioner did indeed take place in March 1955, it is not remembered by Lenshina's followers as a significant moment of conflict, suggesting less importance to the event than Macpherson implied.[95] Lumpa confrontations with the White Fathers did not help relations with the colonial administration, however. The White Fathers constantly warned the colonial administration that the "movement has . . . an anti-white attitude directed primarily at the White Fathers and eventually at all Europeans."[96] Nevertheless, in 1955, although the colonial authorities were uneasy about Lenshina, they were far more tolerant of her movement than the mission churches, whose spiritual authority and followings were actually threatened.

Through the late 1950s, the Lumpa relationship with the colonial administration deteriorated. Colonial officials were concerned that a rather "innocent" movement was being exploited by the nationalists. They thought that teachers such as Robert Kaunda, Sandy Rain, and Lenshina's husband, Petros, manipulated Lenshina and her followers. These concerns reflected an unsurprisingly sexist and patronizing mentality. Colonial officials could not imagine a woman generating such a following and found the presence of any ANC member proof of the manipulation of Lenshina by the nationalists.[97] Reports insinuated that Petros was the real force behind the movement—even while he was in jail. Nonetheless, repeated accounts from colonial officials, anthropologists, and missionaries attest to Lenshina's independence and her lively intelligence. In one telling incident, a visiting Protestant missionary accused Lenshina of distorting God's message and ignoring the Bible. Lenshina responded by asking whether a servant or a master should reprimand another servant. The missionary said, "The master." Lenshina then told him: "You are the servant of Jesus and I am the servant of Jesus, so you cannot dismiss me." To this, the missionary asked whether one servant should warn a blind servant if he notices her walking into a pit. But the missionary was left without an answer when Lenshina replied, "We are all blind."[98] There is little evidence that the nationalists would have fared any better than the missionaries in attempts to persuade Lenshina. At times, especially while she was away on missions or visiting the Copperbelt, her control over the movement may have lapsed and others became influential. Nevertheless, Lenshina did all she could not to upset the colonial administration. When, for example, there were rumors that the movement had become infiltrated by ANC members and was a front for them, Lenshina sent the colonial authorities copies of her commandments, which explicitly stated she was not interested in quarrels and in government.[99] Lenshina's intelligence, charisma, and agency remained the unifying force and inspiration for the movement.

While Lenshina attempted to placate the colonial administration, her spiritual authority and charisma began to upset the chiefs. Lenshina had become such a powerful figure in Chinsali, literally the Queen, that she usurped even the most powerful of the Crocodile Clan chiefs. The popular Lumpa hymn that praised God as the ruler of the world, "Tapali imfumu iyachila ine kano ine neka" (There is no chief above me; I alone am chief), reverberated throughout Bembaland.[100] It reminded all of the collapse of chiefly authority and the replacement of the ancestral tradition with the new spiritual mediator, Lenshina. "Why should Alice Lenshina Mulenga say that there is a chief above Nkula?" Chief Nkula was remembered to have asked. "I, Nkula, am owner of the country. Who is above me?"[101] Encouraged by the White Fathers, the chiefs turned against this powerful rival by the late 1950s.[102] The chiefs could do little to prevent people from going to Lenshina's Sione, but the attempt was made to restrict Lumpa churches in their villages, leading to bitter contestation and rivalry.

In early 1959, the combination of the chiefs' frustration with Lenshina's sacred role, the marginalization of their spiritual resources, and the pressures exerted by the colonial administration led to a confrontation between Nkula and the colonial administration on the one hand and Lenshina's followers on the other. By then, Lenshina's followers had built and opened her church, Kamutola, at Sione, next to Kasomo Village and under Nkula's jurisdiction. The large and lively village defied a system of chiefly authority that had strict controls over settlement through village headmen. Sione was free from taxation and other demands that colonial chiefs made on the villages. Instead, followers volunteered their labor toward the building of the church and celebrated their accomplishments. It was the New Jerusalem. So many new people had arrived that disputes began to occur over resources with the older inhabitants of Kasomo Village. In one incident, Lenshina's goats wandered over to local farms and ate the cassava leaves of local farmers.[103] They complained to Nkula, who used the opportunity to intervene in the affairs of Sione. Shortly after, in May 1959, Nkula, accompanied by his retainers (kapasu), the DC, and a mobile police unit, went to Sione. Nkula insisted that people "clean up the village," return to their villages of origin, and pay their taxes. The Lumpa refused and defended themselves with knobkerries, bows and arrows, and axes. The DC was hit on the side of the head and knocked to the ground, narrowly saved by a loyal Boma employee from being hacked with an ax. The DC then ordered troops to open fire, leading to many injuries and perhaps even fatalities.[104] After capturing nearly two hundred Lumpa, the mobile police unit retreated. A nearby Bisa chief, Chibesekunda, wondered why the Lenshina prisoners had been captured and not speared![105] A court case ensued in which Lenshina hired a prominent lawyer. Sione prevailed—an embarrassing defeat for Nkula, the Crocodile Clan chiefs, and the colonial administration.[106]

After that incident, violent conflicts between the chiefs and Lenshina became too numerous to detail. Chitimukulu outlawed the church in his area and was probably responsible for having two Lumpa churches burned down.[107] Farther east in Lundazi District, in Chief Chikwa's area, the chief's retainers prevented Lumpa members from taking a buffalo that they had killed. Fights ensued over the next several days, resulting in a number of deaths.[108] The most important act in the Lumpa's determined rejection of the Crocodile Clan's ancestral government occurred during December 1963, in response to the killing of several Lumpa, allegedly on the orders of Chief Nkhweto. Young Lumpa men desecrated the burial grounds of the Bemba chiefs at Mwalule by cutting down the sacred *milemba* trees.[109] The Lumpa had attacked the very spiritual center of the Bemba polity.

For Lenshina's followers, the Mwalule sacred grove, the Crocodile Clan's grave and spiritual center, had become an anachronism, a sign of the past; it was transformed from a site of spiritual power and government to one of tradition or perhaps even witchcraft. The ancestral governance of the Crocodile Clan chiefs had been replaced by Lenshina and her access to Jesus and God. Luchele Ng'anga, who had allegedly built the shrine at Mwalule, no longer informed the Crocodile Clan's sacred governance, but shone through the "light of the world," Lenshina. The authority of the chiefs now rested on their attachment to the colonial state. This act of defiance at the center of the Lumpa political imagination represented the final defeat of the Crocodile Clan's ancestral government. By then, as chapter 6 will detail, the Lumpa had new opponents, the nationalists, who were also inspired by the Christian God.

⤳

The politics of Lenshina's movement revolved not around an incipient nationalism, as colonial officials feared and some scholars claimed, nor the revolt of peasants against the petty bourgeois direction of nationalist politicians, nor the restoration of pre–Crocodile Clan sacred chiefs, nor the religious agency of women. Even while all of these explanations reveal different dimensions of the movement, the political agency of Lenshina focused on what is conventionally termed their "religious claims and acts." Lenshina used Jesus and God to cleanse local magic and witchcraft. Lenshina appropriated Luchele Ng'anga from the ancestors of the Crocodile Clan and harnessed him to the narrative of Jesus. Conversely, she took Jesus from the afterlife of the missionaries and attached him to the efforts of women to free themselves from spiritual malaise. She drew on the full range of spiritual technologies of the missions, in particular books and baptism, to mobilize Christian spirits in a battle against the sin of witchcraft.

The rise of Lenshina's movement was a decisive moment in the history of Zambia's political imagination. Future chiefs would still proclaim the politics of tradition and play a limited role in spiritual interventions, especially witchcraft eradication. Yet their spiritual authority could not be mobilized as a significant political resource, and certainly not on the national level. New prophets had emerged. Secular nationalism was not the victor, as is often thought; the authority of the Christian God and his intermediaries offered an alternative to efforts to proclaim a sovereignty that lay outside the spiritual realm. Even the nationalists had to give obeisance to this God and his messengers. Other spiritual agents existed in this political imagination: ancestors still haunted the living, but their presence and agency were increasingly viewed as evil, and leaders had to mediate with the Christian God to deal with the spiritual malaise to which they contributed. The political imagination was still focused on harnessing invisible agents and controlling their influence, even as the form of these invisible agents and the technologies used to approach them had changed.

5 ↭ The Dawn

A GENTLE LIGHT and warmth that banishes darkness, the dawn is an age-old concept that indicates a liminal moment of a new but familiar beginning. In south-central Africa, the dawn was a long-lasting political idiom that associated everyday welfare with the overcoming of fear and uncertainty. Luchele Ng'anga, the solar hero, came from the east and inspired the Crocodile Clan to offer a Luba civilization that promised to join the sky and the earth. The dawn was a prophetic revolution, the conceptualization of a new day and a new order.

In the 1950s, two movements in colonial Zambia's Northern Province imagined a new dawn by reconciling Christianity with vernacular pasts. Popular Christianity, in particular Lenshina's movement, drew on Protestant conversion narratives and older Bemba concepts to invoke the joining of the sky and the earth, and to propose a heaven on earth. The second movement was popular nationalism. It also reconciled biblical narratives and foreign political philosophies with existing identities and networks of power to campaign for a new political order. Nationalism combined its call for popular sovereignty with older campaigns for heaven on earth. "Kwa cha" (It is a new dawn) became the rallying cry of the nationalist movement, so significant that the postindependence national currency, the *kwacha*, would always memorialize this call for revolutionary cleansing of the colonial order.

The history of the nationalist movement in Zambia is well known. The African National Congress (ANC) first grew in response to the imposition of the settler-dominated federation of Southern Rhodesia, Northern Rhodesia, and Nyasaland in 1953 (the Central African Federation [CAF]). The ANC declined or at best stagnated until 1957, when it was reinvigorated by the Zambia ANC (ZANC) and then the United National Independence Party

(UNIP). The historical details of the nationalist mobilization differed from town to countryside, and across rural provinces, districts, and even chiefdoms. By 1960, the Northern Province, especially Chinsali District, which was also the headquarters of Lenshina's church, formed an epicenter of the rural nationalist movement.

Rather than recount the historical details of the nationalist movement, this chapter explores the nationalist moralities and ideologies that enabled the rise of alternative modalities of power to colonialism. In the 1950s, sources of good and evil invested in ancestral spirits, nature, vampires, and witches were joined with other moral and political projects. The mission stations, Watchtower, welfare societies, and Lenshina pioneered this ideological work. The battle against evil morphed into a nationalist political struggle during the campaign against CAF, and then exploded into rural rebellion during the Cha Cha Cha anticolonial uprising. An engagement with a secular and a Christian invisible world informed popular nationalist politics.

A growing historiography on the nationalist movements that contributed to the collapse of European empires after World War II questions the triumphalist narratives that have legitimized postcolonial nationalist regimes. First developed as a critique of dominant nationalist narratives by the "subaltern studies" historians of south Asia, the historiography of nationalism has shifted to an emphasis on alternate and divergent voices, away from the nationalist elites and toward the ideas that inspired broad-based participation in the nationalist project. Where elite accounts are still examined, it is with a critical and counter-hegemonic eye, as in Partha Chatterjee's seminal work on the stages by which nationalist discourse incorporated the peasantry into the anticolonial struggle while marginalizing them from the nationalist modernizing project.[1]

In his early account of the rise of south-central African nationalism, Robert I. Rotberg identified the elite welfare associations that gave way to the nationalist organizations such as UNIP, which were, according to him, distinct from earlier moments of "indigenous protest."[2] A counternarrative to such elitist history suggests that popular elements drove the nationalist mobilization. Because of the depth of colonial and postcolonial anxieties over Mau Mau, scholars of Kenya have led the way in describing the political discourses, moralities, and theocratic commitments that both joined and divided popular and elite components of the nationalist movement.[3] In the case of Zimbabwe, Terence O. Ranger critiques the "patriotic history" that legitimized the liberation movement's leadership and repressed more-democratic possibilities within an older nationalist historiography.[4] In Zambian historiography, Marxist analyses, such as Wim M. J. van Binsbergen's account of the urban-based and petty bourgeois representatives of UNIP versus the peasant base of Lenshina's movement, were some of the first to question the triumphalist nationalist rendition.[5] More recent scholarship has expanded on this theme by highlighting voices that do not fit into patriotic histories. Giacomo Macola, for example, complicates the standard narrative of Harry Nkumbula's character flaws and submission to imperialists, as indicated by UNIP apologists ad nauseam.[6]

Yet there remain many unanswered questions about the spread of popular nationalism, new political cultures, and new notions of sovereignty. Most of all, existing scholarship assumes that concepts such as "freedom" and "independence" were obvious, as if there were a subconscious connection between the post-Enlightenment ideals of democratic republicanism and self-determination spread by the Atlantic Charter and the ordinary people of central Africa. The meanings of such ideas were neither evident nor the same to all. Different concepts of sovereignty were introduced, debated, and fought over in anticolonial nationalist struggles. There is a need to discuss the vernacular meanings and implications of "freedom" and of "independence"; how nationalist concepts were translated, adopted, and adapted in popular struggle. Much scholarship has been concerned with the translation of Christian terms. Yet how were "freedom" and "independence" understood in a society that valued social relationships? Did they imply freedom from forms of debt bondage, forced labor, and slavery? Or were the terms used to refer to "freedom" only from the impositions of the colonial state? How different were they to the salvation promised by Christianity and by older political concepts?

The ChiBemba term for "freedom" was *butungwa*, a cutting off and castration of old kinship ties, whereas "independence" was the process of taking control of oneself, *têkele*. Under the influence of a vernacularized Christianity, these concepts of freedom and independence became a "salvation," a new beginning in which evil and fear were banished. Like Lenshina, the nationalist movement campaigned for a new dawn, for a salvation from evil that would lead to a heaven on earth. Led by a messianic leader, Kenneth Kaunda, the popular nationalist movement would eradicate the evil of colonialism. The most striking campaigns encouraged the burning of colonial property, and especially pieces of paper with supernatural powers—the colonial identity document, the *fitupa*. The new dawn would be achieved by freedom (*butungwa*), literally cutting ties with the colonial state, with all of its exactions, its controls over livelihood, and excessive taxation. This, too, was not unlike Lenshina's claim that she did not want anything to do with "government." In the most striking shared use of terminology, the vernacular and the Christian promise of a new dawn, *kwacha*, became the nationalist cry. As Watchtower adherents had previously declared, the colonial order was satanic; the nationalists innovated this vernacularized Christianity. In other words, they advanced a seemingly secular politics by using Christian concepts.

The popular sovereignty introduced by the nationalists uniformity of the will of the "masses," rather than an institu dissent through an individual's identification with one of a variet parties. Liberal visions, such as those advocated by the multiracial Africa Society, were deemed blasphemous and treasonous.[7] No pers no organization could be autonomous from the UNIP, since the party f in the name of the masses. The UNIP party card, which all were required purchase, indicated that one belonged to this mass movement. Activists con ducted card-checking campaigns to exert the party's sovereignty in place of the colonial state. Political songs or hymns spread nationalist ideas, most of all an absolute conception of alliances: you believed in the nationalist mission or you belonged to the devil, the colonial state. People had the choice of follow- ing the path of evil, the CAF and the colonial state, or the path of righteous- ness, UNIP and its leader, Kenneth Kaunda.

The similarities between popular nationalism, Lenshina's movement, and Watchtower are clear: the charismatic figure, the hymns, the passports to heaven, and the Manichaean morality. But the point is not only that Chris- tianity informed mass nationalism; rather, in addition to arising at the same time and in the same places, popular nationalism was a Christian movement. The division of movements into political and religious obscures this point. Popular nationalism had theocratic claims on truth and morality, with associa- tional structures and strategies of mobilization that were Christian.

The nationalist Christian movement linked its millenarian vision to the capture of the colonial state. Thereby, it sought to replace the instruments that invoked the colonial invisible world, such as the colonial identity document, with its own instruments, especially the party card. Popular nationalism was also an ideological engagement with secular notions of popular sovereignty. In this regard, Stephen Ellis's discussion of Liberia in the 1970s could equally apply to Zambia in the 1950s: "The rhetoric of political liberation . . . used concepts of originally Christian origin, transferred from a mystical to a mate- rial context, allied to Marxist and other secular ideas, to promise a climactic transformation, the creation of a new country and a new politics through an act of political revolution."[8] Similarity between the nationalists and the popu- lar Christians did not, however, mean peaceful coexistence. In terms of their insistence on loyalty, their Manichaean moralities, their millenarianism, and their paranoia of alternative views, the followers of Kaunda and Lenshina were so similar that conflict between them was likely.

In recognizing that Christian and biblical notions were central in the trans- lation of nationalist concepts during acts of popular anticolonial struggle, care needs to be taken not to celebrate the sanguine (and Christian!) view of a popular battle against evil and self-serving colonists. An emphasis on popular

onalism was corrupted from the top down, as if
ern purity. In the voices recovered from lower-
f colonial Christianity prevailed, in particular
cialized in intolerance. It was not difficult
sts into Christian violence, even atrocity; it
activists in the nationalist movement. Such
lerance and political complexity. Perhaps
ace in which Zambians "had grown ac-
oc comes through violence and militancy," as
..eck J. Phiri argues.[9] But Christianity was central to this
.. violence. In a fashion similar to the South African case discussed
by Clifton Crais, subaltern politics was "theodicy" in that it "centered on the
creation of a just world. . . . But it also gave rise to a kind of fundamentalism
that demands unwavering obedience, sees violence as not only necessary but
central to political society, and sustains acts of horror such as necklacing."[10]
The radical and popular aspects of Zambian nationalism harnessed biblical
narratives to formulate a morality that reduced political complexity to good
and evil, encouraging extremism and intolerance. The evidence suggests
that nationalist fervor—in its victory against colonialism but also in its casual
brutality—was driven from below. Popular nationalism's adoption of Christianity gave shape and force to the anticolonial movement.

IMAGINING ZAMBIA

The Zambian nationalist movement coalesced around opposition to the federation of Nyasaland, Northern Rhodesia, and Southern Rhodesia in the early
1950s. Federation became such an explosive national issue because it threatened the status of African land ownership. The fear was that Native Trust land,
communal land under the control of the chiefs, would be converted to Crown
land available for sale to white settlers. This led chiefs, the main beneficiaries
of Native Trust lands, to explicitly petition against federation, providing an opportunity for a broad-based coalition of educated nationalists and chiefs that
stretched from town to countryside. In 1952, chiefs, ANC officials, and trade
unionists met in Lusaka to organize their campaign against federation. Even
then, the Christian basis of the campaign was evident. At a second meeting,
in March 1953, two days of "national prayer" were called. The prospect of
federation with Southern Rhodesia, where white settler interests would prevail, became associated with a sense of evil that far outweighed British imperialism. The appropriate response was prayer—for surely God would not
condone such actions, even if allowed by British imperialism. The national
prayer activities failed to gain widespread support due to the lack of support
by the African Mineworkers Union, probably because urban workers did not

have the same fear of land expropriation as the chiefs—and perhaps because such protest actions would have led to their dismissal.[11] Nevertheless, it was the first of many cases when prayer was invoked as a response to national crisis.

In addition to prayer, the nationalists sought to identify those who represented and embodied evil. The first efforts to do so associated a Northern Province and Copperbelt myth about *banyama* vampire men with the Capricorn Society, educated Africans and progressive Europeans who had advocated for a liberal version of federation.[12] By then, the *banyama* myth had been around for at least twenty years, with *banyama* usually thought to refer to suspicious white men, sometimes Catholic priests and their African allies, who used body parts for occult purposes. Drawing on these ideas, the nationalists claimed that members of the Capricorn Society were *banyama*, vampire men. Political opponents were spiritual others: the Capricorns were vampires who manipulated the lives of others for their selfish benefit. The nationalists thereby associated a political project with a form of witchcraft, just as Lenshina associated witchcraft with sinners who ignored her twelve commandments. The nationalists even appealed for the colonial administration to rid the country of those *banyama* who supported federation.[13]

The development of the broad-based anticolonial national alliance against the evil of federation was found in microcosm in the Chinsali District. In the early 1950s, the Chinsali branch of the ANC was composed of a few young schoolteachers: Kenneth Kaunda, Simon Kapwepwe, Robert Kapasa Makasa, and John Sokoni. Even while they had some support, they did not succeed in mobilizing enough members of their most likely allies, educated civil servants, to strike in protest against the CAF.[14] While chiefs such as Chitimukulu protested against federation, they did not cast their support behind the local ANC branch. The few successful mobilizations of the ANC on the Copperbelt, such as the boycott of racist European shops, found little support in the northern countryside.

The first openly confrontational act by the nationalist teachers was against their closest associates, the Presbyterian Lubwa Mission. In the early 1950s, Fergus Macpherson, the Lubwa missionary recently arrived from Scotland, dismissed more than one hundred teachers from their posts, leading to much dissatisfaction.[15] In the context of these dismissals and growing antagonism possibly related to a pro-federation sermon by Macpherson, the leaders of the Chinsali branch of the ANC, including Kenneth Kaunda, Robert Kapasa Makasa, and Sandy Rain, wrote a remarkably confrontational letter. They chastised Macpherson for his "attitude towards the African political leaders and their organizations. . . . Come to us and advise us in the right way and we shall be ready to discuss your advice—preach against us and we shall preach against you to see who is the stronger of the two of us," the letter warned. Behind the local grievances stood the campaign against the CAF, which had fired the imagination of the Chinsali activists. The nationalists insisted they were not "struggling against the British Government but against the Federal case."[16]

In June 1953, two months before the onset of the CAF in August and three months before Lenshina had her visions in September, the teachers managed to mobilize a broader range of supporters in Chinsali. Discontent over the onset of federation provided the background to their changing influence; yet local conflicts, such as those over trees, the most important agricultural asset, were the sparks that ignited protest. A conflict over one particular tree joined the nationalists' concerns with those of the Bemba royals. It began with an attempt to recognize the coronation of Queen Elizabeth in Chinsali. For the district commissioner (DC), the coronation represented the best aspects of the imperial mission, and he chose to celebrate it with a little pomp and ceremony by planting a tree. Even the troublesome teachers had previously expressed loyalty to the monarch, for them a symbol of British civilization and even justice compared to the racist settlers. Perhaps intentionally the DC chose an indigenous tree of much economic and political importance to the Bemba royalty, and especially to the paramount, Chitimukulu (the "Great Tree"). In the aftermath of the planned imposition of the CAF, however, the teachers were increasingly hostile to the imperial mission. The insensitive celebration of the coronation, the teachers reckoned, would also convince the Bemba royals to join their campaign against colonial rule. After all, the planting of an indigenous tree to celebrate a foreign queen in the land of the proud Bemba royals was a blatant challenge to their claims to control the agricultural cycle upon which any remnants of their sacred authority rested. The teachers formed an "underground movement" to convince the chiefs to refuse to cooperate in the celebrations. The DC invited Helen Kaunda, and then the sisters of chiefs Nkula and Chibesekunda, to plant the tree. All of them refused. Eventually, after the tree was planted by a worker overseen by the DC's wife, it was poisoned. A concrete memorial to the coronation had to be constructed, but even it was destroyed a few years later.[17]

This puerile act of anticolonial opposition seems of little significance—Kaunda never writes of it again, as if he was ashamed, although it is certain that he was in Chinsali for the coronation celebrations.[18] Yet it was the first time that the teachers conducted a campaign that involved a degree of civil disobedience and blatantly challenged colonial notions of sovereignty. To be sure, there were may previous acts of anticolonial resistance across the northern countryside, but the teachers were peripheral to them.[19] The ANC had remained loyal to symbols of empire, even while they were frustrated by their treatment in a colonial society dominated by white settlers.[20] A litany of small insults against this educated elite had eventually led them to question the imperial project. The Kaunda brothers, for example, were embittered by the lack of pension offered to their mother, Helen Kaunda, by the Church of Scotland after their father's long and faithful service to the Lubwa Mission.[21] For the teachers, federation was the final imperial betrayal, heaped upon a pile of smaller grievances. They sought to make federation into a synonym for evil.

Such seemingly insignificant but incremental challenges to colonial rule and to the imperial mission began to amount to a challenge to colonial hegemony. The question of where sovereignty should lie, of who ruled and who should rule, began to be posed. Should sovereignty return to the Bemba royals, even while stories of their brutal nineteenth-century rule were still told and their spiritual powers to combat witchcraft emasculated? Perhaps it was the time for new prophets, for a new queen, Lenshina, who would rule with the blessings of God and his son? The teachers, educated in mission Christianity and Western political philosophies, proposed a third option: sovereignty rested with the people. Of all formulations, this remained the most obscure and foreign. It did nothing to rid the world of the invisible agents that afflicted people. To translate "popular sovereignty" into a *popular* discourse, the nationalists needed to associate the ideas of popular sovereignty with the salvation promised and promoted by Christian discourses.

The connections between popular sovereignty and a Christian dawn were not immediately apparent. In the first half of the 1950s, the idea of popular sovereignty in a nation of equals was contained. Immediately after the unsuccessful fight against federation, there was a lull in nationalist activity in the Northern Province. In 1955 there were only seven ANC branches in the entire province, mostly composed of teachers and civil servants.[22] By 1957, there was a resurgence of activity. Complaints against the ANC began to appear in the colonial record. In one incident, ANC leaders convinced villagers near Chinsali not to give the DC the customary offering of food and insisted on payment.[23] Women's ANC branches became more common.[24] In an indication of what would become normal strategy, ANC activists demanded that market vendors purchase ANC membership cards.[25] The ANC attached ideas of "freedom" and opposition to the CAF to quotidian concerns, such as restrictions on the *chitemene* cutting of trees and the hunting of wild game. Colonial authorities increasingly called upon chiefs to restrict ANC activities in their areas; and ANC branches became involved in the intrigues of chiefly succession, trying to ensure that chiefs sympathetic to the nationalist cause were appointed.[26] Nationalism in the Northern Province still seemed elitist; yet the mobilization of people around everyday issues had begun to give the ANC a popular character. As with Watchtower and the Lumpa ideas, nationalist notions took hold as they became part of people's immediate worlds.

Through the 1950s, the Chinsali teachers who had attempted to spread opposition to federation by boycotting Queen Elizabeth's coronation in Chinsali moved to the Copperbelt and Lusaka. There they became national figures in the still-elitist ANC. Due to dissatisfaction and competition with the ANC leader, Harry Nkumbula, they set out to form a new nationalist movement. In fact, they set out to create a nation. At a meeting held in Kenneth Kaunda's Chilenje house in Lusaka, they began to discuss the problem of naming: Rhodesia, named after the arch-imperialists, Rhodes, would clearly not do. They settled on "Zambia," a variation of "Zambezia," a precolonial Portuguese name for the region. On 24 October 1958, they formally launched the new nationalist organization, the Zambia African National Congress (ZANC), which would campaign for the independence of the renamed colonial territory.[27] They still needed to create "Zambians," people who would consider themselves members of this nation, and who would vest authority in the teachers as the representatives of the new nation.

The ZANC leaders who heralded from the Northern Province sought to spread their ideas in their home region where they could expect to gain the largest number of supporters. Less than one month after ZANC's launch, two of the teachers from Chinsali, Robert Kapasa Makasa and John Sokoni, held meetings in the Northern Province. They told villagers why they had decided to break with Nkumbula and announced that "Sambya" would have self-government by 1960. They encouraged ANC members to surrender their cards, and more than a thousand did so.[28] The meetings continued at different locations, with similar messages; many more ANC cards were surrendered.[29] The activists were encouraged by their reception in the north. A few months later Kapwepwe wrote that in Chinsali, "people only talk about Zambia. . . . They want another party very much right now."[30]

CLEANSING FEDERATION AND CREATING ZAMBIA

For the nationalists, cleansing was achieved through fire. Young ZANC activists began to burn symbols of colonial authority (although the leadership denied that they encouraged such tactics).[31] Even in broad daylight, activists set houses of collaborators on fire, and the colonial authorities sponsored reprisals.[32] Colonial repression increased. The authorities banned public meetings and sent mobile police units into the villages; they arrested activists and beat them until they confessed to the destruction of colonial property.[33] The colonial administration arrested the Chinsali teachers—Kaunda, Kapwepwe, and Makasa—along with most of the rest of the ZANC leadership, and banned ZANC in March 1959.

The movement receded; yet this new nationalist vision, and the centrality of Kaunda and his disciples to it, had become part of the nationalist political imagination infused with a biblical morality. Almost every popular statement of protest referenced the Bible. In a letter to the provincial commissioner, the regional secretary of ZANC insisted that despite beatings, "MEN DIE, BUT ONCE" (emphasis in original). ZANC would not retreat from its "preached Christian Gospel of Non-Violence."[34] In March 1959 a ZANC notice was found nailed to a tree:

> One who reads the bible should know that Jesus Christ was sold by one of his Disciples, and after seeing that he had done a bad thing was ashamed and hanged himself. There will come a time when one who beats and imprisons his brother will also hang himself. You should know that Jesus Christ is not dead, he is still alive. The same as Zambia is not dead. . . . Moses in the bible failed to accompany Israelites but Aron did [sic]. Nkumbula failed to accompany his friends—but Kaunda did.[35]

This was more than a comparison to a biblical narrative. It downloaded a telescoped version of the Old and the New Testaments into a present testimony, with Harry Nkumbula, the ANC leader, as both Moses and Judas, who led the people but then betrayed them. Instead of Nkumbula, Kenneth Kaunda, the new Moses, Aaron, and Jesus Christ, would lead his people to the promised land. The Bible was a long-lasting idiom in which the struggle was understood. More than four decades later, an old ZANC activist, who was arrested and sentenced to eighty years for burning colonial property in the late 1950s, claimed that it is "even written in the Bible that Africa is for the Africans."[36]

In the aftermath of ZANC's banning, several smaller parties emerged, only to unify in September 1959 as the United National Independence Party (UNIP). UNIP positioned itself as the successor to ZANC, the most radical of nationalist movements.[37] Kaunda emerged from jail on 9 January 1960, and by his own account declared, "Freedom! . . . The Zambia ANC was banned but there is no power to ban our desire to be free, to shape our own destiny. . . . I am determined more than ever before to achieve self-determination for Africans in this country."[38] From then on, he made himself inseparable from UNIP and from the idea of an independent and free Zambia. The history of the nation was written in a biblical teleology with Kaunda as Moses. He was the "people's representative," who, according to the *Voice of UNIP*, traveled to the lands of the pharaoh, London, "to press for their God-given rights of a majority rule."[39]

In the Northern Province, UNIP had a decent base of activists to campaign for these rights: 42 branches with 3,895 members, not nearly representative of the Northern Province's 400,000 people, but certainly popular and growing.[40]

UNIP strengthened the position of its branches and attempted to co-opt the chiefs by sending Makasa, Kapwepwe, and Kaunda to negotiate with them.[41] They had some success and the paramount, Chitimukulu, proved sympathetic to UNIP, which led the colonial authorities to suspend his court and to increase the authority of subordinate chiefs more willing to toe the line.[42] However, the most important aspect of the nationalist revolution was its departure from the conversion of elites to the mobilization of what the nationalists liked to term "the masses." To mobilize the masses, colonial instruments of authority had to be destroyed and replaced with the nationalist party card, the song, and the charismatic leader.

The colonial identity document, the *fitupa*, was a technology that invoked the authority of the secular colonial world. Through the *fitupa*, men became colonial subjects who could be taxed; authority could be exerted over their movements and their work habits. The most powerful challenge to the practice of colonial sovereignty was the destruction of the *fitupa* identity document. The *fitupa* took on the quality of an evil document, which, like the bad things (the *bwanga* and *fyabubi*) that Lenshina destroyed, had to be burned. By the middle of 1961, the Chinsali activists claimed to have received orders to burn their documents, which they eagerly implemented:

> On 15 July 1961, we received word from Chairman Geoffrey Mulenga that said that Kenneth Kaunda issued instructions to burn *fitupa* identity certificates . . . we went round our people collecting the *fitupa*. We collected from them, baskets and baskets of *fitupa*. . . . Geoffrey Mulenga . . . took them to the office of the DC [who] ordered the District Messenger to arrest Mulenga. . . . Then Mulenga advised the DC not to have him and the youths arrested . . . because they were ordered to do so by "the leader" K. D. Kaunda in Lusaka. . . . After they finished this exchange, Geoffrey Mulenga took a box of matches from his coat pocket, struck a stick and set the identity certificates on fire by pouring paraffin over them.[43]

After burning their *fitupa*, UNIP branches in the Northern Province coordinated groups of ten to thirty men to burn and destroy all property associated with colonialism, from identity documents to physical infrastructure such as bridges. In Chinsali, the local branch ensured that on the twenty-second of July, "exactly at 9 a.m. everything . . . was set ablaze."[44] Schools, the purveyors of colonial forms of discipline and incubators of the nationalist opposition, were some of the first targets. Activists burned the property of the Roman Catholic missions at Ilondola and Mulilansolo. They slaughtered the cattle of the missionaries and colonists. To prevent the mobile police units from reaching the villages, they destroyed bridges.[45]

The destruction of missionary property is often viewed as an aberration of the anticolonial nationalist project and was criticized by the nationalist leadership. Yet, at the popular level, the burning of missionary property was as central to the nationalist uprising as the destruction of missionary *bwanga* was to Lenshina's Christian revival. The nationalists, not the missionaries, were the true inheritors of Christ's mission on earth. Those missionaries who acknowledged the leadership of the nationalists were not targeted. Lubwa, for example, escaped relatively unscathed. Yet the Catholic missions, the *banyama* vampires and the witches who challenged nationalist claims, became a central target of nationalist fervor.[46]

Colonial counterinsurgency operations were brutal. They attempted to capture UNIP leaders, destroy villages that supported UNIP cadres, and burn food supplies. With typical flair, the *Voice of UNIP* issued a special edition titled "A Grim Peep into the North." It reported on "acts of brutality and bestiality" by the colonial forces that included the burning of villages and food supplies, arbitrary beatings, and torture. Thousands of people, according to UNIP, had left their villages to hide in the bush.[47] The colonial administration denied that such acts took place. Nevertheless, while there may have been some exaggeration, UNIP's claims seem more plausible than those of the Chinsali DC, who suggested that villages were burned by "cooking fires."[48] In fact, the colonial authorities made a concerted effort to break the hegemony of UNIP before general elections: "If elections are to be held then the ban on UNIP will have to be lifted," the DC wrote, "and it is essential that the ringleaders are picked up before then."[49]

As colonial repression increased, the nationalist claim that the colonial regime stood in the way of freedom became more convincing. Colonialism became evil, even satanic. Jameson Chapoloko, a Northern Province activist who headed the Copperbelt UNIP division in 1961, told his followers, "We should watch our steps, is my warning, to lead our people not into temptation, but deliver them from evil yoke [sic] of neocolonialism and imperialism that have oppressed them day and night."[50] Any remnant of the teachers' sympathy for a broader imperial mission disappeared: the May 1962 *Voice of UNIP* declared, "Imperialism is the source of all evil."[51] Of all aspects of evil colonialism and imperialism, the CAF became the worst kind and had to be eradicated.

The UNIP leadership cultivated a group of young activists, child soldiers of liberation, to enforce this vision. In 1962, the UNIP representative in liberated Tanganyika, Kapasa Makasa, introduced several of the young soldiers to the radio broadcaster Andreya Masiye:

He started with a group of nondescript youths wearing an assortment of rags and torn school uniforms. Some of them were barely fourteen years old. . . . The group was made up of politically motivated truants, arsonists, and such. Tough-looking and noisy, the boys looked much older than they were. I then realized that I was shaking hands with youth who had become adults before their age. Some of those hands, I thought, might have committed objectionable acts at home. But this was no time for puritanical sentiments.[52]

In response to Masiyes's call, "One Zambia! One Nation," the youth cried out:

One man, one vote
One boy, one road
One road, one block
One car, one bomb
One man, one stone
One man, one vote[53]

They then sang the popular song "We Are the Stone-Throwers!":

Nifwe bampose-mabwe	[We are the stone-throwers
UNIP yenu mwaleta baKaunda	The UNIP Kaunda brought
Ileleta ubutungwa	Will bring freedom (self-government)
Nifwe bamposa-mabwe	We are the stone-throwers
Bamposa-mabwe besu bafwile	Our stone-throwers kill
Balaleta ubutungwa	They will bring freedom
Ku chalo chonse	To the whole country
Nifwe bamposa-mabwe	We are the stone-throwers.][54]

The violence of the UNIP youth was not unleashed against the colonial state directly. Instead, it focused on those who did not support UNIP, and were thus seen as collaborating in some way with the evil of federation. They were sellouts, colonial stooges, even devils. All non-UNIP members were under threat. The trade union leader and one-time Capricorn member Lawrence Katilungu, for example, had to evacuate his family from the Northern Province for fear they would be burned alive by UNIP activists.[55] UNIP banned the attendance of mission churches, especially the Catholics, who were rumored to have joined with federal forces, and in some cases beat up congregants.[56]

UNIP activists divided people into those who supported the struggle and those who collaborated with the colonial authorities. There was no place for complexity in this vision; the struggle was all embracing. They sang:

Kukaba ubulanda nokulila   [There will be sorrow and crying
Ilyo tukapoka ubutungwa   When we get our freedom
Kapuli ulelemba ifyabufi   The pig who tells lies
Tukamwishiba ulya bushiku   We will know him on that day.]

Mwe bana bamuno Zambia   [Children of Zambia
Imwe bamayo na batata   Mothers and fathers
Bombeleni pamo nga abafita   Work together as black people
Mwilekelesha Kaunda wesu   Don't leave Kaunda alone.][57]

Electoral politics would also be affected by these spiritual forces. In June 1961, when Sokoni invited branch leaders to the Mulungushi conference to elect the leadership of UNIP, he warned that "if your decision falls short of this country's desire and wish you will bear the responsibility of 3 million devils upon your head and if your decision does meet the desires and wishes of this country you will bear the <u>BLESSINGS</u> of the 3 million <u>SOULS</u> of your Mother <u>ZAMBIA</u>" (emphasis in original).[58]

The nationalists had to replace the evil of the colonial state with the good that emanated from UNIP. Just as colonial authority was broadcast through the *fitupa* identity documents, UNIP's authority would spread through the party card. Shame Mulenga, an activist in Kasomo Village adjacent to Lenshina's Sione, remembered, "We had surrendered *fitupa*, and in their place we got [UNIP] cards."[59] An old beer-drinking song that complained of ongoing misfortune, perhaps the result of witchcraft, was inverted, as if the UNIP card now provided protection against such occult forces:

Ine UNIP taishala   [My UNIP card is never left behind
Noko nkalola   Wherever I go
Nkaya nayo   I travel with it
Ine UNIP taishala   My UNIP card is never left behind.][60]

UNIP also began to mimic the administrative procedures of the colonial administration. Their activists sent "tour reports" to national headquarters, in similar fashion to the DC's tour report.[61] UNIP activists claimed they could set up trials and punish individuals for offenses such as disturbing the peace. The guilty had to pay a fine, or were imprisoned.[62] In the northern countryside, UNIP created an invisible world with its own bureaucratic structure: a state with an apparatus of representation, authority, and repression.

If imperial authority was embodied by the British Queen, the Christian sovereignty of the UNIP was embodied by Kaunda. He was a biblical leader. He was not the representative of the people; he was the embodiment of the people. Kasutu, the divisional president of UNIP in Chinsali, hailed Kaunda as "MESIAH OF ZAMBIA LONG LIVE OUR MESIAH K.D. KAUNDA OUR incorruptible Leader [sic]." For Kasutu, all of Zambia belonged to UNIP: "TREES, MOUNTAINS, HILLS, STREAMS, RIVERS, and all LAKES are all UNIP in this Division" (emphasis in original).[63] It was more than a personality cult; Kaunda was the nation:

Katumuchindike Lesa wesu	[Let's respect God
Uwatupele ntungulushi Kaunda	Who gave us Kaunda
Ushakwata akapatulula pa mitundu	Who knows no tribalism
Ala, akesa tulubula nga afuma	He will free us when he comes out
Bonse tuli bana ba Zambia	We're all children of Zambia.][64]

The nationalists were children of Zambia, but they were also *abantu bakwa Kaunda*, "Kaunda's people." And God's will became known through Kaunda. A nationalist prayer called on God, "the creator of Africa," to "bless our Lord Kaunda. Give him the power to lead us to African self-government . . . deliver us from these devil and satanic white settlers from Africa who have come here to rob our Africa and destroy our African nationality."[65]

Kaunda cultivated the image of the sacred patriarch. If, as he declared at a UNIP conference in 1963, "UNIP is the mother and the nation is the child," Kaunda imagined himself to be the stern but generous parent, an image he further developed after independence.[66] Even senior members of UNIP prostrated themselves in front of Kaunda. In a remarkable invocation of the maternal idiom of Bemba politics, Sikalumbi wrote Kaunda in 1963: "Kindly allow me to call myself a suckling baby [who] cannot thank its mother."[67] The teacher from Chinsali had become a *ntambalukuta*, "a person who watches over a large family."

The nation had a scriptural authority linked to Kaunda. Not only did the Bible affirm Kaunda and his vision, but Kaunda also had a book in which the nation and the nationalist struggle were inscribed. "At the time Kaunda began politics and traveled with a book, which he called a black book. He went on to the mountain and played the guitar, crying."[68] Like Lenshina, Kaunda was a skilled musician with exclusive access to the authority of the book. The UNIP program of action was written in this book or scripted in Kaunda's head. At the Mulungushi conference of 1961, which announced the radicalization of UNIP's policies, the activists allegedly asked in what book Cha Cha Cha, UNIP's program of insurgency, was written. Kaunda was said to have answered that Cha Cha Cha was written in his head. It meant, as Mama Chola put it, "real dancing": "Europeans will take part and Africans will take part too. Hens, dogs, and all tamed creatures will join in the dance—even the

Queen will dance Cha Cha Cha." The dance would cause the federal prime minister Roy Welensky's "head to ache."[69]

These tactics enhanced UNIP's standing in the Northern Province. The number of branches increased from 59 at the time of its launch in 1959 to 276 in July 1961, and to 573 by September 1963.[70] Even if not universally accepted, its ideas were certainly popular. UNIP promised a new future that few could resist. No political party could match UNIP's mechanisms of Christian mobilization. Elections at the end of 1963 would lead to a UNIP government and the independence of Zambia on 24 October 1964. It had taken six years to the day for the group of schoolteachers to transform the nation imagined in Kaunda's Chilenje house into an officially recognized entity.

～

The connections between Watchtower, Lenshina, and popular nationalism at the level of the collective political imagination were closer and more profound than appreciated by secular-focused historians. Scholars have viewed African nationalism in secular terms, and secularism as a transparent engagement with the visible world. However, the nationalists who fought in northern Zambia considered themselves in the midst of a battle between good and evil that not only sought to destroy and replace the colonial structures of authority, but also had a Christian dimension: the nationalists had become the representatives of God's will, and they struggled for an end to colonialism as one step in the creation of God's kingdom on earth. In this sense, the history of popular nationalism in Zambia during the 1960s resembles South Africa, where Clifton Crais argues that "Christianity . . . fused with earlier conceptions [of power and authority] . . . to create a terrifying vision of a world awash in an evil and inequity that could be cleansed only by unwavering commitment to God, the ancestors, the 'black nation' . . . and to the eradication of witches."[71] The notion of popular sovereignty was articulated by using Christian discourses of salvation and deliverance from evil.

This proposed popular sovereignty, which claimed to be vested in the God-given rights of people, came to rest on the party, UNIP, and the prophet of the nation, Kenneth Kaunda. The card, the political hymn, and the image of Kaunda were central to this vision: hymns told of a promising future for those who believed, the card identified those who belonged, and Kaunda would lead the righteous to the new dawn, the *kwacha*, of a promised land. "For a long time I have led my people in their shouts of KWACHA. We have been shouting it in the darkness," Kaunda wrote in 1962. "Now there is the grey light of dawn on the horizon and I know that Zambia shall be free."[72]

The nationalist vision was also influenced by the colonial and missionary civilizing mission. In Lenshina's movement some aspects of Bemba identity and cosmology seemed preserved or at least adapted to new realities and ideologies. The nationalists, however, insisted on a complete and radical conversion, a cleansing of an old and backward "tribalism" in favor of the promise of a new civilization. The modernist vision of the nationalists would both celebrate Africa and claim to speak in the name of African people while rejecting vernacular pasts. The irony is hardly surprising: the nationalists, after all, were led by those most thoroughly schooled in the missionary classroom. The teachers viewed their political struggles in the mirror of their particular educations.

The nationalist use of Christianity was thus divided between the popular, prophetic, and revolutionary on the one hand; and the reformist, missionary, and hierarchical on the other. The nationalist teachers represented the reformist impulse: they aimed at guiding the nation toward a new, modern civilization. Yet their joining of ideas of popular sovereignty with Christian spiritual ideas gave opportunity for a revolutionary current to popular nationalism that rapidly overflowed the teachers' political imaginings and expectations. The popular movement employed these Christian discourses to suggest a revolutionary cleansing of the colonial state, salvation, and the establishment of a new heaven on earth. These popular voices did not indicate more tolerant and democratic practices, however. Songs and oral testimonies demonstrate an absolute commitment to party and prophet, an insistence on a world divided into liberators and imperialists, good and evil. Popular and elite nationalist ideas appeared to be opposed to the chauvinism of mission Christianity and to the authoritarianism of the colonial state—and yet they were in dialogue with them, sharing more than they cared to acknowledge. As the missionaries and the colonial state began to withdraw, an intolerant authoritarianism latched onto the ideological debris of popular struggle. By imbuing the dawn with new meanings, Christianity cast a long shadow over it.

6 ⇐ Devils of War

IN JULY 1964, while UNIP controlled the government but the colonial administration was still in charge of security, the interim administration sent in troops to resolve a violent conflict between UNIP cadres and the Lumpa Church. Under orders from the head colonial administrator, Governor Evelyn Hone, and Prime Minister Kenneth Kaunda, the troops insisted that the Lumpa abandon their independent villages. When they refused to submit or surrender their rudimentary weapons, the troops opened fire. Over the next two months, similar military operations took place at eleven other villages and against roaming Lumpa refugees. At the very least, one thousand people died as a direct consequence of troop action, Lumpa retaliatory attacks, and starvation as people fled into the bush. In 1965, a commission of inquiry established the outlines of the conflict, the responsibilities of the various parties, and a diary of events for the most violent period, from 26 June to 15 October 1964.[1]

The narratives of the war espoused by the UNIP and by the Lumpa Church not only diverge significantly but hold different meanings for each of the groups involved in the conflict. In the midst of terror, fear, hunger, and violence, suspicion and rumor gave way to alternative versions of what happened. These alternative versions of events then became enshrined as history through two insular groups. On the one hand, the party and state bureaucracy held to a version of events established by Kaunda and the provincial UNIP officials. This version was based on a few speeches and texts, which became the absolute authority on the Lumpa-UNIP conflict. Few within Zambia were willing to discuss the conflict at all, and when they did they adhered to and referenced these central accounts. On the other hand, in the refugee camps of Zambia and the Congo, where up to twenty thousand Lumpa followers established their homes for between six and thirty years, an equally rehearsed version of the past appeared, around which a Christian community began to base its identity. The nationalists interpreted their history as evidence that Kaunda represented the will of God; Lenshina's followers, by contrast, interpreted their history as evidence that they were God's people who had suffered like Christ. In both cases, the representation of opponents as witches, sinners, and devils allowed people to understand and to rationalize the violence that they had experienced and, in a few cases, perpetrated.

David Anderson's history of the Mau Mau uprising in Kenya demonstrates that the struggle for independence involved multiple factions or nationalist groupings, not simply freedom fighters versus colonial forces.[2] The legacies of such diverse factions formed during the struggle for independence held implications for political alliances and the nature of state-civil society relations in the aftermath of independence. In a similar fashion, the conflict in northern and eastern Zambia constituted Zambia's war of independence, fought not only against the colonial authorities but between African social movements intent on achieving power in the vacuum left by the withdrawal of the colonial administration. The violence committed by UNIP cadres, soldiers, policemen, and Lumpa Church members was aimed not only at achieving control over village life, but also at shaping the invisible world in an independent Zambia. Both the nationalists and the Lumpa members had millenarian visions of a world cleansed of evil—colonialism and the federal government for the former, and sinners and witches for the latter. In contrast to these popular movements, the elite nationalists, who had inherited the colonial state, articulated a different vision. They proposed an ordered and rational march to moral improvement and economic development. Their elite moral reformism aimed to replace the radical and millenarian focus of both the popular nationalist and the Lumpa movements.

Beyond the broader implications of the Lumpa war for the invisible worlds of Zambian history, this chapter demonstrates the links between violent actions and spirits. The Lumpa thought that they were fighting against sinners who were also witches and the nationalists believed that the Lumpa had been corrupted by the evil of the Central African Federation (CAF). The perception by both Lumpa and UNIP members that opponents were possessed by the devil and evil spirits, or agents of a satanic colonial order, led to extreme and often ritualized forms of violence. Spirits also appeared in battle: Lumpa fighters thought that the Holy Spirit prevented bullets from striking the faithful and even if bullets found their target, death did not matter in their spiritual reckoning.

For many Zambians in the Northern Province, by the late 1950s the battle against the evil of "Satani" became a battle against the evil of colonialism, against the CAF and the "Colour Bar." Lenshina and her Lumpa deacons began to lose the exclusive control that they had claimed over the struggle against evil. Tactics changed. Where Lenshina had encouraged evasion and escape from colonial government and the cleansing of the evil of witches, missionaries, and sinners, the nationalist movement confronted the evil of the colonial government directly. Leadership changed from a semiliterate but inspiring woman to the schooled teachers who could converse in the language and the ideologies of the colonizer.

During the 1960–1961 anticolonial Cha Cha Cha revolt, when the nationalists attempted to rid the country of the evil of colonialism, violent practices engulfed northern Zambia, especially the Chinsali District. In reaction to UNIP civil disobedience campaigns, colonial mobile police platoons assaulted villagers suspected of sympathizing with the UNIP. In retaliation, UNIP rebels roamed the province, destroying bridges, colonial infrastructure, and assaulting those who worked with the colonial administration. Arson was a common tactic used by both the security forces and the UNIP. "These incidents of arson are petty in our eyes," the Northern Province's provincial commissioner (PC) wrote, "they are NOT to the chap whose house is burnt."[3] Indeed, for UNIP supporters or colonial agents and informers, acts of arson were serious—sometimes lives were lost, but more often fire destroyed food stores, the results of months of labor, and left villagers destitute and hungry. Burning houses, granaries, and crops was the most effective way of ensuring that villagers toed the line, whether it was colonial or nationalist. By the end of 1961, as UNIP leadership reined in their supporters and the colonial administration doused the last fires of Cha Cha Cha, all villagers were well versed in the tactics and uses of arson, a most effective way of spreading terror and demanding submission. Put a few match heads at the end of a burning cigarette and stuff this live fuse into the thatch roofing. A few minutes later the hut would be up in flames, while the unknown perpetrators had long made their escape. Sometimes the doors would be barricaded, and the inhabitants would be fortunate to die of smoke inhalation before being consumed by flames.[4] In this fearsome time, millenarian prophecies of apocalypse and rebirth found voice and audience.

From early 1961 to May 1962, Lenshina preached to her followers on the Copperbelt. During this period, conflict between UNIP and the Lumpa Church in the Northern Province arose. In some cases, competition over grazing and land allocation—"trivial matters," in the words of one interviewee—lay behind the conflicts.[5] But there were broader, political motivations as well. After UNIP's disappointing performance in the 1962 elections, local UNIP branches were determined to eradicate support for UNIP's political rival, Harry Nkumbula's ANC, which showed signs of limited but growing support in the Northern Province.[6] UNIP wanted to ensure undivided loyalty and perceived any organization to be a threat. During 1961, there had already been conflict with Watchtower Church members who refused to join UNIP. By the end of 1962, the Church of Scotland complained that activists discouraged their congregations from attending church despite their open and acknowledged support for UNIP.[7] The ANC complained of heightened intimidation in the form of "beatings arson woundings and damage to property. . . . People are not at peace now, they do not sleep or move freely but live in fear, the demand for political identity [party cards] in the streets roads bus stops and terminals is extensively going on faster than one expects even worse than Copperbelt."[8] A shadowy group of radical UNIP youths who called themselves the "Unity Front of Zambia" was active in the Chinsali and Kasama Districts, disciplining even those within the party who disagreed with their extreme tactics.[9]

In the midst of this political turbulence, Jameson Chapoloko, then UNIP regional secretary in Mpika and future member of Parliament for Chinsali, emerged as the local UNIP strongman. He attempted to assert UNIP authority over both the district administration and the villages. At the end of 1962, Chapoloko sent a letter to the DCs of Chinsali, Isoka, and Mpika Districts, which demanded:

1. An end to all unlawful mass arrests of leaders and our people.
2. That the die-hard imperialistic minded District Commissioners should take note of the political situation we are in now, and behave.
3. That the imperialistic tactics of dividing the African people into camps will never help these quisling Agents of the now defunct British Colonialism.[10]

In May 1963, when the DC of Chinsali complained to Chapoloko about numerous instances where UNIP members demanded party cards from the public, Chapoloko advised him to ignore the law that disallowed UNIP members to demand cards, so as "not to create a presidency [sic] here where chiefs and ordinary members of the state should consider themselves enemies of the Party leaders."[11] The DC persisted, and after instructions from Simon Kapwepwe, Chapoloko acquiesced, claiming that party cards would no longer be demanded of the public.[12] There is, however, little indication that Chapoloko's acquiescence to the demands of the DC and the national

UNIP leadership actually translated into orders to the UNIP militants and a suspension of the demands for party cards.

Conflict between UNIP and the Lumpa Church intensified, probably because UNIP insisted that the Lumpa attend political meetings on Sundays.[13] The Lumpa refused to buy UNIP cards and burned those that they had already bought. UNIP activists then began to burn Lumpa churches. Acts of arson multiplied. At Kapimpi Village in Chinsali District, Lenshina's followers allegedly set fire to several houses in retaliation for the burning of their churches. On 15 June, Kapwepwe mediated a meeting between nine hundred of Chinsali's UNIP activists and four hundred Lumpa members. At the meeting, Lenshina allegedly agreed to discipline any member calling for or burning UNIP party cards. In exchange, UNIP militants would not burn Lumpa churches or insult Lumpa members. But a few days later Chapoloko complained that Lenshina's followers had reneged on the agreement and were burning UNIP cards. Three Lumpa churches were destroyed by fire, and thirty-seven Lumpa members were arrested and convicted of arson following the burning of seven UNIP houses.[14]

The previous chapter indicated why the party card was so important to UNIP. But why did Lenshina's followers refuse to purchase UNIP cards? And why did they not want to attend UNIP meetings? The Lumpa had a particular understanding of power, of the sovereignty of spirits over people, of God over matters of the world. Even while the Lumpa agreed with the aim of independence, they did not render unto Caesar. They argued that it was a sin to prioritize political meetings, literally to hold them before prayers, which would lead to the spread of evil. To the Lumpa, spiritual matters had to come first, even when it came to the politics of independence:

> When a person is served food, he cannot eat before washing his hands. After we wash our hands, we eat the food. But UNIP insisted that political meetings are in the morning. We refused. We must put God first, so prayers must be put before political meetings. Because independence will be given by God and it will come by the power of God. But Kenneth Kaunda never listened.[15]

In addition to the conflict over meeting times, the followers of Kaunda and the followers of Lenshina clashed over the texts that accessed and empowered different invisible worlds. Lenshina had distributed sacred documents, "passports to heaven," in which people's "names from heaven" were inscribed. (She had also received books from Christ, which were stolen by the missionaries.) The UNIP party card, with its own invisible qualities, challenged the power of Lenshina's control over texts, just as it had challenged the colonial identity document, the *fitupa*. By burning UNIP's cards, the Lumpa rejected UNIP's authority, in the same fashion that UNIP's burning of colonial *fitupa* had rejected colonial authority.

The actions and language of mid-level activists, such as Chapoloko, who led UNIP's struggle against the Lumpa, ratcheted up extremism and led to irreconcilable positions. Chapoloko wrote to the national UNIP leadership, complaining of continued violence by Lumpa members against UNIP. He presented himself as a moderate who appealed for peace and even negotiated another agreement with Lenshina.[16] But at the same time, the White Fathers at Mulanga, hardly friends with the Lumpa, reported that "bands of gangsters . . . required cards everywhere."[17] While Chapoloko preached peace to the national UNIP leadership, he told local UNIP activists that the Lumpa Church was no more than a ploy by the outgoing colonial administration to divide and manipulate Africans, and goaded them on in efforts to eradicate the Lumpa Church:

> At the transfer of power from a Colonialist to indigenous people the British Colonialist do not simply depart peacefully, they usually sow seeds of misunderstandings and these eggs of bitterness hatch immediately after they leave, they linger at one side of the border with a view to come back and pretend to create peace, be alert Comrade. . . . Lenshina and her cult are a floating leave on an ocean through which the British Imperialists are holding their safety to the shores of Colonialism. Do not give them chance, let them be drown for ever.[18]

UNIP activists spread rumors about Lenshina's collaborations with the colonial and the federal governments. They claimed that Lenshina had held discussions with federal prime minister Roy Welensky when she visited Southern Rhodesia, and that the Lumpa Church was Welensky's political arm in the Northern Province. Welensky had allegedly paid Lenshina £8,000 through the colonial Boma. "Lenshina is in the pay of sinister interests in Salisbury," Chapoloko complained to the provincial colonial administration.[19] UNIP cadres also claimed that the Katangese had armed and trained the Lumpa. Regardless of whether there were any ties between Lenshina and the federal government or the Katangan secessionists (the evidence suggests that such ties did not exist or were not influential in determining the course of Lumpa actions), the nationalist perception of these ties transformed Lenshina and her followers into an evil that had to be cleansed for Zambia to be born.[20]

For UNIP cadres, conflict was linked to their desire for absolute control over the villages and loyalty to the party. They could not tolerate an organization that offered an alternative to that of UNIP. For example, a UNIP activist

protested vociferously when a Lumpa deacon allegedly sai̶
distinct line between Lumpa Church and UNIP and the two n̶
in anything."[21] In the buildup to the 1964 elections, which woul̶
the shape of the first postcolonial government, the flouting of UNIP̶
and authority was especially politically sensitive. They perceived the st̶
as one over followers, confounded with how a woman could have more su̶
port than their messianic figure, Kenneth Kaunda:

> We in UNIP thought that people in the Lumpa Church were going to
> get all the people. So we wanted those people back so that we could
> win elections and get independence from the whites. We thought
> that because there were too many people in Lumpa, sometimes even
> white people came to take pictures and interviewed BaMaayo [Len-
> shina] to find out how she received the Holy Spirit and how people
> came to her in large numbers—this made people in UNIP wonder
> why they came to Lenshina. "Why so many people?" This is what
> people wanted to find out—like Kapwepwe and Makasa and even
> Kaunda. All of these people were annoyed and could not understand
> why people were following a woman. . . . So it was a tug-of-war—
> ANC pulling this side, Lumpa this side, Welensky this side. UNIP
> wanted everybody to support them so they could win the elections.
> UNIP wanted to involve BaMaayo in politics. But she had her own
> principles. "I can't worship God and work for the party," she said.
> That brought a lot of trouble because she refused to be part of UNIP.
> She only taught the gospel.[22]

With the buildup to elections at the beginning of 1964, this "tug-of-war" intensified.
    In November 1963, many Lumpa began to leave UNIP-dominated vil-
lages to build their own villages, often without the consent of the chiefs. They
claimed that they did this due to attacks on their members as they made pil-
grimages to Sione or went to the Boma to buy supplies. According to surviving
adherents, Lenshina called a meeting and instructed her followers to form
their own settlements, termed *misumba* (missions/capitals).[23] She gave each
musumba thirty shillings so that they could establish shops and become self-
reliant. Setting up separate settlements, however, perpetuated and heightened
the tensions. Lumpa members had to travel even farther since their new villages were far from their farms, and they had to regularly return to their old
villages to collect food. During these trips, they were frequently attacked and
beaten.[24] Furthermore, Lenshina's followers were severed from their old communities. "Lumpa members lived separately," claimed the 1963 UNIP branch
chairman in the UNIP stronghold of Matumbo Village, "so they did not

ties between communities had ruptured and
:ir insulated and besieged villages, Lenshina's
nmunities and constructed their own versions
nd them.

mber 1963, several battles between UNIP and
Chinsali District. This was the most serious
te, with spears and guns used on both sides. In
ip, UNIP's regional organizing secretary called
act against the church.[26] The colonial authori-
JNIP have been the aggressors, but Lenshina
have done more than just aerend themselves." They identified Robert Kapasa
Makasa, the UNIP election candidate for Chinsali, as one of the key instiga-
tors of the trouble.[27] At least 10 died and up to 100 were wounded.[28] Another
conflict between the villagers of Kalikiti and the Chilanga Lumpa *musumba*
led to at least 2 deaths; 220 terrified villagers took refuge at Mulanga Mission.[29]
UNIP activists, now in control of the newly established rural councils, seized
on these incidents to further their campaign against the Lumpa.[30]

Even given the establishment of independent, stockaded villages and occasional retaliatory attacks, the general demeanor of the Lumpa Church
members prior to June 1964 was defensive, seeking to evade UNIP violence
and isolate themselves—as they had with chiefs and colonial authorities. As
evasion and isolation increased, Lumpa adherents became separated from
sources of established authority; they were seldom heard by the administration, and their views and ideas became insular, convinced of the righteousness
of their suffering. UNIP activists, by contrast, with their similar millenarian
ideas, had become more extroverted, attached to the administration and to the
new government. Articulate and literate UNIP spokespersons communicated
in writing with national leadership and with the press. Through these contacts
and this extroversion, UNIP developed a veneer of moderation and defined to
the world the violent character of the Lumpa Church.

Following the violence of December 1963, Kenneth Kaunda and Grey Zulu
visited Chinsali in an effort to negotiate a truce. Although they instructed their
own branches to be tolerant of the Lumpa, their efforts were directed at the
Lumpa Church, which they viewed as truculent and antagonistic. Kaunda
wanted the Lumpas to abandon their newly established villages and return to
their old villages.[31] At first Lenshina agreed—although her followers still refused to return to their villages, perhaps because Lenshina was insincere and
did not want to disperse her followers, perhaps because of the effort put forth in
building their new villages and planting their nearby fields, but most probably
because Lumpa members were terrified of becoming vulnerable minorities in
UNIP-dominated villages in the face of continued UNIP harassment. Despite

the rulings of Kaunda, UNIP youth planned attacks on Lumpa villages, and "young men were . . . pestering Lenshina people looking for UNIP cards and subscriptions."[32] In fact, the Lumpa secretary general at Sione wrote a letter to the provincial commissioner complaining of several instances where church members had returned to their villages and were attacked by UNIP.[33]

It seemed that UNIP's decisive victory in the January 1964 elections would bring peace. But the opposite was the case. A radical nationalism superseded any tolerant liberal vision.[34] Ecstatic UNIP activists insisted on the absolute sovereignty of the party and fueled a millenarianism brimming with expectations for the postcolonial order. All dissent was quashed in the effort to bring about the new order. Lumpa activists feared for the future. They thought that a final reckoning would come with the declaration of Zambian independence on 24 October 1964, when the colonial government would formally cede power to UNIP.

THE SPIRITS OF WAR

The catalyst for the war began a few months later, in July, with a fight in Kameko Village. Rather than recount the version of events established by the commission, the following is the testimony of one Lumpa member, Paison Nkonde, which gives an indication of the complex, personal, and emotional nature of the conflict:

> At Kameko, children went to school on Sunday after prayers. One day they reached school late. . . . They hid in the bush because they feared that they would be punished by the teacher. Behind them was my wife's brother, who followed them. When he found them he asked, "Why are you not in class?" They said, "Because we are late." So he beat his nephew. The children then went to enter classes. They were there for the week. On Friday, they reported what had happened. Lumpa members said, "That is not good. Why should UNIP people beat our children?" It was my son, Nkonde, who was beaten. When other church members brought the matter to me, I said, "The one who beat my son is his uncle and he beat him because he was late for school." It ended like that.
>
> But the following Sunday, the children went to school again. When they returned, the same man who had beaten his nephew was reported to have beaten another child. The following day, a group of church members came to my house and said, "We are going to investigate why the man who beat your child has beaten another child again." They went to see that man. . . . I followed them and found them arguing. One Lumpa man hit the man who had beaten the

child. But I separated them. Had it not been for my interference there would be a big fight! The man who was beaten, my brother-in-law, reported it to a policeman at Chief Mubanga. Around 1400h, policemen came to the village. They said, "Come here." When we gathered, they called out names. Those called were told to accompany the policemen to Mubanga's palace, where they would sleep. When we reached Mubanga, we were singing, we stayed there until the next morning. We saw vehicles had come from Chinsali and said "All Lumpa members come aboard. All adult members come on the vehicle, we'll pass through Mbesuma and then go to Chinsali." We wanted to refuse, but they insisted. . . . The vehicle went straight to Chinsali and we were thrown in jail. We were jailed without being given a chance to defend ourselves. We were jailed from 1964 to 1965.[35]

Nkonde was among ten men who were taken by Land Rover to Chinsali Boma and jailed. At least five remained, presumably because they could not all fit into the vehicle. A large Lumpa crowd then secured the release of their five compatriots before they could be taken to jail.[36] That afternoon, an armed police patrol went to Kameko Village to arrest those involved. Approximately two hundred Lumpa then attacked the police.[37] Lumpa testimony also records this incident, but views the police as the aggressors and the Lumpa protected by the Holy Spirit:

> The soldiers [police?] came to Kameko. When they shot us, the word was sent by God, and some survived by the power of God. Soldiers fired their guns and it seemed as if young children were in front, so the soldiers couldn't see the older people. They saw children in front and our *musumba* [mission village] in the sky. Instead of firing at us, they pointed their guns towards the sky. Trees lost their leaves. When they reported this, they said, "We saw the Kameko *musumba* on the mountain." But a white man who saw things clearly said, "No, it is on flat land."[38]

Once the rifles were aimed level, they found their targets. According to the commission's *Report*, the mobile police sustained only minor wounds while they killed five Lumpa supporters and wounded another five.[39]

The Kameko incident convinced the Lumpa Church leaders that they needed to take decisive action to defend their church and their villages. For Lenshina and her deacons, it seemed that UNIP and the administration would now act in unison to crush her church. A UNIP spy, who lived in Sione between August 1963 and July 1964 and was accepted as a Lumpa member,

testified that he had heard from both deacons and ordinary L[...]
that the day after the attack on Kameko, Lenshina addressed a g[...]
her courtyard:

> She said that the Police had attacked her followers there and that the
> same thing would happen at other Lumpa villages. She said that they
> should prepare themselves with spears and other weapons to fight
> against the government and that she would send messengers to her
> other villages to warn them and to instruct them also to prepare them-
> selves. She said that men should arm themselves and leave the village
> if the Police came and then if Police attacked the village the men
> should attack them from where they were hiding in the bush. She
> said that if you are fighting the Police you see some of your friends
> fall down—do not be afraid, keep attacking as those people who fall
> down will not die.[40]

A few weeks later, the same spy heard about—but did not witness—a ceremony overseen by Lenshina, where incisions were made on the forehead and
arms of Lumpa church members, into which medicine that would offer protection against bullets was applied. Deacons from other villages took back the
medicines and letters containing instructions from Lenshina to their villages.[41]
A note in ChiBemba, found in the ruins of a Lumpa village, could have been
one way that Lenshina's instructions were distributed from Sione to several
prominent Lumpa villages:

> 1. The enemy is preparing to get hold of all deacons and Mama Len-
>   shina and send them to Mwinilunga. This is the way they will do it.
> 2. They will come to the villages and ask for the deacons. Tell them
>   that they went looking for work.
> 3. They may tell you to leave the village. Tell them that we will not
>   return as we have suffered with them (UNIP) and now they hate
>   us and have burnt our churches and tell us now that they will help
>   rebuild them.
> 4. Give orders to the people, young and old, to stay in the cassava
>   gardens with spears.[42]

The Lumpa Church was preparing for the final battle, for the crescendo of
violence about to descend on their villages.

In July 1964, then prime minister Kaunda coordinated another round of
negotiations. For Kaunda, the destruction of Lumpa settlements and the return of the Lumpa to their original villages was nonnegotiable. On 13 July

ting with a reluctant Lenshina, he allegedly told
es: "Lenshina Villages which are not authorized
i week."[43] Despite the lack of legal basis for this
id police officers thought that after one week they
d to use force to destroy the Lumpa settlements.
remove the Lumpa made a peaceful resolution dif-
npa adherents now knew that the outgoing colonial
e with UNIP activists. They barricaded themselves
iolent onslaught and prayed that God would give
them strength in their battle. On 15 July, about sixty heavily armed soldiers
tried to convince Lumpa members at Chilanga settlement, near the Catholic Mulanga Mission, to return to their original villages. They refused.[44] At
Sione, Lenshina and her followers also refused, blaming UNIP for the violence.[45] Rumors of Lumpa attacks spread. Hundreds of civilians from villages
around Sione, fearing a Lumpa attack, fled to the Chinsali Boma.[46] Fleeing
villagers claimed that women and children from two villages had been forced
into their huts and burned alive.[47] Lumpa members from Siachepa Village
in Chinsali District attacked three UNIP strongholds and killed four UNIP
members on 24 July. Two days later, air reconnaissance reported that up to
thirty villages had been burned in the same area.[48] About twenty-five miles
northeast of Chinsali Boma, also on the twenty-fourth of July, in the remote
Chapaula Village, the Lumpas speared two policemen to death, including
the first European policeman killed, Inspector Smith.[49] In an effort to recover what was probably his badly mutilated body, three mobile police units
attacked the village, resulting in the deaths of twenty-four Lumpas and the
injury of thirteen.[50]

Recording one such event after another does not capture the emotions, the
fear and brutalization, that led mostly Lumpa and UNIP youth, the child soldiers of the war, to violence. The Lumpa believed that they had the Holy Spirit
with them; UNIP believed they were fighting to cleanse Zambia of the evil
remnants of colonialism, those who were in alliance with the federal forces.
An indication of the perceptions, emotions, and spiritual agencies appear in
the testimony of one of the few surviving members of the Lumpa youth, who
described the decisive days in late July as the conflict spiraled into war and led
to the intervention of the colonial army, the Northern Rhodesia Regiment:

> In 1963 we had built Chilanga settlement and moved. . . . [But] in
> 1964 when we went back [to collect food] we were intercepted. The
> UNIP youth apprehended us . . . they took us to Kalikiti. It was 1500h
> when we reached there and found UNIP members had gathered.
> They said, "You have brought them." They started troubling us. They

waited for the sun to go down so they could kill us. When the sun had set, the crowd said, "Escort them." They took us into the bush. "You people of Lenshina, do you know that you are going to die?"

We said, "If that is your wish. We came to look for food, that is all. If you want to kill us, go ahead."

They said, "You are arrogant to talk to us."

They took axes and hacked one Lumpa member. The injured shouted "God," and all of us shouted "Jericho." When we shouted "Jericho," the rope broke. We grabbed axes from the UNIP members. Surprisingly, the UNIP youth became weak and we took their axes. We started hacking them. Each one we confronted was axed and they all fell down. . . . In the confusion we didn't know how many were injured and we ran, reaching the village one by one. When we arrived at the village, we said that we'd been attacked and found that some of us were missing. . . .

Then the mobile police found us. We tried to run away, but they started arresting us. Whoever ran away was caught. They put us in one place and started beating the adults severely. I was afraid of the guns and while hiding between others' legs, one of the policemen kicked me with his boot and I was injured and bleeding. He pushed me and told me to sit. . . . The policeman lifted a gun and asked an old man, "Do I know you?"

"I know you," the old man said.

"Look at my gun; can it shoot water?" the policeman asked.

"Insult me; if you don't I'll shoot you," the policeman said.

The old man said, "In my church we don't insult." He insisted on asking him to insult him—but the old man refused.

The commander of the police came. They took the adults to Chinsali. . . . We [the youth] were annoyed and said, "That village has a chairman who sends youth to kill us." We decided to kill the chairman. That is what we planned. The old people in the village were annoyed with us. But we said, "What are we going to do? Let us protect ourselves." At night we went there and entered the village and attacked. No one survived. We killed all of them—whoever tried to come out of his house, we killed. They didn't have power—we overcame them. They couldn't fight us. We left that village and went to another and in the other village we killed all of them. By the time we were finished killing people at the last village, it was daytime.

We realized we had done wrong and feared that our settlement would be attacked and they would kill many of our members. We said, "What should we do?"

We decided to destroy all the bridges that vehicles would use to come to our settlement. At the Shamusenga River we destroyed the bridge. But as we destroyed the bridge and were going to another, the soldiers [police?] arrived.

When the soldiers arrived, they started to rebuild the bridge and vehicles crossed. We saw [Inspector] Jordan arrive. When he arrived he spoke through a police hailer. We were afraid and ran behind an anthill. Jordan stood on the other side of the river. He said, "You people put down your arms. We want peace." But we saw armed soldiers all over. We thought that we'd all be killed. Jordan was told by his colleagues not to go closer to where we were hiding. . . . But Jordan insisted on crossing the river. As he was about to cross, someone was hidden in the bush with a gun who shot him. He fell down. All of us in hiding came out and shouted, "Jericho, Hallelujah, Hallelujah, Jericho!" As we shouted, soldiers ran away and left their vehicles behind. We even left the body of the white man where he died.

We ran a long way—then they stopped. We said, "We can't leave the body of a white man. If we do that we'll be charged. So if we have to die, let it be with him." We regrouped and returned. We had tried to burn the vehicles but failed. When the soldiers returned they were angry and opened fire. We ran and hid behind the anthill. So we also became annoyed and said, "Let us fight with them." We shouted, "Jericho, Hallelujah," especially the young ones. Then we all came into the open to confront the soldiers. As they fired upon us, their bullets went up in the air. Guns were pointed upwards in the tree when we shouted "Hallelujah." They saw us in the sky and not on the ground. So my group started killing soldiers since they could see the soldiers and the soldiers could not see us.

But when our parents came and wanted to take over the fight and started shouting "Hallelujah," the veil covering the young ones disappeared because the elder people were sinners and witches. So we were exposed and the spirit had left us and soldiers started killing us one by one. Whoever they shot at they killed. So we ran away.[51]

This narrative demonstrates the spiraling of violence, the reaction to humiliation, the view of spiritual agency in warfare, and the perceived righteousness of their struggle. Most striking, though, is the realization that once atrocities have been committed—the massacring of villagers and the killing of the white policeman—there was no turning back. The Lumpa youth knew that they would be hunted down; they fought and fled. The spirits would help them, as long as the Lumpa were pure and not sinners and witches (that they had massacred villagers did not matter in this spiritual reckoning). There was no way to face the policemen's bullets except through spiritual protection; it was, after all, an effective way to confront the real possibility of death. Once violence had replaced law and custom in the reckoning of power and once death was so imminent, spiritual beliefs were crucial to battle.

Immediately after these events, the Central Security Council met and decided on a sustained military operation against the Lumpa. Two battalions of the Northern Rhodesia Regiment (NRR) were to go to Chinsali. On 29 July, the Preservation of Public Security Act was gazetted and Governor Evelyn Hone applied its provisions to the Northern Province and Lundazi District in the Eastern Province, prohibiting any gathering thought to incite or have potential to incite violence. The legal basis for banning church gatherings and forcefully ejecting Lumpa members from their villages was thereby established.[52] Kaunda went to Chinsali to meet with the Provincial Operations Committee. They decided on a military operation against Sione Village. Mobile police squads had proved ineffective in the face of the Lumpa, in part because they believed the Lumpa had powerful magic on their side.[53] The decision to send in soldiers stemmed partly from this police failure. Two thousand soldiers were to be involved in the largest military operation ever on Zambian soil. The First Northern Rhodesia Regiment was instructed to prepare for battle.[54]

The villagers of Sione had decided to defend their village and their magnificent church. "There will be no more talks," a reporter who visited Sione and spoke to Lumpa deacons the day before the battle was told. "The Government and the police have come ready to kill us, and we are ready to die. . . . We are all happy to die for our God. It is not a bad thing to leave this earth."[55] They were armed with spears, bows and arrows, and a few homemade guns. At 0840h on 30 July, on their approach, the NRR paused to allow the DC John Hannah to address the villagers, calling on them to lay down their arms and to surrender those who were considered the Lumpa leaders. The army was attacked on both flanks. The soldiers returned fire with rifles and three machine guns. They entered the village and the church, firing on all who resisted. According to official reports, 75 Lumpa members and 1 soldier were killed, and around 110 Lumpa members and 5 soldiers were wounded. The battle was over by 1005h, although subsequent "mopping up" activities lasted until 1530h.

Mercy Mfula was nineteen years old when she witnessed the attack on Sione. Like most of the Lumpa, she was innocent of the above-mentioned violent acts perpetrated by the youth. Yet the colonial authorities did not consider this silent majority of Lumpa as victims. The soldiers arrived and demanded the surrender of Lenshina and several of the church's leaders. Then, after a short countdown, according to Mercy Mfula:

We heard the sound of guns. We ran into houses to hide. Our friends were being shot. We heard others calling: "Come and see your friends are dead." We ran up and down; we saw people shout, some dying. The guns the soldiers used started from ground level and then rose to treetops. Chickens died, goats died, and trees lost their leaves. We ran up and down. Old people were crying. There was confusion. We kept on saying, "God, what has happened?"

After the operation, the soldiers loaded survivors into trucks and took them to the Chinsali Boma:

> As they brought us to the Boma, there was a large crowd holding branches, which they were shaking and singing, "Well done, Kaunda." They were happy. They took us to a prison by the hill where they kept us. People came to tease us. "You Lumpa said guns would shoot water. Did you see water coming from the guns?"[56]

In the midst of massacre, spirits were not found; in fact, Mercy Mula could not understand why God had abandoned his people. The spirits that turned bullets to water, or made the colonial troops misdirect their fire, applied only to the fighters, not to the victims of the massacre.

In addition to the commission's *Report*, the only documentary evidence of the details of the Sione attack comes from an agreed-upon Provincial Operations Committee release and a timeline of events during the military operation.[57] For the Lumpa villagers, it was a few moments of bravery, confusion, death, and humiliation. The image presented by the Provincial Operations Committee in the formal release was one of law and order confronting savagery:

> Elements of the first battalion NRR and the Police Mobile Unit today moved in on Sione Village, HQ of the fanatical Lenshina religious sect. . . . Some distance from the village the forces halted and Mr. John Hannah the DC addressed the adherents of the sect with a loud hailer. He called upon them in the vernacular to lay down their arms come forward and surrender themselves. A time limit was set for them to do this and they failed to come forward. The forces then advanced in extended order and as they did so they were attacked on both flanks by frenzied villagers carrying bows and arrows, spears and an assortment of firearms. Troops beating off these attacks which were frenzied and pressed home with the utmost ferocity and disregard for personal safety were obliged to use three automatic weapons and it was only at a later stage when it became obvious to the Force Commander that

resistance was weakening that he could safely give instructions that no more use was to be made of these arms. . . . Throughout the whole operation constant appeals were made for the fanatics to see reason but these had no effect and at all times the officers in charge kept the strictest control of the men's fire.[58]

Such reports emphasized the "ferocity" of the "fanatics" of a "sect" in which everyone—women, men, and children—joined in attacks on the security forces. They contrasted with the image of the soldiers and police: unemotional, restrained, and disciplined. Yet there is at least circumstantial evidence that the soldiers were not all disciplined and may have continued firing after being ordered to stop.[59] The idea of Lumpa fanaticism itself inspired intense outbursts of violence. The security operation executed many people, some of them in the church, and many unarmed women and children. Indeed, its efficacy indicates its brutality. Outside the village, where the army attacked at 0840h, fire from rifles and three automatic weapons lasted for approximately fifteen minutes. According to a press report, 65 Lumpas were killed and 50 wounded in the first four minutes of fire.[60] They then advanced into the village, using machine guns for another five minutes. After occasional pauses to allow for Lumpa surrender, the troops resumed firing with single-shot weapons.[61] This lasted for another twenty minutes. By 10h02, the army had occupied the church and cleared it with tear gas. Even if a few Lumpas still wielded spears in the church, the attack inside the church was experienced by most as a massacre. The physical evidence supports this Lumpa experience. One month later, the Special Branch offered a description of the church, "with its walls and doors holed by bullets, and the floors blood stained."[62] The entire operation lasted less than ninety minutes.[63] The army took 436 prisoners, mostly women, but Lenshina escaped.[64] If gauged by the criteria of capturing leaders and perpetrators while preventing harm to innocents, the operation was a dismal failure.

The repercussions of the operation were even worse. As news reached the Lumpa villages of the attack on Sione, most of Lenshina's followers abandoned their settlements and went into hiding in the bush.[65] On the occasion that Lumpa villagers resisted troops, they were again described as "frenzied" and "fanatical." As they had in the previous weeks, Lumpa youth embarked on revenge attacks, especially in the Lundazi District, about one hundred miles to the east of Chinsali, where they attacked several villages, resulting in perhaps 150 deaths. In the most brazen attack, on the night of 3 August, about 200 Lumpa youth from Chipoma Village attacked the Lundazi Boma, seized arms and ammunition from the police station, nearly killed a detective, and did kill his wife and child, together with a number of women and adolescents in the police camp and an Indian trader, resulting in a total of 22 deaths and 28 injured.[66]

The official and press reaction to the Lundazi attack was to contrast good and evil, rational and insane, civilized and savage. The *Northern News* reported that "300 revenge-maddened Lumpa followers raged through the Lundazi District, sacking 18 villagers and killing at least 150 people."[67] Although Kaunda advised against retaliation, he might have encouraged it by his condemnation of the Lumpas for

> bloodthirsty and ungodly brutalities. Lenshina and her followers stand condemned for their madness. . . . [She] taught her followers to do dirty things, to smear themselves in filth to make themselves bullet-proof. . . . Lenshina attackers went to villages while the men were away and locked the women and children in houses which they then set on fire. These are the actions of madmen. They roamed the country killing teachers and children. They stand condemned by their own activities, these mad people.[68]

He called for the capture of Lenshina, dead or alive.

UNIP and government retaliation in Lundazi District was ruthless. Kaunda told the cabinet and Security Council that to prevent local retaliation the government had to take a firm stance against the Lumpa Church. He suggested a combination of "positive action" and a "temporary banning of the church for a limited period of one month."[69] The next day Governor Hone banned the church and the ban was never rescinded.[70] What had begun four days earlier as an operation to arrest the Lumpa involved in the Chinsali disturbances became an all-out assault on the church. The First NRR went to Lundazi District and soldiers attacked Chipoma Village, thought responsible for the attack on the Lundazi Boma. They killed 81 people, at least 23 of whom were women.[71] A few prisoners were taken, but most fled. At Paison Village, 16 were killed and most fled westward into the bush.[72] As the bodies piled up, the office of the prime minister gave permission to the resident magistrate to allow villagers to bury the dead without a coroner's investigation—although an effort was made to record their identity, age, and sex.[73] Following complaints of excessive violence used by the army, the governor delayed an operation against Paishuko Village while the army discussed alternative tactics.[74] When the military arrived, two days after the initial scheduled date, UNIP had already attacked the village. They found 46 dead inhabitants, 36 of whom were women and children. Many showed signs of being raped and tortured before being killed, with grain mortars and stakes thrust into their anuses and vaginas.[75]

On 16 August 1964, a group of UNIP leaders, including Chapoloko; the MP for Abercorn, Sinangwe; the parliamentary secretary, Victor Ngandu; and the minister of Home Affairs, Simon Kapwepwe, addressed a crowd of frightened villagers at Mulanga Mission. Some were victims of Lumpa violence; only a day before a small group of them had briefly returned to their villages to bury the dead. Kapwepwe asked the crowd, "Who has inflicted all of this upon you?" He told them:

> Lenshina, and her adherents. . . . People who eat their dung, washed their bodies with their own urine . . . change into a devil, even 5 times worse than a devil, they actually would be wild beasts. When you find a wild beast feasting in your gardens or trying to kill you: What would you do? You would come together and start to follow it till it is dead. And even after death, you would break its legs, spit on it and roast it above the fire till nothing is left anymore. Our government is determined to destroy this wild beast.[76]

The same evening, Kapwepwe returned to Lusaka to report to Kaunda.[77] The purge of the Lumpa was under way, and UNIP's victory over their most serious rival in northern Zambia assured. The nationalists' vilification of the Lumpa and of Lenshina had transformed Lenshina from a human, *muntu*, into a devil, *mulwani*, which needed not only to be killed but to be ritually defiled—to "break its legs, spit on it and roast it above the fire until nothing is left anymore."

THE SPIRITS OF SUFFERING

In the weeks that followed the attack on Sione, operations were launched against Lumpa villages and roaming Lumpa refugees, leading to hundreds of deaths. Many Lumpa died from starvation after they had abandoned their villages and fled into the bush. For the military, the first priority was the villages in Chinsali, Lundazi, and Mpika Districts, followed by Isoka, Chama, and Kasama Districts. Many villages in these areas, especially in the Kasama District, coexisted peacefully with surrounding areas—yet the government approach was a comprehensive ban on the Lumpa Church and an insistence that all villages be abandoned. Despite attempts to limit casualties after the Chipoma operation in Lundazi, strategies remained similar: a combination of soldiers and police marched to the settlements and demanded that the Lumpas capitulate and accept relocation to their old villages or to resettlement centers. By then, many Lumpa members had already fled into the bush, abandoning their villages. A few Lumpa adherents responded with a show of force, with men in the front brandishing spears and goaded on from behind by women who sang Lumpa hymns; others negotiated. If they refused to surrender, troops opened fire until the Lumpa fled into the bush or surrendered. In general, resistance was greatest in the Chinsali and Lundazi Districts, where the most vicious battles had been fought with UNIP and where the villages were most heavily fortified. In Kasama and Isoka Districts, by contrast, the Lumpa were taken into detention without the use of force. Whether villages were abandoned or surrender was negotiated or forced, the troops set out to destroy all physical remnants of the villages and churches. The last villages were destroyed in the week of 23 to 29 August. The final military operations took place on 10 October 1964, when an encounter between the Second Northern Rhodesia Regiment and a group of roaming Lumpa led to the deaths of 60 Lumpa and 1 soldier, and the arrest of 95 Lumpa.[78] The NRR had to expedite operations if they were to evacuate most of their forces from the Northern Province by 10 September, in time to prepare for the independence celebrations of 24 October in Lusaka.[79]

By the beginning of September, thousands of Lumpa were living as fugitives in the bush or imprisoned in the "cages" next to the Boma district offices. In Chinsali alone, 750 Lumpa followers were in kept in the Boma cage. Lenshina had surrendered on 11 August 1964 in exchange for a guarantee of her personal safety that did not safeguard her from criminal prosecution.[80] While she never faced prosecution regarding the conflict of 1963–1964, Lenshina was detained for the next eleven years. Upon her capture, the government distributed a pamphlet, allegedly dictated by Lenshina, which called on her followers to surrender.[81] The task of resettlement and "rehabilitation" now began. UNIP officials such as Robert Kapasa Makasa, the newly appointed underminister for Northern Province, and Chinsali's member of parliament Jameson Chapoloko played a decisive role in the "rehabilitation committees."

Senior UNIP members and the departing colonial administration still favored the return of Lumpa members to their original villages, and some effort was made to persuade antagonistic villages to accept the Lumpa. This option was unrealistic, however. Lumpa members were afraid, and with good reason. Chiefs and UNIP activists did not favor reintegration of Lumpa members into their villages. At an emergency meeting held at Chinsali Boma on 26 August 1964, Chief Muyombe insisted that all Lumpa members should be arrested: the government "should not mix mad dogs with normal ones." Chapoloko asked "why those spear throwers who in a real sense are criminals should be called refugees."[82]

By October 1964, the legal status of the Lumpas detained at the Boma cages was thrown into doubt. Even under the Preservation of Public Security Act, it was illegal to detain someone for more than twenty-eight days. This led to new legislation that allowed the government to prescribe areas where detention centers could be set up.[83] Following the failure of the original village reintegration schemes, some UNIP members like Kapasa Makasa felt that the only way to "break up the Lenshina cult" was to split its members into single family groups that would be settled in different parts of Zambia, far from their original villages. Makasa's suggestion was not acted upon in the short term (but would be several years later).[84] Instead, the cabinet decided to establish two large detention centers near Mbala and Luwingu, in the north of the country, and one north of Petauke, in the Eastern Province. By March 1965, around four thousand Lumpa were detained at the northern centers and and several hundred at the eastern camp.[85]

At the same time, Lumpa who were not detained had made their way to the Congo. Through intermediaries, especially contacts with Congolese prime minister Moïse Tshombe, the Congolese government invited the Lumpa to settle in Mokambo, near the Zambian border.[86] When Lenshina, then detained at Mumbwa, heard that her followers had been permitted to settle in the Congo, she instructed those who remained in the bush or in the camps to make their way to the Congo.[87] Lumpa members in the detention camps informed the authorities that they were returning to their villagers or to relatives on the Copperbelt; however, their intention was to go to the Congo.[88] By June 1965, the population of the settlement at Mokambo in the Congo had grown to about one thousand.[89] The Lumpa intended to build a new Zion at Mokambo, and from across northern Zambia they made their way to the Congo through Copperbelt safe houses.[90]

In early 1966, the detention camps in Zambia were closed and the Congolese settlement at Mokambo grew to between 15,000 and 20,000.[91] At first the Lumpa resided in one large village, but were soon allocated land to cultivate. Different villages or village sections were named after the *misumba* settlements they had established in northern Zambia.[92] Lenshina's daughter, Elizabeth Ngandu, and her husband, Alfred Kapele, joined a few other prominent deacons to lead the church in the Congo. Far from disintegrating, exile strengthened the corporate nature of the church and solidified Lumpa identity.

Lumpa members identified those who led the initial march through the bush to the Congo, such as Lenshina's nephew, Dixon Mulenga, as "Moses." Even those who did not go on the long march through the bush but joined them after proceeding from the detention camps knew that Moses led God's people through the wilderness to the Promised Land. He even had a staff with which he parted the rivers swollen from the rainy season, or if his staff did not work, he built bridges with ropes made from the bark of trees.[93] Dixon Mulenga became a sacred character; the story of wanderings through the bush were combined with Lenshina's hymns and fragments of biblical reference to create a sacred narrative. "People would drop off one by one and we just covered them with branches and leaves—we had nothing to dig graves with. You'd find people sitting under the tree, who looked alive but were dead." They marched on, occasionally finding food in the farms of villages they passed. At last, they crossed the final river and reached the place they named *Ilondokelo*, "the place of rest."[94]

For the Lumpa, the war and the march to the Congo transformed Lenshina's vision of the transition between life and death into their own lived experience. Instead of the river that Lenshina crossed in her movement from life to death and back again, it was the wilderness of the northern plateau that God's chosen people crossed. It was their faith that guided them across rivers. Men like Dixon "Moses" Mulenga performed miracles, but the people of God reached the other side only through their faith.

In the stories of church members, the fear, terror, and deprivation of the war and the march to the Congo became a sign not of misguided belief or even the tragedy of war, but of the strength of their faith, of their resolution, and that God was on their side:

> As church members, we passed through many difficulties and cannot explain everything. Many *misumba* were attacked and many died because of our church. But we remained determined. Even when Jesus was born, blood was shed. Even those who spread the word of God in those times were killed. Jesus was crucified but he didn't do anything bad; even ourselves, we have remained strong in our faith because we believe a dead person doesn't see his own blood. We will persevere. Jesus promised that he would give us a place in heaven, so even though our friends have been killed, we don't worry about them. . . . That is why our faith is strong and unshaken.[95]

In the new villages around Mokambo, memories of suffering and violence became the bedrock of faith. Prior to the war, being Lumpa was about the purification of spirit, of cleansing the evil of witchcraft. Now, the evil had taken human form. Church members had battled UNIP and Kaunda; they had fled and crossed to the other side. The Manichaean oppositions of Lenshina's hymns had been enacted through the war, where humans had become devils. Tales of the war were proof of Lenshina's visions. The battle against evil in Lenshina's hymns no longer referred only to the struggle against witchcraft; they also referenced the battle against UNIP and the government soldiers.

Exile evoked a new spiritual sensibility of suffering. In the churches that they built in the Congo, the Lumpa sang hymns that remembered the suffering of God's people and the fear and terror of the long march. A frightened young woman sang this hymn on a brief return visit to Zambia in 1972:

Tukaya twanaka, Eye mayo   [We shall go, but we are tired, mother
Pa makasa yaba Tata pe tonta   By foot (we shall go) to the Lord,
                             our savior.][96]

Church texts reference this sacred narrative. The manuscript held by the Chiponya congregation, cited at the beginning of chapter 4, begins with the revelations of Lenshina. Its final "testimony" deals with the war of 1964:

> In the year that government was taken by black people, members of UNIP . . . started burning churches and blocking paths and roads so that those who believe in the prayers of God which Lenshina Mulenga taught were killed because they loved God's things more than things of the world. So they started war wherever the children of God in the Lumpa Church were found.
> Again in 1964 they killed the children of Sione and in all the *misumba* of Sione. So this testimony is great and it shows the truth of all things according to the lord Jesus Christ who said that those who reject me in the last days . . . will suffer. . . . Those who persevere to do good things to the end will be fortunate and will be saved.[97]

Following the final testimony is a renowned and popular Lumpa hymn:

Natemwa bana bandi babebashipa   [I love my children who
                                   are courageous
Ifya shipile Yesu   As Jesus was
Ilyo ifipondo fyamwipwishe   When sinners (the
                                   outcasts) asked
Niwe yesu mwana lesa   Are you the son of God?
Aleti nine wine mwana lesa   He said truly I am the son
                                   of God
Lelo tile kubomba chaabipa   Today we shall do bad things
                                   to you
Aleti bombeni   He said do them.
Nelyo mule bomba chaabipa   Even if you do bad things to me
Ine naba muli tata   I am with my father.]

Chuleni Chuleni   [Suffer, suffer
Efya chulile nomwana wamfumu   That is how the child of the
                                   lord suffered
Umwana wa mfumu alechula   The child of the lord suffered

Kubulwani bwa chalo efyo bwaba	The hatred of this world is like that
Naimwebene chuleni	Even you suffer
Efya chulile nomwana waamfumu	For that is how the child of god suffered
Amen	Amen][98]

The Lumpa considered themselves separated from the new Zambian nation. Lenshina described the situation in her typical familial idiom and with typical emotional understanding. From detention, she sent a message warning her followers to evade the Zambian authorities, as a couple evades one another after a divorce:

> If you are married to a woman and you divorce her, but meet here and there, how do you feel? Jealous? Bitter? Similarly, where you have camped by the road and the Zambian authorities see you every day, they notice you. So you should leave and go far away.[99]

Despite Lenshina's appeals, over the next two decades most of the Lumpa gradually returned to Zambia, sometimes voluntarily and sometimes by force. Lenshina herself died on 7 December 1978, still under government detention. She was buried at the altar of what remained of her church, by then destroyed by the Zambian military (see fig. 6.1, below). The Lumpa movement would, however, survive, and from the 1990s resurrected itself as the New Jerusalem Church. The details of the return of the Lumpa to Zambia and the reemergence of the church, outlined elsewhere, are, however, less important to this analysis.[100]

⌁

The Lumpa-UNIP war demonstrates the interventions of spirits into extraordinary affairs. If, as Carl von Clausewitz put it, "war is a continuation of politics by other means," spirits were everywhere in this violent play for power. The Lumpa and the UNIP fought precisely because church members and political activists recognized the power of the spirits. UNIP activists insisted on the illimitable sovereignty of a party, UNIP, supported by God; Lenshina's followers insisted that Lenshina, not UNIP and Kaunda, was God's intermediary. Lumpa adherents would not recognize UNIP before they prayed to God, and those who prevented them from praying were sinners and witches. For the nationalists, anyone contaminated with an association with colonialism was a Judas; they had to be cleansed, just like a witch. As violence increased, so did death, unpredictability, and spiritual agency. To some, spirits enhanced

Figure 6.1. Remains of Zion church and Lenshina's tombstone. Photo by author, 2005.

fighting prowess and offered physical protection against bullets; to nearly all, spiritual beliefs proved the righteousness of their struggle. Both UNIP and Lumpa were fighting for a revolution, and if they succeeded, a new heaven on earth awaited. After victory, the nationalists imagined that they had become the representatives of God's will; after defeat, the Lumpa believed that their suffering, like Christ's, signaled the strength of their faith.

The Lumpa-UNIP war of 1964 helped to redefine the relationship between the invisible and the visible worlds. With independence, the millenarian popular programs of both Christian and nationalist movements receded, and the urban-based teachers, with their program of moral reform, proposed to guide the masses to an earthly salvation. The nationalist elite tried to establish new boundaries that separated political power from the power of the spirits. They proposed a new slogan, "Lesa ku mulu, Kaunda panshi" (God in heaven, Kaunda on earth). Kaunda had taken over as the ancestor of Zambia, and God was only in control of an afterlife. While the new state elite claimed to be an alternative both to Lenshina and to the excesses of popular nationalism, whenever a political foe appeared, the state and party structures could appeal to this history of millenarian nationalism and mobilize the violence necessary to maintain authority. But the emotional investment of Zambians in the nationalist vision could not be easily contained in the turmoil of a new nation, with its divisions, economic fragility, and unrequited expectations. Fervor did not remain contained by this vision; nor did evil disappear because Kaunda proclaimed it so. With the unmet expectations of independence, people once again turned to personal struggles against the influence of evil.

The Lubemba Plateau—the home of the Crocodile Clan, a number of the Zambian political elites, the Roman Catholic White Father missions, and the Livingstonia Church of Scotland—lost its importance in postcolonial Zambia. The mission of Ilondola survived, sponsored by the Catholic Church, and became a well-known language training institute. But the Presbyterian Lubwa Mission began a period of decline, so that even the old graves of the heroes of Lubwa, Paul B. Mushindo and David and Helen Kaunda, fell into disrepair. Over the decades, many of the mission buildings, homes first to Reverend Mc-Minn and then Fergus Macpherson, began to crumble. During the Lumpa-UNIP war, thousands had left the Chinsali District. There was little reason to return. With the capture of the colonial state, the centers of power shifted to the Copperbelt and to the capital of the new nation, Lusaka.

7 ↤ God in Heaven,
Kaunda on Earth

As THE LAST SOLDIERS of the Northern Rhodesia Regiment withdrew
from the Northern Province, Zambians prepared to celebrate their independence. A new stadium to accommodate thirty thousand people had been built
on the outskirts of Lusaka. The details of the handing over of power followed
a well-rehearsed formula, practiced by the British authorities in their recent
withdrawals from other African colonial territories. A British protocol officer
planned the events in consultation with a government committee. At mid-
night, on the dawn of the new nation, during a ceremony attended by the
Princess Royal, the Union Jack was lowered and the new Zambian flag rose
with an accompanying fireworks display. On the declared Independence Day,
24 October 1964, Zambians cheered to parades, dancing, and a flyover by the
new Zambian air force. Cabinet ministers dressed in "lounge suits" and their
wives in day dresses with hats and gloves—although "National Dress" was
permitted. Events at the stadium ended in the early evening and gave way to
a range of other festivities and ceremonies: a state ball, a beauty pageant, and
a football match. There was also a national service of thanksgiving held at
Cathedral of the Holy Cross. And so as not to forget the old rulers, President
Kaunda held a special reception for chiefs at his new home, State House.
Although Lusaka was clearly the place to be, similar festivities were arranged
across the country and among small expatriate Zambian communities around
the world.[1]

The colonial pomp and ceremony were appropriate. The state had been
captured by the teachers, and in many regards they would continue the civilizing mission of the colonial period. The leaders outlined an economic program
rooted in a sense of social morality that aimed to uplift Zambians from material

157

poverty through hard work and a sense of African communalism, while abstaining from "negative" African traditions such as tribalism and Western influences such as individual selfishness. Despite some of these contradictory imperatives, this was a Christian nation that David Livingstone would have appreciated.[2] Behind the carefully groomed cabinet ministers, however, stood the party activists who had fought for the nationalist New Jerusalem. They had struggled to rid the land of evil and had great expectations for the future. In the first few years of postcolonial Zambia, state elites tried to manage these expectations by guiding the new citizens along a path of moral reform that would lead to a new civilization. By the 1970s, this program of reform proved disappointing and failed to live up to popular expectations; Zambians turned to alternative ways to cure their afflictions. As the state disintegrated, and political and religious leaders denied people the ability to deal with spiritual affliction, the eradication of evil began to be viewed once again as a struggle in the public realm, an effort to purify the land of the postcolonial authorities, who had, like the colonists and missionaries of the past, ignored the presence of spirits and thereby allowed themselves to become agents of evil.

Zambian scholarship has questioned the postcolonial hegemony of Kaunda's United National Independence Party (UNIP), pointing to activist dissatisfaction following what Giacomo Macola terms the "thwarted internal expectations of independence."[3] For example, Miles Larmer outlines opposition by Simon Kapwepwe's United Progressive Party (UPP) and the trade union movement.[4] Similarly, Marja Hinfelaar indicates aspects of Catholic opposition to Kaunda's regime, even while Kaunda co-opted several of the leading Catholic clergy in his social programs.[5] As Gatian F. Lungu points out, the churches, the labor movement, and the press offered occasional critiques of UNIP's government.[6] This literature is a helpful corrective to a view of unchallenged UNIP hegemony, but it does not appreciate the turn by many Zambians to alternative conceptualizations of human struggle that were cast in a spiritual idiom.

This chapter examines the UNIP philosophy of Zambian humanism as a state religion with its own secular invisible world: a modern nation that would resemble heaven. Humanism, Zambians were told, was the path to the creation of heaven on earth. The popular anticolonial nationalist movement and the Lumpa Church both began as attempts to purify the body and body politic of evil; of witchcraft, but also of forms of evil like the Central African Federation and colonialism more generally. Zambian humanism reconceptualized the struggle against evil as a nation-building exercise where individual desires gave way to a progressive social and moral community, a new Zambian nation. Humanism became somewhat popular, but it never satisfied a need to combat evil afflictions, as Lenshina's movement had. It was a moral quest to form a heavenly society that would eradicate allegedly "selfish" individual desires. The slogan "Lesa ku mulu, Kaunda panshi" (God in heaven, Kaunda on earth), drawing on an old idiom of the spirits above and the ancestors who ruled the earth below (see chapter 1, pages 33 to 34), pointed to Kaunda as the ultimate ancestor who had authority on earth. But humanism's failure to deal with individual desires and afflictions led many Zambians to turn to new spiritual Christian tendencies, especially Archbishop Emmanuel Milingo's healing ministry, through the 1970s.[7] The failure or unwillingness of Kaunda to prevent Archbishop Milingo's forced exile, along with socialist tendencies within humanism that denied the agency of spirits, led to the emergence of opposition to Kaunda cast in a spiritual Christian discourse.

HUMANISM AND THE NEW ZAMBIAN

As CAF and Northern Rhodesia disintegrated, the land and the people adopted a new name and a new set of national symbols. Since the teachers who had decided on "Zambia" in 1958 had won the elections at the end of 1963, "Zambia" is what the new cabinet decided the name of the nation should be. They constituted an Independence Celebrations Consultative Committee, which became instrumental in recommending Zambia's national symbols. During their first meeting, the consultative committee settled on the colors of the national flag (black, green, and red), the coat of arms, and the national motto, "One Zambia, One Nation." They decided that the words for the national anthem, set to the music of the "Bantu National Anthem," the spiritual first composed by the South African Enoch Sontonga, were to be determined by a national competition coordinated on the radio. After failing to select a clear winner, an amalgamation of entries was chosen.[8] When the permanent secretary feared that the committee was overstepping its bounds in ruling on such issues, the cabinet took a more direct interest in the national symbols.[9] They chose an eagle, to "symbolize the nation's hopes of rapid progress."[10]

With the keen involvement of Simon Kapwepwe, the cabinet established a Department of Culture.[11] It would see to the spread of Zambian symbols as well as the construction of sites of memory dedicated to the new nation. By 1966, the singing of the new national anthem and saluting the new flag were mandatory at all public events and schools.[12] Religious groups, especially the Jehovah's Witnesses, who refused to submit to these national rituals faced persecution.[13] The National Monuments Commission, under colonial rule and dedicated to early archaeological sites, became focused on identifying sites of memory linked to the new nation. In 1968, they declared Kaunda's house in Lusaka (Chilenje) as well as the Land Rover in which he campaigned against the colonial authorities to be national monuments.[14] A range of symbols drawn from the recent past sculpted a landscape of national memory.

Of all UNIP's and Kaunda's national inventions and creations, the philosophy of humanism took the most intellectual energy and sparked the greatest debate and interest within Zambia. Yet humanism as a philosophy of government and society has received scant scholarly attention. It is often portrayed as a rather uninspired variation of African socialism or as a crude attempt to legitimize Kaunda and UNIP. After an initial wave of enthusiasm, especially by UNIP cadres, missionaries, and economists with a European socialist orientation, Western scholars tended to emphasize the failed promises of humanism.[15] For example, Megan Vaughan claims that the structural features of Zambian society during the First and Second Republic had "nothing to do with 'Humanism' or socialism, except when represented rhetorically by the leadership."[16] The limitations of the post-humanist neoliberalism have inspired some reflection on the moral ambitions of humanism. James Ferguson, for example, argues that humanism's appreciation of economics as a moral problem of "selfishness" versus "sharing," rather than an ostensibly scientific discipline, distinguishes it from neoliberal economic theories (although, contra Ferguson, many UNIP activists did try to equate humanism with scientific socialism, as further explored below).[17] Few scholars have looked beyond this celebration or condemnation to consider humanism as a serious moral and ideological intervention that guided the interactions between individuals and the postcolonial state.

Humanism was part of a struggle to imagine the nation with the tools provided by a European colonial civilizing mission. Its central ideas evolved in dialogue with several European missionaries and clergy, most notably Reverends Colin Morris, James C. Oglethorpe, John Papworth, and G. A. Krapf, all of whom are acknowledged in Kaunda's principal work on humanism.[18] Humanism consolidated the moral reformism of the missionary civilizing mission in which the Kaunda family had been so involved and legitimized this moral discourse by reconciling it with forms of African nationalist ideology found in Ghana, Tanzania, in the liberation movements of southern Africa, and socialist ideology. The contradiction between these ideologies often surfaced, with Zambians divided over the religious and the socialist content within humanism.[19] For Kaunda at least, humanism and its concomitant set of celebrations and rituals related the individual to the new nation. The party would take on the civilizing tasks that had previously been the duty of the mission church. Central to this task was the eradication of exploitation, as well as the development of a work ethic and a sense of self-reliance. "We all know that a man who has developed a genuine sense of self-reliance will not in any way exploit his fellow man," Kaunda wrote in his first guide to humanism. "This is how God wishes it and this is how a humanist responds to this call."[20]

The development of humanism can be traced back to a little more than one month before the proclamation of Zambian independence in October 1964. Then prime minister Kaunda addressed the annual UNIP conference at Mulungushi Rock near Kabwe. UNIP's position as the party that would lead Zambia in the foreseeable future and Kaunda's position at the helm of the party were relatively secure. In a speech lasting four and a half hours, Kaunda outlined the role of UNIP and its relationship to government, to civil society, and to the Zambian citizenry. Kaunda's ambition was no less than to chart a new course for the relationship between the individual, the society, and the state. In this new society, individual desires and needs were subordinate to social ones. The party would identify and guide individuals in their social obligations. The aim was to create a new type of individual, or more precisely, to abolish individual desires, which were considered narrow, selfish, and greedy. Kaunda supposedly acted on this principle in his Mulungushi speech when he refused to become the "Life President" of the party, despite the alleged appeals by party cadres. Instead of individual liberty, the "Government" was to be "a supreme authority, giving instructions to all *and getting instructions from no one on earth.* . . . The Party must be the eyes, ears and mouth of Government. Through the Party, Government must teach common man and through the Party common man must reach Government."[21] Despite Kaunda's refusal to accept the life presidency of the party, he was clear on his personal role within the party as the guardian of a moral quest to protect against evil: "I must warn each of you in the Party that the axe of discipline will fall and fall very heavily on anyone agreeing to being used by any agencies of evil influence." And this quest would be undertaken after the model of the mission school: "As a former headmaster of a big school I knew precisely how the mischievous behaviour of a single student can shake the foundations of the school to the core. . . . I am sure it is your intention as good citizens to allow me a margin of firmness that might not be very palatable at times."[22]

The Mulungushi UNIP conference took place in the immediate aftermath of the Lumpa-UNIP conflict, which had resulted in the largest military operations ever within Zambia, with around one thousand dead, massive social disruption in the Northern Province, and the proclamation of emergency regulations that remained in force up until 1990. The conflict convinced Kaunda that the party should be a sovereign instrument of morality and guidance for his sometimes confused Zambian flock. If the new nation and its new civilization needed a foil, an "Other," an example of the chaos and violence that would result from evil, selfish individuals and their misguided followers, it was Lenshina and her Lumpa Church. "Of late the nation has been disgraced by a woman called Lenshina . . . [who] for her own *selfish* reasons, left a blot on our record and it will be a long time before we can erase it." In addition to Kaunda's condemnation of Lenshina as "selfish," which contrasted with Kaunda's social vision, Kaunda also evoked a familiar opposition between "savagery" and "civilization"; he warned of what could be expected should the new nation lose its moral guide. Far from the official government policy of "reconciliation" toward or even "rehabilitation" of the Lumpa, Kaunda repeated his old condemnation and conjured an image of horrific savagery:

> We are, in fact, dealing with not only fanatics, but lunatics. . . . They have become anti-society. They have been known husband and wife, to plan to kill their own parents because they were non-Lumpa and this they have done. . . . These evil people have gone on the rampage in a manner known only to the barbarians of the Middle Ages. Innocent villagers and children trying to escape from their burning homes have been captured by followers of Lenshina and thrown back into the flames.[23]

Kaunda's representation of the Lumpa Church as antisociety, evil, selfish, mad, and savage reverberated across Zambian society, legitimizing the quest for a civilized morality. Zambians came to refer to the Lumpa as *tumpa*, a Bemba insult meaning "foolish" or "stupid." Kaunda and the party would guard against such outbreaks of misguided selfishness.

Kaunda's Mulungushi speech, together with his condemnation of Lenshina, was published in the October 1964 edition of the UNIP publication *Voice of UNIP*. Here the editor commented on Kaunda's "greatness and sincerity . . . which makes him a giant among leaders in this continent." On his decision to refuse the life presidency of the party, Kaunda was "gifted with a foresight lacking in some of Africa's leaders."[24] Kaunda's supposedly selfless act only further promoted the messianic portrayal of him. Less than one year later, Kaunda's birthday was celebrated in the *Voice of UNIP* with a poem:

> If I were asked
> Who is the most selfless leader?
> I would say Kaunda of Zambia
>
> If I were asked
> Which leader cares for the Common Man
> I would say Kaunda of Zambia
>
> . . . .
> If I were asked
> Which is the Founder's Day in Zambia

I would say 28th April
Kaunda's Birthday.[25]

An enthusiastic follower rewrote Psalm 21: "The King (President Kaunda)
shall joy in thy strength. . . ." Following the psalm, Kaunda's prophetic role
was declared: "His Excellency and President of the free Republic of Zambia
is not only the receiver and spendor of God's blessing; but like the patriarch,
he is the distributor. He, as the son of God, is conceived as not only enjoying
the presence of the Lord at this birthday, but also as living in the presence of
favour of the lord and so as ever joyful and gladness."[26]

Not all Zambians agreed with this vision of Kaunda's supreme and divinely
inspired role. By the late 1960s, as Giacomo Macola and Miles Larmer have
shown, there were challenges to Kaunda from both within and outside the
UNIP, especially from activists who felt they had been inadequately compen-
sated for their role in the freedom struggle.[27] Yet unmet economic expectations
are only part of the story. The representation of Kaunda as a messianic hero,
a representative of God, needs to be taken seriously. Many Zambians thought
that Kaunda would rid the evil that afflicted society. Although Kaunda did not
claim to perform miracles or heal afflictions with spiritual interventions, he
did promise to foster heaven on earth. It would be as difficult for Kaunda to
meet the expectations of this New Jerusalem as it was for Lenshina.

The moral vision offered by humanism carried out the struggle against
evil through the subordination of individual interests to social ones. Kaunda's 1964 speech formed a blueprint for the later articulation of humanism.
The first formal published record of humanism was a series of "letters" to the
European missionary, ally, and friend of Kaunda, Colin Morris, which were
published in 1966 as A Humanist in Africa. In the letters Kaunda reflected
on the particularities of nationalism in postcolonial Africa, drawing inspiration from postcolonial African leaders that ranged from Senghor to Nyerere.
Kaunda argued that African society emphasized communalism and placed
"Man," as opposed to material objects, at its center. This allowed postcolonial
African society a special ability to develop a new type of society that cherished
humans above selfish and narrow individual interests.[28] In April 1967, UNIP's
National Council adopted humanism as Zambia's national philosophy, and
six months later, Kaunda presented his thoughts on humanism in a pamphlet
submitted to the UNIP national conference:

> Africa's gift to world culture must be in the field of Human Rela-
> tions. . . . The traditional community was a mutual aid society. . . .
> Human need was the supreme criterion of behaviour. The hungry
> stranger could, without penalty, enter the garden of a village and take,

say, some peanuts, a bunch of bananas, a mealie cob or a cassava plant root to satisfy his hunger. His action only became theft if he took more than was necessary to satisfy his needs. . . . The high valuation of MAN and respect for human dignity which is a legacy of our tradition should not be lost in the new Africa. However "modern" and "advanced" in a Western sense this young nation of Zambia may become, we are fiercely determined that this humanism will not be obscured.[29]

Humanism thus combined a concern for supposedly African communalism with the developmentalist vision of the colonial state and the civilizing mission of the Christian churches. A humanist moral vision guided an economically and politically integrated unit, the new nation-state, toward a society defined by the absence of individual interests. For Kaunda, this moral project should not be left to religious institutions. "We need religious leaders to give us guidelines," Kaunda acknowledged. "But moral and spiritual development must be part and parcel of the Party and Government programme. Hence, it is seriously proposed that the Party's programme include moral and spiritual teaching."[30] In this humanist program, Kaunda combined the two elements of his own background: the son of a missionary and the leader of a nationalist movement.

Unlike European humanist ideas or Marxist-Leninist forms of socialism, Kaunda's humanism did not deny the presence of God. However, the most influential UNIP intellectuals were influenced by Marxism, and thus struggled to define the spiritual component of humanism. The emphasis was always on "man" as the object of social reform, even while God was sometimes recognized to have created and inspired man.[31] One book, titled *Zambian Humanism: Some Major Spiritual and Economic Challenges*, hardly discusses "spiritual," except to indicate that it was a sense of social alienation that resulted from the exploitation of men.[32] A list of "humanist terminology" defined *religion* as a "fantasy reflection in people's minds of external forces dominating over them in every day life, a reflection in which earthly forces assume non-earthly forms."[33] For Timothy Kandeke, a leading influence in the socialist camp, the "spiritual life of Society (Social Consciousness) is a reflection of material life (Social Being)."[34] Kandeke went on to claim that humanism recognized Zambian "traditions," but this "does not mean going back to witchcraft, necromancy (sorcery), idolatory." For just like a driver who only looks in a rearview mirror, Kandeke argued, "a nation that keeps its mind fixed on past traditional ways of life without looking 'in front' is committing a crime against 'progress' and is more than likely to end up in a 'crash.'"[35] Many Zambians of this era shared Kandeke's desire for a secular and scientific modernity.

As opposition to Kaunda's dominance within UNIP emerged in the late 1960s, factions within UNIP competed to offer more-aggressive versions of humanism. For example, Kaunda had to rein in the enthusiastic UNIP youth brigade, thugs who implemented Kapwepwe's "Cultural Revolution" by attacking women who wore short skirts.[36] After Kapwepwe and his followers formed the United Progressive Party (UPP) in 1971, which was outlawed in 1972 with the advent of the one-party system, humanism became even more closely associated with the persona of Kaunda. Humanism became more than a philosophy; it promoted itself as a religion, with Kaunda as its chief prophet. Loyal cadres described Kaunda as a *ntambalukuta*, meaning "someone who watches over a large family," in the "father-chief" idiom common to many African political leaders.[37] There was a renewed effort to identify national rituals, symbols, and even memories. The party encouraged supporters to carry a slim volume of selections of Kaunda's speeches, titled *Kaunda's Guidelines*, as if it were a Bible.[38] The Joint Publications Bureau of Zambia, the creation of an alliance between the state and missionary educational efforts, became the Kenneth Kaunda Foundation. Its chief researcher, the missionary who had "stolen" Lenshina's book, Fergus Macpherson, was brought under the stricter control and guidance of loyal UNIP cadres, such as Henry S. Meebelo.[39] Upon witnessing the dress code of Mobutu's militants in Zaire, UNIP officials suggested that UNIP develop a similar national dress code.[40] Kaunda declared a "Humanist Week" around the time of the annual independence celebrations, when all Zambians were "expected to practice Humanism in their private homes, at work, on the roads . . ." There were to be television shows, radio talks, films, and articles in the national newspapers about humanism in Zambia. Kaunda wanted people to visit the sick, to "show respect for human dignity," and to discuss what the philosophy meant to everyday life in general. The Ministry of Development Planning and National Guidance coordinated events, which involved all aspects of government and civil society, from the armed services to the churches.[41]

In the aftermath of the banning of opposition parties in 1972 and the declaration of the "one-party participatory democracy" in 1973, the repressive and intrusive tendencies of humanism became pronounced. A 1975 speech that Kaunda named the "Watershed Speech" drew on Kapwepwe's earlier "Cultural Revolution" to further restrict immoral and un-Zambian media and behavior: "cowboy," "Kung-Fu," and "love-making" films were to be proscribed in television and in theaters. "This is Zambia with its own way of life and not Europe. This is Zambia and not the United States of America. We take our cultural values seriously," Kaunda instructed UNIP cadres, continuing:

> There is a nude picture. Now when you publicise such things, you are appealing to the instinct of men. You are sabotaging their morality— that is what you do in a permissive society. I cannot respect people

who do such things; who own such papers for money calling themselves civilized and Christians. How do you do such things? What do
you promote? You are promoting prostitution in the nation. You are
appealing to the most base instincts of man, destroying him morally,
and do you expect me as President of the Party to accept such things
in our society?[42]

Soon after the Watershed Speech, Kaunda introduced a Zambian Humanist
Moral Code with seventeen specific points, based on a document produced
by UNIP's research bureau.[43] Socialist UNIP members under the influence
of the South African communist Jack Simons, in particular Timothy Kandeke
and Joseph Musole, and with the support of the UNIP secretary, A. G. Zulu,
campaigned for the more aggressive adoption of scientific socialism and for
UNIP to become a vanguard party in the Marxist-Leninist sense.[44] Perhaps in
response to these initiatives, Kaunda announced greater party intervention
in the media, including the takeover of the independently minded *Times of
Zambia* from Lonrho, which was finally achieved in 1981.

Humanism was not simply an instrument of state propaganda, however. Its
moral vision allowed for greater flexibility, for a bending of its direct political
purposes, at least compared to, say, Mobutu's Authenticité or even Nyerere's
Ujamaa. In a sensitive but unpublished study of religion in Zambian political
life, scholar and White Father missionary J. L. Calmettes argued that the religious dimension to Kaunda's personality allowed him to stay in power without
much bloodshed.[45] Appeals to humanism could curb excessive political preda-
tion and act as court of moral appeal. As James Ferguson discovered during his
fieldwork in the mid-1980s, despite the "intensely interested, self-serving, and
very often fraudulent" aspects of humanism, mine workers could still draw
on humanist tenets to criticize the government for "selfishness."[46] Moreover,
while there were certainly abuses of human rights and acts of political disen-
franchisement in UNIP's Zambia, given the context of Zambian independence, surrounded by antagonistic European settler regimes (and from the
1970s nations embroiled in civil war), some restraint was displayed. The ability
to draw on these humanist ideas may also have curbed patronage politics and
provided a possibility for oppositional politics. Kapwepwe, for example, criticizing the elite *apamwamba* (the new class of prosperous politicians), claimed
that "if you cannot have pity on these people [the downtrodden], then you are
a disciple of the devil—EVIL."[47] Humanism provided a blueprint for a public morality. Of course, like most state religions, the fact that the clergy and
the political elite were one and the same or closely allied, with few independent intellectuals, ensured that any rebuke humanism offered to state power
was tepid.

The most spectacular failure of humanism was in its attempts to provide for the individual who faced spiritual afflictions. In the 1960s and 1970s, Kaunda had defined the struggle against evil as a struggle against imperialism. The character of evil was "selfishness"—greed was what made imperialism evil. The biblical message of a New Jerusalem was linked to a united effort to create an unselfish society without exploitation. The political class expressed widespread support for this idea. In a eulogy for Kapwepwe after his death in 1980, Musonda Chambeshi appealed for all Zambians to struggle for the promised land: "You must lead our people from the corruption, nepotism and moral decay of today into the new promised land, where a better sense of purpose will create fraternity as Jesus Christ proclaimed many years ago, and about which so much is said these days but so little is done."[48] Yet, for many Zambians, this morality never became persuasive, or was at least incomplete. The moral struggle and teleology of humanism did not address the personal afflictions of spirits.

The conventional explanation for the failure of Kaunda's regime focuses on political challenges in the context of the declining economic circumstances through the 1970s. While there is much truth in this explanation, the inability of Kaunda to offer a convincing intervention in the forces of spiritual good and evil that afflicted individuals also undermined his rule. Kaunda not only denied spiritual forces in this world; his social vision denied individual desires. As economic and political circumstances worsened through the 1970s and people lost faith in a socialist modernity, UNIP was less fervently followed and Kaunda's efforts to develop a humanist public morality collapsed. The problem of spiritual affliction was amplified: a spiritual discourse expressed a common feeling of disempowerment. The healing ministry of the Catholic Archbishop of Lusaka, Emmanual Milingo, demonstrates the beginnings of new efforts to deal with this sense of disempowerment.

HEALING SPIRITS

As a state religion, humanism was brought into competition and sometimes conflict with the churches. What was the role of the church if humanism guided the morality of citizens? Given the missionary role as promoter of education, civilization, and morality, could the postcolonial churches that grew out of these mission societies cede these roles to UNIP? Most of all, the churches had to decide what it meant to be involved in the affairs of heaven, while Kaunda and the party were the guardians of morality on earth. They had to adapt or at least respond to "Lesa ku mulu, Kaunda panshi" (God in heaven, Kaunda on earth), a slogan that disempowered the church as a guide for moral actions here on earth. Even as Kaunda did his utmost to reconcile Christianity with humanism, Zambians asked what was God's role if "man" and "society" were at the center of the humanist moral vision. Competition between Christianity and humanism became even more fraught as socialist Zambians educated in the Soviet Union and Eastern Europe, along with members of the exiled southern African liberation movements, began to emphasize a scientific socialism, with an invisible world guided by class struggle, as the basis for human action.[49]

Shortly after independence, most of the mainline Protestant churches combined to form the autonomous United Church of Zambia (UCZ). The advantage of this arrangement was that African clergy quickly played a leading role; the disadvantage was that UCZ, without an international structure, was chronically underfunded and often unable to remain independent of the Zambian state.[50] In the better-funded Catholic Church, by contrast, expatriate clergy still played a dominant role, with only a few of the prominent positions allocated to Africans. Emmanual Milingo became Archbishop of Lusaka in 1969, and Elias Mutale became Archbishop of Kasama in 1973. Both played a major role in the development of the relationship between the Catholic Church and the Zambian state. In a sign of the more autonomous and sometimes assertive role of the Catholic Church, in 1972, largely with Catholic sponsorship, Zambia's three major church bodies—the evangelical and Pentecostal Evangelical Fellowship of Zambia (EFZ), the mainline Protestant Council of Churches in Zambia (CCZ), and the Catholic Zambia Episcopal Conference (ZEC)—launched a monthly newspaper, the *National Mirror*. The newspaper would offer independent assessments of Kaunda's government in years to come.

Besides the overt and open development of the churches as a significant element of civil society, there were several spiritual movements that moved through Zambian society at an almost subterranean level, coming into the open when the fractured postcolonial polity was at its most vulnerable. The movements shared many similarities with the Lumpa Church, most strikingly in their concern with the problem of evil possession. The most widespread and popular of these movements was Archbishop Emmanuel Milingo's healing ministry. After he announced his first healing of a woman who suffered from spirit possession in April 1973, Milingo was inundated by crowds, especially of women, who wanted to experience individual exorcism. Despite attempts to limit his activities in the face of hostility from the Vatican, demands for his services increased through the 1970s. His movement grew in popularity as he joined healing rituals with social works. From 1976, he allied his healing ministry with international efforts to spread charismatic renewal through the Catholic Church. Thousands came to be freed from possession: at just one monthly healing mission around 1,300 came to be healed; Milingo could expect visits from another 200 individuals per week. In 1979, under pressure from the Zambian bishops (and probably the Vatican), he conducted his final public healing session in Zambia.[51]

Milingo wrote extensively about his healing ministry. For him, evil had a very real spiritual existence. Drawing on a range of sources, from Zambian concepts of the spiritual world to biblical commentary, ethnographies, Machiavelli, and even the film *The Exorcist*, Milingo sought to demonstrate the presence of spiritual evil and the need to combat it.[52] Milingo believed that evil operated in the material world through living beings possessed by spirits. In Zambia, demons had possessed people, most explicitly through the "Church of the Spirits," which was, according to Milingo, "a group of people who have been given spiritual power by the devil, and whose aim is unquestionably to wage war against the holy people of God."[53] He viewed his duty, and that of the clergy more broadly, to be the purification of members of the "Church of Spirits" who had fallen under the control of the devil. Milingo explicitly criticized the clergy who claimed to believe in Jesus and God, but not in Satan. This willful dismissal of evil spiritual forces, Milingo argued, obstructed attempts to do battle with the devil. "They have accepted somehow a co-existence with the enemy, the devil."[54]

Milingo's views of the presence of evil spirits ran contrary to modern Catholic orthodoxy. Even a priest as sympathetic to Milingo as his one-time secretary Hugo F. Hinfelaar would later write, "The Church holds that a steady faith in Christ as the Son of God is incompatible with an equal belief in the power of evil spirits. . . . Faith in Christ makes the presence in a hidden, let alone stronger, power irrelevant."[55] Such formal Catholic denial of the presence of spiritual evil and the ability to rid the world of such spiritual evil contributed to a sense of disappointment and disillusionment with the established churches.

Milingo adapted a Zambian vocabulary to the spiritual battle between good and evil. He termed the spirits *mashawe*, which referred to foreign spirits, and were commonly found in possession cults among the Shona in Zimbabwe.[56] In this sense, he extended the ideas first developed by Lenshina, who perceived the vernacular spirit world as an evil that could be cleansed by God and Jesus. He acknowledged the beneficent role of some indigenous ancestral spirits, or "guardian" spirits, but argued that Christian conversion involved the replacement of such ancestral spirits with Jesus and God, who alone were responsible for the battle against evil. "The living-dead ancestors are cultured and well-mannered people. They will give way when Jesus comes in, provided that Jesus guarantees protection and guardianship to the living members of the clan and tribes. . . . We are marrying Jesus with our ancestors."[57] Milingo thereby made the presence of God crucial to efforts to cleanse the world of spiritual affliction.

Spirit possession had a gendered and even sexual component. Not only were women disproportionately possessed by the spirits, but the spirits were said to have literally "married" women. Another faith healer and prominent supporter of Milingo, a Baptist Church minister and chairman of the Zambia Evangelical Association, Rev. Malekeni Mulimine, was told by the spirits that they frequented Zambia because Zambian women were so beautiful. He claimed that if a woman had agreed to marry such a spirit, he could cast the spirit out, but only after a struggle. Christian women, he emphasized, were less susceptible to such possession.[58]

Despite the need for and popularity of such spiritual healing, Milingo faced pressure from bishops inside and outside of Zambia to end his healing ministry. On 25 February 1979, he held his final healing session. According to press reports, some four thousand people attended, forcing the service outside the Roma Cathedral and into the churchyard. To the disapproval of the crowd, Milingo announced that he had been directed to end his healing sessions. As he did not want scandal and division in the church, he had agreed. Nearly half the audience of mostly women was possessed by "demons and evil spirits," as Milingo and his helpers exorcised them for the last time.[59] The letter columns of the *Times of Zambia* were inundated with complaints against those expatriate clergy who had stopped Milingo's healing sessions. Mr. Chimbalang'ondo of Kabwe, who was paralyzed by *mashawe* spirits, wrote that he was "shocked at decision of Milingo to stop healing. . . . As a Christian I am not convinced the bishop's [sic] decision is fair. Bishops you are unfair to us, the sick. Some of us believe in the power of Christ and we don't want to go to the witch-doctors for healing. Now you have stopped us going to Milingo. . . . Kindly explain why you made such an inconsiderate decision."[60] Those who had already been healed by Milingo expressed dismay at the decision. One hundred women who had been healed by Milingo sent a petition to the Catholic secretariat, insisting that they stop "persecuting" Milingo.[61] Many thought that the European clergy were jealous of Milingo's healing powers and had thus ordered him to end his healing ministry.[62]

The expansion of Milingo's healing mission took place during a decade of increasing political authoritarianism and disenchantment with humanism. Milingo's first healings occurred in 1973, the year of the declaration of the one-party state and immediately following the crackdown on Kapwepwe's UPP. They spread as Kaunda and UNIP aggressively promoted humanism, yet the nation was thrown into economic turmoil by rising oil prices and falling copper prices. And toward the end of the 1970s, Zambians came under military attack from the settler regimes of Rhodesia and South Africa. Disillusionment with the nationalist vision, the inability to resolve the individual-social relationships despite the moral proclamations of humanism, the uneven economic and social benefits of the postcolonial state, and even Zambia's precarious regional and international position, all encouraged Zambians in their quest for individual salvation through the purification of evil spirits.[63] However, popular perceptions that the government, with the aid of the established churches, had reined in those who could deal with spiritual malaise led to the greatest emotional dissatisfaction. By the 1980s, Zambians thought that they would have to combat secular powers directly if they were to eradicate the spiritual evil that afflicted them. *Cleansing and combating spiritual evil would involve a direct political struggle.* The struggle between UNIP, the churches, and the trade union movement in the early 1980s illustrates how political struggles became entwined with spiritual ones.

STRIKES AND SPIRITS

In 1980–1981, the UNIP attempted to incorporate and subordinate the Zambia Congress of Trade Unions (ZCTU). When the unions resisted by dismissing shop stewards who competed in UNIP ward elections, Kaunda dismissed ZCTU's leadership, including its general secretary, Frederick Chiluba. Zambian workers then embarked on the most widespread and economically harmful strikes since independence. Only through a program of co-option and repression, which included the detention of the ZCTU leadership, did Kaunda manage to contain the strikes. Nevertheless, ZCTU had proved that it would remain autonomous from UNIP and act as a check on UNIP through the 1980s. The strike of 1981 is conventionally regarded as a significant manifestation of popular urban opposition to Kaunda's regime, which culminated a decade later in multiparty elections and the landslide victory, especially on the Copperbelt, by Chiluba's Movement for Multiparty Democracy (MMD) in the first multiparty elections of 1991.[64]

As in the 1930s and 1940s, declining real wages lay behind worker dissatisfaction at the outset of the 1980s. But workers were not simply concerned with wages. Their most vocal grievance, and the issue over which they came to clash with Kaunda, was their autonomy. Workers wanted to ensure that the union movement remained autonomous from UNIP. On the other hand, UNIP militants insisted on the unification of all organs of government in an Orwellian-termed policy, "decentralisation." By combining party position with local administration, which had previously been managed independently, the unions would lose their ability to bargain independently from UNIP. Workers thus opposed "decentralisation." The Mineworkers Union of Zambia (MUZ) prohibited its officials from participating in party elections; they expelled ten members who did so, much to the distress of UNIP officials. In retaliation, UNIP expelled seventeen union leaders from UNIP and withdrew their passports, including Chiluba. Since the officeholders had to be UNIP members, the legal effect was to dismiss the leading unionists from their official positions.[65]

Zambian workers remained steadfast behind their leaders, especially Chiluba, whom they viewed as uncompromising martyrs to their struggle. When the union leadership was expelled from UNIP, workers embarked on a series of strikes across a range of industries (156 strikes with 556,408 man-days lost), which were a blow to an increasingly fragile and indebted Zambian economy.[66] While there were material interests in the insistence on union autonomy, there were other paths to ensure better wages and conditions: Why not, for example, work within UNIP and thereby influence wage policy? To a certain extent, the inspiration for a strong and autonomous union derived from regional and international ideological currents. Zambian newspapers reported daily on the Polish union, Solidarity, which supported workers and opposed the Polish Communist Party. Yet, as in Poland, churches, as the last vestiges of autonomous civil society, inspired new moral directions and strategies. Zambian workers were disenchanted with humanism and UNIP's program of development, and mobilized alternate moral discourses. Christian arguments focused on development and activism independent of the party, that the definition of "good" was not tied to official humanist ideology, but to the Christian and biblical injunctions. Examine, for example, this worker's complaint to the Times of Zambia:

> The action taken by MUZ shop stewards is justified. Those who call themselves Christians and believe in the bible and all that the bible teaches cannot blame MUZ officials for the action they took. There is a verse in the bible which states clearly that man cannot serve two masters. He must either worship God or the demon, not both. MUZ, like any other union, represents the interests of the miners.[67]

The break with humanism was not complete, however, especially for leaders of secular institutions. Before 1981, public Christian pronouncements by secular leaders were rare. Instead, humanism guided public morality in areas traditionally considered to be in the secular sphere. When it did appear, Christianity seemed somewhat veiled, a force from below rather than above, and espoused only rarely by leaders. Prior to 1980, Chiluba, for example, did not cite Christian inspirations and instead described his political philosophy as a "pragmatism" that works for the "betterment of man."[68] Such "pragmatism" was a direct challenge to the idealism of humanism. Nevertheless, in its progressive and secular vision it shared aspects of Zambian humanism, and contrasted with the explicit Christian philosophy that Chiluba introduced in years to come.

The controversy between the churches and UNIP over scientific socialism would change the secular orientation of oppositional politics.[69] Previously, the mainline churches and the state had a fairly good relationship, agreeing to collaborate on projects of national development under the rubric of humanism. In the early 1970s, they clashed over the enactment of an abortion law, the Termination of Pregnancy Act of 1972, which was seen to benefit young men and the male elite. Archbishop Milingo, representing the views of many Zambian women, vocally opposed the legislation. The promotion within UNIP of an authoritarian form of socialism, which they termed "scientific socialism," began, however, to draw the clergy, including Milingo, into a direct confrontation with the state. Fearful of tendencies to deny Christianity and God's moral guidance in the world, and even perhaps the freedom of worship, the three major church bodies published a pamphlet in 1979, *Marxism, Humanism and Christianity: A Letter from the Leaders of the Christian Churches to All Their Members about Scientific Socialism*. In the pamphlet, church leaders attempted to dissociate humanism from scientific socialism, especially given the tendency of the latter to deny religion as a legitimate spiritual experience guided by the clergy.[70] Occurring at the same time as the curtailment of Milingo's exorcisms, Zambians began to associate scientific socialism's denial of God with the denial of Milingo's healing sessions. Conspiratorial, perhaps satanic, forces were depriving them of opportunities for dealing with spiritual malaise.

When the UNIP National Council proved reluctant to formally endorse scientific socialism, radical cadres advocated for its introduction as a high school subject, which they imagined would lead to greater support for a socialist program.[71] Instead, this issue ignited further Christian opposition to UNIP. Christianity increasingly became an alternative ideology to the more repressive tendencies of humanism, or at the very least Christianity was posed as that element of humanism that protected individual rights.[72] In the immediate aftermath of the mine workers' strike, a prominent Christian leader who was also the chairman of the board of the *National Mirror* and general manager of Barclays Bank, Francis Nkhoma, argued:

> Christians should feel free to speak out whenever they felt that the fundamental rights of the people were threatened by politicians and other leaders. . . . Christians [should] expose the underlying tendencies by some leaders towards socialism at the expense of the liberty and fundamental rights of the people. To this effect measures must be taken to ensure that the freedom of the individual was held sacrosanct.[73]

Nkhoma also criticized one of UNIP's most respected intellectuals, Henry S. Meebelo, for blaming Zambia's economic ills on capitalism.[74] The *National Mirror* carried a series of articles on "The True Zambian Humanism," which opposed the scientific socialist version of humanism espoused in the "Humanist Corner" of the government (or party?)-run *Times of Zambia*, written by Joseph Musole, one of the leading advocates for scientific socialism.[75] The *National Mirror*'s editorial declared:

> There are unfortunately in our midst today those who have chosen to hijack Zambian Humanism and give it the ideological mantle of Soviet Russia, the leading monolithic communist state in which men are forcibly held down and their dignity and everything else are relative to the state. . . . Those Party members using public media to indulge in platitudes, doublespeak or pretentious obscurantism should SHUT UP. (emphasis in original)[76]

Injustice began to be linked to scientific socialism. Willie Sakala of Kabwe asked, "Why should people be detained for having different opinions? Is this what we call democracy or is it Scientific Socialism type of democracy?" Conversely, justice and morality emerged from the teachings of Jesus. Sakala went on to question whether it was hypocritical to accuse apartheid South Africa of injustice, since "we should sweep our country clean first. . . . Jesus said 'Why see the speck in your friend's eye without taking out the one in your eye first?'"[77]

Elements within UNIP, encouraged by ideological currents in southern Africa's liberation movements, reacted by further affirming the principles of Marxist-Leninism. Activists attempted to prove the popularity of UNIP by increasing party membership. Party militants insisted on the purchase of party cards, much as they had during other moments of contestation. The party card signified patriotism and belonging to the nationalist vision. A card-checking campaign in Ndola was aimed at "rooting out undesirable elements in view of the current wrangle between the Party and the labour movement over the decentralisation issue. . . . The Party would now adopt methods used during Zambia's independence struggle." The campaign involved the youth wing of the party at all markets, bus stations, bars, and homes.[78] Those who did not purchase the cards were traitors, subverted by racist South African agents to destabilize Zambia.

Kaunda mediated between these radical party activists and those who espoused Christian humanism. Using his missionary background to his advantage, Kaunda tried to demonstrate the consistency between humanism and Christianity. To church concerns that humanism placed man at the center of existence instead of God, an editorial on Kenneth Kaunda's fifty-seventh birthday in 1981 replied that under Zambian humanism, "man is a spiritual being."[79] Holding talks with the US envoy to the region, Chester Crocker,

Kaunda emphasized the Christian basis of resistance to apartheid.[80] He also attempted to co-opt the Catholic and mainline Protestant churches by appointing leading Catholic and Protestant clergy to government and party positions, and making a select few his personal advisers.[81] Politicians took their place next to clergy at church gatherings and espoused the need for collaboration. For example, Kaunda addressed Catholics alongside Archbishop Milingo, and told them to combine "good works" with "faith," an appeal to cooperate with programs of national development.[82] Kaunda affirmed the church as one of the "pillars" of the nation and even praised the role of the early missionaries.

Mainstream church leaders and scholars tended to argue that humanism built on Christian principles. "The religious dimension is something that permeates the entire political philosophy of Zambian humanism through and through," claimed the Zambian theologian Clive M. Dillon-Malone.[83] The socialist-inclined members of UNIP, perhaps under pressure from Kaunda, backed down. Even Henry S. Meebelo acknowledged that, "according to Zambian Humanism, the spiritual is prior to the material."[84] In reply to a question as to why Zambia should have scientific socialism, Mainza Chona, then prime minister and a respected Catholic, replied, "This is like asking why we should have Christianity in the country. It is the way to heaven."[85] At an Anglican ceremony, the succeeding prime minister, Nalimuno Mundia, dismissed arguments by some "Zambian intellectuals and theologians" that humanism was a cover for Marxism: "No philosophy . . . is better equipped to serve mankind than Humanism," he told the clergy. In response to Mundia's arguments, Bishop Stephen Mumba affirmed his church's loyalty to the party and government, and yet in a message addressed to Kaunda insisted that "criticism from the Church should be seen as a patriotic effort to right some of the evils of society. . . . Patriotism which did not discriminate between right and wrong was not true patriotism."[86] Christianity had emerged as an autonomous and potentially oppositional discourse. In the early 1980s, the previously secular-oriented trade union leader Frederick Chiluba began to regularly attend church to indicate his opposition to scientific socialism.[87]

The most interesting critique, a signal of what was to emerge in the late 1980s, came from ordinary Zambians struggling against spiritual evil. Scientific socialism itself had become satanic, not because of its claims for economic justice, but because it denied people's ability to combat spiritual evil. Chama John Powell of Ndola insisted:

We are against the infringement of freedom by Marx's satanic doctrinal principles. I am more Marxist than Marx himself. Marx's principles, for example, equalitarianism, are very much in line with our born-philosophy—"Christianity." But he goes far by denying God's existence and furthermore indoctrinating his staunch followers to regard faith in God as an opium.[88]

Many Zambians were concerned with the denial of God. They complained of too much "political" programming on the Zambian broadcasting services, and not enough attention to "spiritual programs."[89] Both Kaunda and the mainline clergy ruminated on the "evils of society," but not the evils of the spirit world that afflicted the individual. It was at the most immediate and personal level that Zambians felt the need for spiritual intervention. The mainline clergy refused to acknowledge the presence of Satan, and, even worse, the scientific socialists denied the presence of God, the most effective way to combat individual afflictions. For many Zambians, Satan had indeed infiltrated the land.

The final straw in this denial of spiritual agency was the Vatican's recall of Archbishop Emmanuel Milingo in May 1982 for a period of respite, reflection, and theological training. The press, reflecting widespread Zambian sentiment, contended that Milingo's recall was engineered by racist white clergy, perhaps with the consent of the Zambian government, who feared such an independent rival. And even if UNIP did not actually conspire to exile Milingo, UNIP's unwillingness to intervene on his behalf demonstrated their culpability.[90] "Is it a sin to cast out demons in the name of the Lord?" a letter to the *Times of Zambia* asked. "It seems there is a conspiracy to make the Archbishop mad. Is it because he is against scientific socialism? If someone is declared mad for speaking the truth, is that fair?"[91] Similarly, an opinion piece in the *Sunday Times of Zambia* compared the treatment of Milingo to the crucifixion of Christ: "As Jesus was deprived one of his disciples, Peter, the Zambia Episcopal Conference and the Party have washed their hands of Archbishop Milingo who is being held in virtual detention in a monastery in the Vatican. Why? The mind boggles. . . . Has there been a conspiracy between the throne of St. Peter in the Vatican and the local church and state authorities?"[92] Milingo's recall to Rome indicated a conspiracy by the state and established clergy to get rid of a rival who had the potential to heal ordinary Zambians.

Many Zambians maintained that spirits affected the living—and they thought that their government should support them in dealing with the afflictions of the spirits. The curtailment of Milingo's healing mission in 1979 and his recall to Rome in 1982 took place at the same time as the promulgation of a more aggressive and materialist version of humanism based on scientific socialism, and as the Zambian state failed to meet the expectations of its citizenry. Humanism, especially when influenced by scientific socialism, denied people the ability to deal with the harm that evil spirits caused in the individual. Social and economic distress made such spiritual malaise evident. And the established clergy, including the Catholic Church, denied the presence of this evil. For many Zambians, Kaunda and UNIP's unwillingness to intervene in the Milingo affair demonstrated that they cared little for the spiritual well-being of people and that they feared or were jealous of Milingo's healing powers.

↩

By the 1980s, Zambian humanism was already a hollow-sounding philosophy to impoverished Zambians who searched for a way to control the invisible forces that affected their lives. Humanism had not dealt with the problem of spiritual evil, in the same fashion that the mission churches from which humanism had inherited its moral reformism had failed to deal with the problem of witchcraft. Like the mission churches, humanism viewed evil and sin as a moral problem, antisocial behavior that had to be corrected and reformed, rather than evidence of spiritual evil. The slogan "God in heaven, Kaunda on earth" contradicted the experiences of people who felt the agency of spirits in the world. Scientific socialists seemed especially nefarious since they denied the presence of all spirits, even God, in the world of the living and the dead. Even the mainline church leaders who criticized the scientific socialist tendencies within humanism underestimated the fervor with which many Zambians opposed such ideas. Political and religious leaders had abandoned their attempts to intervene in the spirit world, and many Zambians felt a profound sense of disempowerment.

With rising socioeconomic dissatisfaction, the spiritual dimensions of evil were increasingly viewed in terms of a public debate about the righteousness of Kaunda's rule. The inability or unwillingness of Kaunda's government to prevent Milingo's exile, along with the reluctance of the mainline churches to rid people of evil spirits, convinced many that spirits had to become a matter of state politics. The Pentecostal movement, examined in the next chapter, would most convincingly link this problem of spiritual evil to the welfare of the nation. Just as the individual needed to be possessed by the Holy Spirit and be born again, so did the nation. But before the individual and the nation could be born again, those who, under the influence of Satan, had denied God and Christ's agency needed to be born again. And if they failed to open themselves to the Holy Spirit, the state itself would have to be captured. In other words, the road to spiritual empowerment traversed the political kingdom.

8 ᔒ A Nation Reborn

IN 1981, the South African–based faith healer and evangelist Reinhard Bonnke, founder of Christ for All Nations (CfAN), planned a crusade in Zambia. He liaised with existing church networks and sent "prayer warriors" to prepare for mass conversions and healing sessions. For two weeks that July, Zambians flocked to the ten-thousand-person tent in Lusaka to hear Bonnke's preaching and to experience his healing. "Indeed, miracles have been happening this week," declared an editorial in the Christian weekly, the *National Mirror*. "Empty wheelchairs and excited faces, which have regained sight after long periods of blindness, were tangible evidence of miracles. Dozens of people claim they have been healed spiritually while others say demons have left them." The editorial endorsed Bonnke's healing mission and thanked those who brought him to Zambia: "CfAN is fulfilling Christ's message of nearly 2000 years ago: 'Go ye into the world and preach the Gospel to every creature. . . . And these signs shall follow them that believe. In my name they shall cast out devils . . . They shall lay hands on the sick and they shall recover' (Mark 16:15–18)."[1] Bonnke's intercessions with the spirit world contrasted with the denial of spiritual agency by the scientific socialists and humanists of Kaunda's regime. The only disappointment expressed in the *National Mirror*'s editorial was that Zambians did not have their own preachers who could perform such miracles, a clear reference to the curtailment of Archbishop Milingo's healing ministry and a call to a new generation of Zambians who were empowered by the Holy Spirit.[2]

Bonnke's rallies did inspire a cohort of young Zambian born-again Christians who had already been studying and propagating an evangelical revival.[3] Following the crusade, Bonnke paid for his translator, Nevers Mumba, to attended Bible college at Christ for the Nations in Dallas, Texas. After Mumba's 1984 graduation, he returned to Zambia to inaugurate a series of Victory Bible churches, a Bible college in Kitwe, and to embark on crusades with prominent international speakers.[4] The future bishop of the Pentecostal Assemblies of God in Lusaka, Joshua Banda, was a councilor for CfAN in Zambia. In 1982, he studied for a degree at Northwest University (Kirkland, Washington, USA), before he became the founding principal of Trans-Africa Theological Bible College in Kitwe, Zambia. He envisaged Zambia as a Christian stronghold in a battle against a Muslim advance across Africa.[5] After attending Bible colleges in Kenya and the United Kingdom, Joseph Imakando, future head of the Evangelical Fellowship of Zambia (EFZ), the umbrella body for most Pentecostal and charismatic churches, organized the popular Bread of Life Ministries in Lusaka, promising prosperity to urban Zambians desperate for a sign that God had not abandoned their "expectations of modernity," even if anthropologists had.[6] A young Pentecostal missionary of German origins, Helmut Reutter, worked with the Zambian Apostolic Faith Mission for ten years, before branching out to form Chreso Ministries and the Gospel Outreach (GO) center in Lusaka.[7] These are only a sampling of the many Pentecostal leaders who emerged during the 1980s across urban Zambia.

The evangelical Christian advance from the 1970s was a global phenomenon, occurring across the Americas, Asia, and Africa. While it has become commonplace to reflect on the evangelical influence on US politics—where they provided activists for the conservative wing of the Republican Party—their influence on politics in other parts of the world remains little understood and mired in preconceptions drawn from the US example. Certain aspects of evangelical politics associated with US conservative causes such as anti-abortion and the restriction of homosexual rights give the impression that Pentecostalism in Africa is simply an import of the US "religious right."[8] Yet the politics of the African Pentecostalism has not been limited to such right-wing causes. Their broader political influences need to be considered afresh in each context since evangelical Christianity engaged with different political and religious cultures. Even while they have formed strategic alliances with Western conservative Christians, their politics cannot be lumped together with them.

In an edited collection published in 2008, Terence O. Ranger and a cohort of African scholars (a few of them evangelicals) argue that evangelicals have formed a distinctive African civil society. In his introduction to the volume, Ranger argues that an "evangelical democratic culture" fostered democratic *participation*, as opposed to the straightforward *opposition* to authoritarian regimes typical of many churches. According to the contributors to the volume, the engaging and personal nature of the evangelical experience may have inspired a democratic culture that goes beyond the conventional opposition to political authoritarianism fostered by mainline Christian networks.[9] They also associate Pentecostalism in Africa with a new Protestant ethic. Pentecostal churches, with their focus on the prosperity gospel, on an engaged and "purpose-driven" life, on individuality, and on the avoidance of conspicuous consumption, encourage the growth of an autonomous middle class that can assert itself against state elites. A recent synthesis report on Pentecostalism in South Africa similarly concludes by celebrating the role that Pentecostal churches have played in "protecting the social fabric from further decay, and giving people who are otherwise sidelined in our society a sense of purpose and mission."[10] Pentecostalism, in this view, has provided a framework, an ideology, and an inspiration for participation both in politics and in the free market neoliberal order.

Paul Gifford, in his many studies of the public role of African Christianity, has offered a more cautionary interpretation. Gifford's analysis points to how Pentecostalism may obfuscate social relations and real structural forms of exploitation. Not only is the "prosperity gospel" (or "faith gospel") profoundly disempowering in the sense that it advocates a rather naive faith in faith alone as the path to prosperity, but the new Christianity also does not necessarily involve a reformulation of civil society, personal morality, and consciousness (even while it claims to do so). Cultural impacts are probably overstated: many people go to church for enjoyment, to meet friends, for the excellent music, and for the excitement of services. Even if the churches are involved in cultural changes, these have had little effect on the broader forces influencing African societies, or so Gifford implies. The new churches have not been able to overcome or replace existing social identities and practices, such as ethnicity and clientelism, which still structure and saturate African political and civil society—in fact, they often replicate such practices. While Gifford acknowledges that there exists the potential for evangelical Christianity to critique forms of exploitation, he argues that it is misleading to claim that the new evangelical movement empowers an autonomous and democratic civil society.[11] Similarly, rather than a celebration of women's leadership roles, recent literature has pointed to a more sober assessment of the complicated gender dynamics in the new Pentecostal churches.[12]

Whether scholars wish to celebrate or criticize the potentials of the new Christianity, their analyses have to be better located in place and time. At first glance, the Zambian case would seem to support the argument for Pentecostalism's role in promoting democratization and the transition to free market capitalism. Zambian Pentecostals claim that they were at the forefront of bringing an end to Kaunda's socialist regime. They also claim to have promoted prosperity for their members and churches, which have become some of the wealthiest indigenous corporations in Zambia today. Zambian scholars are more cautious. While Isabel Apawo Phiri suggests that evangelicals may have contributed to political activism, Austin M. Cheyeka argues that "charismatic" churches have offered "uncritical loyalty" to government, in contrast to an older "church cooperation which always took a critical stand in public affairs."[13] Critics point to the fact that even if the Pentecostal movement played a role in the coming to power of Frederick Chiluba, the Christian leader of Zambia's transition to multiparty politics in 1991, the government of Chiluba became mired in corruption and fraught with authoritarian tendencies. The promises of Chiluba's "Christian nation" were never delivered. Despite its claims, Pentecostalism was not the harbinger of a vibrant civil society, free market prosperity, and democratic politics. It seems that in Zambia, as elsewhere, the new Christianity has exhibited tendencies that encouraged both democratic engagement and patrimonial authoritarianism.[14]

Scholarship on Pentecostalism and the new evangelical churches argues that a new Protestant ethic is driving the creation of capitalism in the developing world.[15] In Zambia, Pentecostalism produced spiritual interventions aligned with a neoliberal order; it was not, however, a Weberian Protestant ethic, precisely because of the dominance of spirits within this Pentecostal ethic. Pentecostalism offered opportunities for church members to invoke spiritual agencies in the neoliberal environment, to intervene in the prospects of business ventures in the here and now, rather than the promises of a heavenly afterlife. As Jean Comaroff and John L. Comaroff point out, the "neo-protestant" ethic is not content to wait for the rewards of afterlife, but instead seeks to separate salvation from saving.[16]

The emphasis on success in this Pentecostal ethic overcame older moralities of individual sacrifice tied to mission Christianity and to Kaunda's humanism. This morality of success highlighted the power of personal transformation in the presence of the Holy Spirit. Through Pentecostalism, many Zambians engaged with the transition from a socialist society in which the party reigned supreme to a capitalist society in which God exerted sovereignty. Zambia's neoliberal transformation was welcomed as a Pentecostal spiritual rebirth. Like the liberal's celebration of the agency of the invisible hand, however, the celebration of the agency of the Holy Spirit did not necessarily lead to the actual emergence of a wealthy and autonomous middle class. Pentecostalism encouraged individuals to view their lives and their actions anew, but often in ways that mimicked deep-seated historical patterns.

Zambian Pentecostals wanted to rid the world of evil spirits, to defeat those who used spirits to bewitch others, and to harness the Holy Spirit to achieve prosperity. These ideas spread beyond the diverse collection of evangelical churches to Protestants and even to Roman Catholics. Through new media, especially independent Christian television broadcasts, Pentecostal spiritual beliefs empowered Zambians and directed their political agency. At first, like many of the other movements discussed in the book, evangelical Christians distanced themselves from state politics, but increasingly through the late 1980s, they confronted it directly. By insisting on an autonomous relationship with God, Pentecostals offered an alternative morality to humanism. In part, Kaunda's regime succumbed to a revolution based on these Pentecostal ideas. Instead of leading to a neoliberal multiparty democracy that entrenched individual rights, however, a politics of spiritual patrimonialism emerged. Blessing in this world devolved from prophets who had access to the spirit world. Those who sought power in this world, in the form of wealth or political influence, had to cultivate relationships with the spirit world through a new class of Pentecostal "big men" and "big women."

THE GROWTH OF ZAMBIAN PENTECOSTALISM
SINCE THE 1970S

In the 1970s a new Pentecostal movement in Zambia superseded the established Pentecostal churches that grew from missionary efforts following the Pentecostal revivals of the early twentieth century. Internal and external agents promoted the new Pentecostalism. Internally, a student-run movement in high schools called the Scripture Union met at least once a week to discuss the Bible and readings termed "Daily Power," published by the Scripture Union headquarters in Kitwe. On the weekends, the students organized evangelical campaigns in their communities. At the end of each school semester, Student Union groups held weeklong Bible camps at the homes of like-minded missionaries, where they met members of the Scripture Union from across the country. The Scripture Union at Hillcrest School in Livingstone was especially influential. Here, future luminaries in Zambia's Pentecostal movement met: the vice president of Zambia and Victory Ministries founder Nevers Mumba; the minister of information and head of Trinity Broadcasting Network and Dunamis Ministries, Dan Pule; and the head of Northmead Assemblies of God, Bishop Joshua Banda. Members of the Scripture Union fellowship further consolidated their ties during compulsory national military service in the late 1970s. After national service, the same young men took part in the formation of Christian fellowships at the University of Zambia.[17]

The external forces that contributed to the Pentecostal expansion began with a seven-day Billy Graham crusade in 1967 and culminated in the popular crusades of Reinhard Bonnke in the 1980s. The international crusades inspired widespread participation by Zambians in the Pentecostal movement. The young leaders who had met and trained in the Scripture Union movement found that they had both international patrons and an eager local clientele. After studying in Bible colleges in South Africa or the United States, they pastored their own churches. The interaction between the international crusades, the popular demand for healing and prosperity, and existing student movements gave shape to Pentecostalism in Zambia.

Charismatic tendencies within Catholic and mainline Protestant churches also began to appear, provoking vigorous discussion and dissent. Archbishop Milingo had a history of ties to the charismatic renewal movement going back to at least 1976. In 1981, despite the curtailment of his healing ministry, he held discussions with Gideon Simwanga's evangelical and interdenominational "Operation Rescue Group for Ministry of Christ."[18] In the mainline Protestant churches, youth movements became the most vocal supporters of charismatic worship.[19] In the United Church of Zambia (UCZ), the 1980 formation of the Christian youth movement led to charismatic worship, much to the consternation of the UCZ leadership, which by 1987 had "banned" all youth fellowship groups.[20] The language used by the general secretary of UCZ, Joel Chisanga, indicated the threat that this youthful rebellion posed to established forms of governmental and church authority:

> Because of the rudeness of young people due to the misinterpretation of the Doctrine of Regeneration, the Ministry of National Guidance is collecting facts with a view to identifying the expatriate culprits who are brain-washing Zambians and making them unpatriotic citizens of this nation. For example: A certain so called "Born Again" Youth came to me the other day and told me point blank that because he was a new being in Christ, he would not be in a position to mix freely with sinners or accept the advice of his sinful parents. He further stated that he would also be reluctant to share meals with those who are not born again, for fear of contamination. (emphasis in original)[21]

Through the 1980s and early 1990s, UCZ headquarters resisted charismatic renewal, dissociating themselves from the proliferation of youth fellowships that propagated charismatic practices. In the most significant breakaway from the mainstream UCZ, the UCZ youth wing established Grace Ministries in 1993.[22] Only in the late 1990s, under popular pressure and the influence of then president Chiluba, did the UCZ decide to embrace charismatic worship.[23]

The youth not only rejected the established mainline churches; they rejected their families as well. In one interview after the next, Pentecostals described how they had to defy their parents to be born again. For example, in the words of an Assemblies of God elder, Gibstar Makangila, on his decision to leave the Anglican Church of his father:

I went through persecution in the home. My father was proud of me in all areas—I was clever at school, good boy, everything. But in 1983, he said for the first time I disappointed him by leaving his church, which was our church as a clan, and joined this church of young people. . . . On one particular evening just before an exam, my dad came, he was a bit drunk, and he called me. He said if I don't renounce that church I was going to cease to be his child. Now, he meant well, but they were strong words. . . . Then I picked up the Bible, and flipped the Bible. I turned to a portion in the Gospels where Christ said that if you follow me you may have to reject father, reject mother. I continued reading until I came to another passage that said, "Blessed be you when men persecute you for my namesake." That is how the Lord spoke to me that night, and that issue didn't even matter because God had spoken to it. From then on I've been very zealous.[24]

That these churches were composed of zealous youth explains why there was not a sudden decline in the membership of other mainline churches as the Pentecostals increased in number. Parents remained with their old churches; their children turned to the Pentecostal churches. By the mid-1980s, evangelical churches still represented a minority of Zambian Christians. Yet they were the most youthful and popular churches in Zambia's urban centers, spreading from the Copperbelt to Lusaka, and composed of the middle-class and working-class elite.

As the student leaders became pastors, they changed from Pentecostal youth to Pentecostal "big men."[25] These big men, and in several cases big women, acquired their authority and influence by linking to international Christian networks while at the same time promoting their local churches. All of the prominent urban leaders had international training in Bible colleges or universities in South Africa, the United Kingdom, or the United States. Connections with prominent Nigerian and South African preachers provided a pan-African dimension to the Pentecostal networks. In some cases, such as that of Nevers Mumba, the ability to draw on international Christian networks to organize big-name crusades provided the substance of authority. For others, such as Prophetess Elfrida Mhusambazi of Barak Ministries, the growth of the church was linked to the careful cultivation of a local following, with occasional support from prominent US or Nigerian evangelists.[26]

The lack of national and international hierarchies meant that there were remarkable opportunities for Pentecostal big men and big women to advance their positions through international connections. A church could accept funds for specific projects without subordinating itself to international hierarchies or agendas, at least compared to mainline churches that retained control over church positions. Despite boasting of international connections, Nevers Mumba prided himself on not "living on handouts," which would lead to international control over the church. "Such ungodly control is the devil's principle," Mumba wrote.[27] National affiliations also reflected the lack of hierarchical control. Either most of the churches became affiliated with the EFZ, established in 1964, or they joined the Independent Church Organization of Zambia (ICOZ) after it was established in 2001. However, they remained autonomous in matters concerning their individual churches.[28] By the late 1980s and especially in the 1990s, hundreds of independent Pentecostal and charismatic churches appeared in Zambia's urban areas.

Within the individual churches, patrimonial and hierarchical relationships developed. With the proliferation of titles, greater possibilities for numerous positions in these church structures appeared. For each prophet or prophetess, there could be several apostles, then bishops, then pastors, then evangelists, teachers, and elders. There was an inflationary pressure on the titles: as more pastors appeared, their value diminished. More leaders wanted to be bishops, then apostles, and so on. This contributed to unstable hierarchies that needed to be maintained by patrimonial relationships. In older churches, such as the Evangelical Church of Zambia, constitutional governance and regular elections had long been a standard feature of church organization.[29] In many of the new churches led by these inspirational figures, however, democratic practices gave way to patrimonial ones. In such churches members professed absolute loyalty to the founding figure for their spiritual gifts and for their material help.[30] As Gifford speculates, the nature of these Pentecostal leaders may have replicated that of other political elites.[31]

The Pentecostal big man or big woman had a spiritual role, but he or she was not tied to doctrine or to any doctrinaire form of Christianity. Pastor Reutter claimed that his church was "not interested in religion"; instead, it was about personal relationship with God.[32] The heads of the two principal umbrella bodies that represented Pentecostal and charismatic churches in Zambia, the EFZ and the ICOZ, expressed little interest in matters of church doctrine.[33] Church was there only to ignite the personal relationship with God. Of course, there were certain people, the pastors and prophets, who could provide the fuel that best sustained this passionate relationship.

While a church title could be striking, it was only as impressive as the size and wealth of a church's following. Churches targeted sections of civil society that ensured followings substantial in numbers and in wealth. Cultivating a membership composed of students at the University of Zambia guaranteed that future prominent members of Zambian society would form part of their churches. In the late 1980s, Pentecostal students broke away from the mainline Protestant University Christian Fellowship and the Zambia Fellowship of Evangelical Students to form a Chi Alpha campus fellowship. Soon after, prominent Lusaka churches established their own student fellowships on campus. The Northmead Assemblies of God, led by the academically inclined Bishop Banda, became popular with the students. By the 1980s, the secular student activist Owen Sichone lamented that the "'Born Again Full Gospel Breakfast' type of commercialized evangelism, with its unashamedly capitalist values," was everywhere on campus.[34] As the students graduated, they became influential members of Zambian society and their churches.[35] Other churches focused on aspirant businesspeople, holding seminars and prayer meetings to remove curses on businesses and to ensure entrepreneurial success. With the support of a few successful businesspeople and a following of numerous aspirants, church finances were secured.[36]

As the bankrupt Zambian state withdrew from providing basic education and health care to Zambians, churches augmented followings by providing such services. Most of the churches provided healing clinics and sometimes even hospitals. Some of them even distributed condoms and promoted the use of antiretroviral therapy for HIV-positive Christians. Prophetess Mhusambazi began Barak Ministries with healing and counseling centers focused on sick Zambians.[37] Churches established orphanages for the children of parents who died of AIDS. They offered some of the finest schools in Lusaka (Northmead Assemblies of God boasted that the minister of education sent his children to their school). Churches also established connections with secular international aid organizations. For example, Pastor Reutter of the Chreso Ministries Gospel Outreach (GO) center was a frequent recipient of German aid for his health initiatives. Once established, the reputation of a church further encouraged such connections (Laura Bush visited the GO center's clinic to demonstrate US commitment to antiretroviral distribution).[38] American Pentecostals helped to promote Christian education in the schools. The churches engaged directly with international aid organizations, sidestepping the state in the provision of health and educational services. The clinics, schools, and orphanages in turn provided the churches with devout members, indebted to their pastors and patrons. In privatizing the social services provided previously by the state, the churches fueled neoliberal transformations.

These strategies to generate followings led to a rapid increase in the influence of Pentecostal churches. In the early 1990s, Gifford estimated a relatively modest number of urban born-again churches.[39] By the late 1990s, the number had increased dramatically: one estimate put Pentecostals at 10 percent of the Zambian population, or 43 percent if we include the broader evangelical and charismatic categories (almost half of the total 85 percent of Christians).[40] Even if a far more modest number is estimated, however, the Pentecostal and charismatic churches were composed of wealthy urbanites. Compared to other denominations, their influence exceeded their overall membership due to the wealth, resources, and enthusiasm of their followers. As other autonomous organs of civil society such as the trade unions weakened in the face of the onslaught of the party and the collapse of state-run enterprises, Pentecostal fellowships of believers became the most influential component of civil society.[41] This civil society was characterized by patron-client relationships, rather than more democratic forms of organization. In this respect, Gifford's cautionary arguments about the prospects of the new evangelicals for democratization may be more apt than Ranger's optimism. However, the promotion of democracy may be an inappropriate yardstick to measure the political efficacy of Pentecostalism. After all, the Pentecostals were more concerned with the efficacy of government's intervention in the world of the spirits.

NEOLIBERAL SPIRITS

Pentecostalism focuses on the spiritual agencies that ensure personal success and prosperity in this world. The "prosperity gospel," as this belief is often termed, has been most closely associated with the West African and American churches. In Zambia, Pentecostal leaders were ambivalent toward aggressive versions of the prosperity gospel. Even those reticent about its materialist claims made some form of individual prosperity a central feature of their spiritual activism, however. For example, Pastor Reutter and Bishop Banda expressed misgivings with an exclusive focus on material wealth. Nonetheless, Pastor Reutter's Gospel Outreach center, with its acronym, the GO center, and its television program, *Run to Win*, made the focus on prosperity clear— even if prosperity was defined more broadly than monetary gain. In his televised weekly sermons, Bishop Banda also focused on the prosperity that God's presence brings to the individual. He had his church read and discuss chapters of Rick Warren's *The Purpose-Driven Life* as part of weekly church activities.[42]

The Pentecostals aimed to create a community defined by successful individuals, quite different from the ascetic morality of Kaunda's humanism. The aim was not the Armageddon, as Watchtower would have it; nor the cleansing of the sin of witchcraft, as Lenshina's followers desired; nor the eradication of selfishness, as proposed by Kaunda's socialism. Pentecostalism promised individual prosperity through spiritual interventions. The means and the end of spiritual actions were brought closer together in the form of direct individual salvation. The community did not matter, as long as the correct relationship with God was developed by the individual. Spiritual interventions were focused on the wealth and well-being of the individual instead of the collective.

Evil obstructed prosperity. Manichaean moral oppositions and the focus on exorcizing evil have been central to international Pentecostalism. Yet in its focus on evil spirits, Penteconstalism in Zambia combined local concerns about spiritual power with older Christian missionary condemnations of ancestral spirit veneration. The Zambian Pentecostal focus on witchcraft eradication was thereby the outcome of a history of Christian attempts to identify the sins of the African past combined with long-held attempts at spiritual government, similar to those practiced by Watchtower and Bamuchape in the early twentieth century. This multilayered approach to witchcraft can be appreciated by looking at how one of Lusaka's most popular witchcraft-eradication prophetesses, Elfrida Mhusambazi, described the problem. First, there was her conventional missionary Christian condemnation of past practices:

> For us in Africa, we cannot deny that there is witchcraft. . . . It is there in families; it is there in churches. Because of our foundations in Africa, wrong foundations. Many of them worshipped idols; they prayed to the moon; they prayed to the sun; they worshipped the dead. They would go to the grave to worship the dead, pour beer on the dead. Any African person would agree that someone down the line of their family there is a witch. It may not be your direct father, but your grandfather; it may not be your mother, but your aunt. So in African community, we live with it.[43]

The treatment of what an earlier generation of Christian missionaries would have termed "pagan practices" was thus located in a particular notion of spiritual progress. It also went beyond the conventional healing and laying on of hands found in US or European Pentecostal churches. With a few subtle differences, notably the increased role of God and the primary social unit being the church rather than the family or clan, the way of describing and dealing with such spiritual aberrations was remarkably similar to older forms of witchcraft purification:

> We catch a witch in church and have proof that he is practicing witchcraft, we talk to them. But you see, one of the spirits of witchcraft is stubbornness. People don't acknowledge unless by divine intervention. There are people who won't say yes. So we counsel them. And if they don't stop their operation, we make them leave church. We say that we don't want you here attacking others while they worship. So if you are not ready to stop what you are doing and we help you through prayers through deliverance, I am afraid you cannot remain in the service.[44]

The Zambian content of such forms of witchcraft eradication meshed comfortably with American healing and demonology; with increased Nigerian and independent African appropriations of American Pentecostalism, the focus on individual witches and witchcraft cleansing increased (Nigerian evangelists became especially sought after in Zambian efforts to eradicate witchcraft).[45] Through such witchcraft eradication, Pentecostals appropriated Western features of Pentecostalism to solve pressing spiritual concerns related to their historical contexts. While not all the Pentecostal churches focused on problems of witchcraft, the campaign against evil, sometimes referred to Satanism, pervaded most of them. For some pastors, it was about getting rid of evil in your heart; that was how you would begin to "do good," as Pastor Reutter put it. For Nevers Mumba, "witchcraft" and "Satanism" stemmed from the jealousy that would provoke evil thoughts.[46] Zambian Pentecostalism's struggle against evil built on several layers of previous spiritual discourses.

Just as evil could be understood only by appreciating past and present moralities enmeshed in local and global ideologies, so it was with good. Good flowed from a personal relationship with God through the Holy Spirit. The relationship was felt in prayer and in glossolalia, speaking in tongues. Good was not only personal; there were good actions that built and healed the Christian community, the body of Christ. Giving to the church was obviously one such action. Then, there was "development," education, visiting the sick, and healing. Health and prosperity were evidence of goodness. An HIV-positive Christian may use medication, but if she or he had a "strong enough" relationship with God, they were encouraged to terminate their medication and "stand alone." Business prosperity was a sign of being good. However, prosperity was not a reward for being good; it was the goodness that flowed from God. "Standing alone" with God, without any physical aids from this world, was a sign of God's presence in a person's life.

Good came most decisively through power, influence, signs, and miracles. These spiritual gifts indicated a strong relationship with God and the Holy Spirit. Gifts were manifested in several ways, most typically visions, dreams, faith healing, and prophecy. In Zambia, spiritual gifts of visions and dreams were especially common. Prophetess Mhusambazi received instructions from an angel during a dream, which inspired her to begin a ministry. Bishop Banda had visions that guided his choice in planting his first church and his dedication to spread Christianity across Africa to contain a Muslim advance— to "possess the land, reaching unreached peoples and nations," as his church's slogan puts it. This effort, he claims, was his primary reason for changing the Pentecostal Assemblies of God Bible College in Kitwe into the interdenominational Trans-Africa Theological College.[47] At the age of seventeen, Nevers Mumba claimed to have a vision of himself preaching the gospel to a "sea of black faces." He then heard God's voice: "Go, son, go and do it."[48]

Services represented, performed, and enacted such good spiritual power, the power to find the Holy Spirit, to heal, and to perform miracles. Modern sound equipment, bands, and choirs stimulated this power. There were few rehearsed rituals; this was chasing the Holy Spirit through inspiration. The performative aspect was emphasized, the spoken word instead of the written. Outside church, Christian entrepreneurs sold audio tapes and compact discs instead of books; pamphlets of prayers to be recited instead of passages to be studied.[49] People went to church because it was fun, not due to a this-worldly ascetism in the hope of the pleasures of an afterlife, but because fun was good; it led to excitement, and perhaps to an ecstatic possession by the Holy Spirit, the height of goodness.

Upon closer examination, notions of good, just like evil, innovated a local spiritual imagination. Speaking in tongues and possession by the holy spirits has a Zambian history. In the territorial cults such as Butwa, people were possessed by *ngulu* spirits after dancing sessions. Both these old and new forms of possession healed, provided prosperity, and cleansed evil forces. Dreams and visions provided guidance for the prophets of such territorial cults, as they did for Pentecostals with spiritual gifts.[50] Of course, Zambian Pentecostals, intent on distinguishing their Christianity from the sin of past practices, would deny such continuities; nevertheless, a corporeal mnemonics has made possession by the Holy Spirit, the role of dreams, and being born again in Christ familiar terrain for Zambians.[51]

Zambian Pentecostal morality also built on the moral reformism of humanism. Even while Pentecostals criticized humanism for denying God's presence in this world, some of the most prominent churches included a social gospel in their church activities that resembled aspects of Christian humanism. "The Bible I was reading showed me that Jesus cared for the people around him; that is why he told the story of the Good Samaritan," according to Bishop Banda. In response, together with his wife, Bishop Banda's church embarked on projects to help street children, sex workers, and HIV/AIDS patients.[52] Bishop Banda even became chairman of Zambia's National AIDS Council. These activities were justified and explained in a language that built on both humanism and an older mission Christianity.

For the Pentecostals, the personal orientation toward good and evil occurred by being born again, the ultimate intervention of good spirits into an individual's life. Possession by the Holy Spirit and being born again in Christ was a decisive and life-altering moment that defined a relationship with Christ. Even if one had belonged previously to a mainline church, the journey as a true Christian began upon feeling the presence of the Holy Spirit, dedicating one's life to Christ, and being born again. Pentecostals remembered the date of this event; it was when they began a new life. In Zambia, being born again built on multilayered past approaches to ideas about and practices that dealt with spiritual good and evil. The act of being born again was related conceptually and corporeally to older forms of cleansing by the Bamuchape, baptism by Lenshina, and healing by Milingo. Zambian Pentecostals appropriated a global discourse on possession by good and evil spirits and adapted it to their particular concerns with the world of the spirits.

A REBORN NATION

In the early 1980s the Pentecostals did not openly confront UNIP and were not at the forefront of the critique of scientific socialism.[53] The evangelical student movement of the 1970s and early 1980s was known for its political complacency, compared to the strident demands made by the politically conscious students at the time.[54] Instead, Zambian evangelicals emphasized that religion and politics "don't mix"; they were autonomous of each other. "Jesus Christ said you cannot serve two masters," claimed one "worried" Christian from Kitwe. "You either please one and disappoint the other, and if we have to follow the New Testament, we have to adhere to its full meaning. . . . Steps to feature politics and religion can only culminate in falling away from the truth."[55] Gideon Simwanga, the founding member of Operation Rescue Group for Ministry of Christ, which began in 1979 to preach at crusades, told his readers that instead of criticizing politicians, the duty of a Christian was to bring Christ into the lives of politicians:

> We long to see the time when every political-minded Church leader will stop criticizing politicians and unite with other Christians in fasting and prayer in order to reach leaders in the Party and Government with the Gospel. If Church leaders join politics we very much doubt who is going to preach the word of God to those who are still without hope for salvation. I tell you the truth. Politicians too need Christ in their lives more than anything else so that they can do their work honestly.[56]

The claim that morality came from a personal relationship with God, and not from the party, was nevertheless subversive of the humanist project. The implications of this Pentecostal argument for moral autonomy were profound. Morality came from God, not a political philosophy such as humanism, whether influenced by Christian or socialist principles. Despite the lack of direct political engagements, the idea that people improve through personal relationships with a spiritual God was more incompatible with the nationalist project than Catholic and mainline Protestant theology, which, for all their critiques of scientific socialism, shared a sense of salvation through good actions in this world. Instead, the evangelicals proposed a cleansing of sin and evil, a giving of oneself over to God, a getting rid of the demons, as a basis for health and well-being in this world. P. Musonda of Kitwe warned fellow born-again Christians of being misled by the emphasis on persecution and injustice espoused by liberation theology found in the Christian Marxist League of many Zambian churches; for Musonda, this theology failed to solve any "personal" problems.[57] "The battlefield is the mind," wrote Clive Mwalwanda of Lusaka. "It is against imaginations, thoughts and every high thing that exalts itself . . . against the knowledge of God. . . . Decisions about God must be settled by individuals. . . . The battle is spiritual. The enemy is invisible yet very real."[58]

The emphasis on the spirit world as a path to health, wealth, and righteousness contributed to an insistence on the autonomy of the individual from the party and the government. Even while elements of the established mainline churches were critical of the party, they were co-opted into programs of national improvement and development. The born-agains presented a new challenge. By 1984, the general secretary of UCZ, Joel Chisanga, complained of "Christians who shout at the top of their voices that they have been saved, they have been born again, they have the holy spirit. . . . They have been telling people that they cannot establish hospitals, schools and they cannot contribute to agricultural projects because they have been born again."[59] In reply, Moffat Mbewe of Luanshya insisted that born-again Christians were not against national development, but were "engaged in a *spiritual battle* to have a better Zambia."[60] According to Ernest Musase of Mufilira, "We the 'born-agains' believe the Word of God as being so powerful that whoever believes and obeys it enjoys many benefits (promises of God) while still in this wicked world."[61] Moral improvement and well-being were spiritual quests guided by the individual's relationship with God, and not by the party. In socialist Zambia, such ideas marked a distinct departure from previous humanist moral notions. Pentecostal doctrines, especially the struggle for autonomy and individual agency in the pursuit of a prosperous life, collided directly with UNIP's socialist vision. Opposition to Kaunda's regime became cast in a Pentecostal spiritual theology.

The political role of Pentecostalism was manifest most directly with President Frederick Chiluba's declaration of the Christian nation after defeating Kenneth Kaunda in the first multiparty elections in 1991. Marja Hinfelaar has argued that the idea of a Christian nation was nothing new; it has a long history, dating back to Catholic and even humanist discourses.[62] From the perspectives of the Pentecostals, who were the main proponents of the Christian nation, however, it was an exciting event that broke decisively with the past in cleansing Zambia and committing the nation to Christ. The declaration has to be evaluated in the light of the practices of the Pentecostals, their prayers, personal morality, and most importantly, the notion of being born again.

The idea of a Christian nation began to be actively pursued by the evangelical community in 1990, as UNIP's one-party state disintegrated. The Evangelical Fellowship of Zambia (EFZ), led by Joseph Imakando and with significant input from Pastor Reutter, began to advocate for a Christian nation and a Christian national philosophy. At the beginning of 1991, the EFZ argued that Zambia should be declared a Christian nation, and that humanism should no longer be the national philosophy.[63] Their critique of humanism went far beyond the earlier ecumenical critique of the scientific socialist elements of humanism. The Pentecostals rejected the very basis of the idea of humanism. "Humanism is a disaster," declared Pastor Reutter. "A philosophy which puts man at the center of society instead of God never works. Most Zambians don't even understand humanism anyway. It is only suitable for some individuals at the top."[64] Bishop Banda criticized humanism for "deifying man."[65] Pentecostal leaders gained confidence with a growth in the popular appeal and influence of Pentecostalism, promoted by an increase in televangelism and mass crusades that linked the personal quest for goodness with the redemption of the Zambian nation.

The Pentecostal call for national redemption focused on areas of evil that had to be cleansed. In addition to the philosophy of humanism, evil came to be embodied in President Kaunda himself, especially since Kaunda had embarked on his own spiritual quest, which was widely distrusted. In the 1980s, Kaunda had formed a close relationship with Dr. M. A. Ranganathan, his guru and adviser, which had led to the establishment of the David Universal Temple (named after his father, the Lubwa missionary David Kaunda) at State House.[66] If such actions were meant to recapture the spiritual ground ceded to the Christian movement, they were entirely unsuccessful. To many born-again Christians, Kaunda's actions were "tantamount to blasphemy."[67] Instead of ridding Zambia of evil, televised attempts by Kaunda to make Zambia "Heaven on Earth" proved that Kaunda had allied with the devil, who had "mobilized his forces of darkness to fight against, and perhaps destroy, the nation of Zambia."[68] It was almost as if Kaunda had allowed himself to be unwittingly possessed by evil. A regular contributor to the *National Mirror*, Austin Kaluba, expressed widespread Zambian fears when he wrote:

> To many Zambians, President Kaunda has masqueraded as a God-fearing leader, but the unholy alliance with the Indian cultist Dr. Ranganathan and the David Universal Temple Cult, which is at State House, would make one wonder if Dr. Kaunda is a true Christian. People who have entered the temple have described early experiences and talked of ancient and oriental images they saw in the temple. The halo that Dr. Ranganathan described seeing around Kaunda's

head in his book when the President was lighting candles could not have come from God but from the devil. . . . The embracing of the David Universal Temple cult by a head of state is tantamount to blasphemy. . . . Dr. Ranganathan's practices are not from God, but from the devil who is a great deceiver.[69]

So at the heart of Kaunda's rule was something far more sinister than humanism, which denied the centrality of God: Kaunda's relationship with Ranganathan and his promotion of a scheme with Maharashi Mahesh Yogi to make Zambia "Heaven on Earth" were denounced as Satanism. For the Pentecostals, only their prayers and Christian leadership would allow Zambia to prosper.

Pentecostals advocated a cleansing of evil and a dedication to Christ through prayer. Most of the churches opposed Kaunda and favored Frederick Chiluba's Movement for Multiparty Democracy (MMD) in the elections scheduled for October 1991. But Pentecostals expressed their political preferences through prayer, not through the public pronouncements and pastoral statements typical of the mainline Protestants and the Catholic Church. Letters written to the newspapers now rejected the earlier separation of religion and politics and declared it essential that "God's Children" pray for victory in the upcoming elections.[70] John Mambo, overseer of the Church of God and a member of the Zambia Elections Monitoring Coordinating Committee, headed by EFZ's Joseph Imakando, called a national day of prayer on 27 October, a few days before the elections at the end of the month.[71] For the Pentecostals, prayer and miraculous intervention would bring about change. UNIP would be defeated only by a miracle:

> Former President [Kaunda] had so much power . . . his army, the intelligence, they would easily have disregarded the election result, but the prayers of the Christians which had gone on before were so powerful. I believe that the hearts of Kaunda and his people were melted by God. It was not politically possible to remove him and his henchmen that time except it had to be an act of God.[72]

On 31 October 1991, in the first multiparty elections since 1968, Zambians elected Chiluba's MMD in a landslide victory over UNIP, especially in the urban areas.[73] "Christians consider President Chiluba's victory as an answer to their protracted prayers," declared Rev. Ronald Mwape in an article titled "Zambia Returns to God." "So in the scramble for Zambia Christians prayed and Satanists meditated . . . suspended in mid air. At the end of the day, Christ's forces prevailed against the kingdom of darkness, for it is written: The forces of Hell shall not prevail against the Church."[74]

Intervention in the spirit world was high on the list of priorities of Chiluba's new government. A first task was to get rid of the evil forces and lead the nation to be born again in Christ: the evil of the past had to be cleansed before a new beginning could be declared. On 10 November, under the direction of Imakando, Stephen Mumba of the Anglican Church anointed Chiluba.[75] A new Christian column titled "Encounter" replaced the weekly "Humanism Corner" in the state-owned daily newspaper, the *Times of Zambia*. The minister without portfolio (later vice president), Godfrey Miyanda, accompanied four evangelists to State House to cleanse it of evil spirits. Security officers raided the David Universal Temple.[76] A Ndola-based Assemblies of God evangelist, Stan Kristafor, became minister of information and banned a popular Zairean musician's show, which he claimed was "pornographic," from Zambian television. He also put an end to a Muslim program on Zambian radio and to the national slogan "One Zambia, One Nation," which appeared after news broadcasts, presumably because of its association with Kaunda and humanism.[77] Zambia established diplomatic ties with Israel—which may have "broken hearts in ANC and PLO camps," but would lead to the "blessing of Zambia."[78]

On 29 December 1991, in the presence of prominent Pentecostal leaders—but in the absence of other church representatives—Chiluba declared Zambia to be a Christian nation. He claimed that Zambia's transition to democracy was possible only through God and that "the hour has come to wake up from our slumber because salvation is near." Imakando, in turn, thanked God for "raising a Bible-believing Christian to leadership of this land." Bishop Banda was invited to attend the event: "The experience was exhilarating," he recalled. Pastor Reutter, who also witnessed the declaration, described "jubilation" among those present.[79]

The declaration subjected the nation to the Pentecostal discourse of being born again in Christ. It was thought to have healed the nation, and set it on a path to prosperity in the same fashion as a born-again individual. Not only was it witnessed by Pentecostal leaders, its political theology was distinctly Pentecostal. The Catholic and mainline Protestant leadership was less enthusiastic and even critical of the Christian nation declaration.[80] In part, they resented not being consulted and invited to the ceremony. But more profoundly, they saw no purpose in it, underestimating its importance from the perspective of Pentecostals for whom the declaration of the Christian nation was a long-overdue commitment by government to God and to combat the influence of Satan in the life of the nation. It marked the beginning of a new era of prosperity. "The hour has come," as the MMD slogan put it. Now it was time for Zambia to prosper with its new commitment to Christ. Anthropologist James Ferguson noted the millenarian aspect of the MMD victory; as with much other millenarianism, the victory implied a spiritual cleansing, purification, and rebirth.[81]

The downfall of Kaunda and the declaration of the Christian nation gave force to the Pentecostal movement and laid the groundwork for the continued political involvement of Pentecostal "big men." The most fervent and influential was Nevers Mumba, the former translator of Reinhard Bonnke and founder of Victory Ministries. Mumba had already established his *Zambia Shall Be Saved* television program in 1990, crucial for the spread of Pentecostal ideas in Zambia, modeled on Bonnke's "Africa Shall Be Saved" programs.[82] After the 1991 elections, Bonnke returned to Zambia and, with sponsorship by the Billy Graham Foundation, led a seminar to explore opportunities for additional Christian television.[83] Mumba organized a series of conventions and crusades, for example, Victory '94, which supported Chiluba's government.[84]

The high expectations set by Pentecostal efforts to rid the nation of evil led Pentecostals to offer critical voices rather than consistently stand behind a single party or candidate. By 1996, Mumba began to lead an oppositional Christian movement. Disillusioned with corruption and with the broken promises of Chiluba's cohort, Mumba claimed to be attracted to the place where he perceived the greatest darkness, politics:

> I had burdens for a more darker [sic] part of life. . . . I said this Christian power can be used somewhere else, and at that time identified politics as one of the very dark areas, where it was even a known thing that politics is a dirty game. . . . [I would use] politics as a mission to heal, to bring the gospel, the light.[85]

Using "politics as a mission to heal" was not meant in the sense of national reconciliation, but in the sense of healing during a mass crusade against evil, when demons are cast out of the body. As part of his mission, Mumba launched the National Christian Coalition in 1996 (renamed the National Citizens Coalition in an effort to reach out to non-Christians), which campaigned on a platform of moral and spiritual righteousness.[86]

Other Pentecostal leaders also criticized Chiluba's government. Bishop Banda, who had witnessed and celebrated the Christian nation declaration, warned of the lack of transparency in leadership and told a class of graduating pastors not to "flow with the current."[87] Church leaders complained of a lack of access to Chiluba.[88] When Chiluba managed to amend the preamble to the constitution in 1996 to declare Zambia a Christian nation, the EFZ, together with the other church bodies, expressed misgivings, despite support from some Pentecostals such as the Assemblies of God.[89] Bishop Mususu, who took over the leadership of EFZ from Imakando, claimed to have always been suspicious of Chiluba's Christianity, especially since he appointed politicians known for corruption and drug-trafficking to his cabinet.[90] In 1997, "Captain Solo," who claimed to have received instructions from an angel, launched a failed coup code-named "Operation Born Again."[91] By 2001, almost all of Chiluba's old Pentecostal allies had abandoned him, following his failed attempt to change the constitution to allow a third term in office.[92] Even after Chiluba agreed not to stand for a third term, the EFZ, the Catholic and mainline Protestant church associations, and other NGOs contested the results of the 2001 elections, which were widely perceived to have been rigged in favor of Chiluba's chosen successor, Levy Mwanawasa. Nevers Mumba, after a failed presidential bid in the 2001 elections, became a spokesperson for the opposition to the new president, Mwanawasa. By 2003, Mumba had, however, reconciled with Mwanawasa and became vice president. (Mumba was dismissed one year later due to his unilateral actions, especially his accusations that opposition candidates were corrupt.)

Pentecostalism did not legitimize a single candidate or government; instead, it provided the spiritual discourse appropriate to discussions over the onset of multiparty democracy and a neoliberal economy. Since 1991, the idea of a Zambia freed from evil and blessed by the power of the Holy Spirit has been a core aspect of Zambian political discourse. The ability of a candidate to intercede with the spirit world for the good of the nation is central to his or her political program and appeal. Pentecostal "big men" are called upon to intervene in national political strife. Prayer is considered the appropriate response to elections or events that result in political upheaval, such as the death of President Mwanawasa in 2008. Individual and national prosperity, as opposed to the sense of social responsibility and comradeship of humanism, defines righteousness. Good is about prosperity, in particular personal wealth, not altruism and service. The morality of "God's People" celebrates the success that God's agency in the world delivers to the powerful. As Kaunda's regime fell in 1991, so did humanism: Pentecostal spirituality became the imaginative landscape upon which Zambian politics would be contested.

Pentecostal ideas and practices spread from the church faithful to the broader community, facilitating distinctive engagements with democratic politics and with the neoliberal economic order. The emphasis on individual salvation in born-again Christian doctrines developed the idea of the individual as the sovereign unit in a struggle between good and evil, and not the party; it cultivated the idea of autonomy from the party in moral and organizational spheres; and it legitimized an individual quest for wealth and well-being as a path to righteousness. Typical of what David Maxwell terms Pentecostalism's "capacity for individuation . . . enabling believers to rewrite their own personal narrative and break with the past," Pentecostalism offered a way for individuals to reimagine themselves and their relationship to the state in the neoliberal order.[93]

In Zambia, this personal political engagement took the form of a struggle for democracy, which would lead to a nation reborn and prosperous. Kaunda had to be deposed because he was under the influence of Satan and denied the influence of God. Pentecostals thought that by defeating Kaunda, they would end witchcraft and Satanism; democratic elections would lead to a government that devoted Zambia to God and thereby blessed the nation. In this sense, the promotion of and participation in multiparty democratic elections was less of a democratic ideology, a sign of intrinsic Pentecostal civic engagement, than a tool in a campaign against the influence of the evil spirits that obstructed prosperity in a neoliberal world.

Pentecostalism gave the transition to capitalism and multiparty democracy a particular character by promoting spiritually gifted politicians who imagined a new community, a reborn nation. In contrast to humanism's suppression of individual desires, Pentecostal morality celebrated autonomous and successful individuals empowered by the Holy Spirit. Either through its many churches or through its indirect influence, Pentecostalism's spiritual beliefs spread until they became a significant ideological component of urban Zambian civil society. Like Watchtower in the 1930s, the use of a novel media, this time broadcast television and radio instead of pamphlet literature, extended Pentecostalism far beyond its organizational base. By the 1990s, as Pentecostals promoted the takeover of the state by those with spiritual gifts such as Frederick Chiluba, spiritual beliefs appeared to become a legitimizing ideology of rule. However, as Chiluba soon discovered, spirits are fickle allies. They are more likely to offer alternative paths to power than to legitimize the status quo.

The Spirit Realm of Agency

> By Christian humanism, I mean that we discover all that is worth
> knowing about God through our fellow men and unconditional
> service of our fellow men is the purest form of the service of God.
> I believe that Man must be the servant of a vision which is bigger
> than himself; that his path is illumined by God's revelation and
> that when he shows love towards his fellow men, he is sharing the
> very life of God, who is Love. When Man learns, by bitter experi-
> ence if in no other way, that the only hope for peace and happi-
> ness of the world is to give political and economic expression to
> love for others we shall have entered not the Kingdom of Man but
> the Kingdom of God.
>
> — Kenneth Kaunda, 1966

> On behalf of the people of Zambia, I repent of our wicked ways of
> idolatry, witchcraft, immorality, injustice and corruption. I pray
> for the healing, restoration, revival, blessing, and prosperity for
> Zambia. On behalf of the nation, I have now entered a covenant
> with the living God. . . . I submit the Government and the entire
> nation of Zambia to the Lordship of Jesus Christ. I further declare
> that Zambia is a Christian Nation that will seek to be governed
> by the righteous principles of the Word of God. Righteousness
> and justice must prevail in all levels of authority, and then we
> shall see the righteousness of God exalting Zambia.
>
> — Frederick Chiluba, 1991

SOME OF THE MOST SIGNIFICANT political movements and moments in
Zambian history—Bemba chieftaincy, Bamuchape, Watchtower, Lenshina's
church, popular nationalism, Kaunda's humanism, and Chiluba's reborn
Christian nation—have been part of an ongoing Zambian debate about the
relationships between the individual, the community, the state, and the spirits. By talking about spirits, people made sense of the worlds that enveloped
their lives, and, in turn, transformed these worlds. In this regard, the ideas of
Zambia's first and second presidents, Kenneth Kaunda and Frederick Chiluba, shortly after they came to office, represent two conflicting notions of the
spirit world dealt with by this book. Both were concerned with the relationship

between God and the Zambian people, but in very different ways. For Kaunda, through bitter experience people would follow God's path in showing love toward one another. Kaunda's humanism struggled against exploitation, greed, excess, and injustice in a moral language faithful to its Protestant roots.

For Chiluba, the evil was found within, and good would come through direct spiritual intervention, "a covenant with the *living* God." Chiluba made this spiritual salvation a condition for the possibility of a public utopia. In a formulation that would be familiar to Archbishop Emmanuel Milingo or even to Lenshina, Chiluba recognized that spiritual evil afflicted Zambians and promised to cleanse it. For many Zambians, Chiluba's declaration represented an important corrective to a humanist vision that viewed spirits as populating another world, heaven and hell, which could inspire moral actions in this world but did not intervene in it directly.

In precolonial forms of governance, the centrality of spirits to political rule and conflict was accepted; after all, the most important duties of government, the provision of agricultural fecundity and human fertility, rested on the relationship of the spirits to living rulers. The colonial state created a dissonance in this regard: it claimed a secular sovereignty and ruled through the "traditions" of chiefs, which were divorced from the spirit world. To the colonial administrators who lorded over the chiefs, spiritual powers were at best a source of embarrassment and arcane anthropological interest; they had to be discouraged, repressed, sometimes prohibited, or at the very least removed from the quotidian running of the administration. In this sense, even while indirect rule seemed to give chiefs power, the chiefs were spiritually and thus politically disempowered.

Christian missionaries aided in this civilizing mission. They claimed that since the world of the living was separate from the world of the dead, spirits did not inhabit and influence this world. Coming from a European tradition that sought to separate the church and state, the missionaries accepted a formal division between politics and religion, at least in theory (in practice, their local standing was tied to the colonial administration). For the missionaries, spiritual interventions, the miracles of the distant biblical past, rarely occurred, and if they did, they were performed by a chosen few within church hierarchies that excluded Africans. For the most part, the stories of the Bible were to be understood as symbolic, intended to demonstrate how to lead a moral life free from sin. Beliefs in the immediate presence and influence of spirits in everyday affairs of health, wealth, and power were rejected as false superstitions.

From an African perspective, the separation of secular power from sacred power was not convincing. Spirits could not be banished by the proclamations of the colonists and the missionaries. Since people prospered and suffered through the agency of spirits, governments had to deal with spirits. The loss of spiritual power by the chiefs inspired new political movements, which, in turn, further disempowered the chiefs. These movements confronted an increasingly populated spiritual landscape, inhabited now not only by natural and ancestral spirits, but also by God, Jesus, and Satan, who existed not only in the spiritual afterlife recognized by the missionaries but also in the everyday of living people. These Christian spirits were relevant to a colonial world of hardship and foreign oppression. Christianity did not banish the spirits, as the missionaries hoped; instead, spirits took on a Manichaean character, became associated with Christian rituals, narratives, and conflicts, and engaged with life under colonialism. Colonial Christianity gave further rein to the spirits.

The dialogue between missionaries and Africans over the existence of sin and its eradication indicated that even in agreement there were misunderstandings that confirmed alternative spiritual ideas. For the missionaries, Africans were sinners because of their marital practices, their alleged sloth, their idolatry, and innumerable unfamiliar cultural practices. Africans could change their behavior, the missionaries thought; after all, agency to end sin lay in the reform of human behavior, not with spiritual interventions. Sin was pervasive, Africans agreed, but this was due not only to human actions that should be confessed, reformed, and rejected. Rather, there were many spirits, often employed by living witches, who dominated and even killed others, or made people act in antisocial ways. Witchcraft was the most prevalent sign of sin. For the missionaries, however, belief in witchcraft was further indication of ignorance and sin, and so they spoke more fervently of sin, even as they discouraged people from eradicating witchcraft.

In the postcolonial period, the missionary-trained nationalists took up the colonial civilizing mission in an effort to guide the morality of their citizens and develop their nation. In their attempts to exert the hegemony of the nationalist party and the chosen leader, they also denied the agency of the spirits in this world. The political class proclaimed their faith in forms of progressive secularism, such as scientific socialism, that relegated spirits to an irrational past. Yet this civilizing mission was not widely believed and was not convincing in the context of a failed modernist program: people still prospered or suffered because of capricious spirits. Under popular pressure and faced with challenges to their rule, even the nationalist elite came to acknowledge the powers of the spirits, occasionally initiating their own spiritual interventions. The collapse of the party-guided moral reformism in the 1980s witnessed an open resurgence of spirits in political and economic life.

Historians have imposed their own civilizing mission on the spirits that refuse to abide by the constraints of a post-Enlightenment historical imagination. They have separated out the spiritual from the secular, recasting spiritual beliefs as symbolic systems, statements about something else, metaphors for economic struggles, indigenized manifestations of class consciousness, or viewed only their limited functions (such as "healing"). Some political historians have not even bothered with the spirits, considering them to be legitimizing devices (ignoring why they provide legitimacy), beliefs that can be explained away by focusing on the secular, on supposed material interests, on forms of power and patronage politics familiar to them. In their attempts to record a history of a sphere of politics distinct from spirits, the civilizing mission of such historians shares a genealogy with the missionary and the postcolonial nationalist.

The premise of this book is that for many central Africans, spirits have power, and thus accounts of human agency must involve spirits. This premise becomes even more interesting when the nature of the agency that spirits have facilitated and encouraged is examined. In the colonial and post- (or neo-) colonial periods, rulers emphasized a secular civilizing mission as the basis of government; the spiritual beliefs of the movements examined here inspired alternative modalities of power. Spiritual discourses became the consciousness of resistance. Even when they were appropriated by rulers, nondoctrinal and capricious spirits mobilized critique and opposition. If secular government and the rule of law attempted to control people in a consistent fashion, spirits offered alternative routes to power that conformed to uneven, and often disappointing, experiences. But these spirits not only represented the conditions of life; they encouraged people to challenge the instruments of the secular invisible world, human-made laws, and their living intermediaries, the rulers and functionaries of states.

The conventional history of the organization of power in Europe and the modern West after the Enlightenment imagines that spiritual beliefs have changed from a source of political authority to a private realm separate from politics and public life. African politico-religious constellations have not allowed spirits to become a matter of private faith, however. Since spirits are a source of power in this world, the divorce of the spirit world from the political world is often challenged. The overlapping and intertwining of these different sources of power contributes to the rich character of historical agency across much of Africa. This paradigm of invisible agency may be the African Renaissance: a theory of power that emerges from an ancient history, engages with colonial and neocolonial modernities, and insists on the invisible inspirations of our actions.

Notes

INTRODUCTION: SEEING INVISIBLE WORLDS

1. A survey of 25,000 conducted by the Pew Research Center in 2008–2009. Pew Forum on Religion and Public Life, *Islam and Christianity in Sub-Saharan Africa* (Washington, DC: Pew Research Center, 2010).

2. The distinction and characteristics of sacred and profane have been widely discussed. For critique of the distinctions, see the discussion by Talal Asad, *Formations of the Secular: Christianity, Islam, Modernity* (Stanford, CA: Stanford University Press, 2003), esp. 30–37.

3. Kwame Anthony Appiah, *In My Father's House: Africa in the Philosophy of Culture* (New York: Oxford University Press, 1993), 134.

4. Monica H. Wilson used the term "shade" in *Communal Rituals of the Nyakyusa* (London: Oxford University Press, 1959); it was further employed by the Rhodes-Livingstone Institute anthropologists. See, for example, Victor Turner, *The Forest of Symbols: Aspects of Ndembu Ritual* (Ithaca, NY: Cornell University Press, 1970), esp. 9–10.

5. A copious literature that includes John S. Mbiti, *African Religions and Philosophy* (Oxford: Heinemann, 1969); Terence O. Ranger, "African Traditional Religion," in *The Study of Religion, Traditional and New Religions*, ed. Stewart Sutherland and Peter Clarke (London: Routledge, 1991), 106–14; Jacob K. Olupona, ed., *African Traditional Religions in Contemporary Society* (New York: Paragon House, 1991).

6. Asad, *Formations of the Secular.*

7. Stephen Ellis and Gerrie ter Haar, *Worlds of Power: Religious Thought and Political Practice in Africa* (New York: Oxford University Press, 2004); Peter Geschiere, *The Modernity of Witchcraft: Politics and the Occult in Postcolonial Africa*, trans. Peter Geschiere and Janet Roitman (Charlottesville: University of Virginia Press, 1997); Adam Ashforth, *Witchcraft, Violence, and Democracy in South Africa* (Chicago: University of Chicago Press, 2005); Birgit Meyer and Peter Pels, *Magic and Modernity: Interfaces of Revelation and Concealment* (Stanford, CA: Stanford University Press, 2003).

8. Callum G. Brown argues that the death of Christian Britain occurred only in the cultural revolution of the 1960s, and not during the Enlightenment, in *The Death of Christian Britain: Understanding Secularisation, 1800–2000* (London:

Routledge, 2001). For a similar argument located around the Lourdes shrine in France, see Ruth Harris, *Lourdes: Body and Spirit in the Secular Age* (New York: Penguin, 1999).

9. Terence O. Ranger, "Connexions Between 'Primary Resistance' Movements and Modern Mass Nationalism in East and Central Africa: Parts 1 and 2," *Journal of African History* 9, nos. 3–4 (1968): 437–53, 631–41.

10. Robert I. Rotberg, *The Rise of Nationalism in Central Africa: The Making of Malawi and Zambia, 1873–1964* (Cambridge, MA: Harvard University Press, 1972); Henry S. Meebelo, *Reaction to Colonialism: A Prelude to the Politics of Independence in Northern Zambia, 1893–1939* (Manchester: Manchester University Press, 1971).

11. David Lan, *Guns and Rain: Guerrillas and Spirit Mediums in Zimbabwe* (Berkeley: University of California Press, 1985).

12. Terence O. Ranger, "Religious Movements and Politics in Sub-Saharan Africa," *African Studies Review* 29, no. 2 (1986): 1–69.

13. Terence O. Ranger, "Scotland Yard in the Bush: Medicine Murders, Child Witches and the Construction of the Occult: A Literature Review," *Africa* 77, no. 2 (2007): 272–83; and the response by Stephen Ellis and Gerrie ter Haar, "The Occult Does Not Exist: A Response to Terence Ranger," *Africa* 79, no. 3 (2009): 399–412.

14. Michael G. Schatzberg, *Political Legitimacy in Middle Africa: Father, Family, Food* (Bloomington: Indiana University Press, 2001), 70–110.

15. For example, see Clifton Crais, *The Politics of Evil: Magic, State Power, and the Political Imagination in South Africa* (Cambridge: Cambridge University Press, 2002), esp. 115–44.

16. Especially in Paul Gifford's work, which covers both possibilities, most notably contrast his edited collection: Paul Gifford, ed., *The Christian Churches and the Democratisation of Africa* (Leiden: Brill, 1995); for his more critical position, especially of evangelical churches, see Gifford, *African Christianity: Its Public Role* (Bloomington: Indiana University Press, 1998).

17. Cynthia Hoehler-Fatton, *Women of Fire and Spirit: History, Faith, and Gender in Roho Religion in Western Kenya* (New York: Oxford University Press, 1996); Dorothy L. Hodgson, *The Church of Women: Gendered Encounters between Maasai and Missionaries* (Bloomington: Indiana University Press, 2005); Phyllis M. Martin, *Catholic Women of Congo-Brazzaville: Mothers and Sisters in Troubled Times* (Bloomington: Indiana University Press, 2009). For an important emphasis on spiritual power, see Jane E. Soothill, *Gender, Social Change, and Spiritual Power: Charismatic Christianity in Ghana* (Leiden: Brill, 2007). For a Zambian example, see Hugo F. Hinfelaar, *Bemba-Speaking Women of Zambia in a Century of Religious Change (1892–1992)* (Leiden: Brill, 1994).

18. For the interpretative translation of religion and the transformation of political to spiritual concepts, see Paul S. Landau, *The Realm of the Word: Language, Gender, and Christianity in a Southern African Kingdom* (Portsmouth, NH: Heinemann, 1993); and more recently his *Popular Politics in the History of South Africa, 1400–1948* (Cambridge: Cambridge University Press, 2010), 74–107. For translations, see

Derek R. Peterson, *Creative Writing: Translation, Bookkeeping, and the Work of Imagination in Colonial Kenya* (Portsmouth, NH: Heinemann, 2004).

19. Harris, *Lourdes*, xvii.

20. Robin Horton argues that symbolic approaches to religion miss the elements of "explanation/prediction/control," in other words, power, at the center of religious thought. Much of his work is collected in *Patterns of Thought in Africa and the West: Essays on Magic, Religion and Science* (Cambridge: Cambridge University Press, 1993). For a further philosophical critique of the Western and Christian emphasis on the symbolism of African religion, see Appiah, *In My Father's House*, 107–36.

21. Jean Comaroff and John L. Comaroff, *Of Revelation and Revolution: The Dialectics of Modernity on a South African Frontier*, vol. 2 (Chicago: University of Chicago Press, 1997). But also includes other work on more recent Christian movements, such as Comaroff and Comaroff, "Second Comings: Neo-Protestant Ethics and Millennial Capitalism in Africa, and Elsewhere," in *2000 Years and Beyond: Faith, Identity and the Common Era*, ed. Paul Gifford (London: Routledge, 2002), 106–26. J. D. Y. Peel, *Religious Encounter and the Making of the Yoruba* (Bloomington: Indiana University Press, 2000), esp. 278–309; Landau, *Realm of the Word* and *Popular Politics*; Elizabeth Elbourne, *Blood Ground: Colonialism, Missions, and the Contest for Christianity in the Cape Colony and Britain, 1799–1853* (Montreal: McGill-Queen's University Press, 2002).

22. Ruth Marshall, *Political Spiritualities: The Pentecostal Revolution in Nigeria* (Chicago: University of Chicago Press, 2009), 22. For further critique of symbolic approaches in anthropology, see Todd Sanders, *Beyond Bodies: Rain-Making and Sense-Making in Tanzania* (Toronto: University of Toronto Press, 2008).

23. Karen E. Fields, *Revival and Rebellion in Colonial Central Africa* (Princeton, NJ: Princeton University Press, 1985). For elaboration of the theoretical arguments, see Fields, "Political Contingencies of Witchcraft in Colonial Central Africa: Culture and the State in Marxist Theory," *Canadian Journal of African Studies* 16, no. 3 (1982): 567–93.

24. Luise White, *Speaking with Vampires: Rumor and History in Colonial Africa* (Berkeley: University of California Press, 2000), 206.

25. For example, as James L. Giblin has pointed out in his review, there is little to link rumors of vampires with class struggle in the copper mines. Giblin, "Vampires and History," *African Studies Review* 44, no. 1 (April 2001): 83–87.

26. Wyatt MacGaffey points out that spiritual technologies often worked through metaphor and metonymy, in *Kongo Political Culture: The Conceptual Challenge of the Particular* (Bloomington: Indiana University Press, 2000), 84.

27. Stephen Ellis, *The Mask of Anarchy: The Destruction of Liberia and the Religious Dimension of an African Civil War*, 2nd ed. (New York: New York University Press, 2006).

28. See this criticism in Gary Kynoch's review of Ashforth in "Living with Witches in South Africa: Review of Adam Ashforth," H-SAFRICA, H-Net Reviews (June 2005), http://www.h-net.org/reviews/showrev.php?id=10591.

29. Emile Durkheim, *The Elementary Forms of Religious Life*, trans. Karen E. Fields (New York: Free Press, 1995), 425–26.

30. Karen E. Fields, "Witchcraft and Racecraft: Invisible Ontology and Its Sensible Manifestations," in *Witchcraft Dialogues: Anthropological and Philosophical Exchanges*, ed. George Clement Bond and Diane M. Ciekawy (Athens: Ohio University Press, 2001), 283–315.

31. The single most important and representative collection of thinking on this subject was Meyer Fortes and Edward E. Evans-Pritchard, eds., *African Political Systems* (London: International Africa Institute, 1940). From the perspective of religious thought and practice, see Evans-Pritchard, *Witchcraft, Oracles and Magic Among the Azande* (Oxford: Clarendon Press, 1937).

32. G. Wilson to M. Fortes, 20 August 1940, B4/3, BC1081, University of Cape Town Manuscripts and Archives (henceforth UCTMA).

33. Neil Kodesh, *Beyond the Royal Gaze: Clanship and Public Healing in Buganda* (Charlottesville: University of Virginia Press, 2010), esp. 14–20.

34. Willy De Craemer, Jan Vansina, and Renée C. Fox, "Religious Movements in Central Africa: A Theoretical Study," *Comparative Studies in Society and History* 18, no. 4 (1976): 458–75.

35. Christopher Ehret, *An African Classical Age: Eastern and Southern Africa in World History, 1000 B.C. to A.D. 400* (Charlottesville: University of Virginia, 1998), 158–60. Also see Ehret, *The Civilizations of Africa: A History to 1800* (Charlottesville: University of Virginia Press, 2002), 50.

36. Jan Vansina, *How Societies Are Born: Governance in West Central Africa Before 1600* (Charlottesville: University of Virginia Press, 2004), 51, 167–68, 193–94.

37. Jan Vansina, *Paths in the Rainforests: Toward a History of Political Tradition in Equatorial Africa* (Madison: University of Wisconsin Press, 1990), 95. A helpful reconstruction of early western Bantu terms for spirits and religious experts can be found on pages 297–301.

38. Kairn A. Klieman, *"The Pygmies Were Our Compass": Bantu and Batwa in the History of West Central Africa, Early Times to c. 1900 C.E.* (Portsmouth, NH: Heinemann, 2003), 81–86.

39. As cited by Wyatt MacGaffey, "Dialogues of the Deaf: Europeans on the Atlantic Coast of Africa," in *Implicit Understandings: Observing, Reporting, and Reflecting on the Encounters Between Europeans and Other Peoples in the Early Modern Era*, ed. Stuart B. Schwartz (Cambridge: Cambridge University Press, 1994), 249–67; and John K. Thornton, *The Kongolese Saint Anthony: Dona Beatriz Kimpa Vita and the Antonian Movement, 1684–1706* (Cambridge: Cambridge University Press, 1998).

40. For ethnography of Kongo beliefs, also see MacGaffey, *Kongo Political Culture*; and his earlier *Religion and Society in Central Africa: The BaKongo of Lower Zaire* (Chicago: Chicago University Press, 1986).

41. For oral traditions of south-central Africa, see Luc de Heusch, *The Drunken King; or, The Origin of the State* (Bloomington: Indiana University Press, 1982); Thomas Q. Reefe, *The Rainbow and the Kings: A History of the Luba Empire to*

1891 (Berkeley: University of California Press, 1981). Among the eastern Lunda, see David M. Gordon, *Nachituti's Gift: Economy, Society, and Environment in Central Africa* (Madison: University of Wisconsin Press, 2006); and Gordon, "History on the Luapula Retold: Landscape, Memory and Identity in the Kazembe Kingdom," *Journal of African History* 47, no. 1 (2006): 21–42. For an example of Luba artifacts, see Mary Nooter Roberts and Allen F. Roberts, eds., *Memory: Luba Art and the Making of History* (New York: Museum for African Art, 1996).

42. For the latter, see accounts of Audrey I. Richards and Godfrey Wilson, as reported by Megan Vaughan, "'Divine Kings': Sex, Death and Anthropology in Inter-War East/Central Africa," *Journal of African History* 49, no. 3 (2008): 383–401, esp. 399.

43. A quality of love in Africa ignored in the modern-focused volume by Jennifer Cole and Lynn M. Thomas, eds., *Love in Africa* (Chicago: University of Chicago Press, 2009).

44. Geschiere, *Modernity of Witchcraft*.

45. For the best example, see the case of Ovambo in northern Namibia in Meredith McKittrick, *To Dwell Secure: Generation, Christianity, and Colonialism in Ovamboland* (Portsmouth, NH: Heinemann, 2002).

46. For an elaboration of this argument, see Lamin Sanneh, *Whose Religion Is Christianity?: The Gospel Beyond the West* (Grand Rapids, MI: Eerdmans, 2003); contra Terence O. Ranger, introduction to *Themes in the Christian History of Central Africa*, ed. Terence O. Ranger and John Weller (Berkeley: University of California Press, 1975), 86.

47. A recent reflection on this changing global nature of Christianity appears in Gerrie ter Haar, *How God Became African: African Spirituality and Western Secular Thought* (Philadelphia: University of Pennsylvania Press, 2009).

48. Fieldwork; and David M. Gordon, "A Community of Suffering: Narratives of War and Exile in the Zambian Lumpa Church," in *Recasting the Past: History Writing and Political Work in Modern Africa*, ed. Derek R. Peterson and Giacomo Macola (Athens: Ohio University Press, 2009), 191–208. For a discussion of such practices from the West African context, which European missionaries condemned as "transvaluation" and "transgression," see J. D. Y. Peel, *Religious Encounter*, 162–63.

49. In central Africa these range from the seventeenth-century Dona Beatriz Kimpa Vita, as described by Thornton, *Kongolese Saint Anthony*; to the twentieth-century Simon Kimbangu, as described in Wyatt MacGaffey, *Modern Kongo Prophets: Religion in a Plural Society* (Bloomington: Indiana University Press, 1983); and the Congolese political opposition in the late twentieth century, as in Filipe de Boek and Marie Françoise Plissart, *Kinshasa: Tales of the Invisible City* (Ghent, Belgium: Ludion, 2004), 110–11.

50. For the failure of writing and bureaucracy to undermine the powers of the spirits in central African Christianity, see Thomas G. Kirsch, *Spirits and Letters: Reading, Writing and Charisma in African Christianity* (New York: Berghahn Books, 2008).

51. Fields, *Revival and Rebellion*. Also similar to South Africa and west Africa. For South Africa, see Crais, *Politics of Evil*, 129. For west Africa, see Birgit Meyer, *Translating the Devil: Religion and Modernity among the Ewe in Ghana* (Edinburgh: Edinburgh University Press, 1999), esp. 83–111.

52. Michael G. Schatzberg, "La sorcellerie comme mode de causalité politique," *Politique Africaine* 79 (October 2000): 33–47.

53. James Ferguson, *Expectations of Modernity: Myths and Meanings of Urban Life on the Zambian Copperbelt* (Berkeley: University of California Press, 1999).

54. Crawford M. Young and Thomas Turner, *The Rise and Decline of the Zairian State* (Madison: University of Wisconsin Press, 1985); Michael G. Schatzberg, *The Dialectics of Oppression in Zaire* (Bloomington: Indiana University Press, 1988).

55. Ashforth, *Witchcraft*.

56. See the revealing case of Kinshasa's child witches in Boek and Plissart, *Kinshasa*, 155–209.

57. Luis Nicolau Parés and Roger Sansi, eds., *Sorcery in the Black Atlantic* (Chicago: University of Chicago Press, 2011), 9.

58. Morten Bøås and Kevin C. Dunn, *African Guerrillas: Raging Against the Machine* (Boulder, CO: Lynne Rienner, 2007).

59. The Lord's Resistance Army in northern Uganda and the DRC is an obvious case, as is the Pentecostal influence on eastern Congo rebels such as Laurent Nkunda. Heike Behrend, *Alice Lakwena and the Holy Spirits: War in Northern Uganda, 1986–97* (Athens: Ohio University Press, 1999). For similar Muslim and Christian religious agents and violence in Nigeria, see Toyin Falola, *Violence in Nigeria: The Crisis of Religious Politics and Secular Ideologies* (Rochester, NY: University of Rochester Press, 1998). A comparable survey of Christian political mobilization does not exist for central Africa. Also see Bøås and Dunn, *African Guerrillas*, 25–27.

60. For rain, see Lan, *Guns and Rain*. For struggles against taxation, see Sean Redding, *Sorcery and Sovereignty: Taxation, Power, and Rebellion in South Africa, 1880–1963* (Athens: Ohio University Press, 2006). For Shembe's spirit church, see Bengt G. M. Sundkler, *Bantu Prophets in South Africa* (Oxford: Oxford University Press, 1961). Also see more recent work by Elizabeth Gunner, *The Man of Heaven and the Beautiful Ones of God: Umuntu Wasezulwini Nabantu Abahle Bakankulunkulu; Writings from Ibandla Lamanazaretha, a South African Church* (Leiden: Brill, 2002). For the political role of mainline Christianity, see Daniel R. Magaziner, *The Law and the Prophets: Black Consciousness in South Africa, 1968–1977* (Athens: Ohio University Press, 2010); for postapartheid witchcraft in Soweto, see Ashforth, *Witchcraft*. For the northern lowveld, see Isak A. Niehaus, "Witches of the Transvaal Lowveld and Their Familiars: Conceptions of Duality, Power and Desire," *Cahiers d'Études africaines* 35 (1995): 513–40; and Niehaus, "The ANC's Dilemma: The Symbolic Politics of Three Witch-Hunts in the South African Lowveld, 1990–1995," *African Studies Review* 41, no. 3 (1998): 93–118.

61. For Ghana, see Meyer, *Translating the Devil*; and Paul Gifford, *Ghana's New Christianity: Pentecostalism in a Globalizing African Economy* (Bloomington:

Indiana University Press, 2004). For Nigeria, most recently, see Marshall, *Political Spiritualities*.

62. Ellis, *Mask of Anarchy*.

63. Jean Allman and John Parker, *Tongnaab: The History of a West African God* (Bloomington: Indiana University Press, 2005).

64. For the Caribbean, see Stephan Palmié, *Wizards and Scientists: Explorations in Afro-Cuban Modernity and Tradition* (Durham, NC: Duke University Press, 2002); Joan Dayan, *Haiti, History, and the Gods* (Berkeley: University of California Press, 1998). For North American, see early twentieth-century Pentecostal revivals, esp. in Grant Wacker, *Heaven Below: Early Pentecostals and American Culture* (Cambridge, MA: Harvard University Press, 2001).

65. John C. Holt, *Spirits of the Place: Buddhism and Lao Religious Culture* (Honolulu: University of Hawaii Press, 2009); John Pemberton, *On the Subject of "Java"* (Ithaca, NY: Cornell University Press, 1994); Mary Margaret Steedly, *Hanging without a Rope: Narrative Experience in Colonial and Postcolonial Karoland* (Princeton, NJ: Princeton University Press, 1993).

66. For the repression of *bori* spirit possession, see Adeline Masquelier, *Prayer Has Spoiled Everything: Possession, Power, and Identity in an Islamic Town of Niger* (Durham, NC: Duke University Press, 2001). Other recent studies of Islamic political influences in the region include: Donal B. Cruise O'Brien, *Symbolic Confrontations: Muslims Imagining the State in Africa* (London: Hurst, 2003); see Leonardo A. Villalón, *Islamic Society and State Power in Senegal: Disciples and Citizens in Fatick* (Cambridge: Cambridge University Press, 1995).

67. Barbara M. Cooper, *Evangelical Christians in the Muslim Sahel* (Bloomington: Indiana University Press, 2006).

68. Gordon, *Nachituti's Gift*.

69. Giacomo Macola, "Literate Ethnohistory in Colonial Zambia: The Case of 'Ifikolwe Fyandi na Bantu Bandi,'" *History in Africa* 28 (2001): 187–201, esp. 189. Hugo F. Hinfelaar's most influential scholarship includes *Bemba-Speaking Women of Zambia*. Others include Jean-Loup Calmettes and Louis Oger, who have written in many nonacademic contexts. Most of their writings are deposited in the White Fathers Archives, Lusaka (henceforth WFA).

70. Louis Etienne, "A Study of the Babemba and Neighbouring Tribes" (1948), 1/M/Co4, WFA.

71. At first in Audrey I. Richards, *Land, Labour and Diet in Northern Rhodesia: An Economic Study of the Bemba Tribe* (Oxford: Oxford University Press, 1939).

72. Her last article on the Bemba was Audrey I. Richards, "Keeping the King Divine," *Proceedings of the Royal Anthropological Institute of Great Britain and Ireland* (1968): 23–35. Her field notes are deposited in the London School of Economics (henceforth LSE).

73. For the role of Zambians in the development of colonial-era anthropologists, see Lyn Schumaker, *Africanizing Anthropology: Fieldwork, Networks, and the Making of Cultural Knowledge in Central Africa* (Durham, NC: Duke University Press, 2001).

74. For critique of RLI tendencies to focus on "permanent urbanization," see Ferguson, *Expectations of Modernity.*

75. This tendency was not universal among the RLI anthropologists. For example, see the valuable empirical work by Elizabeth Colson, with her study of religion culminating in *Tonga Religious Life in the Twentieth Century* (Lusaka: Bookworld, 2006).

76. Zambia, *Report of the Commission of Enquiry into the Lumpa Church* (Lusaka, 1965).

77. Andrew Roberts, *A History of the Bemba: Political Growth and Change in North-Eastern Zambia before 1900* (London: Longman, 1973).

78. Rotberg, *Rise of Nationalism.*

79. Henry Meebelo, *Reaction to Colonialism.*

80. For example, consider Henry S. Meebelo's argument that the failure of the unions to embrace UNIP was the fault of the unions' megalomaniacal leaders rather than UNIP's authoritarian tendencies, in *African Proletarians and Colonial Capitalism: The Origins, Growth and Struggles of the Zambian Labour Movement to 1964* (Lusaka: Kenneth Kaunda Foundation, 1986), esp. 414–50.

81. Robin Palmer and Neil Parsons, eds., *The Roots of Rural Poverty in Central and Southern Africa* (Berkeley: University of California Press, 1977).

82. Wim M. J. van Binsbergen, *Religious Change in Zambia: Exploratory Studies* (London: Kegan Paul, 1981).

83. Samuel N. Chipungu, ed., *Guardians in Their Time: Experiences of Zambians under Colonial Rule, 1890–1964* (London: Macmillan, 1992).

84. For the relationship between this new generation of anthropologists and the RLI, see David M. Gordon, "Rites of Rebellion: Recent Anthropology from Zambia," *African Studies* 62, no. 1 (2003): 125–39.

85. Karen Tranberg Hansen, *Keeping House in Lusaka* (New York: Columbia University Press, 1997); and Hansen, *Salaula: The World of Second-hand Clothing in Zambia.* (Chicago: University of Chicago Press, 2000).

86. James A. Pritchett, *The Lunda-Ndembu: Style, Change, and Social Transformation in South Central Africa* (Madison: University of Wisconsin Press, 2001); and Pritchett, *Friends for Life, Friends for Death: Cohorts and Consciousness among the Lunda-Ndembu* (Charlottesville: University of Virginia Press, 2007).

87. Henrietta L. Moore and Megan Vaughan, *Cutting Down Trees: Gender, Nutrition, and Agricultural Change in the Northern Province of Zambia, 1890–1990* (London: James Currey, 1994).

88. Jan-Bart Gewald, Marja Hinfelaar, and Giacomo Macola, eds., *One Zambia, Many Histories: Towards a History of Post-Colonial Zambia* (Leiden: Brill, 2008), 9.

89. Giacomo Macola, "Harry Mwaanga Nkumbula, UNIP and the Roots of Authoritarianism in Nationalist Zambia," in Gewald, Hinfelaar, and Macola, *One Zambia, Many Histories,* 17–44.

90. For the underground UPP opposition after 1972, see Miles Larmer, "Enemies Within?: Opposition to the Zambian One-Party State, 1972–1980," in Gewald,

Hinfelaar, and Macola, *One Zambia, Many Histories*, 98–128. His thorough account of the trade union movement is Miles Larmer, *Mineworkers in Zambia: Labour and Political Change in Post-Colonial Africa* (London: Taurus, 2007).

91. Marja Hinfelaar, "Legitimizing Powers: The Political Role of the Roman Catholic Church, 1972–1991," in Gewald, Hinfelaar, and Macola, *One Zambia, Many Histories*, 129–43. In the same volume, Austin M. Cheyeka pointed to the political influences of the charismatic churches: "Towards a History of the Charismatic Churches in Post-Colonial Zambia," in Gewald, Hinfelaar, and Macola, *One Zambia, Many Histories*, 144–63.

CHAPTER 1: THE PASSION OF CHITIMUKULU

1. The generic Luba forms of such staffs are discussed in Mary Nooter Roberts and Allen F. Roberts, *Memory: Luba Art and the Making of History* (New York: Museum for African Art, 1996), 162–74. For the Bemba staff in this genre and the claim that it represents Chilimbulu, see Andrew Roberts, *A History of the Bemba: Political Growth and Change in North-Eastern Zambia before 1900* (London: Longman, 1973), plate 4, p. 30. Also see pages 344–45 for relationship of the staff to other relics.

2. V. Y. Mudimbe, *Parables and Fables: Exegesis, Textuality, and Politics in Central Africa* (Madison: University of Wisconsin Press, 1988), esp. 86–123.

3. Roberts, *History of the Bemba*, 44.

4. See J. Matthew Schoffeleers's study of the Mbona cult in *River of Blood: The Genesis of a Martyr Cult in Southern Malawi, c. A.D. 1600* (Madison: University of Wisconsin Press, 1992).

5. Several of the Roman Catholic White Father missionaries drew on their own mission experiences, a series of mission surveys, and previous missionary notes. The original manuscript from which most of the mission studies seem to be drawn is Nicolas Garrec, "Croyances et coutumes religieuses." Photocopy of the original that is in Rome, Padre Bianchi 260 via Aurelia, catalogue n. 453, manuscript 453, orig. 1916, 1/M/C50, White Fathers Archives, Zambia (henceforth WFA). The most widely cited and influential is a translation and edited version of Edouard Labrecque manuscripts, *Beliefs and Religious Practices of the Bemba and Neighbouring Tribes*, trans. and ed. Patrick Boyd (Chinsali, Zambia: Ilondola Language Center, 1982). The parts that focus on spiritual beliefs are based on two typescripts written in 1934. Edouard Labrecque, "La religion du Noir infidele" and an edited "Coutumes matrimoniales des Babemba de la Rhodesie du Nord," 1/M/C19–20, WFA. These in turn draw from Garrec, above. The Viciarité de Bengweulu undertook extensive fieldwork about Bemba and related customs from 1934 to 1938. The findings were written in 1948, as Louis Etienne, "A Study of the Bemba and Neighbouring Tribes," 1/M/C4, WFA. For spiritual beliefs of the nearby Luba, first written in the 1930s, but published only in its original English form, see William F. P. Burton, *Luba Religion and Magic in Custom and Belief* (Tervuren, Belgium: Musée royal de l'Afrique centrale, 1962).

6. Audrey I. Richards, *Land, Labour and Diet in Northern Rhodesia: An Economic Study of the Bemba Tribe* (Oxford: Oxford University Press, 1939), 359.

7. Hugo F. Hinfelaar, *Bemba-Speaking Women of Zambia in a Century of Religious Change (1892–1992)* (Leiden: Brill, 1994), 1–19. For further discussion of the differences between Hinfelaar and Richards, also see Henrietta L. Moore and Megan Vaughn, *Cutting Down Trees: Gender, Nutrition, and Agricultural Change in the Northern Province of Zambia, 1890–1990* (London: James Currey, 1994), 9–10; Megan Vaughan, "'Divine Kings': Sex, Death and Anthropology in Inter-War East/Central Africa," *Journal of African History* 49, no. 3 (2008): 383–401.

8. Harold Scheub, *Story* (Madison: University of Wisconsin Press, 1998), 21.

9. Godfrey Wilson, "The Analysis of Religious Behaviour," D 4/6, University of Cape Town Manuscripts and Archives (henceforth UCTMA).

10. Richards, *Land, Labour and Diet*, 359.

11. Emile Durkheim, *The Elementary Forms of Religious Life*, trans. Karen E. Fields (New York: Free Press, 1995), 275.

12. For the liminal aspects of the oral tradition, see Kevin B. Maxwell, *Bemba Myth and Ritual: The Impact of Literacy on an Oral Culture* (New York: Peter Lang, 1983), 39.

13. For an evaluation of the factual basis of the oral tradition and the approximate dating of the founding of Chitimukulu, see Roberts, *History of the Bemba*, 56–65.

14. We have several twentieth-century attempts to write down the oral tradition in its entirety. The version here is based on a summary of the earliest and most complete recording: Edouard Labrecque, "La tribu des Babemba, 1: Les origines des Babemba," *Anthropos* 28 (1933): 633–48. Paul B. Mushindo presents a version as *A Short History of the Bemba (As Narrated by a Bemba)* (Lusaka: National Educational Company of Zambia, 1977). Labrecque's version was widely circulated and used as a blueprint for Francois Tanguy, *Imilandu ya BaBemba* (Lusaka: African Literature Committee, 1948). A school reader of Bemba history was published as White Fathers, *Ifyabukaya* (Chilubula, n.d.). The influence of the Catholic White Fathers' *Ifyabukaya*, used as a primary school textbook, is widespread and renders further collection of the precolonial form of the oral tradition by present-day researchers at best problematic. Labrecque's version, published before the dissemination of *Ifyabukaya*, is free from the influence of *Ifyabukaya*. For a discussion of these accounts, see Roberts, *History of the Bemba*, 9–11. Another rich version, with unclear origins, is "Manuscript of Bemba Origins," in Audrey Richards Papers, 1/67, London School of Economics (henceforth LSE). For an account based on a compilation of early colonial officials, but in which the summation of the oral tradition of genesis differs substantially from other versions, see Cullen Gouldsbury and Hubert Sheane, *The Great Plateau of Northern Rhodesia: Being Some Impressions of the Tanganyika Plateau* (New York: Negro University Press, 1968), 80–98.

15. See, for example, the story of Kimpimpi, in Leon Verbeek, *Le monde des esprits au sud-est du Shaba et au nord de la Zambie* (Rome: Libreria Ateneo Salesiano, 1990), 89–112.

16. A substantially different version omits the story of the tower and instead discusses father-son discord, brought about by a strict father and unruly sons who refused to clean the royal shrines, in Mushindo, *Short History*, 2–4. The seeds included that of the most commonly grown crop, finger millet (*Eleusine corecana*), and the most desirable royal crop, sorghum (*Sorghum* sp.), which grew only in fertile soils, and was closely associated with ritual and royalty. A continuation of the story of Chilufya deals with her seduction by her half brother, Kapasa.

17. This symbolic interpretation in Luc de Heusch, *The Drunken King; or, The Origin of the State*, trans. Roy Willis (Bloomington: Indiana University Press, 1982), 235–36. The rising sun in the east is indeed an important religious concept across the region. East of the Bemba polity, the fertility *ngulu* Nakabutula was associated with the rising run and with good fortune. Interview: Peter Kanyembo Chikoko, Kanaya, Luapula, 16 July 2002; Simon Kalumba Shindiliya, Kazembe, 24 July 2002.

18. According to Labrecque, the chief's "head wife" danced with Chilimbulu's skin; this is not actually inconsistent with the idea of a "virgin," as, according to Richards, the "head wife" who performs many ritual acts is expected to be chaste and past child-bearing age. Audrey I. Richards, "Keeping the King Divine," *Proceedings of the Royal Anthropological Institute of Great Britain and Ireland* (1968): 23–35, esp. 32.

19. Labrecque, *Beliefs and Religious Practices*, 35.

20. Such as the staff of Mwamba in Roberts, *History of the Bemba*, plate 4, p. 30.

21. W. Vernon Brelsford collected a more detailed version of the relationship of Kabotwe and Chimbala, their origins, and the transactions that led to the creation of the title "Shimwalule," in "Shimwalule: A Study of a Bemba Chief and Priest," *African Studies* 1, no. 3 (1942): 207–23, esp. 208–9.

22. For Luba *mulopwe* and earth priests, see Thomas Q. Reefe, *The Rainbow and the Kings: A History of the Luba Empire to 1891* (Berkeley: University of California, 1981), esp. 46.

23. *Mfumu* chieftainship among the Bemba seems to have been a Crocodile Clan innovation. The term has old proto-Bantu origins, and probably spread through the region from the lower Kwilu in the thirteenth and fourteenth centuries, in Jan Vansina, *How Societies Are Born: Governance in West Central Africa Before 1600* (Charlottesville: University of Virginia Press, 2004), 241–44. For the affective aspects of *mfumu* in deep Bantu-speaking history, see Kathryn M. de Luna, "Fame as Fortune: Emotion and the Politics of Knowledge in Central Africa" (paper presented to African Studies Association Meeting, New Orleans, 16–19 November 2009).

24. As claimed in the version written by Mushindo, *Short History*, and accepted by Roberts, *History of the Bemba*, 39, 68. Contra Wim M. J. van Binsbergen, who ignores this evidence in his claim that Luba divine kingship replaced territorial cults, in *Religious Change in Zambia: Exploratory Studies* (London: Kegan Paul, 1981), 119–24.

25. For further explication of the vertical and horizontal cosmogenic axes in the story, see de Heusch, *Drunken King*, 236–37.

26. David Livingstone, *The Last Journals of David Livingstone, in Central Africa: From 1865 to His Death* (New York: Harper and Brothers, 1875), 279.

27. For association between *ngulu* and the sky, see Louis Oger, "Spirit Possession Among the Bemba" (paper presented at Conference on Central African Religions, Lusaka, 30 August–8 September 1972), 1/M/C59, WFA; Louis Etienne, "A Study of the Bemba and Neighbouring Tribes" (1948), 93, 1/M/C4, WFA. The "Bangulu" among the Luba are also related to the sky, in Burton, *Luba Religion and Magic*, 73–74.

28. Wyatt MacGaffey *Astonishment and Power: The Eyes of Understanding: Kongo Minkisi* (Washington: Smithsonian Institution Press, 1993), 75.

29. Allen Roberts, personal communication.

30. For claims by chiefs to know correct mortuary rites in the colonial period, see Walima T. Kalusa, "Death, Christianity, and African Miners: Contesting Indirect Rule in the Zambian Copperbelt, 1935–1962," *International Journal of African Historical Studies* 44, no. 1 (2011): 89–112, esp. 97–98.

31. Historical linguistics suggests that the use of *ngulu* is more recent than *mipashi*. Given the tendency of religious terminology to diffuse, however, use of historical linguistics in this instance is imprecise; oral traditions and testimony suggest that *ngulu* was present at least prior to the rise of the Bemba polity. Eastern ChiBemba dialects, such as ChiMambwe and ChiLungu, as well as the more distinctive ChiChewa and ChiNyanja languages, used the *–zimu* root as a general term for ancestors and associated *–pashi* exclusively with royal ancestors, perhaps as a result of Bemba conquests, in Douglas Werner, "Some Developments in Bemba Religious History," *Journal of Religion in Africa* 4, no. 1 (1971): 1–24, esp. 91–93. For nineteenth-century evidence of *–zimu* east of the Bemba, see Antonio C. P. Gamitto, *King Kazembe and the Marave, Cheva, Bisa, Bemba, Lunda and Other Peoples of Southern Africa*, trans. Ian Cunnison (Lisbon: Junta de Investigações do Ultramar), 73–76.

32. Oger, "Spirit Possession Among the Bemba," 1/M/C59, WFA; interview: Simon Kalumba Shindiliya, Kazembe, 24 July 2002.

33. Referred to as *ukupyana* "succession." Etienne, "Study of the Bemba," 72–75, 1/M/C4, WFA. For *mipashi* inheritance by a crying child, see H. Barnes, "Survival after Death among the Ba-Bemba of North-Eastern Rhodesia," *Man* 25–26 (1922): 41–42.

34. Oger, "Spirit Possession Among the Bemba"; and "Interview with Stephen Chipalo, Keeper of relics at Nkula," 1/M/C59, WFA. For *bena ngandu* not being possessed by *ngulu*, see Louis Oger, "Handwritten Notes on Van Binsbergen" 5/PP/36, WFA; Roberts, *History of the Bemba*, 70–77. Werner, "Some Developments"; van Binsbergen, *Religious Change in Zambia*, 121. For the eastern Lunda, see David M. Gordon, "History on the Luapula Retold: Landscape, Memory and Identity in the Kazembe Kingdom," *Journal of African History* 47, no. 1 (2006): 21–42.

35. Richards, *Land, Labour and Diet*, 356–57. Livingstone, *Last Journals*, 279. Such places of variation had a number of different names, several that reference

the home or places of rest, such as *nfuba, nsaka, tupeshi, tekeshi,* as listed in Verbeek, *Le monde des esprit,* 27.

36. Verbeek, *Le monde des esprit,* 17, 27.

37. The best account of such *bwanga* is in Etienne, "Study of the Bemba," esp. 82, for harvest ceremony, 1/M/C4, WFA. For other objects used for *bwanga,* see Reginald J. B. Moore, "'Bwanga' among the Bemba," *Africa: Journal of the International African Institute* 13, no. 3 (July 1940): 211–34. For analysis, see Moore, "'Bwanga' among the Bemba, Part 2," *Bantu Studies* 15, no. 1 (1941): 37–41. For the use of similar charms, including detailed descriptions of their composition and use among the Luba, see Burton, *Luba Religion and Magic,* 100–126.

38. Etienne, "Study of the Bemba," esp. 82, for harvest ceremony, 1/M/C4, WFA; Richards, *Land, Labour and Diet,* 355–56; Labrecque, *Beliefs and Religious Practices,* 35–39.

39. Richards, "Keeping the King Divine," 26–30.

40. The *babenye* relics were not exclusively located at Mwalule, and were probably relocated to Lubemba through the twentieth century. The traditional residence of *bamukabenye* indicates that they were previously held at Mwalule. Labrecque, *Beliefs and Religious Practices,* 15–16; Brelsford, "Shimwalule," 212; Richards, *Land Labour and Diet,* 358–59; Audrey Richards Papers, "Supernatural Powers of Chiefs," 1/4/1/13, LSE.

41. The version above is found in Labrecque's and Mushindo's narrations. For an alternative version of the founding of Nkhweto and the meaning of Chilinda, see the "Transcription of "tape-recording by Chief Nkweto Mulenga, 17 May 1965," in Roberts, *History of the Bemba,* 378–80.

42. Labrecque, *Beliefs and Religious Practices,* 10. For mention of Chishimba and how shrines developed through negotiation between conquest chiefs and locals, see Douglas Werner, "Miao Spirit Shrines in the Religious History of the Southern Lake Tanganyika Region: The Case of Kapembwa," in J. M. Schoffeleers, ed., *Guardians of the Land: Essays on Central African Territorial Cults* (Gwelo, Zimbabwe: Mambo Press, 1978), 89–130. Audrey Richards, "Religion and Magic," 1/4/1/30, LSE.

43. R. F. Burton, trans., *The Lands of Cazembe: Lacerda's Journey to Cazembe in 1798* (New York: Negro University Press, 1969), 127. For reference in 1868, see Livingstone, *Last Journals,* 279.

44. For linguistic evidence that dates "Lesa" to an antiquity similar to the *pashi* root, see Werner, "Some Developments," 8–9.

45. As argued by Maxwell, *Bemba Myth and Ritual,* 101–12, esp. 104. For an elaboration based on linguistic evidence, see Christine Saidi, *Women's Authority and Society in Early East-Central Africa* (Rochester, NY: University of Rochester Press, 2010), 92–95.

46. Findings from 1934 to 1938 research, in "Table d'enquete: Existence de Dieu," 1/M/C11, WFA.

47. The first recording of this narrative in Garrec, "Croyances et coutumes religieuse," 1/M/C49, WFA.

48. For example, see Maxwell, *Bemba Myth and Ritual*, 106–10; Labrecque, *Beliefs and Religious Practices*, 5–7; Reginald J. B. Moore "The Development of the Conception of God," *International Review of Missions* 31, no. 124 (1942): 412–20, esp. 414–16.

49. Oger, "Spirit Possession Among the Bemba." According to Mulumbwa Mutambwa and Leon Verbeek, *chiwa* were not living-dead, but rather simply evil spirits, in *Bulumbu: Un mouvement extatique au sud-est du Zaire à travers la chanson traditionelle* (Tervuren, Belgium: Musée royal de l'Afrique centrale, 1997), 17. *Chiwa* and *chibanda* might actually refer to the same root word; observers tend to alternate between "b" and "w" in ChiBemba orthography. These evil spirits are conflated in J. H. West Sheane, "Some Aspects of the Awemba Religion and Superstitious Observances," *Journal of the Anthropological Institute of Great Britain and Ireland* 36 (January–June 1906): 153.

50. For *mipashi* ancestors occupying newborn babies, see Barnes, "Survival after Death," 41–42.

51. Interview: Fergus Macpherson with Donald Siwale, Isunda, Nakonde, 22 December 1966; interview: Yafet Mugara, 22 December 1966, Macpherson Collection, Box 3–4, Center for Study of Christianity in the Non-Western World, Edinburgh (henceforth CSCNWW). Among the Valley Bisa from fieldwork in the 1960s, see Stuart A. Marks, *Large Mammals and a Brave People: Subsistence Hunters in Zambia* (New Brunswick, NJ: Transaction Publishers, 2005), 36–37.

52. Interview: Fergus Macpherson with Donald Siwale, Isunda, Nakonde, 22 December 1966, CSCNWW.

53. Labrecque, *Beliefs and Religious Practices*, 25. Labrecque's use of the term "occult" to describe these practices long predates its recent use among anthropologists, best known in Peter Geschiere, *The Modernity of Witchcraft: Politics and the Occult in Postcolonial Africa* (Charlottesville: University of Virginia Press, 1997).

54. Labrecque convincingly argues that such witches (*baloshi*) and associations actually existed; they were not simply the scapegoats of witchcraft accusations in "La sorcellerie chez les Babemba," *Anthropos* 33 (1938): 260–65. Labrecque claims that the most successful witches were able to pass the *mwavi* ordeal unscathed, as they had knowledge of emetics that would ensure they vomited the *mwavi* poison. For the Luba, among whom the *mwavi* ordeal seemed less evident, see Burton, *Luba Religion and Magic*, 132–35.

55. Oger, "Spirit Possession Among the Bemba." For similar possession in the *bulumbu* cult to the west of the Bemba, where "*ngulu*" is the vehicle for recognizing the spirit, rather than the spirit itself, see Mutambwa and Verbeek, *Bulumbu*, 18–24.

56. Sheane, "Some Aspects of the Awemba Religion," 152.

57. Hinfelaar, *Bemba-Speaking Women*, 6–8; Jan J. IJzermans, "Music and Theory of the Possession Cult Leaders in Chibale, Serenje District, Zambia," *Ethnomusicology* 39, no. 2 (1995): 245–74, esp. 251–52.

58. Daniel Crawford, *Thinking Black: 22 Years without a Break in the Long Grass of Central Africa* (New York: George H. Doran, 1912), 229–53, especially

234–35. Ian G. Cunnison also refers to a women's secret society that had died out by the time he did his fieldwork in the 1940s, in Cunnison, *The Luapula Peoples of Northern Rhodesia: Custom and History in Tribal Politics* (Manchester: Manchester University Press, 1959), 204.

59. The *chisungu* rites were abbreviated and changed by the time they were witnessed by outsiders in the early twentieth century. My interpretation of their precolonial forms is based on a careful reading of the testimony presented in these twentieth-century accounts. Based on observations in 1931 and additional commentary in 1933, see Audrey I. Richards, *Chisungu: A Girl's Initiation Ceremony among the Bemba of Zambia* (London: Routledge, 1995). Based on observations in 1960, see J. J. Corbeil, *Mbusa: Sacred Emblems of the Bemba* (London: Ethnographica, 1982).

60. Richards, *Chisungu*, 80.

61. *Mutwale umwana ku ngwena.* Corbeil, *Mbusa*, 38.

62. The origins of *chisungu* is associated with the oral tradition of the Crocodile Clan in accounts reported by Corbeil, *Mbusa*, 7. Initiation rites and songs are prevalent across the ChiBemba-speaking area: Leon Verbeek, *Initiation et marriage dans la chanson populaire des Bemba du Zaire* (Tervuren, Belgium: Musée royal de l'Afrique centrale, 1993), esp. 10; and among the Bisa, F. M. Thomas, *Historical Notes on the Bisa Tribe of Northern Rhodesia* (Lusaka: Rhodes-Livingstone Institute, 1958), 22. The Luba did have an equivalent ceremony, termed "Butanda," but there is not the same evidence of the use of *mbusa*; Burton, *Luba Religion and Magic*, 151–53; Allen Roberts, personal communication. The linguistic evidence is decisive on the ancient east-central African and pre–Crocodile Clan origins of *mbusa*-based initiation rites, Saidi, *Women's Authority*, 101–27.

63. Hinfelaar, *Bemba-Speaking Women*, 33.

64. See Labrecque's description of *mbusa* in *Beliefs and Religious Practices*, 44–50.

65. Contra Hinfelaar, *Bemba-Speaking Women*, 19–33.

66. For Shimwalule's details, see Brelsford, "Shimwalule," 207–23. Further details in "Mwalule and the Shimwalule, " SEC 2/751. Annexure 3 Tour Report 5/1939, NAZ.

67. Brelsford, "Shimwalule," 219.

68. Roberts, *History of the Bemba*, 128–29.

69. The political process is best covered in Roberts, *History of the Bemba*, 125–63. For trade, see pages 168–214. For "constitutional" changes in Bemba polity after 1860, roughly linked to increase in trade, see Richard P. Werbner, "Federal Administration, Rank, and Civil Strife among Bemba Royals and Nobles," *Africa: Journal of the International African Institute* 37 no. 1 (January 1967): 22–49. For the Chitimukulu's proclaimed conquests by 1883, see Victor Giraud, *Les lacs de l'Afrique équatoriale: Voyage d'exploration executé de 1883 à 1885* (Paris: Libraire Hachette, 1890), 264.

70. Livingstone, *Last Journals*, 147.

71. Ibid., 164.

72. Giraud, *Les lacs de l'Afrique équatoriale*, 238.

73. Roberts, *History of the Bemba*, 312.

74. Mushindo, *Historical Notes*, 68.

75. Mushindo's rendition of this "prayer" is probably influenced by his own Christian background; nevertheless, it gives us an impression of spiritual appeals in times of war. Mushindo, *Short History*, 76.

76. For slavery and judicial system, see Martin Chanock, *Law Custom and Social Order: The Colonial Experience in Malawi and Zambia* (Porstmouth, NH: Heinemann, 1998), 163–64. Interview evidence suggests use of the judicial mechanisms to acquire slaves. Interview: Macpherson with Chief Shaibila, Mkushi, 14 August 1974; Macpherson with Patson Chipili, Mukupa Katandula, 27 November 1974, CSCNWW. Payment of people to solve witchcraft cases was noted in the early colonial period, in James Chisholm, "Letter to Friends," *Livingstonia News* 3, no. 2 (1910).

77. Richards, *Land, Labour and Diet*, 361.

78. To my knowledge, no Bemba representations of royalty can be found in Western museum collections.For similar representations of royalty invented and celebrated in this period among the Tabwa to the north, see Allen Roberts, "Female Figures," in *Treasures from the Africa-Museum Tevuren*, ed. Gustaaf Verswijver et. al. (Tevuren, Belgium: Royal Museum for Central Africa, 1995), 65–369. For the Luba staff held by Bemba chiefs, see Roberts, *History of the Bemba*, plate 4, p. 30.

79. The association between "forgiven" and "vomiting" was an obvious one, repeated in *mwavi* poison ordeals. For the notion of *mfumu ya muluka* as "forgiven," see Brelsford, "Shimwalule," 219.

80. For the most detailed account of precolonial burial practices, see Audrey Richards, "Death and Burial of Chiefs," n.d. (1930s?); and Paul Mushindo, "Traditional Overnight Funeral Stops for Chiti's Funeral," 1934, ARP 1/1, LSE. A decade later, these rites were again recorded in W. Vernon Brelsford, *Aspects of Bemba Chieftainship* (Livingstone, Northern Rhodesia: Rhodes-Livingstone Institute, 1944), 27–37. Brelsford claims that a man who had been sacrificed and "vomited out" by the chief was still alive in the 1930s, and that the last human sacrifices took place at the death of Chitimukulu Sampa (d. 1896; see report cited below by BSAC administrator), reinforcing the probability that they were at their height around the time of the death of Chitapankwa. Brelsford, "Shimwalule," 219. Also see District Commissioner's Report on "The Burial of Chitimukulu IX Mubanga," SEC 2-307, NAZ; Aaron Mwenya, "The Burial of Chitimukulu Mubanga," *African Affairs* 46, no. 183 (April 1947): 101–4. When the BSAC administrator visited Mwalule in 1896, he heard rumors of "atrocities" committed during the burial of Chitimukulu Sampa, in Bell to P. W. Forbes, 24 November 1896, A 1-1 Ikawa Collector, NAZ.

81. Sheane identifies *tulubi* almost exclusively among the Bisa in "Some Aspects of the Awemba Religion," 150–58.

82. For the use of *mikishi* among Aushi, Lamba, and Lala, see Mutambwa and Verbeek, *Bulumbu*, 16. Livingstone found the term *mikishi* to be widespread in *Last Journals*, 279.

83. Roy Philpot, "Makumba—The Baushi Tribal God," *Journal of the Royal Anthropological Institute of Great Britain and Ireland* 66 (January–July 1936): 189–208; Verbeek, *Le monde des esprits*, 18–20, 75–88.

84. As observed in 1868 by Livingstone in *Last Journals*, 353.

85. For a description, see Allen Roberts, "Standing Figures," in *African Art from the Menil Collection*, ed. Kristina van Dyke (New Haven, CT: Yale University Press, 2008), 224.

86. Mwelwa C. Musambachime, "The Ubutwa Society in Eastern Shaba and Northeast Zambia to 1920," *International Journal of African Historical Studies* 27, no. 1 (1994): 77–99; Gordon, "History on the Luapula," 29–30. Interviews: P. Lary with Aron Mwenya, Mbereshi, 27 October 1973; P. Lary with James Kakonko Lendengoma, Lendengoma Village, 26 October 1973; P. Lary with Chinyanta, Mununshi, Luapula, 20 October 1973, CSCNWW. For Butwa songs, see Mutambwa and Verbeek, *Bulumbu*, 331–33. For "territorial cults," see J. M. Schoffeleers, introduction to *Guardians of the Land*, 8. For Zambian examples, see Wim M. J. van Binsbergen, "Explorations in the History and Sociology of Territorial Cults in Zambia," in *Guardians of the Land*, 47–88, and his *Religious Change in Zambia*, 100–134.

87. "Bulumbu" refers to similar practices of spirit possession across the region, in Mutambwa and Verbeek, *Bulumbu*. Also see the similar Luba *Bumbudye* society in Burton, *Luba Religion and Magic*, 154–67.

88. Mushindo, *Short History*, 53–54.

89. Thomas, *Historical Notes*, 49.

90. Ibid., 43–46; Mushindo, *Short History*, 51–53, 87–88. Around 1883, Giraud claims Chitimukulu sold two hundred slaves captured in wars against the Bisa to Swahili slave traders, in *Les lacs de l'Afrique équatoriale*, 245–55.

91. Jean-Jacques Corbeil, "Notes on Ubwanga," 1/M/C87, WFA; Thomas, *Historical Notes*, 52; Labrecque, *Beliefs and Religious Practices*, 34.

92. For example, see defeat of the Mambwe, Chitongwa, and Chifuta in Mushindo, *Short History*, 87.

93. For taking of heads, see R. O'Ferrall, "An Old War Song of the Babemba," *Bulletin of the School of Oriental Studies* 4, no. 4 (1928): 839–44. For skulls on stockades, see Giraud, *Les lacs de l'Afrique équatoriale*, 253–55, 369–71, 531–32.

94. A Bemba *ilamfya* is held by the National Museum of Scotland, and duplicated in Roberts, *History of the Bemba*, plate 6. Sarah Worden, National Museum of Scotland, personal communication. A photo and description the use of what appears to be the same *ilamfya* is in Gouldsbury and Sheane, *Great Plateau*, 92.

95. J. H. West Sheane, "Wemba Warpaths," *Journal of the Royal African Society* 11, no. 41 (1911): 21–34.

96. For example, the spirit of Mwela in western Lubemba, in Roberts, *History of the Bemba*, 70–71.

97. Etienne, "Study of the Bemba," 93–95.

98. Labrecque, *Beliefs and Religious Practices*, 12.

CHAPTER 2: CHRISTIAN WITCHES

1. Karen E. Fields, *Revival and Rebellion in Colonial Central Africa* (Princeton, NJ: Princeton University Press, 1985), esp. 65–66.

2. Brian Garvey, *Bembaland Church: Religious and Social Change in South Central Africa, 1891–1964* (Leiden: Brill, 1994), 28–39.

3. Dupont's diary entries of the establishment of the mission celebrates his heroism in this endeavor, and are repeated in Francois Tanguy, "Kayambi: The First White Father Mission in Northern Rhodesia," *Northern Rhodesia Journal* 2, no. 4 (1954): 73–78. For a more balanced account, see Garvey, *Bembaland Church*, 50–51.

4. Garvey, *Bembaland Church*, 56–58. Also see the celebratory and embellished account of Dupont, by W. F. Rea, *The Bemba's White Chief* (Salisbury, Rhodesia: Historical Association of Rhodesia and Nyasaland, 1964).

5. The legality of this and other allocations by the BSAC was always under question, given the directives to allow the freedom of missionary operations, as stipulated in the Berlin Agreement of 1885–1886. For the process of allocation, see A 3-10-7 United Free Church Scotland, Livingstone Mission, NAZ. Also see George Prentice, U. Free Church of Scotland, Foreign Mission Committee, *Report on Our Central African Fields*, n.d. (1922–1923?), Acc. 9269, Livingstonia, National Library of Scotland, Edinburgh (henceforth NLS).

6. *Aurora: A Journal of Missionary News and Christian Work* 9 (June 1906).

7. Quote from National Archives of Malawi, as cited in At Ipenburg, "All Good Men": *The Development of Lubwa Mission,Chinsali, Zambia, 1905–1967* (Frankfurt: Peter Lang, 1992), 34. Based on these sources, Ipenburg claims that twenty-four native teachers went to Bembaland, while a report in the *Aurora* claims fifty: "A Visit to Chinsali," *Aurora* 10 (June 1907).

8. "Visit to Chinsali," *Aurora* 10 (June 1907).

9. Ipenburg, "All Good Men," 35–45; W. V. Stone, "The Livingstonia Mission and the Bemba," *Bulletin of the Society for African Church History* 2 (1965–1968): 311–22.

10. Garvey, *Bembaland Church*, 96–97.

11. For example, see Emilio Mulolani's Catholic movement, in Garvey, *Bembaland Church*, 159–71; L. Oger, "Mutima Church of Emilio Mulolani," Mimeograph, Ilondola, n.d.

12. James Chisholm to George Smith, Edinburgh, 3 April 1901, MS 7884, NLS.

13. *Livingstonia News Report*, 1902, 30–31. Quoted in Ipenburg, "All Good Men," 50.

14. David J. Cook, "The Influence of Livingstonia Mission upon the Formation of Welfare Associations in Zambia, 1912–31," in *Themes in the Christian History of Central Africa*, ed. Terence O. Ranger and John Weller (London: Heinemann, 1975), 98–134, esp. 99.

15. Tessier to Livinhac, Chilubula, 24 October 1980. Quoted in Garvey, *Bembaland Church*, 90.

16. Garvey, *Bembaland Chuch*, 105–12.

17. Ibid., 159. The first accurate census figures in 1963 total 563,995 people in Northern Province, reported in Zambia, *May/June 1963 Census of Village Population* (Lusaka: Central Statistics Office, 1965).

18. Jean Comaroff and John L. Comaroff, *Of Revelation and Revolution: The Dialectics of Modernity on a South African Frontier*, vol. 2 (Chicago: University of Chicago Press, 1997).

19. For limited Catholic education initiatives during BSAC rule, see Garvey, *Bembaland Church*, 140–42.

20. For numbers of pupils from 1909 to 1925, see Ipenburg, "All Good Men," 66.

21. The distinction was made by the Native Schools (Amendment) Ordinance of 1927. A "school" was an assembly (not necessarily in a built structure) that devoted not less than 120 days to teaching, according to a code approved by the director of Native Education and the Advisory Board on Native Education. All other assemblies that taught secular subjects were "sub-schools." According to the Native Educational Department, *Annual Report 1927*. Cited in Peter D. Snelson, *Educational Development in Northern Rhodesia, 1883–1945* (Lusaka: National Educational Company of Zambia, 1974), 160.

22. *Livingstonia News*, 4 August 1913.

23. For MacMinn's prolific linguistic work, see C. M. Doke, "The Linguistic Work and Manuscripts of R. D. MacMinn," *African Studies* 18, no. 4 (1959): 180–89.

24. An interpretation that formed a precursor to the arguments for the "pre-Christian" monotheistic basis of African religions made by theologians, especially John S. Mbiti, *African Religions and Philosophy* (London: Heinemann, 1969). Robin Horton critiques this "theological" position in "Judaeo-Christian Spectacles: Boon or Bane to the Study of African Religions?" *Cahiers d'Etudes africaines* 24, no. 96 (1984): 391–436.

25. Ipenburg, "All Good Men," 23.

26. The general noun *devil* is sometimes translated as "kasebenya," perhaps derived from "kase," a spirit that caused death. White Fathers, *The White Fathers' Bemba English Dictionary* (Ndola, Zambia: Mission Press, 1991).

27. The list of titles is in Snelson, *Educational Development*, 161.

28. John Fraser, "Report on the Lubwa Campaign," B/314, Livingstonia Rhodesia General 1953–1957, Acc. 7548, NLS.

29. In the notes Audrey Richards records that if a man slept with his daughter or sister, he was considered a witch; and yet the ChiBemba verb to express this action was *bembuka*, "to commit sin." Audrey Richards Field Notes, 1934, Audrey Richards Papers, 2/17, London School of Economics (henceforth LSE).

30. The *–pondo* root was used for sin in Lenshina's hymns. See, for example, the hymn on page 153 in chapter 4. White Fathers, *White Fathers' Bemba-English Dictionary*.

31. Louis Etienne, "A Study of the Bemba and Neighbouring Tribes" (1948), 1–2, 1/M/C4, WFA.

32. MacMinn, Chinsali, to Ashcroft, Edinburgh, 5 January 1921, MS 7884, NLS.

33. Garvey, *Bembaland Church*, 143.

34. Ibid, 157–58.

35. Lubwa Mission Reports 1927, CS 13-2, United Church of Zambia Archives, Mindolo, Kitwe (henceforth UCZA).

36. Lubwa Mission Reports 1934, CS 13-2, UCZA.

37. Garvey, *Bembaland Church*, 123; Calmettes, "Lumpa Sect," 95, 107.

38. Lubwa Mission Reports, 1937, CS 13-2, UCZA.

39. First Bemba version published in 1942, in Lubwa Mission Reports, 1942, CS 13-2, UCZA; Minutes, Church of Scotland, Livingstonia Mission Council, 28 June 1943, Acc. 7548, Central African Correspondence, NLS.

40. Garvey, *Bembaland Church*, 150–54.

41. Notes on Spirit Possession, Audrey Richards Papers 1/34, LSE.

42. Luise White's focus on the vampire *banyama* accusations against the White Fathers tends to conflate *banyama* with *baloshi* witches. Evidence suggests that the White Fathers were accused of being both, although *baloshi* witchcraft accusations were more frequent. Luise White, *Speaking with Vampires: Rumor and History in Colonial Africa* (Berkeley: University of California Press, 2000), 175–207. For the harboring of witches, see Mambwe Diary, 23 November 1892, WFA. The mission's role in harboring witches is allegedly the origin of a Bemba saying, "cuba ndoshi" (The missions are the refuge of sorcerers). According to Louis Oger, *Forget Me Not: Saved from Slavery; He Became a Missionary to Zambia* (Ndola, Zambia: Mission Press, 1992), 6, 42n9.

43. Comments of Albert Muyao, Audrey Richards Papers 1/16, LSE.

44. According to an account dictated to Stewart Gore-Brown by his cook. "The Apocalypse of Dr Chiboko," Audrey Richards Papers, 1/15, LSE.

45. Annexure 1 Tour report 7/1939, SEC 2/751, NAZ.

46. Ibid.

47. From a selection of cases recorded by Audrey I. Richards, in Audrey Richards Papers 1/34, LSE.

48. Audrey I. Richards, "A Modern Movement of Witch-Finders," *Africa: Journal of the International African Institute* 8, no. 4 (1935): 448–61, esp. 460.

49. Extract from Minutes of Presbytery of Livingstonia, 25 June 1940, located in Native Secretariat files, SEC 2/427, NAZ.

50. Richards, "Modern Movement," 458, is the most thorough published account. Also see Field Notes, 4/1934, Audrey Richards Papers 1/16, LSE. Differences in some details, such as the founder (claims that he was South African before organizing his following in Malawi) and payment for the Muchape potion can be found in several court cases and DC reports in WP 1/14/7, NAZ.

51. Cases and official correspondence on Bamuchape, in WP 1/14/7, NAZ.

52. Richards, "Modern Movement," 450.

53. This change in policy would culminate in Ordinance 47 of 1948: "An Ordinance to Amend Witchcraft Ordinance." Colonial views were influenced by anthropologists, especially Godfrey Wilson, in "Notes on Witchcraft Ordinance," 28 November 1939. The notes and policy discussions recorded in SEC 2/247, NAZ.

54. Francois Tanguy, "Mucapi Business," 9 March 1935, 1/M/C46, WFA.

55. Report of Native Clerk Edward Shaba, Ufipa District, 3 March 1934, WP 1/14/7, NAZ.

56. J. Van Sambeek to Audrey Richards, 14 April 1932, Audrey Richards Papers, 2/15, LSE. For complaints regarding the burning of *mfuba* shrines by Catholics, also see Garvey, *Bembaland Church*, 99.

57. Richards, Handwritten Manuscript, n.d. (1934?), Audrey Richards Papers 1/16, LSE.

58. Richards, "Tribal Government in Transition: The Babemba of Northeastern Zambia," Supplement to *Journal of the Royal African Society* 34, no. 137 (1935): 1–27. Contra Fields, *Revival and Rebellion*, esp. 65–66, who associated the "customary" codes of indirect rule with spiritual power.

59. Brelsford argued directly against Richards's association of the sacred ties between the Crocodile Clan and the land. Aspects of the argument, especially the permanent associations between the Crocodile Clan and the land, are convincing, but Brelsford's argument ignores the fact that the most important aspect of conquest and succession was the capture of the *babenye* relics that made the land and people fertile. W. Vernon Brelsford, *Some Aspects of Bemba Chieftainship* (Livingstone, Northern Rhodesia: Rhodes Livingstone Institute, 1944), esp. 1–9.

60. For example, the accusations that Chitimukulu was a *banyama* vampire, in Lewis H. Gann, *A History of Northern Rhodesia: Early Days to 1953* (New York: Humanities Press, 1969), 231.

61. Terence O. Ranger, "The Mwana Lesa Movement of 1925," in *Themes in the Christian History of Central Africa*, ed. Terence O. Ranger and John Weller (Berkeley: University of California Press, 1975), 45–75; Fields, *Revival and Rebellion*, 162–93.

62. W. Vernon Brelsford, "Shimwalule: A Study of a Bemba Chief and Priest," *African Studies* 1, no. 3 (1942): 207–23, esp. 211. The original DC's report by Brelsford upon which the above article was based, but with considerably more details, including rumors of European deaths at Mwalule, can be found in Annexure 3 Tour Report 5/1939, SEC 2/751, NAZ.

63. Fields, *Revival and Rebellion*, 161.

64. Based on the Audrey Richards Papers 1/34, LSE, Megan Vaughan details Chandamali's anger over the death of the messenger, Chanda, in "'Divine Kings': Sex, Death and Anthropology in Inter-War East/Central Africa," *Journal of African History* 49, no. 3 (2008): 383–401, esp. 395–96.

65. Tour Report No. 6 of 1935, NP 1/1/3, NAZ.

66. Annexure 3 Tour Report 5/1939, SEC 2/751, NAZ.

67. PC Comments on Chinsali Tour Report 5/39; TF Standford, Acting Chief Sec. to PC, Kasama, 12 January1940, SEC 2/731, NAZ.

68. Annexure 2, Tour Report 1/1940, SEC 2/752, NAZ.

69. Brelsford, "Shimwalule," 223.

70. Tour Reports 2–3, 1948, NP 1/1/22, NAZ.

71. Ipenburg, *"All Good Men,"* 123–24.

72. Tour report 2 of 1948, NP 1/1/22, NAZ.

73. "Supernatural Powers of Chiefs," Audrey Richards Papers, 1/4/1/13, LSE.

74. Annexure 3 Tour Report 5/1939, SEC 2/751, NAZ.

75. DC to AR, 16 October 1934, Audrey Richards Papers, 1/1, LSE.

76. L. Oger Notes, 5/ZWF/PP/36, WFA.

77. DC to AR, 16 October 1934, Audrey Richards Papers 1/1, LSE.

78. TS. Fox–Pitt to AR, 21 September 1934, Audrey Richards Papers 1/1, LSE. In contrast to the White Fathers mission correspondence on this issue, as found in Garvey, *Bembaland Church,* 127.

79. KTQ Chinsali District Notebooks, 2/1 Vol IV, NAZ.

80. L. Oger Notes, 5/ZWF/PP36, WFA.

81. Annexure 1 of Tour 4/1937, SEC 2/750, NAZ. Also published as R. P. Bush, "The Installation, August 1937," in Brelsford, *Some Aspects of Bemba Chieftainship,* 41–48, esp. 45–46.

82. W. Vernon Brelsford, "A Description of the Housebreaking Ceremony at Chief Nkula's Village, Chinsali," 1938, SEC 2/750. Also published in Brelsford, *Aspects of Bemba Chieftainship,* 49–55, esp. 50.

83. Malole Diary, 20 February 1944, WFA; Garvey, *Bembaland Church,* 159.

84. Father Oger in particular was called upon to pray for rain. Oger's Notes, 5/ZWF/PP36, WFA. For the use of body parts to make rain, see *mafyeka* traditions of Isoka District, "Memorandum Concerning Bamyama and Mafyeka," 1943, SEC 2/429, NAZ. For the replacement of *mafyeka* with *banyama* in colonial reports, see White, *Speaking with Vampires,* 25–26.

CHAPTER 3: SATAN IN THE CITY

1. From a note in ChiBemba at Nkana mine posted on 4 April calling for strike and translated from ChiBemba by an African clerk, in Northern Rhodesia, *Report of Commission to Inquire into Disturbances in the Copperbelt, Northern Rhodesia, October 1935* (Lusaka: Government Printer, October 1935), 18. More details on the report in CO 795/76/11 Part II, 1936, National Archives of the United Kingdom (henceforth NAUK).

2. For a timeline of the strike, see *Report of Commission,* 8–32.

3. For origins of workers, see "Schedule Showing Tribal Distribution of Employees on the Copper Mines," in Northern Rhodesia, *Evidence Taken by the Commission Appointed to Inquire into the Disturbances in the Copperbelt, Northern Rhodesia, July–September 1935* (Lusaka: Government Printers, July–September 1935), 649.

4. J. Clyde Mitchell, *The Kalela Dance: Aspects of Social Relationships among Urban Africans in Northern Rhodesia* (Manchester: Manchester University Press, 1956).

5. J. C. Chiwale, "Brief History of How the Joking Relationships Came About between the Ngoni and Bemba Speakers" (unpublished paper, n.d.), held at Institute for Social and Economic Research, Lusaka.

6. Wallace D. Best, *Passionately Human, No Less Divine: Religion and Culture in Black Chicago, 1915–1952* (Princeton, NJ: Princeton University Press, 2005).

7. For an emphasis on economics, see Godfrey Wilson, *An Essay on the Economics of Detribalization in Northern Rhodesia* (Livingstone, Northern Rhodesia: Rhodes-Livingstone Institute, 1941–1942). For new cultural identities, see J. Clyde Mitchell, *African Urbanization in Ndola and Luanshya* (Lusaka: Rhodes-Livingstone Institute, 1954); Mitchell, *Kalela Dance*; and Arnold L. Epstein, *Politics in an Urban African Community* (Manchester: Manchester University Press, 1958). Epstein's later work, *Scenes from African Urban Life: Collected Copperbelt Essays* (Edinburgh: Edinburgh University Press, 1992), includes a valuable chapter on Watchtower in the 1950s.

8. James Ferguson, *Expectations of Modernity: Myths and Meanings of Urban Life on the Zambian Copperbelt* (Berkeley: University of California Press, 1999), but despite a discussion on cosmopolitanism hardly mentions Christianity, spirits, or religion, missing an entire category of understanding for workers. For witchcraft as poisoning, see Ferguson, *Expectations of Modernity*, 118–21.

9. Luise White, *Speaking with Vampires: Rumor and History in Colonial Africa* (Berkeley: University of California Press, 2000), esp. 269–305.

10. Walima T. Kalusa, "Death, Christianity, and African Miners: Contesting Indirect Rule in the Zambian Copperbelt, 1935–1962," *International Journal of African Historical Studies* 44, no. 1 (2011): 89–112.

11. J. Merle Davis, ed., *Modern Industry and the African: An Enquiry into the Effect of the Copper Mines of Central Africa upon Native Society and the Work of the Christian Missions* (London: Frank Cass, 1967). Also see Reginald J. B. Moore, a missionary engaged by the London Missionary Society (LMS) in the 1930s, who wrote an impressionistic and liberal overview of the spiritual life of Copperbelt: *These African Copper Miners: A Study of the Industrial Revolution in Northern Rhodesia, with Principal Reference to the Copper Mining Industry* (London: Livingston Press, 1948). A thorough work based on fieldwork and surveys, and also sponsored by the International Missionary Society, is John V. Taylor and Dorothea A. Lehmann, *Christians of the Copperbelt: The Growth of the Church in Northern Rhodesia* (London: SCM Press, 1961).

12. According to Ranger, the movement built on particular Lala notions of millennial witchcraft eradication, thus offering a striking contrast to Ranger's earlier analysis of "nationalist" expansion of scale in his study of the religious aspects of the Shona and Ndebele uprisings farther south. Terence O. Ranger, "The Mwana Lesa Movement of 1925," in *Themes in the Christian History of Central Africa*, ed. Terence O. Ranger and John Weller (Berkeley: University of California Press, 1975), 45–75.

13. Karen E. Fields, *Revival and Rebellion in Colonial Central Africa* (Princeton, NJ: Princeton University Press, 1985), 269.

14. Sholto Cross's unpublished dissertation attempts a thorough investigation of central African Watchtower in all its diversity in "The Watchtower Movement in South Central Africa, 1908–1945" (PhD diss., Oxford University, 1973).

15. John Higginson, *A Working Class in the Making: Belgian Colonial Labor Policy, Private Enterprise, and the African Mineworker, 1907–1951* (Madison: University of Wisconsin Press, 1989); and Higginson, "Liberating the Captives: Independent Watchtower as an Avatar of Colonial Revolt in Southern Africa and Katanga, 1908–1941," *Journal of Social History* 26, no. 1 (1992): 55–80.

16. Charles Perrings, *Black Mineworkers in Central Africa: Industrial Strategies and the Evolution of an African Proletariat in the Copperbelt, 1911–1941* (London: Heinemann, 1979), 214–17; Jane L. Parpart, *Labor and Capital on the African Copperbelt* (Philadelphia: Temple University Press, 1983), 55–56, 67–68.

17. The first lead and zinc mining operations began in Broken Hill (Kabwe) in 1916. The principal copper mines began in Bwana Mkubwa (1926); Kansanshi (1927); Nkana (1927); Luanshya (1929); and Mufulira (1929). For background on the growth of the Copperbelt, see Perrings, *Black Mineworkers*, esp. 73–98. For growth in colonial Zambia, see Parpart, *Labor and Capital*, 19–23.

18. Davis, *Modern Industry and the African*, 151. For a discussion of numbers, see Perrings, *Black Mineworkers*, 76–77.

19. The best account of the formation of the associations, informed by substantial oral evidence, is David J. Cook, "The Influence of Livingstonia Mission upon the Formation of Welfare Associations in Zambia, 1912–31," in Ranger and Weller, *Themes in the Christian History of Central Africa*, 98–134. For a limited account, see Robert I. Rotberg, *The Rise of Nationalism in Central Africa: The Making of Malawi and Zambia, 1873–1964* (Cambridge, MA: Harvard University Press, 1972), 124.

20. Cook, "Influence of Livingstonia Mission," 111–20. For the Muwamba brothers, see pp. 118, 132n76. Also see Nyasaland government report, cited in Roderick J. MacDonald, "Religious Independency as a Means of Social Advance in Northern Nyasaland in the 1930s," *Journal of Religion in Africa* 3, no. 1 (1970): 106–29, esp. 115–16. Henry S. Meebelo, *African Proletarians and Colonial Capitalism: The Origins, Growth and Struggles of the Zambian Labour Movement to 1964* (Lusaka: Kenneth Kaunda Foundation, 1986), 47, cites correspondence between Muwamba and Kadalie. The contents of the letters, deemed "of a propagandist or subversive nature," are unclear. The Northern Rhodesian documentation claims that Muwamba was Kadalie's "uncle," in Criminal Investigation Department Report on Watch Tower Preaching, Broken Hill, 20 April 1932, SEC 2/434, NAZ.

21. Criminal Investigation Department (CID) Report on Watch Tower Preaching, Broken Hill, 20 April 1932, SEC 2/434, NAZ.

22. J. F. Rutherford, *Preparation: The revelation of the Prophecy by Zechariah showing Jehovah and his enemies preparing for the final war, and describing the great battle and the conclusion thereof in a glorious victory and the establishment of peace on earth and good will toward men, and the everlasting vindication of Jehovah's name* (Brooklyn: Watch Tower Bible and Tract Society, 1933). Further evidence of the spread of these ideas is found in the exhaustive list of banned Watchtower publications, in SEC 2/434, NAZ.

23. Criminal Investigation Department CID Report on Watch Tower Preaching, Chisamba, 8 May 1932; CID Report on Watch Tower Preaching, Broken Hill,

20 April 1932, SEC 2/ 434, NAZ. For an account of Watchtower ideology in the 1930s, see Griffith Quick, "Some Aspects of the African Watch Tower Movement in Northern Rhodesia," *International Review of Missions* 29 (1940): 216–26.

24. Quick, "Some Aspects of the African Watch Tower Movement," 217–18.

25. "Testimony of Frederick William Eaton," *Evidence taken by the Commission, 1935*, 394.

26. "Testimony of Sam Kawinga Kamchacha Mwase," *Evidence taken by the Commission, 1935*, 753.

27. "Testimony of A. J. Cross," *Evidence Taken by the Commission, 1935*, 848–52.

28. CID Report on Watch Tower Preaching, Broken Hill, 20 April 1932, SEC 2/ 434, NAZ.

29. DC, Lusaka, to PC, 11 March 1932; Report of Jacob Ngulube, 11 March 1932; CID Report on Watch Tower Preaching, Broken Hill, 20 April 1932, SEC 2/ 434, NAZ.

30. Testimony of Chiwakawaka and Chuifuwe to CID at Chisamba, 6 May 1932; Report of Petros Mukambwa to CID, Broken Hill, 20 April 1932, SEC 2/434, NAZ.

31. Second Report of Jacob Ngulube, 12 April 1932, SEC 2/434, NAZ. According to Rutherford, the clergy had "stolen the Word of God and taken away the key of knowledge," in *Preparation*, 79.

32. Report of Native Detective Petros Mukambwa, CID, Broken Hill, 20 April 1932, SEC 2/434, NAZ.

33. Second Report of Jacob Ngulube, 12 April 1932, SEC 2/434, NAZ.

34. Ibid.

35. Report of Jacob Ngulube, 11 March 1932; CID Report on Watch Tower Preaching, 20 April 1932, SEC 2/ 434, NAZ.

36. For widespread rejection of authority among Watchtower in 1930s, see Quick, "Some Aspects of the African Watch Tower Movement," 222–23.

37. Acting Director of Native Education to Chief Secretary, 15 August 1931, SEC 2/434, NAZ.

38. Assistant Commissioner Police to Chief Sec., 13 May 1932, SEC 2/434, NAZ.

39. The commission devoted nine pages to describe Watchtower's subversive influences, in *Report of the Commission to Enquiry into the Disturbances, 1935*, 42–51.

40. Perrings, *Black Mineworkers*, 216; Cross, "Watchtower Movement," 386–88. Also see Parpart, *Labor and Capital*, 67–68. Contra Meebelo, *African Proletarians*, 94, who, contrary to all evidence, claims that Watchtower in 1935 was mostly "a rural social phenomenon . . . patently anti-social and a great nuisance to both the colonial and the traditional authorities."

41. "Testimony of Lefati Mwambula," *Evidence Presented to Commission of Inquiry into the 1935 Strike*, 134–42. According to de Jager, Mwambula wrote to the Cape Town headquarters on 2 June, three days prior to his arrest, denying any Watchtower involvement in the strike. "Testimony of Petrus Johannes de Jager";

"Testimony of Glynn Smallwood Jones," *Evidence Presented to Commission of Inquiry into 1935 Strike*, 196, 580.

42. "Testimony of William Ngandu," *Evidence Presented to Commission of Inquiry into 1935 Strike*, 815.

43. "Testimony of Lefati Mwambula," *Evidence Presented to Commission of Inquiry into 1935 Strike*, 137.

44. "Testimony of Anna Nkulukusa," *Evidence Presented to Commission of Inquiry into 1935 Strike*, 856.

45. Phillips, General Secretary of South African Branch of Jehovah's Witnesses, to Chief Secretary, Northern Rhodesia, 1 July 1935, SEC 2/434, NAZ.

46. "Testimony of P. J. de Jager," *Evidence Presented to Commission of Inquiry into 1935 Strike*, 225.

47. Phillips to Chief Secretary, NR, 3 July 1935; GR. Phillips, W Tower, Cape Town to Sec. to Gov, Lusaka, NR, 27 July 1935; Chief Secretary, NR, to Colonial Secretary, 22 July 1935, SEC 2/434, NAZ.

48. P. J. de Jager to Chief Sec., NR, 31August 1935, SEC 2/434, NAZ. *Northern Rhodesia Advertiser*, 31 August and 7 September 2008.

49. PC, Western Province to Chief Sec. Lusaka, 12 September 1935; Chief Sec. NR to Secretary, Watch Tower, 23 September 1935; de Jager to Chief Sec., NR, 14 February 1936, SEC 2/434, NAZ.

50. Sec., Watch Tower, to Chief Sec. NR, 2 October 1935, 17 June 1936, SEC 2/434, NAZ.

51. In a letter to Phillips, the secretary of the Watch Tower Society insists that "no true Christian can indulge in the practice of bowing down . . . or grovel at the feet of another creature." Secretary Watch Tower, to Phillips, 11 March 1938, 12 April 1938. The conflict over Watchtower refusal to bow down to chiefs was reported by DC, Kasempa, 5 February 1938 to PC, WP, 5 February 1938, 22 May 1939, 7 December 1939. For Watch Tower Society response, see Phillips, "Statement of Watch Tower position in the Kasempa District, 7 November 1939, SEC 2/434, NAZ.

52. Governor NR to Sec. of State, 18 September 1935; Sec. State to Governor NR, 20 September 1935. The Executive Council Minute, 6 August 1935, recorded the prohibition of the Watch Tower publication the *Crisis*. The Executive Council Minute of 7 August 1936 banned two further publications. SEC 2/434, NAZ.

53. Secretary of Native Affairs to Chef Secretary, 23 June 1934, SEC 2/434, NAZ.

54. Governor, NR to Sec. of State for Colonies, 13 August 1937, NAUK.

55. J. R. Hooker, "Witnesses and Watchtower in the Rhodesias and Nyasaland," *Journal of African History* 6, no. 1 (1965): 91–106, esp. 102–3.

56. The Native/African Literature Committee was established in General Notice 146 of 1937. Minutes of their first meetings can be found in SEC 2/1138–39, NAZ. Also see Giacomo Macola, "Historical and Ethnographical Publications in the Vernaculars of Colonial Zambia: Missionary Contribution to the 'Creation of Tribalism,'" *Journal of Religion in Africa* 33, no. 4 (2003): 343–64.

57. Brian Garvey, *Bembaland Church: Religious and Social Change in South Central Africa, 1891–1964* (Leiden: Brill, 1994), 158.

58. DC, Mufulira, to PC, WP, 1 December 1936, SEC 2/434, NAZ.

59. Davis, *Modern Industry and the African.*

60. For the establishment of UMCB, see *UMCB First Annual Report, 1936–37*, UMCB 13, UCZ Archives, Mindolo (henceforth UCZA). For the formation of CCAR, see CCAR 05, UCZA. For UCCAR, see UCCAR 05 UCZA. For UCZ, see "Statement on Consummation of UCZ," 10 May 1965, UCZ 9, UCZA. The different church unions are thoroughly covered in Peter Bolink, *Towards Church Union in Zambia: A Study of Missionary Co-Operation and Church-Union Efforts in Central-Africa* (Sneek, Netherlands: T. Wever–Franeker, 1967).

61. Kalusa, "Death, Christianity, and African Miners."

62. Michael O'Shea, *Missionaries and Miners: A History of the Beginnings of the Catholic Church in Zambia with Particular Reference to the Copperbelt* (Ndola, Zambia: Mission Press, 1986), 280.

63. The letter, intercepted by the colonial administration, reproduced in NR Police, Staff Officer to Chief Sec., 7 August 1935, SEC 2/434, NAZ.

64. For stabilization and the 1940 strike, see Parpart, *Labor and Capital*, 75–95; Perrings, *Black Mineworkers*, 217–24. Details of the strike from Northern Rhodesia, *Report of the Commission Appointed to Inquire into the Disturbances in the Copperbelt, Northern Rhodesia, July 1940* (Lusaka, 1940).

65. Northern Rhodesia, *Report of the Commission*, 40–43.

66. Julius Lewin, *The Colour Bar in the Copper Belt* (Johannesburg: Pub. for the Southern African Committee on Industrial Relations by the South African Institute of Race Relations, 1941), esp. 9–10.

67. Parpart, *Labor and Capital*, 83.

68. For critique of teleology of progressive views of stabilization, permanent urbanization, and worker consciousness, see Ferguson, *Expectations of Modernity.*

69. Moore, *These African Copper Miners.* Moore was certainly on the progressive limits of missionary opinion; see Sean Morrow, "'On the Side of the Robbed': R. J. B. Moore, Missionary on the Copperbelt, 1933–1941, *Journal of Religion in Africa* 19, no. 3 (1989): 244–63.

70. For example, see the series of *John Christian* publications, especially *John Christian Looks at the Colour Bar*; also, George Hewitt, Sec. of Christian Council, "An Appeal to Men of Reason and Religion," n.d. (1947–49?), Acc. 7548/B318, National Library of Scotland, Edinburgh (henceforth NLS).

71. UMCB Annual Report, 1939–1940, UMCB 13, UCZA; Minutes of Exec. Meeting, Gen. Missionary Conference of Northern Rhodesia, Lusaka, 3 June 1941, Acc. 7548/B317, NLA.

72. Parpart, *Labor and Capital*, 105–6. For urban advisory councils, see F. M. N. Heath, "The Growth of African Councils on the Copperbelt of Northern Rhodesia," *Journal of African Administration* 5, no. 3 (1953): 123–32.

73. Arnold L. Epstein, *The Administration of Justice and the Urban African: A Study of Urban Native Courts in Northern Rhodesia* (London: H. M. Stationery,

1953), 90. As quoted in Elena L. Berger, *Labour, Race, and Colonial Rule: The Copperbelt from 1924 to Independence* (Oxford: Clarendon Press, 1974), 92.

74. From the administration's perspective, unionization is most thoroughly covered in Berger, *Labour Race, and Colonial Rule*, 73–96. For an emphasis on workers' agency, see Parpart, *Labor and Capital*, 96–113. For the broader context of colonial labor policies, see Frederick Cooper, *Decolonization and African Society: The Labor Question in French and British Africa* (Cambridge: Cambridge University Press, 1996), esp. 336–48.

75. Hooker, "Witnesses and Watchtower," 105.

76. The ARC was abolished in 1958. While the nationalists condemned the ARC through the 1950s, many leaders were members of subsidiary bodies such as the Urban Advisory Councils, which elected members to the ARC. Bizeck J. Phiri, *A Political History of Zambia: From the Colonial Period to the Third Republic* (Trenton, NJ: African World Press, 2006), 80–83. For urban advisory councils, see Heath, "Growth of African Councils."

77. "A Study of African Social and Political Development in Ndola," 20 August 1951; DC, Chingola, to PC, Western Province, with PCs comments, forwarded to DCs Mufulira, Ndola, Luanshya, and Kitwe, 21 September 1951, WP1/11/25, NAZ.

78. For an overview, see Rotberg, *Rise of Nationalism*, 179–302; Andrew Roberts, *A History of Zambia* (New York: Africana Publishing, 1976), 208–11; Lewis H. Gann, *A History of Northern Rhodesia: Early Days to 1953* (New York: Humanities Press, 1969), 423–33.

79. Taylor and Lehmann, *Christians of the Copperbelt*, 230.

80. Meebelo, *African Proletarians*, 203, 289–90.

81. Epstein, *Scenes from African Urban Life*, 120.

82. According to the public relations officer of the Watchtower Society, as reported in Taylor and Lehmann, *Christians of the Copperbelt*, 227.

83. The survey conducted by Taylor and Lehmann reported 29.4 percent compared to 25.6 percent Catholic and 15.7 percent CCAR, in *Christians of the Copperbelt*, 60. The Catholics and CCAR represent a higher proportion of children, probably due to their schools.

84. Taylor and Lehmann, *Christians of the Copperbelt*, 227–28.

85. Cross, "Watchtower Movement," 396.

86. Taylor and Lehmann, *Christians of the Copperbelt*, 237; Epstein, *Scenes from African Urban Life*, 120.

87. Ian G. Cunnison, "A Watch Tower Assembly in Central Africa," *International Review of Missions* 40 (1951): 456–69, esp. 460.

88. Taylor and Lehmann, *Christians of the Copperbelt*, 228.

89. The last section has benefited from my fieldwork in Zambia over the last ten years. While I conducted many formal interviews with Watchtower members, especially in Luapula during the 1990s, none of them focused explicitly on Watchtower beliefs and activism. Nevertheless, my ideas have been informed by many discussions with Watchtower members and attendance of Watchtower church services.

90. For the liberal position, see Rotberg, *Rise of Nationalism*. For the Marxists, see Parpart, *Labor and Capital*; Perrings, *Black Mineworkers*; and, in Katanga, Higginson, *Working Class in the Making*.

CHAPTER 4: A NEW JERUSALEM

1. Kampamba Mulenga, *Blood on Their Hands* (Lusaka: Zambia Education Publishing House, 1998), 3–4.

2. This version is from a manuscript held by a Lumpa church in Chiponya Village, near Mkushi, Zambia. It was allegedly recited by Lenshina to her son-in-law, Alfred Kapele, who distributed the written version to Lumpa deacons. Henceforth referred to as the Chiponya Manuscript.

3. Similar but slightly contradictory interview testimony confirms the outlines of this story. Interviews: Agnes Mafupa, Lubwa, 12 July 2005; Maggie Nkonde, Chandamali, Chinsali, 9 July 2005. A contemporary version, shorn of some of the details but confirming many of the themes, was recorded by the Lubwa missionary Fergus Macpherson, whom Lenshina visited immediately after her awakening, in Fergus Macpherson and W. V. Stone, "The Alice Movement in Northern Rhodesia" (Occasional Papers Issued by Department of Mission Studies, London, August 1958), 2–3. Copies of the document are held by Andrew Roberts and in NP 3/12/3, NAZ.

4. Interviews: Dixon Mulenga, Chinsali, 7 July 2005; Maggie Nkonde, Chandamali, Chinsali, 9 July 2005. The story of the two books was also recorded by White Father Pascal Kakokota in 1954, Letter to L. Oger, and Short Report, Lubushi 23 February 1962, 1/M/Hi31, White Fathers Archives, Zambia (henceforth WFA).

5. Macpherson and Stone, "Alice Movement," 2–3.

6. According to Maggie Nkonde, who was one of the girls that accompanied Lenshina to Lubwa; interview: Maggie Nkonde, Chandamali, Chinsali, 9 July 2005. The first documentary evidence of the accusation that Macpherson stole the book of life is in PC, Kasama, to DC, Kasama, 1 March 1955, NP 3/12/3, NAZ.

7. Interview: Dixon Mulenga, Chinsali, 7 July 2005; Jennifer Ngandu, Lusaka, 25 March 2005. Macpherson's refusal to allow her to preach in the chapel is confirmed by discussions between Audrey Richards and the mission in "Lenshina visit, 28 Aug. 1957," 1/16, Audrey Richards Papers, London School of Economics (henceforth LSE).

8. Mushindo's version is in "Report by Paul Mushindo to the Presbytery of CCAR," quoted at length in John V. Taylor and Dorothea A. Lehmann, *Christians of the Copperbelt: The Growth of the Church in Northern Rhodesia* (London: SCM Press, 1961), 249–50. I have been unable to locate Mushindo's original report.

9. I have not found any evidence to verify Mushindo's baptism of Lenshina, as claimed by Andrew Roberts, *The Lumpa Church of Alice Lenshina* (Lusaka: Oxford University press, 1972), 12.

10. Detailed by a Protestant, and not a Lenshina follower, interview: Agnes Mafupa, Lubwa, 12 July 2005. Mushindo's account of Lenshina is conspicuously absent in his autobiography, Paul B. Mushindo, *The Life of a Zambian Evangelist*:

The Reminiscences of the Reverend Paul Bwembya Mushindo (Lusaka: Institute for African Studies, 1973).

11. Kenneth Mackenzie and Paul Mushindo to Alice, 24 February 1955; Kenneth Mackenzie and Paul Mushindo to Chinsali CCAR Elders, 24 February 1955, Andrew Roberts Collection. Translated with the help of Kampamba Mulenga.

12. DC's Handwritten Notes on meeting Lenshina, 2 March 1955, NP 3/12/3, NAZ. Macpherson blames the DC's meeting with Alice for her alienation from the mission, claiming that the DC mocked the veracity of Lenshina's encounter. This is unlikely, and Macpherson in any event was on furlough when Lenshina split from the Lubwa Mission. Macpherson and Stone, "Alice Movement," 3–4.

13. DCC Church Elders to BanaKangwa [Alice Lenshina], 25 December 1955, Andrew Roberts Papers. Translated with the help of Kampamba Mulenga.

14. Chinsali Intelligence Report, February 1955, NP 3/12/3, NAZ.

15. From mission diaries in WFA and Mission Reports in Acc. 7548, National Library of Scotland, Edinburgh (henceforth NLS). For the best overview of numbers, see Jean Loup Calmettes, "The Lumpa Sect, Rural Reconstruction, and Conflict" (master's thesis, University College of Wales, Aberytswyth, 1978), 38.

16. Tour Report No. 5, 27 March 1957, NP 3/12/3, NAZ.

17. Dorothea A. Lehmann, "Alice Lenshina Mulenga and the Lumpa Church," in Taylor and Lehmann, *Christians of the Copperbelt*, 248–68. Another early account was Robert I. Rotberg, "The Lenshina Movement of Northern Rhodesia," *Rhodes-Livingstone Journal* 29 (1961): 63–78.

18. *Report of the Commission of Inquiry into the Lumpa Church* (Lusaka, 1965).

19. Roberts, *Lumpa Church*, esp. 4. In doing so, Roberts built on the interpretation of two influential accounts: Rotberg, "Lenshina Movement," 63–78; and Lehmann, "Alice Lenshina Mulenga and the Lumpa Church."

20. Roberts, *Lumpa Church*, 29.

21. The rules are referenced in numerous sources and publications. The first account of them is in a letter to the governor of Northern Rhodesia: Letter from Alice Lenshina to Governor of NR, 18 April 1957, NP 3/12/3, NAZ. The first ChiBemba version, dated 13 December 1957, was given to Catholic priest L. Oger, after the return of their Catholic congregants, and appears in L. Oger, "The Lenshina Movement in NR: Religious Sect Founded by Alice Lenshina," 1955–1960. Mimeograph, n.d. (1960?), 26–27. The same version is found in *Report of Commission of Enquiry*, 17.

22. Wim M. J. van Binsbergen, *Religious Change in Zambia: Exploratory Studies* (London: Kegan Paul, 1981), 271.

23. Ibid., 267–316, esp. 299.

24. Calmettes, "Lumpa Sect," 196–97.

25. Hugo F. Hinfelaar, "Women's Revolt: The Lumpa Church of Lenshina Mulenga in the 1950s," *Journal of Religion in Africa* 21 (1991): 99–129.

26. Kwame Anthony Appiah, *In My Father's House: Africa in the Philosophy of Culture* (New York: Oxford University Press, 1993), 114.

27. Karen E. Fields, *Revival and Rebellion in Colonial Central Africa* (Princeton, NJ: Princeton University Press, 1985).

28. For smallpox outbreak, see Annandale Hospital, Lubwa, Report 1953, Acc. 7548, NLS; also found in Annandale Hospital Reports, CCAR 13/8, United Church of Zambia Archives, Kitwe (henceforth UCZA); Mulanga Mission Diary, 24 January 1956, 5/WF/ MD59; Kayambi Mission Diary, July 1956, Calmettes Box 7, WFA.

29. The effects of migration of men to urban areas was first discussed in Audrey I. Richards, *Land, Labour and Diet in Northern Rhodesia: An Economic Study of the Bemba Tribe* (London: Oxford University Press, 1939). See recent qualifications of Richards in Henrietta L. Moore and Megan Vaughan, *Cutting Down Trees: Gender, Nutrition, and Agricultural Change in the Northern Province of Zambia, 1890–1990* (London: James Currey, 1994).

30. A number of letters written to Lenshina where "BaMulopwe," "Lubuto lwa chalo," or even "Lubuto mulopwe" were used interchangeably. For associations between Lenshina's use of light symbols and Luchele Ng'anga, see Hugo F. Hinfelaar, *Bemba-Speaking Women of Zambia in a Century of Religious Change (1892–1992)* (Leiden: Brill, 1994), 83–84.

31. Letter from Alice Lenshina to Governer of NR, 18 April 1957, NP 3/12/3, NAZ.

32. Calmettes, "Lumpa Sect," 115.

33. For more extensive discussion of influences of *The Pilgrim's Progress* on Lenshina's visions, see David M. Gordon, "Community of Suffering: Narratives of War and Exile in the Zambian Lumpa Church," in *Recasting the Past: History Writing and Political Work in Modern* Africa, ed. Derek R. Peterson and Giacomo Macola (Athens: Ohio University Press, 2009), 191–208. For the general influence of *Pilgrim's Progress*, see Isabel Hofmeyr, *The Portable Bunyan: A Transnational History of "The Pilgrim's Progress"* (Princeton, NJ: Princeton University Press, 2004), esp. 137–50. The ChiBemba versions of *The Pilgrim's Progress* were *Ulwendo lwa mwina-Kristu mu ciloto* (new ed., Mbeleshi, 1953; first ChiBemba ed., 1925, published by London Mission at Mbereshi; rev. 1944). The only existing copies I have found are in 3/P/R36, WFA.

34. J. L. Calmettes, "Church Music in The Chinsali District, 1954–1974: The Lumpa Church" (unpublished ms in Calmettes Boxes, WFA, 14).

35. Calmettes, "Church Music," 15.

36. Report on DC Visit to Kasomo, 10 August 1956, NP 3/12/3, NAZ.

37. Ibid. The DC provides a sketch map of Kasomo Village and *tempile*, under the *museshi* tree, where Lenshina first had visions.

38. Ilondola Annual Report, 1955–1956, WFA.

39. Quotation in Report on DC Visit to Kasomo, 10 August 1956; also see Report by DC Investigating Officer, August 1956, NP 3/12/3, NAZ.

40. Kayambi Mission Diary, 12 June 1956, WFA.

41. For blessing of seeds, see Louis Oger, *The Lenshina Movement in Northern Rhodesia: Religious Sect Founded by Alice Lenshina, 1955–1960*, 14, WFA; "Report by Paul Mushindo," in Taylor and Lehmann, *Christians of the Copperbelt*, 250.

42. "I call on you, come and enter; In the house of Seed" (Namwita seni mwingile; Munganda ya lubuto); in Calmettes, "Lumpa Sect," 24.

43. "Lenshina visit, 28 August 1957," 1/16, LSE.

44. Interview: Jennifer Ngandu and Elizabeth Lutanda (Lenshina's daughters), Lusaka, 25 March 2005.

45. See reference 21.

46. J. J. Corbeil, *Mbusa: Sacred Emblems of the Bemba* (London: Ethnographica, 1982), 24.

47. According to the Registrar of Societies, October 1958, and reported in Special Branch, "Report on the Lenshina Movement," n.d. (1959?), 7, NP 3/12/3, NAZ.

48. Calmettes, "The Lumpa Sect," 144. For "kafundisha" teachers in 1956, see Chinsali Tour Report No. 6 of 1956, NP 3/12/2, NAZ. Interviews: Dixon Mulenga "Kachimona," Choshi, 15 July 2005; William "Kalomba muli Lesa," Chiponya Village, 29 July 2005.

49. Fergus Macpherson recalls the "pruning" of 100 of 115 paid evangelists in the late 1940s and early 1950s, in *North of the Zambezi: A Modern Missionary Memoir* (Edinburgh: Handsel Press, 1998), 87–88.

50. Robert Kaunda was a teacher at Lubwa and Luanshya before being dismissed by Lubwa missionaries in 1949. Rev. G. Fraser, Luanshya, to Rev. J. W. C. Dougall, 19 September 1956, Acc. 7548 / B320, NLS.

51. Special Branch, "Report on the Lenshina Movement," n.d. (1959?), 7, NP 3/12/3, NAZ.

52. Sandy Rain, "What I Think of Lenshina," quoted in Taylor and Lehmann, *Christians of the Copperbelt*, 251–52.

53. "The Alice Movement in Northern Rhodesia," n.d. (1956?); Special Branch, "Report on the Lenshina Movement," n.d. (1959?), 7, NP 3/12/3, NAZ.

54. Calmettes attempts to date and locate some of the hymns in "Church Music in the Chinsali District, 1954–1974," WFA.

55. For Robert Kaunda's musical talents, see Rev. G. Fraser, Luanshya, to Rev. J. W. C. Dougall, 19 September 1956, Acc. 7548 / B320, NLS. His manuscript of church hymns is edited by L. Oger and J. L. Calmettes, "Lumpa Hymnal," Calmette Box 1, WFA.

56. "Amashina yaba Church Choir," n.d. (1960s?), Andrew Roberts Papers.

57. Calmettes, "Church Music in the Chinsali District," 19, WFA.

58. Report, "Portrait of a Problem," Acc. 7548/ B326, NLS.

59. Interview: Dixon Mulenga, Choshi, Chinsali, 7 July 2005.

60. Report of Visit to Alice, 17 May 1958, Andrew Roberts Papers.

61. The description of the Kamutola Church is from photos taken by Fergus Macpherson and found at the CSCNWW. The photos were held by a scholar in the CSCNWW and were not included as part of the Macpherson collection. The inscription on the foundation reads "*Lenshina M, 25 Oct 1953 Afwa 26 Abuka ku Bafwa 27 Bamonene na Yesu apelwe imilimo tata nakula pebwe.*" Also see description in Roberts, *Lumpa Church*, 26. As indicated in chapter 6, the church was destroyed in the 1970s. For building the church, interviews: Maggie Nkonde,

Chandamali, Chinsali, 9 July 2005; Dixon Mulenga, Choshi, Chinsali, 7 July 2005; Agre Chewe "Kusensala," Choshi, 4 July 2005. For the first service, see Mulenga, *Blood on Their Hands*, 19.

62. Kenneth Mackenzie and Paul Mushindo to Alice, 24 February 1955, Andrew Roberts Collection.

63. Kayambi Mission to Lord Bishop, Ilondola Mission Diary, 1 April 1955, 5/WF/MD63, WFA.

64. Kayambi Mission to Lord Bishop, Ilondola, 1 April 1955, Calmettes Box 7. At Ilondola the statue of Our Lady of the Rosary was stolen, in Ilondola Misson Diary, 6 September 1955, WFA.

65. Ilondola Mission to Rev. Father Kohle, Chalabesa, 31 May 1955, Calmettes Box 7, WFA.

66. Kayambi Diary, 18 August 1955, Calmettes Box 7, WFA.

67. See allegation against the missionary who prayed for Lenshina in "Report to a Visit to Alice," 17 May 1958.

68. Religious Organization Reports, August 1956, NP 3/12/13, NAZ.

69. Mulanga Diary, 4 August 1955, 5/WF/MD59, WFA.

70. Report to PC, Kasama, 4 April 1957; DC to Sec. Native Affairs, 22 June 1957, NP 3-12-3, NAZ. For "Rosary Campaigns," see Chalabesa Annual Report, 1955–1956, Calmettes Box 7, WFA.

71. Brian Garvey, *Bembaland Church: Religious and Social Change in South Central Africa, 1891–1964* (Leiden: Brill, 1994), 177.

72. Kayambi mission diary, 12 May 1956, Calmettes Box 7, WFA.

73. Francois Tanguy, "Intervention at Chitimukulu, re : Lenshina," from White Fathers Archives Rome 52/268, 1/M/Hi/56, WFA.

74. Ilondola Mission to Father Kohle, Chalabesa, 31 May 1955; Ilondola Annual Report, 1955–1956, WFA.

75. Chalabesa Annual Report, 1955–1956, Calmettes Box 7, WFA.

76. Abercorn Vicariate, Circular No. 4, April 1957, as quoted in Calmettes, "Lumpa Sect," 25.

77. Kenneth Mackenzie and Paul Mushindo to Alice, 24 February 1955; Kenneth Mackenzie and Paul Mushindo to CCAR Elders, Andrew Roberts Collection.

78. Lubwa Elders to Alice, 15 December 1955, Andrew Roberts Papers.

79. Macpherson and Stone, "Alice Movement"; V. Stone to Watt, 5 January 1958, Acc. 7548/B310; William Mackenzie to Dougall, 28 June 1956, Acc. 7548/B314, NLS.

80. Lubwa Mission Annual Report, 1956, Acc. 7548/C17, NLS.

81. John Fraser, "Report on the Lubwa Campaign," Acc. 7548/B/314, NLS.

82. CCAR Minutes of Presbytery 1956, 9. As quoted and discussed in Calmettes, "Lumpa Sect," 124–25.

83. For "chibolya," see Kenneth Mackenzie, Chitambo, to JAR Watt, 2 January 1956, Acc. 7548/B310, NLS. But with the arrival of the ChiBemba Bible at Lubwa, under missionary pressure and the accompanying celebrations, Lenshina withdrew her instructions not to read the Bible. Lubwa Annual Report, 1956, Acc. 7548/C17, NLS.

84. DC, Chinsali, Report to PC, Kasama, 4 April 1957, NP 3/12/3, NAZ.

85. Calmettes, "Lumpa Sect," 133–34. Mushindo seems to have reconciled with Lenshina in the early 1960s, sending her a book and a letter. Lenshina to Paul Mushindo, 29 July 1962, Andrew Roberts Collection. Translated with the help of Kampamba Mulenga.

86. PC Intelligence Reports, 16 September 1956; PC Situation Report, 22 September 1956, NP 3/12/3 NAZ. DC to Father Superior, Ilondola Mission, 13 September 1956, Calmettes Box 7; Ilondola Diary, 11–12 September 1956, WFA. For subsequent sentencing of Petros and the colonial official perspective, see "Report on Religious Organisation/Lenshina," 1956, NP 3/12/3, NAZ.

87. Ilondola Diary, 12 September, WFA.

88. W. V. Stone, Lubwa Annual Report, 1957, C/21, Acc. 7548, NLS.

89. *Subileni bonse, umwine ale isa; Iseeni mumwimbile; Tapali mfumu iyacila ine kamo ine neka; Iseeni mumwimbile. Uwashama eka, Uwashama eka; Ewuka filwa kupalama kwi sano; Nelyo wa filwa, iwe; Ukalola kwi?* Interviews: Jennifer Ngandu, Lusaka, 25 March 2005; Stephanie Nguni, Chiponya, 19 July 2005.

90. Minutes of seventy-third meeting of Nchenje Council held at Musumba, 1 June 1955; Kasama Intelligence Report, March 1955, NP 3/12/3, NAZ. A letter from a White Father indicates that Chitimukulu felt unable to combat various forms of "magic," in extract from letter from Francois Tanguy to Directeur de l'École de Catechists, Ilondola, 22 May 1955, from White Fathers Archives Rome 52/268, 1/M/Hi56, WFA.

91. Calmettes, "Lumpa Sect," 180. Kayambi Mission Diary, 23 May 1955, Calmettes Box 7, WFA.

92. Chinsali Tour Report 10, 1955, NP 3/12/3, NAZ.

93. Report on the Lenshina Movement, n.d. (1955–1956?), NP 3/12/3, NAZ.

94. Macpherson and Stone, "Alice Movement," 3–4. The encounter is embellished in his memoir: Macpherson, *North of the Zambezi*, 120–21.

95. DC's Handwritten Notes on Meeting with Lenshina, 2 March 1955, NP 3/12/3, NAZ.

96. Abercorn Tour Report 7, 1955, NP 3/12/3, NAZ.

97. At first the tendency was to attribute agency to Petros. For example, DC's Report on Lenshina, n.d. (1956?). By the late 1950s, nationalists were deemed most important, DC, Chinsali, to Ministry of Native Affairs, 14 August 1959, NP 3/12/3, NAZ, who argues that Petros, Kaunda, and Rain were the decision makers and authorities behind the movement.

98. N.a., "Report on Visit to Alice," 17 May 1958, Andrew Roberts Papers.

99. Alice Lenshina to Governor of NR, 18 April 1957, NP/12/3, NAZ.

100. Interview: Dixon Mulenga, Chinsali, 7 July 2005; interview: Agnes Chanda, Chinsali, 14 July 2005; interview: Jennifer Ngandu, Lusaka, 25 March 2005.

101. Interview: Dixon Mulenga, Chinsali, 7 July 2005.

102. For White Father concern and instructions to prevent collaboration between chiefs and Lenshina, see Francois Tanguy to Directeur de l'École de

Catechists a Ilondola," 22 May 1955, from White Fathers Archives Rome 52/268, 1/M/Hi56, WFA.

103. Interview: Dixon Mulenga, Chinsali, 7 July 2005.

104. Statement by Dennis Frost, DO, at Kawambwa Boma, 16 July 1959, NP 3/12/3, NAZ; interview: Dixon Mulenga, Chinsali, 7 July 2005; Ilondola Mission Diary, 6–7 April 1959, WFA.

105. For Chibesekunda's claim, see Wilson to Friends, 10 May 1959, B 310, Acc. 7548, NLS.

106. The legality of the use of the mobile police unit was questioned by the Colonial Office. For a full report of incident, see Governor Lusaka to Sec. of State of State London, 24 June 1959, CO 1015/2045, NAUK.

107. Mulilansolo Mission Diary, 21 August 1963, WFA. Intelligence reports claim that Chitimukulu "may have ordered the burning of the churches." Central Intelligence Committee, Monthly Reports, September 1963, DO 183/138, NAUK. Cf. *Report of Commission*, 11.

108. Interview: Alfred Mvula, Lusaka, 13 March 2005; Telegram: Lusaka (Gov.) to Central Africa Office, 8 October 1963, DO 183/134, NAUK; Central Intelligence Committee, Monthly Reports, September 1963, DO 183/138, NAUK.

109. Interview: Dixon Mulenga, Choshi, 7 July 2005; Telegram: Lusaka (Gov.) to Central Africa Office, 28 December 1963, DO 183/134, NAUK.

CHAPTER 5: THE DAWN

1. Partha Chatterjee, *Nationalist Thought and the Colonial World: A Derivative Discourse* (Tokyo: Zed Books, 1986).

2. Robert Rotberg, *The Rise of Nationalism in Central Africa: The Making of Malawi and Zambia, 1873–1964* (Cambridge, MA: Harvard University Press, 1972).

3. Among others, see the work of John Lonsdale, "The Moral Economy of Mau Mau: Wealth, Poverty and Civic Virtue in Kikuyu Political Thought," in *Unhappy Valley: Conflict in Kenya and Africa; Book Two: Violence and Ethnicity*, ed. Bruce Berman and John Lonsdale (Athens: Ohio University Press, 1992), 315–504; Derek R. Peterson, *Creative Writing: Translation, Bookkeeping, and the Work of Imagination in Colonial Kenya* (Portsmouth, NH: Heinemann, 2004). For contested historiography and memories of Mau Mau, see in particular E. S. Atieno-Odhiambo, "The Production of History in Kenya: The Mau Mau Debate," *Canadian Journal of African Studies* 25, no. 2 (1991): 300–307.

4. Terence O. Ranger, "Nationalist Historiography, Patriotic History and the History of the Nation: The Struggle over the Past in Zimbabwe," *Journal of Southern African Studies* 30, no. 2 (June 2004): 215–34.

5. Wim M. J. van Binsbergen, *Religious Change in Zambia: Exploratory Studies* (London: Kegan Paul, 1981), 267–316.

6. Giacomo Macola, "Harry Mwaanga Nkumbula, UNIP and the Roots of Authoritarianism in Nationalist Zambia," in *One Zambia, Many Histories: Towards a History of Post-Colonial Zamiba*, ed. Jan-Bart Gewald, Marja Hinfelaar, and

Giacomo Macola (Leiden: Brill, 2008), 17–44; and most recently, Macola, *Liberal Nationalism in Central Africa: A Biography of Harry Mwaanga Nkumbula* (New York: Palgrave Macmillan, 2010).

7. Bizeck J. Phiri, *A Political History of Zambia: From the Colonial Period to the Third Republic* (Trenton, NJ: Africa World Press, 2006), esp. 61–129.

8. Stephen Ellis, *The Mask of Anarchy: The Destruction of Liberia and the Religious Dimension of an African Civil War*, 2nd ed. (New York: New York University Press, 2006), 301.

9. Phiri, *Political History of Zambia*, 117.

10. Clifton Crais, *The Politics of Evil: Magic, State Power, and the Political Imagination in South Africa* (Cambridge: Cambridge University Press, 2002), 122.

11. Andrew Roberts, *A History of Zambia* (New York: Africana Publishing, 1976), 211; Kenneth D. Kaunda, *Zambia Shall Be Free: An Autobiography* (London: Heinemann, 1962), 147–48.

12. Phiri, *Political History of Zambia*, 31–59.

13. For reports of *banyama* in the Northern Province during the 1930s, see DC, Mpika, "Report on Banyama Rumours in the Lake Chaya Area, 1938"; DC, Mpika, to PC, NP, Kasama, 6 March 1939, "Memorandum concerning "Banyama" and "Mafyeka" with special reference to the Provincial Commissioner, Kasama's Confidential File on "Banyama" and to incidents in the Isoka District in the Latter Part of 1943"; *Mutende* 38 (1939) "Banyama: Copperbelt Myth"; in SEC 2/429, NAZ. Also see Luise White, *Speaking with Vampires: Rumor and History in Colonial Africa* (Berkeley: University of California Press, 2000), 302–4; Mwelwa C. Musambachime, "The Impact of Rumor: The Case of the Banyama (Vampire Men) Scare in Northern Rhodesia, 1930–1964," *International Journal of African Historical Studies* 21, no. 2 (1988): 201–15, esp. 211–12.

14. Kenneth Kaunda held a meeting in Mpika and urged a strike and protest against federation on 1–2 April, but no government employees were present. In general, there was limited or no participation by civil servants in the strike despite detailed preparations made by the administration; DC, Mpika, to PC, Kasama, 27 March 1953, NP 3/15/2, NAZ.

15. Fergus Macpherson, *North of the Zambezi: A Modern Missionary Memoir* (Edinburgh: Handsel Press, 1998), 87–88.

16. Executive Branch, NR ANC, Chinsali Branch, to Rev. F. Macpherson, Lubwa Mission, Chinsali, 25 March 1952. B/313, Acc. 7548, NLS. The same letter is referred to in Kaunda, *Zambia Shall Be Free*, 146–47.

17. Interview: Robert Kapasa Makasa, Lubu River Home, Chinsali, 15 July 2005; John Malama Sokoni, "The Causes of Cha Cha Cha," ms., HM 74/ PP/ 1, NAZ; Rotberg, *Rise of Nationalism*, 273. Kapasa Makasa, *Zambia's March to Political Freedom* (Nairobi: Heinemann, 1981), 48–50.

18. Kaunda sent a letter, noting that Chief Chibesakunda refused to allow his sister to plant the coronation tree. Kennie to VG Secretary, ANCO, Lusaka, 25 May 1953. Macpherson Collection, Box 7, CSCNWW.

19. For resistance before 1939, see Henry S. Meebelo, *Reaction to Colonialism: A Prelude to the Politics of Independence in Northern Zambia, 1893–1939* (Manchester: Manchester University Press, 1971).

20. According to the Constitution of the ANC, in Macpherson Collection, Box 7, CSCNWW.

21. Audrey Richards Fieldnotes, 2/25/34, LSE.

22. ANC circular 1.9 (November 1955) Macpherson Collection Box 11, CSC-NWW; NP 3/15/3, NAZ.

23. R. K. Makasa, Provincial President, ANC to PC, NP, 9 June 1955, NP 3/15/3, NAZ.

24. Audrey Richards Fieldnotes, n.d. (1950s), Audrey Richards Papers 2/25, LSE.

25. DC, Kasama, to PC, Kasama, 6 August 1957, NP 3/15/2, NAZ.

26. Audrey Richards Fieldnotes n.d. (1950s), Audrey Richards Papers 2/25, LSE.

27. It is unclear who first came up with "Zambia." Interviews identify Sikalumbi or Kapwepwe. Fergus Macpherson, Interview with Reuben Kamanga, 1971, Macpherson Collection, Box 1, CSCNWW. Rotberg claims Arthur Wina first used "Zambia" in a poem he wrote while at Makerere College in 1953: Rotberg, *Rise of Nationalism*, 291. Interview: Robert Kapasa Makasa, Lubu River Home, Chinsali, 15 July 2005. Also covered in Makasa, *Zambia's March*, 97–102; Kaunda, *Zambia Shall Be Free*, 98–99. A letter from N. Tembo to Sikalumbi indicated a preference for "Zambia," with the abbreviation "ZA," an effective catchphrase for the "simple-minded villager," in Jack Simon Collection, W2, Universtity of Cape Town, Manuscripts and Archives (henceforth UCTMA).

28. Report by District Messenger Benson Mutale on meeting on 23 November 1958 at Kasama, NP 3/15/3, NAZ.

29. Report by District Messengers R. Chiboo and M. Kaengel on Congress meeting, on 30 November 1958, NP 3/15/3, NAZ.

30. Mwansa to Sikalumbi, 15 June 1959, HM 76/PP/1, NAZ.

31. Acting Sec. for Native Affairs to PC, Kasama, 24 November 1958, NP 3/15/3, NAZ. Interview: Rodwell Mwansabama, Chandamali, 9 July 2005.

32. Mwansa to Sikalumbi, 15 June 1959, HM 76/PP/1, NAZ.

33. Report by M. Musa Kabwe, 2 December 1958; Taishi, ZANC Regional Sec. to PC, Kasama, 12 January 1959; J. C. M Ng'andu to DC, Chinsali, 23 January 1959, NP 3/15/3, NAZ. Interview: Rodwell Mwansabama, Chandamali, 9 July 2005.

34. Regional Secretary, ZANC, to PC, Kasama, 23 January 1959, NP 3/15/3, NAZ.

35. DC to PC, Kasama, 26 March 1959, NP 3/15/3, NAZ.

36. Interview: Rodwell Mwansabama, Chandamali, 9 July 2005.

37. Minutes of First Central Comm. Meeting, 15 October 1959, UNIP 8/1/1, UNIPA.

38. Kaunda, *Zambia Shall Be Free*, 138.

39. *Voice of UNIP*, December 1960.

40. Branch numbers from UNIP First territorial Emergency Conference, 3–4 September, Lusaka. UNIP 3/1/1, UNIPA. The approximate number of 400,000 from Northern Rhodesia, *An Account of the Disturbances in Northern Rhodesia* (Lusaka, 1961), 4.

41. Confidential Tour Reports, NP 3/2/11, NAZ.

42. A. J. Soko to Sikalumbi, 25 November 1959, Sikalumbi Papers, HM 76, NAZ. "Changes in Bemba Administration, September 1959," Audrey Richards Papers 1/32/30–32, LSE.

43. Interview: Fergus Macpherson with Robert Kaunda, n.d., 197, Macpherson Box 1, CSCNWW. According to Sokoni, the instructions to burn *fitupa* came from the national leadership, "The Causes of Cha Cha Cha," mss. Sokoni Papers, HM 74, NAZ.

44. Interview: Fergus Macpherson with Robert Kaunda, n.d., MacPherson Collection Box 1, CSCNWW.

45. Ibid.

46. Mulanga Mission Diary, 8 August 1961, 5/WF/MD 59; Ilondola Mission Diary, 24 April; 10, 14, 18, 31 August 1961, 5/WF/MD63, WFA. William Mackenzie, Lubwa, to Rev. JM Hamilton, Gen Sec., Foreign Mission Council, 29 August 1961, B/311, Acc. 7548, NLS.

47. *Voice of UNIP*, "A Grim Peep into the North."

48. DC, Chinsali, "Allegations in the 'Voice of UNIP,'" 28 October 1961, NP 3/12/9, NAZ. The colonial administration seems correct, however, in its assertion that UNIP activists carried out violent actions, before the colonial counterinsurgency. A colonial report on the "disturbances" appeared in the *Tanganyika Standard*, 4 January 1962. UNIP responded in a press statement authored by Makasa, 4 January 1962. Macpherson Collection Box 9, CSCNWW.

49. "Review of the Military Situation — Northern Province as at 9 Sept., 1961," NP 3/12/9, NAZ.

50. Presidential Address to Third Divisional Exec. Committee, Ndola, 29 April 1961, *Dawn*, UNIP 14/1/3, UNIPA.

51. *Voice of UNIP*, May 1962.

52. Andreya S. Masiye, *Singing for Freedom: Zambia's Struggle for African Government* (Lusaka: Oxford University Press, 1977), 100.

53. Ibid.

54. Ibid., 87.

55. I. H. Wether, DC, Kasama, to PC, Kasama, 8 August 1961, CO 1015/2447, NAUK.

56. A rumor spread that the Bishop of Kasama would join with Welensky to destroy UNIP. Marcel Daubechies, Bishop Kasama, to Divisional Pres. UNIP, 10 January 1962; A. Kemmink, Santa Maria Mission to Div. Pres. UNIP, 16 December 1961, UNIP 5/1/1/12, UNIPA.

57. Masiye, *Singing for Freedom*, 95. My translation differs slightly from Masiye's translation.

58. Sokoni to Constituency Secretaries, 6 June 1961, UNIP 5/1/1/12, UNIPA.

59. Interview: Shame Mulenga, Bright Village, Chinsali, 9 July 2005.

60. Masiye, *Singing for Freedom*, 32.

61. Several found in UNIP 5/1/1/12, UNIPA.

62. For example, the case detailed in C. M. Chikwenda, Constituency Secretary to DC, Kasama, 30 July 1963, UNIP 5-1-1-12, UNIPA.

63. Kasatu to National Leader on Tour, 2 August 1961; UNIP Newsletter 4 July 1961, UNIP 5/1/1/12, UNIPA.

64. Masiye, *Singing for Freedom*, 73.

65. Calmettes Assorted Correspondence, n.d. (late 1950s?), Calmettes Box 7, WFA.

66. Address by Kenneth Kaunda to Party conference on 3 September 1963, as quoted in "The Struggle for Independence," n.d., UNIP 2/2/2, UNIPA.

67. Kaunda had sent money to Sikalumbi's wife. Sikalumbi to Kenneth Kaunda, Lusaka, 24 November 1963, HM 76, NAZ.

68. Interview: John Chabula, Kasomo, 9 July 2005.

69. Interview: F. Macpherson with Mama Chola, UNIP Regional Women's Sec., Mwense, 15 February 1970, MacPherson Collection, Box 1, CSCNWW.

70. Intelligence Report, September 1962, DO 183/138, NAUK.

71. Crais, *Politics of Evil*, 144.

72. Kaunda, *Zambia Shall Be Free*, 160.

CHAPTER 6: DEVILS OF WAR

1. Zambia, *Report of the Commission of Enquiry into the Lumpa Church* (Lusaka, 1965). The original security reports upon which the diary of events in the *Report* is based can be found, as "Diary of Events from 25 June to 15 October," 16 October 1964, in MHA 1/3/10 in National Archives of Zambia (NAZ). The MHA 1/3/10 Lenshina file is not yet cataloged. It was viewed with the permission of the director of the National Archives. The number of those killed due to the conflict is unclear. Based on hospital records, the *Report* cites 707 killed and 404 wounded "during security operations" in northern and eastern provinces (probably between June and September 1964). The *Report* gives only a few "approximate" figures for the earlier period and none for the period before June 1963. It also does not include those who died after security operations and those who starved in the bush or during the march to the Congo. In my view, the *Report* also underestimates the number killed by UNIP cadres. I have attempted impartial rendition of the war of 1963–1964, in David M. Gordon, "Rebellion or Massacre: The UNIP-Lumpa Conflict Revisited," in *One Zambia, Many Histories: Towards a History of Post-Colonial Zambia*, ed. Jan-Bart Gewald, Marja Hinfelaar, and Giacomo Macola (Leiden: Brill, 2008), 45–76.

2. David Anderson, *Histories of the Hanged: The Dirty War in Kenya and the End of Empire* (New York: Norton, 2005).

3. PC's report on "Review of the Military Situation—Northern Province as at 9 Sept. 1961"; for burning of Watchtower churches, see DC's report on "Allegations in the "Voice of UNIP," 28 October 1961; for burning of chiefs' houses in Chinsali, see Report by DC (Chinsali), 1 November 1961, NP 3/12/9, NAZ.

4. The technique was described by informants of a colonial officer in Annexure to Chinsali Tour Report 16 of 1960, NP 3/2/11, NAZ.

5. Interview: John Bwalya Mfula, Bright Village, 9 July 2005.

6. The ANC's Provincial Secretary General's report of 1962 claimed that support for the party was growing in the Northern Province and many held UNIP cards only for protection; ANC 2/10 United National Independence Party's Archives, Lusaka (henceforth UNIPA).

7. Clerck to UNIP Regional Secretary, 3 December 1962, UNIP 12/1/8, UNIPA. By contrast, the Mulanga Mission seems to have been on better terms with UNIP activists through 1963, following many violent confrontations in 1961–1962. See entries in Mulanga mission diary for 2 November 1962 and 10 February 1963, 5/WF/MD59, White Fathers Archives, Lusaka (henceforth WFA).

8. Memorandum presented to the PC (Northern Province), 14 October 1963, ANC 2/10, UNIPA.

9. "ANC Warning to Members of ANC and Other Peoples of Goodwill," n.d. (end 1963), ANC 2/10 UNIPA.

10. Chapoloko to DCs (Chinsali, Isoka, and Mpika), 19 December 1962, UNIP 5/1/2/1/4, UNIPA.

11. Chapoloko to Priestley, 22 June 1963; Priestley to Chapoloko, 21 May 1963; Manager (Mbesuma Ranch) to UNIP Regional Secretary, 18 May 1963, UNIP 5/1/2/1/4, UNIPA. For demanding of party cards, also see Mulanga Mission Diary, 26 August 1963, Lusaka, 5/WF/MD/59, WFA.

12. Priestley to Chapoloko, 18 June 1963; Chapoloko to Priestley, 29 June 1963, UNIP 5/1/2/1/4, UNIPA.

13. As claimed in the oral testimony of Jennifer Ngandu and many others. This accusation has become church orthodoxy. Interviews with Jennifer Ngandu, Lusaka, 25 March 2005; Helena Mulenga, Leonard Mutonga, Lusaka, 12 March 2005; Dixon Mulenga, Choshi, 3 July 2005; Felix Chimfwembwe Mumba, Choshi, 10 July 2005; Denise Chilufya, Choshi, 10 July 2005; Stephanie Nguni, Chiponya, 19 July 2005.

14. An account of the agreement and Chapoloko's complaints in Chapoloko to Mama Mulenga, 29 June 1963, UNIP 5/1/2/1/4, UNIPA. The meeting and some of the preceding events are covered in the *Report*, 11. For the meeting and arson, see Central Intelligence Committee, Monthly Reports, June 1963, DO 183/138, NAUK.

15. Interview: Dixon Mulenga, Choshi, 3 July 2005.

16. Chapoloko to M. M. Chona, Lusaka, 28 August 1963, UNIP 16/6/145, UNIPA.

17. Mulanga Mission Diary, 26 August 1963, WFA.

18. Chapoloko to UNIP Constituency Secretaries (Mpichi Region), 29 August 196, UNIP 16/6/145, UNIPA.

19. DC, Isoka, to PC, Northern Province, 6 October 1963, NP 3/12/1, NAZ.

20. Interviews in Chinsali suggest that UNIP activists believed there was an alliance between Lenshina and Welensky. Ten UNIP activist interviewed in different

villages in Chinsali District insisted that Lenshina received money from the Katangese. No Lumpa members indicated an alliance with Welensky or the ANC. There is no documentary evidence to support this claim, although a few Lumpa-ANC meetings probably took place, probably on matters of security. See, for example, the letter written by Lenshina to the ANC cited in Kampamba Mulenga, *Blood on Their Hands* (Lusaka: Zambia Educational Publishing House, 1998), 49. I have been unable to find this letter in its cited location, MHA 1/3/10, NAZ. After 1964, certain members of the Lumpa Church had discussions with Moïse Tshombe, which facilitated their move to the Congo. Interview: Dixon Mulenga, Choshi, 15 July 2005 (detailed below). Fergus Macpherson claims that the Lumpa Church was funded by Welensky and trained by federal or Kantangan armed forces. The evidence he presents is an interview with one-time Lumpa member Robert Kaunda, but who was in the UNIP camp by the early 1960s. In this interview Robert Kaunda explicitly states that the Lumpa who prepared weapons were not from elsewhere. Fergus Macpherson and Julius Chabala's interview with Robert Kaunda, 26 February 1969, Macpherson Collection, Box 1.2, Center for the Study of Christianity in the Non-Western World, Edinburgh (henceforth CSCNWW).

21. Chola to Lenshina Mulenga, 26 June 1963, UNIP 5/1/2/1/4, UNIPA.

22. Interview: Lazerus Chewe Chanika, Kasomo, 5 July 2005.

23. A chief's capital is referred to as a *musumba*. This was also the term the missionaries adopted to describe their missions.

24. More than twenty Lumpa members who witnessed events made these claims. The most instructive and detailed interviews include: Dixon Mulenga, 7 July 2005; Felix Chimfwembwe Mumba; Mercy Mfula, Choshi, 10 July 2005; Paison Nkonde, Kapiri Mposhi, 20 July 2005. Some documentary evidence substantiates their testimony of beatings and the burning of their churches. See, for example, attacks on Lumpa reported in Mulanga Mission Diary, 13 June 1963, 28 July 1963, 26 August 1963, 28 August 1963, WFA.

25. Interview: Sebastian Chewe Filamba, Matumbo Village, 18 July 2005.

26. UNIP Regional Organizing Secretary to M. M. Chona, 24 December 1963, UNIP 16/6/145, UNIPA. The *Report*, 12, does not provide or further clarify the background of the December incidents.

27. Telegram: Lusaka (Gov.) to Central Africa Office, 28 December 63, DO 183/134, NAUK.

28. *Report*, 12.

29. Mulanga Mission Diary, 16–29 December 1963, WFA.

30. For example, at a meeting of Chinsali's Rural Council, they compiled a list of twenty-five violent acts in which the Lumpa Church had been involved across the colony since 1955. Minutes of Chinsali Rural Council, 12–14 December 1963, NP 3/12/10, NAZ.

31. *Report*, 13.

32. Mulilansolo Mission Diary, 28 December 1963, WFA.

33. Since this letter was addressed to the provincial commissioner personally, and he was transferred and returned to England, it followed him to England and

only appeared in the Commonwealth Relations Office (CRO) in the middle of August. The letter also claims that the designate minister of state for defense, L. Changufu, had "talked with confidence that Mama Lenshina and some of her church elders would soon be in custody." A. G. H. Kapelekasubila to PC (Northern Province), 26 June 1964, DO 183/135, NAUK.

34. As argued by Bizeck J. Phiri, A Political History of Zambia: From the Colonial Period to the Third Republic (Trenton, NJ: Africa World Press, 2006), 119–21.

35. Interview: Paison Nkonde, "Lisuwe mumilimo yakwa Lesa" (the train in the work of God), Kapiri Mposhi, 20 July 2007.

36. Contra the Report, 20, which does not record those taken to jail. Documentary evidence supporting the fact that eight to ten men were jailed in "Testimony of John Hannah," John Hudson Papers.

37. Report, 20. Cf. Mulenga, Blood on Their Hands, 51–52. Also see details recorded in Mulilansolo Mission Diary, 26 June 1964, WFA.

38. Interview: Monica Nkamba, Chiponya, Mpika, 19 July 2005.

39. Report, 20. According to the DC Hannah, six Lumpa died in this action: "Testimony of John Hannah," John Hudson Papers.

40. Appendix C: Statement of Anderson Chintankwa taken on 22 September 1964, MHA 1/3/10, NAZ.

41. Ibid.

42. Appendix B: Translation of Bemba Note, MHA 1/3/10, NAZ.

43. I have been unable to locate this statement in the archives, probably because before the Preservation of Public Security Act was promulgated fourteen days later, the government had no legal basis to make such an order. Evidence of it may have been removed from the files. However, the order was submitted to the Appeals Court as evidence in "Mutambo and Five Others v The People," in Zambia Law Report 1965 (Lusaka, 1972), 15–59, esp. 20, 43. In this case, the judge ruled that the order was legal since "one could regard the document as a circular of advice put out by the administration for the information of the local people." On 11 July, Chinsali DC John Hannah informed the White Fathers at Mulanga that the government intended to threaten the Lumpas to make them go back to their original villagers. Mulanga Mission Diary, 11 July 1964, WFA. In Hannah's testimony, he clearly thought that it was necessary to disperse the Lumpa, and to use force to do so. "Testimony of John Hannah," John Hudson Papers.

44. Mulanga Mission Diary, 13–16 July 1964, WFA.

45. Report, 21.

46. Message no. 7 from Bond Disops to Compol, 27 July 1964, MHA 1/3/10, NAZ.

47. Northern News, 30 July 1964.

48. Message no. 28 from Disops Chinsali to Compol, 27 July 1964, MHA 1/3/10, NAZ.

49. Six men were tried and sentenced to hang for the death of Inspector Smith. Their failed appeal, which contains much detail about the killing of Inspector Smith, can be found in "Mutambo and Five Others v The People," Zambia Law Report 1965, 15–59.

50. Several interviewees claimed that Inspector Smith's body was mutilated. The documentary evidence does not state this explicitly, although it does demonstrate that the Lumpa villagers resisted giving up the body. The numbers of dead, from the correspondence: Message no. 28 from Disops Chinsali to Compol, 27 July 1964, MHA 1/3/10, NAZ; Telegrams: Troops Lusaka to Ministry of Defence (MOD), 27 July 1964; Lusaka (Gov.) to CRO, 27 July 1964, both in DO 183/135, NAUK. The Commission's *Report* reports on only 14 deaths and 15 wounded; *Report*, 22–23. Hannah reports "approximately 25," in "Testimony of John Hannah," John Hudson Papers.

51. Anonymous interview. For a UNIP perspective, see interview: Sebastian Chewe Filamba, Mutambo Village, 18 July 2005. The confrontation occurred on the twenty-seventh of July 1964. The trial of youth involved in the Chilanga battle is reported in *Northern News*, 20 October 1964, but no judgment is recorded. Trial records are unavailable. The *Report*, 29–30, confirms many details of the conflict.

52. Preservation of Public Security Act, Gazetted on 29 July 1964, Government Notice no. 375 of 1964, in MHA 1/3/10, NAZ.

53. According to the deputy governor's office, "At least one platoon ran away from the enemy through fear of witchcraft. If this fact were widely known it would have a very unsettling effect on the European community. It would, moreover, undermine Kaunda's prestige as the minister responsible for the police and armed services." Molyneaux to Jamieson, 7 September 1964, DO 183/135, NAUK.

54. "Diary of Events," 5, MHA 1/3/10, NAZ; *Report*, 23–24.

55. *Northern News*, 30 July 1964.

56. Interview: Mercy Mfula Choshi, 10 July 2005. A second eyewitness, the daughter of the prominent deacon "Chonkela," who was wanted and was shot by the police, offers similar testimony; interview: Denise Chilufya, Choshi, 10 July 2005.

57. "Message from Chinsali," 30 July 1964, MHA 1/3/10, NAZ. The *Report* is similar to the "Message from Chinsali" with a few details and names excluded; *Report*, 24. The timeline is in "Messages from Chinsali," 30 July 1964, MHA 1/3/10, NAZ and demonstrates the rapidity of the operation, which is underemphasized in the agreed-upon release and the *Report*. The account of the attack on Sione also in "Testimony of John Hannah," John Hudson Papers.

58. "Message from Chinsali," 30 July 1964, MHA 1/3/10, NAZ.

59. The Northern Rhodesian Department of the Commonwealth Relations Office heard of several cases in which the "officers found it extremely difficult to get them [the soldiers] to stop firing and that consequently there were many more casualties than there should have been." Jamieson to Molyneaux, 2 September 1964, DO 183/135, NAUK.

60. *Rhodesia Herald*, 31 July 1964.

61. According to John Hannah, eight appeals for surrender were made. "Testimony of John Hannah," John Hudson Papers.

62. Report by Special Branch on "Feelings of the Followers of the Lumpa Church Towards the Church Building at Sione," 4 September 1964, MHA 1/3/10, NAZ.

63. Provops to Mainops, Sitrep messages from Chinsali, 30 July 1964, MHA 1/3/10, NAZ.

64. "Testimony of John Hannah," John Hudson Papers.

65. "Messages concerning Chinsali," 2 August 1964, MHA 1/3/10, NAZ.

66. "Messages from Chinsali and Lundazi," 4–5 August 1964, MHA 1/3/10, NAZ. Seven Lumpa members were sentenced to hang for the attack on Lundazi. Trial records are not available, but some details are in *Northern News*, 3, 6, 7, 9, 10 October 1964.

67. *Northern News*, 4 August 1964.

68. Ibid. Kaunda's allegations are not substantiated in official military or intelligence reports.

69. Records of a meeting held at government house, 3 August 1964, MHA 1/3/10, NAZ.

70. Societies Ordinance, 3 August 1964, MHA 1/3/10, NAZ.

71. The commission reports 81 dead; military messages from the attack report 51 men and 23 women dead at the time of the operation. *Report*, 26; "Messages from Chinsali and Lundazi," 4 August 1964, MHA 1/3/10, NAZ.

72. "Messages from Chinsali and Lundazi," 4 August 1964, MHA 1/3/10, NAZ.

73. Acting registrar to resident magistrate (Lundazi), 4 August 1964, MHA 1/3/10, NAZ. A list of those buried in Lundazi can be found in the UNIP archives; UNIP 5/5/2/7/2, UNIPA.

74. Minute by governor to permanent secretary (Office of Prime Minister), 11 August 1964, MHA 1/3/10, NAZ.

75. John Hudson, *A Time to Mourn: A Personal Account of the 1964 Church Revolt in Zambia* (Lusaka: Bookworld, 1999), 48–49; "Messages from Chinsali and Lundazi," 8–9 August 1964, MHA 1/3/10, NAZ.

76. As reported in Mulanga Mission Diary, 15 August 1964, WFA.

77. Ibid.

78. Troops Lusaka to MOD, 17 October 1964, DO 183/135, NAUK; *Report*, 35.

79. Telegram army HQ to permanent secretary (Office of the Prime Minister) and "all DIVOPS," 21 August 1964, MHA 1/3/10, NAZ.

80. A. S. Bennet, "Alice Lenshina Giving Herself Up," 13 August 1964, MHA 1/3/10, NAZ. The government guarantees to Lenshina are to be found in "Letter to Alice Lenshina," 12 August 1964, MHA 1/3/10, NAZ.

81. "Mwe Lukuta Lwakwa Lesa Umfweni Ifyo Ndesosa," MHA 1/3/10, NAZ.

82. Minutes of an emergency meeting held at Chinsali rural Boma, 26–27 August 1964, NP 3/12/10, NAZ.

83. According to the *Preservation of Public Security Ordinance, Amendment no. 4*. Memorandum, Office of Magistrate, 12 October 1964, NP 3/12/10, NAZ.

84. Makasa to Kaunda, 3 February 1965, NP 3/12/11, NAZ. Kaunda disagreed with Makasa, arguing that the Lumpa would create problems across the country. Kaunda to Makasa, 4 May 1965, NP 3/12/11, NAZ.

85. K. P. Gill, "Memorandum Containing Proposals for the Eventual Resettlement of Lenshina Present at Katito and Lunzuwa Camps," March 1965, NP 3/12/11, NAZ.

86. Lumpa leaders claim that Bulala Wina showed them where to settle and how to conduct themselves in the Congo. He was fluent in French and Swahili and was friendly with the Congolese authorities. Interviews: Dixon Mulenga, 15 July 2005; Lewis Mumba, Chiponya, 19 July 2005; Monica Nkamba, Chiponya, 19 July 2005.

87. The police intercepted John Museba, who had been in Katanga, with a letter from Lenshina instructing her followers to go to Mokambo. Namulongo to district secretary (Chinsali), 29 April 1965, NP 3/12/11, NAZ. Interview: Dixon Mulenga, 15 July 2005.

88. Rehabilitation Officer to Permanent Secretary (Office of the President), 31 May 1965, NP 3/12/11, NAZ. Interviews: David Mpuku, Choshi, 6 July 2005; Mercy Mfula; Aida Lukonde, Choshi, 10 July 2005; Monica Nkamba; Gabriel Chimfwembe, Kapiri Mposhi, 20 July 2005.

89. Minutes of the Ninth Meeting of Central Security Council, 12 June 1965, NP, 3/12/11, NAZ.

90. Social Welfare Officer (Katito) to Makasa, 18 February 1966; Zambia police telegram Disops Chinsali to Provops Kasama and Mainops Lusaka, 1 February 1965, NP 3/12/11, NAZ. Interview: Gabriel Chisanga, Choshi, 10 July 2005.

91. The closure of the camps is not documented in detail, but camp authorities declared their determination to close the camp by the end of March 1966. Mulala to Permanent Secretary (Office of the President), 16 February 1966, NP 3/12/11, NAZ. Several interviewees claim that tear gas was fired into the camp and they were forced to leave. This probably is a reference to an attempt to close the camp in October 1965 with the use of the military, which resulted in many fleeing the camp. Interviews: Mercy Mfula; Aida Lukonde; Monica Nkamba, Choshi, 10 July 2005. "Record of conversation with Mr. D. A. Penn on 1 November 1965," DO 183/814, NAUK.

92. Interviews: Paison Nkonde; Dixon Mulenga, 15 July 2005; and Elizabeth "Lutanda" Ngandu, Lusaka, 25 March 2005.

93. Interview: Dixon Mulenga, Choshi, 7 July 2005. Mulenga's claims to be Moses were repeated by several Lumpa members, Field Observations, June to July 2005.

94. Anonymous interview: Choshi Village, Chinsali.

95. Interview: Stephanie Nguni, Chiponya, 19 July 2005.

96. J. L. Calmettes, "Church Music in Chinsali District, 1954–1974: The Lumpa Church; 64 Hymns Recorded, Translated, and Explained," unpublished paper, J. L. Calmettes Box 8, WFA.

97. Chiponya Manuscript, Chiponya Village New Jerusalem Congregation, Zambia, 11.

98. Ibid., 12.

99. The story of the divorce in interview: William "Kalomba muli Lesa," Chiponya, Mpika, 29 July 2005; and Dixon Mulenga, Chinsali, 15 July 2005.
100. Gordon, "Rebellion or Masssacre."

CHAPTER 7: GOD IN HEAVEN, KAUNDA ON EARTH

1. Programme for Independence Celebrations, Box 85 A, NAZ. For discussions and detailed protocol over independence celebrations, see Independence Arrangements and Coordination, Cabinet Office 2/1/3, NAZ. *Independence Celebrations Background* (Lusaka: UNIP, 1964), UNIP 14/3, UNIP Archives, Zambia (henceforth UNIPA). Further details on Lusaka, local and international festivities in UNIP 13/1/1, 2, 3, UNIPA.

2. Contra Robert I. Rotberg, *Christian Missionaries and the Creation of Northern Rhodesia, 1880–1924* (Cambridge, MA: Harvard University Press, 1965), esp. 147, who argues that even though the nationalists were mission-trained, they had come to disavow or ignore the church by independence.

3. Giacomo Macola, "'It Means as If We Are Excluded from the Good Freedom': Thwarted Expectations of Independence in the Luapula Province of Zambia, 1964–1966," *Journal of African History* 47, no. 1 (2006): 43–56.

4. Miles Larmer, "'A Little Bit Like a volcano': The United Progressive Party and Resistance to One-Party Rule in Zambia, 1964–1980," *International Journal of African Historical Studies* 39, no. 1 (2006): 49–83; Larmer, "Enemies Within?: Opposition to the Zambian One-Party State, 1972–1980," in *One Zambia Many Histories: Towards a History of Post-Colonial Zambia*, ed. Jan-Bart Gewald, Marja Hinfelaar, and Giacomo Macola (Leiden: Brill, 2008), 98–128; and Larmer, *Mineworkers in Zambia: Labour and Political Change in Post-Colonial Africa* (London: Taurus, 2007).

5. Marja Hinfelaar, "Legitimizing Powers: The Political Role of the Roman Catholic Church, 1972–1991," in Gewald, Hinfelaar, and Macola, *One Zambia, Many Histories*, 129–43.

6. Gatian F. Lungu, "The Church, Labour and the Press in Zambia: The Role of Critical Observers in a One-Party State," *African Affairs* 85, no. 340 (July 1986): 385–410.

7. This chapter does not provide a thorough account of Archbishop Milingo's healing ministry, which has been dealt with in Gerrie ter Haar, *Spirit of Africa: The Healing Ministry of Archbishop Milingo of Zambia* (Trenton, NJ: Africa World Press, 1992).

8. UNIP Press Release, 6 May 1964, UNIP 7/22/7, UNIPA; National Anthem, CO 2/1/2, NAZ.

9. Note by P.S. on Consultative Committee, 7 March 1964, CO 2/1/3, NAZ.

10. Cabinet Minutes, 12 May 1964, CO 3/1/70, NAZ.

11. According to "Proceedings of Exploratory Conference on Cultural Affairs in Zambia," 9 February 1969, in Box 172 A, NAZ.

12. According to the Public Order Amendment Bill, in *Times of Zambia* (henceforth TOZ), 14 December 1966.

13. *TOZ*, 7 December 1966; Record of a Meeting Between the Minister of State for Presidential Affairs, A. M. Milner, and Leader's of Jehovah's Witnesses held on 6 December 1967, FA 1/221, NAZ.

14. National Monuments Commission Annual Report for 1968, Box 112, NAZ.

15. For celebratory accounts by UNIP cadres, see Henry S. Meebelo, *Main Currents of Zambian Humanist Thought* (Lusaka: Oxford University Press, 1973); Justin B. Zulu, *Zambian Humanism: Some Major Spiritual and Economic Challenges* (Lusaka: National Educational Company of Zambia, 1970); Timothy K. Kandeke, *Fundamentals of Zambian Humanism* (Lusaka: National Educational Company of Zambia, 1977). For the wave of enthusiasm by economists and missionaries, especially following the socialist 1968 Mulungushi reforms, see Bastiaan de Gaay Fortman, *After Mulungushi: The Economics of Zambian Humanism* (Nairobi: East Africa Publishing House, 1969). Two of the four non-Zambian contributors to this celebratory volume were clergy.

16. Megan Vaughan, "Exploitation and Neglect: Rural Producers and the State in Malawi and Zambia," in *History of Central Africa: The Contemporary Years Since 1960*, ed. David Birmingham and Phyllis M. Martin (London: Longman, 1998), 178.

17. James Ferguson, *Global Shadows: Africa in the Neoliberal World Order* (Durham, NC: Duke University Press, 2006), 75–77.

18. Kenneth D. Kaunda, *Humanism in Zambia and a Guide to Its Implementation: Part II* (Lusaka: Division of National Guidance, 1974), vi. For the clergy advisory role in other aspects of government policy, see William Tordoff and Robert Molteno, "Government and Administration," in William Tordoff, ed., *Politics in Zambia* (Manchester: Manchester University Press, 1974), 261.

19. These divisions are most evident in the long struggle of Jack Simon, South African Communist Party activist and Zambian political educator, to consolidate the socialist element within humanism and UNIP, as indicated in his correspondence and notes in Simon Collection, W10-19, BC1081, University of Cape Town Manuscripts and Archives (henceforth UCTMA).

20. Kaunda, *Humanism in Zambia*, 50.

21. Kaunda, Speech to the Annual Conference of the UNIP at Mulungushi, 12–13 September 1964, esp. 13–14, UNIP 3/1/1, UNIPA.

22. Ibid., 51–52.

23. Ibid., 54–55.

24. *Voice of UNIP*, October 1964.

25. A J. Kangwe, "Ken's Birthday: 28th April," in *Voice of UNIP*, May 1965.

26. *Voice of UNIP*, May 1965.

27. Macola, "It Means as If We Are Excluded from the Good Freedom"; Larmer, "A Little Bit Like a Volcano."

28. Kenneth D. Kaunda, *A Humanist in Africa: Letters to Colin M. Morris from Kenneth D. Kaunda, President of Zambia* (Nashville: Abingdon Press, 1966).

29. *Humanism in Zambia*, pamphlet prepared by K. D. Kaunda for National Council of UNIP held in Lusaka on 26 April 1967, UNIP 1/3/2, UNIPA. For the

adoption of humanism by UNIP's National Council, see *Zambia Mail*, 28 April 1967, and also cited in Meebelo, *Main Currents*, 15.

30. Kaunda, *Humanism in Zambia*, 118–19.

31. As discussed in Meebelo, *Main Currents*, 15–27.

32. Zulu, *Zambian Humanism*, 6–16.

33. "Humanist Terminology: A Supplement to Lectures on Party Organization," UNIP 2/3/1, UNIPA.

34. Kandeke, *Fundamentals of Zambian Humanism*, 50–51. South African communist Jack Simons was in dialogue with Kandeke, and offered a reader's report for Kandeke's book; Jack Simons, "Review of Problems of Building Socialism," W/15, BC1081, UCTMA.

35. Kandeke, *Fundamentals of Zambian Humanism*, 56–57.

36. For Kapwepwe's "Cultural Revolution," see Goodwin B. Mwangilwa, *The Kapwepwe Diaries* (Lusaka: Multimedia Publishers, 1986), 110–11. For UNIP leadership instructions to desist from attacks, see M. Chona to all Reg. Sec., 19 July 1967, UNIP 7/1/3, UNIPA.

37. For the "father-chief" idiom, see Michael G. Schatzberg, *Political Legitimacy in Middle Africa: Father, Family, Food* (Bloomington: Indiana University Press, 2001), 145–73.

38. Titus B. Makupo, ed., *Kaunda's Guidelines* (Lusaka: TMC Publicity, 1970).

39. See Meebelo's correspondence, which criticizes Macpherson's independent research agenda, in UNIP 2/7/2, UNIPA.

40. Mudenda to Kalula, Chair Soc. Cultural Comm., 17 December 1973, UNIP 8/7/2, UNIPA.

41. Presidential Circular Minute to All Cabinet Ministers, UNIP, 10 October 1972, UNIPA. For Ministry of National Guidance and Humanism activities and publications, see Box 110ABC, NAZ.

42. Kaunda, "Speech by Kaunda to National Council at Mulungushi, June 30 to July 3, 1975," UNIP 1/3/20, UNIPA.

43. Research Bureau, "The Zambia Moral Code—A Programmatic Approach." Lusaka, Freedom House, 1975, in UNIP 2/3/3; "The Moral Code of a Humanist Socialist 18 Commandments," n.d. (1977?), UNIP 2/3/3 Programmes, 1975–1977, UNIPA.

44. Jack Simons, "Handwritten Notes from a Meeting at [Robert?] Molteno's Flat, 26 April 1975, W18; Jack Simons, "My First Reactions to Our Meeting as a Group," 3 May 1975; J. W. Musole to Director, Research Bureau, 22 May 1975, W17, BC1081, UCTMA.

45. J. L. Calmettes, "Politique, Religion et Ideologie en Zambie, 1964–1987" (ms, May 1988), Calmettes Box 6, WFA.

46. Ferguson, *Global Shadows*, 76.

47. Kapwepwe quoted in Mwangilwa, *Kapwepwe Diaries*, 191.

48. Quoted in Mwangilwa, *Kapwepwe Diaries*, 186–87.

49. Such "scientific socialist" perspectives began to appear in the *Times of Zambia*, especially in the editorial "Humanism Corner." For an indication of the scientific socialist impact on humanism, see Kandeke, *Fundamentals of Zambian*

Humanism, along with the documentation of Jack Simons, Simons Collection, W10 to W19, BC 1081, UCTMA.

50. A process covered in Peter Bolink, *Towards Church Union in Zambia: A Study of Missionary Co-Operation and Church-Union Efforts in Central-Africa* (Sneek, Netherlands: T. Wever–Franeker, 1967).

51. Ter Haar, *Spirit of Africa*, 13–28, esp. 26.

52. An edited collection of this extensive pamphlet literature can be found as Emmanuel Milingo, *The World in Between: Christian Healing and the Struggle for Spiritual Survival*, ed. Mona Macmillan (London: Hurst, 1984).

53. Ibid., 32–33.

54. Ibid., 52. For guardian spirits, also see p. 42.

55. Hinfelaar wrote these comments in the context of an article about Catholic efforts in the 1990s to rid rural Zambia of witchfinders, which in his view were used by the elite to manipulate the poor; "Witch-Hunting in Zambia and International Illegal Trade," in *Imagining Evil: Witchcraft Beliefs and Accusations in Contemporary Africa*, ed. Gerrie ter Haar (Trenton, NJ: Africa World Press, 2007), 229–45.

56. Ter Haar, *Spirit of Africa*, 124–25.

57. Milingo, *World in Between*, 87.

58. *Sunday Times of Zambia*, 18 March 1979.

59. *TOZ*, 26 February 1979.

60. *TOZ*, 23 February 1979.

61. *TOZ*, 19 November 1980.

62. *TOZ*, 25 February, 13 March, 19 April 1979.

63. Ter Haar finds further political purposes to Milingo's mission and even compares Milingo to Kapwepwe as a Zambian savior in *Spirit of Africa*, 219–20.

64. On the Copperbelt, support for the MMD measured approximately 87 percent with a 49 percent turnout, compared to a national average support of 72 percent with a 43 percent turnout. Adapted from Zambia Independent Monitoring Team Secretariat, "Summary of Parliamentary Results," November 1991.

65. Per Nordlund, *Organising the Political Agora: Domination and Democratisation in Zambia and Zimbabwe* (Uppsala: Uppsala University, 1996), 72–83; Larmer, *Mineworkers in Zambia*, 119–26.

66. Republic of Zambia, Ministry of Labour and Social Services, Annual Reports of the Department of Labour, as quoted in Nordlund, *Organising the Political Agora*, 74.

67. *TOZ*, 8 January 1981.

68. *TOZ*, 7 December 1980.

69. For a detailed analysis of this conflict from the Catholic perspective, see Hinfelaar, "Legitimizing Powers"; Calmettes, "Politique, Religion, et Ideologie," 33–48.

70. Zambia Episcopal Conference, Christian Churches in Zambia, and Zambia Evangelical Fellowship, *Marxism, Humanism and Christianity: A Letter from*

the Leaders of the Christian Churches in Zambia to Their Members about Scientific Socialism (Lusaka: Teresianum Press, 1979).

71. The strategy first outlined after failure to adopt aggressive socialist program at Ninth UNIP National Council, in Joseph Musole, "Postmortem or Observations of the Leaders' Seminar and the 9th National Council of UNIP," Confidential Memo, 30 September 1976, W/10. For recommendation to introduce as high school subject, T. K. Kandeke, "A Guide to the Study of Scientific Socialism," 18 February 1977," Simons Collection, W/15, BC1081, UCTMA.

72. For concern over introduction of Marxism into the school curriculum, see *National Mirror*, 23 October–3 November 1981.

73. *TOZ*, 1 February 1981.

74. Ibid.

75. *National Mirror*, 17–30 July, 14–27 August 1981. For Musole's writing of the "Humanist Corner" in the early 1980s, see Musole, introduction to "Dialectics of Humanism: A Lecture at the Ideological Workshop for Senior Staff in the Ministry of the National Commission for Development and Planning, 21–28 May 1982," Simons Collection, W/19, BC1081, UCTMA.

76. *National Mirror*, 20 November–3 December 1981.

77. *National Mirror*, 28 August–10 September 1981.

78. *TOZ*, 16 January 1981. For complaints against forced purchase of party cards, see *National Mirror*, 4–17 December 1981.

79. *TOZ*, 28 April 1981.

80. *TOZ*, 12 April 1981.

81. For a list of prominent clergy appointments, see Hinfelaar, "Legitimizing Powers," 131.

82. *TOZ*, 22 April 1981.

83. Clive M. Dillon-Malone, *Zambian Humanism, Religion, and Social Morality* (Ndola, Zambia: Mission Press, 1989), 4.

84. Henry S. Meebelo, *Zambian Humanism and Scientific Socialism: A Comparative Study* (Lusaka: Government Printer, 1987), 19.

85. *National Mirror*, February 1979. Quoted in Hinfelaar, "Legitimizing Powers," 138.

86. *TOZ*, 1 June 1981.

87. *Africa Confidential*, 12 May 1980, as cited in Hinfelaaar, "Legitimizing Powers," 139.

88. *National Mirror*, 6–19 November 1981.

89. *TOZ*, 26 April 1981.

90. *Sunday Times of Zambia*, 16 May 1982; *TOZ*, 10 May 1982.

91. *TOZ*, 18 May 1982.

92. *Sunday Times of Zambia*, 19 September 1982.

CHAPTER 8: A NATION REBORN

1. *National Mirror*, 17–30 July 1981; *TOZ*, 19 September 1981; interviews: Elder Gibstar Makangila, Lusaka, Northmead, 16 September 2008; Bishop Joshua

Banda, Lusaka, Zambia, 10 September 2008. For background on Bonnke, see Paul Gifford, "Africa Shall Be Saved: An Appraisal of Reinhard Bonnke's Pan-African Crusade," *Journal of Religion in Africa* 17, no. 1 (February 1987): 63–92.

2. For example, see "Our Comrade Says," *National Mirror*, 14–27 August 1981.

3. I use "evangelical" as an umbrella category for Pentecostal and charismatic movements. In addition to "charismatic" influences in mainline churches, in Zambia church leaders distinguish formal, international, and "Bible-based" churches as "Pentecostal," and local and experiential churches as "charismatic." I have tried to use the term that the churches use to self-identify, rather than impose a formal definition.

4. Student interview with Nevers Mumba, UNZA, Lusaka, n.d. (2006?). Tape held by Prof. A. Cheyeka, UNZA; Nevers Mumba, *Integrity with Fire: A Strategy for Revival* (Tulsa, OK: Vincom, 1994), 79–80. Also see Isabel Apawo Phiri, "President Frederick Chiluba and Zambia: Evangelicals and Democracy in a 'Christian Nation,'" in *Evangelical Christianity and Democracy in Africa*, ed. Terence O. Ranger (Oxford: Oxford University Press, 2008), 108–9; Paul Gifford, *African Christianity: Its Public Role* (Bloomington: Indiana University Press), 233–43.

5. Interview: Bishop Joshua Banda, Northmead Assemblies of God, Lusaka, Zambia, 10 September 2008.

6. For unmet "expectations of modernity," see James Ferguson, *Expectations of Modernity: Myths and Meanings of Urban Life on the Zambian Copperbelt* (Berkeley: University of California Press, 1999). For Imakando and Bread of Life Church in Zambia, see http://www.bolci.org/.

7. Interview: Pastor Reutter, Lusaka, 16 September 2008.

8. For example, "Slain By the Spirit: The Religious Right in East Africa," in *Economist* (July 2010): 44–45.

9. Terence O. Ranger, introduction to *Evangelical Christianity and Democracy in Africa*, ed. Terence O. Ranger (Oxford: Oxford University Press, 2008), 3–35.

10. Centre for Development and Enterprise, *Under the Radar: Pentecostalism in South Africa and Its Potential Social and Economic Role* (Johannesburg: Centre for Development and Enterprise, March 2008).

11. Gifford, *African Christianity*, esp. 181–245; most recently Paul Gifford, "Evangelical Christianity and Democracy in Africa: A Response," in Ranger, *Evangelical Christianity and Democracy in Africa*, 225–30.

12. Jane E. Soothill, *Gender, Social Change, and Spiritual Power: Charismatic Christianity in Ghana* (Leiden: Brill, 2007).

13. Phiri, "President Frederick Chiluba and Zambia," 95–129. As the previous chapter indicates, Cheyeka may overestimate older church criticism of government and the extent of "charismatic" support for MMD regimes. Austin M. Cheyeka, "Towards a History of the Charismatic Churches in Post-Colonial Zambia," in *One Zambia, Many Histories: Towards a History of Post-Colonial Zambia*, ed. Jan-Bart Gewald, Marja Hinfelaar, and Giacomo Macola (Leiden: Brill, 2008), 144–63, esp. 162–63.

14. For an example from Zimbabwe, see David Maxwell, *African Gifts of the Spirit: Pentecostalism and the Rise of a Zimbabwean Transnational Religious Movement* (Oxford: James Currey, 2006), 219–20.

15. For example, Timothy Samuel Shah, preface to Ranger, *Evangelical Christianity and Democracy in Africa*, xi.

16. Jean Comaroff and John L. Comaroff, "Privatizing the Millennium: New Protestant Ethics and the Spirits of Capitalism in Africa, and Elsewhere," *Afrika Spectrum* 35, no. 3 (2000): 293–312, esp. 309.

17. Interview: Bishop Paul Mususu, Lusaka, 15 September 2008; interview: Bishop Joshua Banda, Northmead Assemblies of God, Lusaka, Zambia, 10 September 2008; interview: Bishop Teddy Kamfwa, Campus Crusades, Lusaka, 16 September 2008; interview: Elder Gibstar Makangila, Lusaka, 16 September 2008; interview: Bines Bwali Lusaka, 21 September 2008; student interview with Nevers Mumba.

18. Gerrie ter Haar, *Spirit of Africa: The Healing Ministry of Archbishop Milingo of Zambia* (Trenton, NJ: Africa World Press, 1992), esp. 20–43. For meeting with Simwanga, see *National Mirror*, 30 January–12 February 1981.

19. For an overview of youth involvement in African Pentecostalism, see Ogbu Kalu, *African Pentecostalism: An Introduction* (Oxford: Oxford University Press, 2008), 87–102.

20. A. Muwowo, Director of Youth Work, UCZ, to Joel Chisanga, General Secretary UCZ, 25 February 1987; Joel Chisanga, General Secretary UCZ, to Donald Walker, Synod Department of Evangelism UCZ, 20 February 1987, UCZ 9/15, United Church of Zambia Archives, Mindolo, Kitwe, Zambia (henceforth UCZA). One of the first breakaway groups to be dissociated from UCZ was the "Free Church in Christ," TOZ, 19–20 October 1980.

21. Joel Chisanga, General Secretary UCZ, to Donald Walker, Synod Department of Evangelism UCZ, 20 February 1987, UCZ 9/15, UCZA.

22. Gifford, *African Christianity*, 232.

23. *Christianity Today*, 23 April 2001. Also see UCZ Working Group, "Report on Charismatic Worship," n.d. (1999?), UCZ 9/15, Mindolo, UCZA.

24. Interview: Elder Gibstar Makangila, Lusaka, Northmead, 16 September 2008.

25. For Pentecostal big men, see Kalu, *African Pentecostalism*, 113–14. Maxwell also develops the term "Pentecostal big man" in his study of Ezekiel Guti and the Zimbabwe Assemblies of God Africa (ZOAGA); Maxwell, *African Gifts of the Spirit*.

26. Interview: Elfrida Mhusambazi, Lusaka, 11 September 2008.

27. Mumba, *Integrity with Fire*, 11–12.

28. After 2001, in opposition to the EFZ's condemnation of Chiluba's bid for a third term in office, the ICOZ was formed. See interview: Reverend David Musondo Masupa, ICOZ, Lusaka, 18 September 2008. For EFZ, see Bishop Paul Mususu , EFZ, Lusaka, 15 September 2008, and the EFZ website, accessed 12 November 2008, http://www.evafeza.org.zm/.

29. Interview: Bishop Mususu, Lusaka, 15 September 2008.

30. Interviews with members of Barak Ministries on 16 September 2008.

31. Gifford, "Evangelical Christianity," 22.

32. GO Fellowship Pamphlet, n.d. (2008?).

33. Interviews: Reverend David Musondo Masupa, ICOZ, Lusaka, 18 September 2008; Bishop Paul Mususu, EFZ, Lusaka, 15 September 2008.

34. Owen Sichone, "The Sacred and the Obscene: Personal Notes on Political Ritual, Poverty and Democracy in Zambia," in *African Democracy in the Era of Globalisation*, ed. Jonathan Hyslop (Johannesburg: Witwatersrand University Press, 1999), 152–66, 158.

35. Interviews: Elder Gibstar Makangila, Lusaka, Northmead, 16 September 2008; Bishop Joshua Banda, Northmead Assemblies of God, Lusaka, Zambia, 10 September 2008; Bines Bwali, Lusaka, 21 September 2008. Fieldwork and interviews with Northmead Assemblies of God.

36. Fieldwork and interviews with Barak Ministries.

37. Interview: Prophetess Elfrida Mhusambazi, Lusaka, 11 September 2008.

38. Interview: Pastor Reutter, Lusaka, 16 September 2008; White House Press Release, accessed 15 November 2008, http://www.whitehouse.gov/news/releases/2007/07/20070725-5.html

39. Discussion of numbers in Gifford, *African Christianity*, 183–88.

40. These numbers are approximate. The Zambian census has no report on church affiliation. The numbers are from the evangelical missionary publication, Patrick Johnstone and Jason Mandryk, *Operation World* (Carlisle, UK: Paternoster Lifestyle, 2001), 686.

41. A survey conducted in 1991 found that 75.6 percent of Zambians belonged to a Christian church; the next most important forms of associations were cooperatives (7.1 percent), sports clubs (3.1 percent), women's clubs (2.4 percent), and trade unions (2.4 percent). Those who claimed to have joined their associations over the last ten years totaled 53.9 percent, indicating an expansion through the 1980s. Michael Bratton and Beatrice Liatto-Katundu, "Political Culture in Zambia: A Pilot Survey" (working papers on Political Reform in Africa, Michigan State University, 1994), 9–10.

42. Interview: Jennifer Kasamanda, Lusaka, 21 September 2008; see Rick Warren, *The Purpose-Driven Life* (Grand Rapids, MI: Zondervan, 2002).

43. Interview: Elfrida Mhusambazi, Lusaka, 11 September 2008.

44. Ibid.

45. Contrary to argument by Gifford, "Africa Shall Be Saved," 79. But in agreement with his reflections in "Evangelical Christianity," 229.

46. Mumba, *Integrity with Fire*, 64–66.

47. Interview: Elwida Mhusambazi, 11 September 2008; interview: Joshua Banda, 10 September 2008.

48. Mumba, *Integrity with Fire*, 14.

49. For oral and experiential component to Pentecostal services, also see Gifford, "Africa Shall Be Saved," 82–83.

50. Contra Gifford, who emphasizes the difference between older practices and Pentecostalism in *African Christianity*, 234.

51. For corporeal mnemonics, see Paul Connerton, *How Societies Remember* (Cambridge: Cambridge University Press, 1989).

52. Interview: Bishop Joshua Banda, Northmead Assemblies of God, Lusaka, 10 September 2008.

53. Gifford's argument regarding EFZ's critique of humanism has to be placed in the context of the longer history of Catholic and mainline Protestant critiques of humanism. Gifford, *African Christianity*, 191. See above, chapter 7.

54. For his personal account of Zambian student politics in the 1970s, see Sichone, "The Sacred and the Obscene," 154–58.

55. *National Mirror*, 6–19 November 1981.

56. *National Mirror*, 27 March–6 April 1981.

57. *National Mirror*, 4–17 December 1981.

58. *National Mirror*, 5–18 November 1982.

59. *National Mirror*, 10–23 February 1984.

60. *National Mirror*, 23 March–5 April 1984.

61. *National Mirror*, 9–22 March 1984.

62. Marja Hinfelaar, "Legitimizing Powers: The Political Role of the Roman Catholic Church, 1972–1991," in Gewald, Hinfelaar, and Macola, *One Zambia, Many Histories*, 129–43.

63. *TOZ*, 17 January 1991; 4 April 1991.

64. *National Mirror*, 10–16 June 1991.

65. Interview: Bishop Joshua Banda, Lusaka, 10 September 2008.

66. M. A. Ranganathan, *The Political Philosophy of President Kenneth D. Kaunda of Zambia* (Lusaka: Kenneth Kaunda Foundation, 1986).

67. *National Mirror*, 28 October–3 November 1991, 5. Also quoted in Gifford, *African Christianity*, 191.

68. *National Mirror*, 6–12 October 1991, 4. Also quoted in Gifford, *African Christianity*, 191.

69. *National Mirror*, 28 October–1 November 1991.

70. For example, *TOZ*, 19, 29 October 1991; *National Mirror*, 10–16 June 1991.

71. Perceived as a threat, Mambo was detained by Kaunda on 24–25 October; *TOZ*, 20, 24–25 October 1991.

72. Interview: Elder Gibstar Makangila, Lusaka, 16 September 2008.

73. On the Copperbelt, support for the MMD measured approximately 87 percent with a 49 percent turnout, compared to a national average support of 72 percent with a 43 percent turnout. From Zambia Independent Monitoring Team Secretariat, "Summary of Parliamentary Results," November 1991.

74. *National Mirror*, 18–24 November 1991.

75. *TOZ*, 11 November 1991; *National Mirror*, 10–17 November 1991. For an alternative account based on an interview in 2000, see Phiri, "President Chiluba and Zambia," 102.

76. *TOZ*, 19 December 1991. Based on an interview from 2000, Phiri claims that "fifty Christians from evangelical fellowships" cleansed State House, in "President Chiluba and Zambia," 101.

77. *National Mirror*, 12–16 January 1992. Kristafor was widely criticized for this censorship, and after accusations of racism he was dismissed in 1992. *National Mirror*, 3–9 August 1992.

78. *National Mirror*, 18–24 November 1991.

79. *TOZ*, 30 December 1991. Interviews: Bishop Banda, Lusaka, 10 September 2008; Pastor Reutter, Lusaka, 16 September 2008. Gifford's account in *African Christianity*, 197–98, is based on a 1994 article in *TOZ*, 20 February 1994.

80. *National Mirror*, 30 December 1991.

81. The spiritual dimension is ignored in James Ferguson, *Global Shadows: Africa in the Neoliberal World Order* (Durham, NC: Duke University Press, 2006), esp. 119–20.

82. Mumba, *Integrity with Fire*, 20.

83. *National Mirror*, 18–24 November 1991.

84. Gifford, *African Christianity*, 204, 233–34.

85. Student interview with Nevers Mumba.

86. Phiri, "President Chiluba and Zambia," 109–10.

87. *National Mirror*, 3–10 August 1992.

88. Cheyeka, "Towards a History of the Charismatic Churches," 158.

89. Isaac Phiri, *Proclaiming Political Pluralism: Churches and Political Transitions in Africa* (Westport, CT: Praeger, 2001), 43–44; Phiri, "President Chiluba and Zambia," 106–7.

90. Interview: Bishop Mususu, Lusaka, 15 September 2008.

91. Phiri, "President Chiluba and Zambia," 108.

92. Ibid., 120–22. A number of leaders from "charismatic" churches supported Chiluba. Since the EFZ opposed Chiluba, another "mother body" for "independent" Pentecostal and charismatic churches, the Independent Church Organization of Zambia (ICOZ) was formed; in Cheyeka, "Towards a History of the Charismatic Churches," 160–62; interview: David Masupa, Lusaka, 18 September 2008.

93. Maxwell, *African Gifts of the Spirit*, 224.

CONCLUSION: THE SPIRIT REALM OF AGENCY

First epigraph: Kenneth D. Kaunda, *A Humanist in Africa: Letters to Colin M. Morris from Kenneth D. Kaunda, President of Zambia* (Nashville: Abingdon Press 1966), 39.

Second epigraph: This quote is attributed to the declaration of the Christian Nation on 29 December 1991, but appears only in *Times of Zambia*, 20 February 1994. Extracts cited in Paul Gifford, *African Christianity: Its Public Role* (Bloomington: Indiana University Press, 1998), 197–98; and full text in Isabel Apawo Phiri, "President Frederick J. T. Chiluba of Zambia: The Christian Nation and Democracy," *Journal of Religion in Africa* 33, no. 4 (2003): 401–28, esp. 407.

Glossary of Select Spiritual Terms

Definitions and orthography differ across south-central Africa. This glossary refers to usage in the ChiBemba-speaking areas of northern Zambia. For nouns in different classes, I have indicated their most common usage, followed by the plural or singular. The initial vowel for nouns has been excluded.

babenye. Royal relics, in particular those held by Bemba rulers and used to ensure fertility and fecundity.

badikoni. Deacons, in particular those of the Lumpa Church.

baloshi (sing. *muloshi*). Witches. Living beings who manipulate spiritual forces to harm others.

bamuchapi. The cleansers. Witchfinding and purification movement (from ChiNyanja).

bangulu. A living being who may have spiritual gifts and is possessed by a *ngulu* spirit.

banyama (sing. *munyama*). Living beings who consume or trade in human flesh.

buloshi. The practice of witchcraft, often associated with groups of witches.

Butwa. An association prevalent outside of the Bemba polity, which recognized the spiritual authority of the original inhabitants of the land, the "Batwa," and specialized in interactions with *ngulu* spirits.

bwanga. Objects that can mobilize forces from the invisible world to change the visible world.

chibanda (pl. *fibanda*). Spirits, in particular the living dead, who for certain reasons harm the living.

chibyalilo. Planting ceremony conducted by Bemba paramount and taken over by certain Christian churches.

Chilimbulu. Mythic heroine with beautiful scarifications who seduces the first *Chitimukulu*.

Chitimukulu. Title for the Bemba paramount and head of the Crocodile Clan.

chiwa (pl. *fiwa*). Spirits who harm the living. Often associated with evil.

ilamfya. A horn with *bwanga* used to mobilize invisible forces to aid in warfare.

Lesa. Nature spirit associated in legends with the origins of humanity. Term used to refer to the Christian God.

lubuto lwa chalo. Light of the world. Title for prophets, used to refer to Alice Lenshina.

lubuto mulopwe. The light king. Prophetic title, used to refer to Alice Lenshina.

Luchele Ng'anga. Mythic Bemba hero. The white magician who leads the Bemba eastward.

mfuba. Personal shrines where offerings are made to spirits, often near homes and villages.

mfumu. Title for a leader with somatic and spiritual qualities.

mfumu sha kale. The ancestral spirit of an old ruler who was not inherited nor appropriated by living rulers.

mfumu ya mipashi. Leader of *mipashi* ancestral spirits. An important ancestral spirit.

mikishi (sing. *mukishi*). Spiritual forces held in objects that were representative of communal cults. Generally found outside the area ruled by the Bemba Crocodile Clan.

mipashi (sing. *mupashi*). Ancestral spirits. May harm or help the living beings usually of the same family. For Christians, refers to the Holy Spirit.

mulopwe. Living rulers, especially those with spiritual power and celestial genealogies, among Luba-related peoples.

musumba (pl. *misumba*). A palace, such as the capital of a Bemba ruler, a mission station, or one of Lenshina's villages.

muti. Medicine used for interventions with the invisible world.

Mwalule. The burial ground of the Bemba Crocodile Clan royalty.

mwavi. Poison ordeal. Generally identifies and administers justice to witches.

ngulu. Disembodied spirits, related to animals and other natural features. May possess living people termed *bangulu.*

nsengo. Horns used to contain *muti* medicines and *bwanga.*

shimapepo. Preachers, in particular those of the Lumpa Church.

Shimwalule. Title for the "father" of the Mwalule burial ground, and hence the caretaker of the royal ancestors.

shinganga. Fathers of *bwanga.* Specialists in the use of *bwanga* to mobilize invisible forces.

Sione. Zion. For the Lumpa Church, this referred to the Kamutola church building and the surrounding area.

tempile. Temple of the Lumpa Church, outside of which *bwanga* was placed and inside of which people were cleansed. Distinct from the Kamutola Church at Sione.

ukusemuka (v., infinitive form). Rhythmic whimpers, usually made by those possessed by *ngulu.*

ukusesema (v., infinitive form). Glossolalia, often due to possession by *ngulu* or by the Holy Spirit.

Bibliography

PUBLISHED BOOKS AND ARTICLES

Allman, Jean, and John Parker. *Tongnaab: The History of a West African God.* Bloomington: Indiana University Press, 2005.

Anderson, David. *Histories of the Hanged: The Dirty War in Kenya and the End of Empire.* New York: Norton, 2005.

Appiah, Kwame Anthony. *In My Father's House: Africa in the Philosophy of Culture.* New York: Oxford University Press, 1993.

Asad, Talal. *Formations of the Secular: Christianity, Islam, Modernity.* Stanford, CA: Stanford University Press, 2003.

Ashforth, Adam. *Witchcraft, Violence, and Democracy in South Africa.* Chicago: University of Chicago Press, 2005.

Atieno-Odhiambo, E. S. "The Production of History in Kenya: The Mau Mau Debate." *Canadian Journal of African Studies* 25, no. 2 (1991): 300–307.

Barnes, H. "Survival after Death among the Ba-Bemba of North-Eastern Rhodesia." *Man* 25–26 (1922): 41–42.

Bayart, Jean-François. *The State in Africa: The Politics of the Belly.* London: Longman, 1993.

Behrend, Heike. *Alice Lakwena and the Holy Spirits: War in Northern Uganda, 1986–97.* Athens: Ohio University Press, 1999.

Berger, Elena L. *Labour, Race, and Colonial Rule: The Copperbelt from 1924 to Independence.* Oxford: Clarendon Press, 1974.

Best, Wallace D. *Passionately Human, No Less Divine: Religion and Culture in Black Chicago, 1915–1952.* Princeton, NJ: Princeton University Press, 2005.

Bøås, Morten, and Kevin C. Dunn. *African Guerrillas: Raging Against the Machine.* Boulder, CO: Lynne Rienner, 2007.

Boek, Filipe de, and Marie Françoise Plissart. *Kinshasa: Tales of the Invisible City.* Ghent, Belgium: Ludion, 2004.

Bolink, Peter. *Towards Church Union in Zambia: A Study of Missionary Co-Operation and Church-Union Efforts in Central-Africa.* Sneek, Netherlands: T. Wever–Franeker, 1967.

Bozzoli, Belinda. *Theatres of Struggle and the End of Apartheid.* Athens: Ohio University Press, 2004.

Bradford, Helen. *"Akukho ntaka inokubhabha ngephiko elinye* (No bird can fly on one wing): The 'Cattle-Killing Delusion' and Black Intellectuals, c. 1840–1910." *African Studies* 67, no. 2 (2008): 209–32.

Bratton, Michael, and Beatrice Liatto-Katundu. "Political Culture in Zambia: A Pilot Survey." Working papers on Political Reform in Africa, Michigan State University, 1994.

Brelsford, W. Vernon. "Shimwalule: A Study of a Bemba Chief and Priest." *African Studies* 1, no. 3 (1942): 207–23.

———. *Some Aspects of Bemba Chieftainship.* Livingstone, Northern Rhodesia: Rhodes-Livingstone Institute, 1944.

Brown, Callum G. *The Death of Christian Britain: Understanding Secularisation, 1800–2000.* London: Routledge, 2001.

Burton, R. F., trans. *The Lands of Cazembe: Lacerda's Journey to Cazembe in 1798.* New York: Negro University Press, 1969.

Burton, William F. P. *Luba Religion and Magic in Custom and Belief.* Tervuren, Belgium: Musée royal de l'Afrique centrale, 1962.

Calmettes, Jean Loup. "The Lumpa Sect, Rural Reconstruction, and Conflict." Master's thesis, University of Wales, Aberystwyth, 1978.

Centre for Development and Enterprise. *Under the Radar: Pentecostalism in South Africa and Its Potential Social and Economic Role.* Johannesburg: Centre for Development and Enterprise, March 2008.

Chanock, Martin. *Law, Custom and Social Order: The Colonial Experience in Malawi and Zambia.* Cambridge: Cambridge University Press, 1985.

Chatterjee, Partha. *Nationalist Thought and the Colonial World: A Derivative Discourse.* Tokyo: Zed Books, 1986.

Cheyeka, Austin M. "Towards a History of the Charismatic Churches in Post-Colonial Zambia." In Gewald, Hinfelaar, and Macola, *One Zambia, Many Histories*, 144–63.

Chiluba, Frederick J. T. *Beyond Political Rhetoric: Balancing Political and Economic Reforms.* Compiled and edited by Richard L. Sakala. Lusaka: ZPC Publications, 1998.

———. *Democracy: The Challenge of Change.* Lusaka: Multimedia Publications, 1995.

———. *Politics of Poverty and Underdevelopment: Speeches by President Frederick H. T. Chiluba on Development Politics, Poverty Reduction, and Economic Recovery.* Compiled and edited by Richard L. Sakala. Lusaka: Sentor Publishing, 2001.

Chipungu, Samuel N., ed. *Guardians in Their Time: Experiences of Zambians under Colonial Rule, 1890–1964.* London: Macmillan, 1992.

Cole, Jennifer, and Lynn M. Thomas, eds. *Love in Africa.* Chicago: University of Chicago Press, 2009.

Colson, Elizabeth. *Tonga Religious Life in the Twentieth Century.* Lusaka: Bookworld, 2006.

Comaroff, Jean, and John L. Comaroff. *Of Revelation and Revolution: The Dialectics of Modernity on a South African Frontier.* Vol. 2. Chicago: University of Chicago Press, 1997.

———. "Privatizing the Millennium: New Protestant Ethics and the Spirits of Capitalism in Africa, and Elsewhere." *Afrika Spectrum* 35, no. 3 (2000): 293–312.

———. "Second Comings: Neo-Protestant Ethics and Millennial Capitalism in Africa, and Elsewhere." In *2000 Years and Beyond: Faith, Identity and the "Common Era,"* edited by Paul Gifford, 106–26. London: Routledge, 2003.

Comaroff, John L. "Images of Empire, Contests of Conscience: Models of Colonial Domination in South Africa." In *Tensions of Empire: Colonial Cultures in a Bourgeois World,* edited by Frederick Cooper and Ann Laura Stoler, 163–97. Berkeley: University of California Press, 1997.

Comaroff, John L., and Jean Comaroff, eds. *Civil Society and the Political Imagination in Africa: Critical Perspectives.* Chicago: University of Chicago Press, 1999.

Connerton, Paul. *How Societies Remember.* Cambridge: Cambridge University Press, 1989.

Cook, David J. "The Influence of Livingstonia Mission upon the Formation of Welfare Associations in Zambia, 1912–31." In Ranger and Weller, *Themes in the Christian History of Central Africa,* 98–134.

Cooper, Barbara M. *Evangelical Christians in the Muslim Sahel.* Bloomington: Indiana University Press, 2006.

Cooper, Frederick. *Colonialism in Question: Theory, Knowledge, History.* Berkeley: University of California Press, 2005.

———. *Decolonization and African Society: The Labor Question in French and British Africa.* Cambridge: Cambridge University Press, 1996.

Corbeil, J. J. *Mbusa: Sacred Emblems of the Bemba.* London: Ethnographica, 1982.

Crais, Clifton. *The Politics of Evil: Magic, State Power, and the Political Imagination in South Africa.* Cambridge: Cambridge University Press, 2002.

Crawford, Daniel. *Thinking Black: 22 Years without a Break in the Long Grass of Central Africa.* New York: George H. Doran, 1912.

Crehan, Kate. *The Fractured Community: Landscapes of Power and Gender in Rural Zambia.* Berkeley: University of California Press, 1997.

Cross, Sholto. "The Watchtower Movement in South Central Africa, 1908–1945." PhD diss., Oxford University, 1973.

Cunnison, Ian G. *The Luapula Peoples of Northern Rhodesia: Custom and History in Tribal Politics.* Manchester: Manchester University Press, 1959.

———. "A Watch Tower Assembly in Central Africa." *International Review of Missions* 40 (1951): 456–69.

Davis, J. Merle, ed. *Modern Industry and the African: An Enquiry into the Effect of the Copper Mines of Central Africa upon Native Society and the Work of the Christian Missions.* London: Frank Cass, 1967.

Dayan, Joan. *Haiti, History, and the Gods*. Berkeley: University of California Press, 1998.

De Craemer, Willy, Jan Vansina, and Renée C. Fox, "Religious Movements in Central Africa: A Theoretical Study." *Comparative Studies in Society and History* 18, no. 4 (1976): 458–75.

Dillon-Malone, Clive M. *The Korsten Basketmakers: A Study of the Masowe Apostles, an Indigenous African Religious Movement*. Manchester: Manchester University Press, 1978.

———. *Zambian Humanism, Religion, and Social Morality*. Ndola, Zambia: Mission Press, 1989.

Doke, C. M. "The Linguistic Work and Manuscripts of R. D. MacMinn." *African Studies* 18, no. 4 (1959): 180–89.

Durkheim, Emile. *The Elementary Forms of Religious Life*. Translated by Karen E. Fields. New York: Free Press, 1995.

Edgar, Robert R., and Hilary Sapire. *African Apocalypse: The Story of Nontetha Nkwenkwe, a Twentieth-Century South African Prophet*. Athens: Ohio University Press, 1999.

Ehret, Christopher. *An African Classical Age: Eastern and Southern Africa in World History, 1000 B.C. to A.D. 400*. Charlottesville: University of Virginia, 1998.

———. *The Civilizations of Africa: A History to 1800*. Charlottesville: University of Virginia Press, 2002.

Elbourne, Elizabeth. *Blood Ground: Colonialism, Missions, and the Contest for Christianity in the Cape Colony and Britain, 1799–1853*. Montreal: McGill-Queen's University Press, 2002.

Ellis, Stephen. *The Mask of Anarchy: The Destruction of Liberia and the Religious Dimension of an African Civil War*. 2nd ed. New York: New York University Press, 2006.

Ellis, Stephen, and Gerrie ter Haar, "The Occult Does Not Exist: A Response to Terence Ranger." *Africa* 79, no. 3 (2009): 399–412.

———. *Worlds of Power: Religious Thought and Political Practice in Africa*. New York: Oxford University Press, 2004.

Epstein, Arnold L. *The Administration of Justice and the Urban African: A Study of Urban Native Courts in Northern Rhodesia*. London: H. M. Stationery, 1953.

———. *Politics in an Urban African Community*. Manchester: Manchester University Press, 1958.

———. *Scenes from African Urban Life: Collected Copperbelt Essays*. Edinburgh: Edinburgh University Press, 1992.

Evans-Pritchard, Edward E. *Witchcraft, Oracles, and Magic among the Azande*. Oxford: Clarendon Press, 1937.

Falola, Toyin. *Violence in Nigeria: The Crisis of Religious Politics and Secular Ideologies*. Rochester, NY: University of Rochester Press, 1998.

Ferguson, James. *Expectations of Modernity: Myths and Meanings of Urban Life on the Zambian Copperbelt*. Berkeley: University of California Press, 1999.

———. *Global Shadows: Africa in the Neoliberal World Order*. Durham, NC: Duke University Press, 2006.

Fields, Karen E. "Charismatic Religion as Popular Protest." *Theory and Society* 11, no. 3 (1982): 321–61.

———. "Political Contingencies of Witchcraft in Colonial Central Africa: Culture and the State in Marxist Theory." *Canadian Journal of African Studies* 16, no. 3 (1982): 567–93.

———. *Revival and Rebellion in Colonial Central Africa*. Princeton, NJ: Princeton University Press, 1985.

———. "Witchcraft and Racecraft: Invisible Ontology and Its Sensible Manifestations." In *Witchcraft Dialogues: Anthropological and Philosophical Exchanges*, edited by George Clement Bond and Diane M. Ciekawy, 283–315. Athens: Ohio University Press, 2001.

Fortes, Meyer, and Edward E. Evans-Pritchard, eds. *African Political Systems*. London: International Africa Institute, 1940.

Fortman, Bastiaan de Gaay. *After Mulungushi: The Economics of Zambian Humanism*. Nairobi: East Africa Publishing House, 1969.

Frazer, James George. *The Golden Bough: A Study in Magic and Religion*. New York: Macmillan, 1922.

Gamitto, Antonio C. P. *King Kazembe and the Marave, Cheva, Bisa, Bemba, Lunda and Other Peoples of Southern Africa*. Translated by Ian Cunnison. Lisbon: Junta de Investigações do Ultramar.

Gann, Lewis H. *A History of Northern Rhodesia: Early Days to 1953*. New York: Humanities Press, 1969.

Garvey, Brian. *Bembaland Church: Religious and Social Change in South Central Africa, 1891–1964*. Leiden: Brill, 1994.

Gertzel, Cherry, ed. *The Dynamics of the One-Party State in Zambia*. Manchester: Manchester University Press, 1984.

Geschiere, Peter. *The Modernity of Witchcraft: Politics and the Occult in Postcolonial Africa*. Translated by Peter Geschiere and Janet Roitman. Charlottesville: University of Virginia Press, 1997.

Gewald, Jan-Bart, Marja Hinfelaar, and Giacomo Macola, eds. *One Zambia, Many Histories: Towards a History of Post-Colonial Zambia*. Leiden: Brill, 2008.

Giblin, James L. "Vampires and History." *African Studies Review* 44, no. 1 (April 2001): 83–87.

Gifford, Paul. *African Christianity: Its Public Role*. Bloomington: Indiana University Press, 1998.

———. "'Africa Shall Be Saved': An Appraisal of Reinhard Bonnke's Pan-African Crusade." *Journal of Religion in Africa* 17, no. 1 (February 1987): 63–92.

———, ed. *The Christian Churches and the Democratisation of Africa*. Leiden: Brill, 1995.

———. "Evangelical Christianity and Democracy in Africa: A Response," in Ranger, *Evangelical Christianity and Democracy in Africa*, 225–30.

———. *Ghana's New Christianity: Pentecostalism in a Globalizing African Economy.* Bloomington: Indiana University Press, 2004.

Giraud, Victor. *Les lacs de l'Afrique équatoriale: Voyage d'exploration exécuté de 1883 à 1885.* Paris: Libraire Hachette, 1890.

Gluckman, Max. *Custom and Conflict in Africa.* Oxford: Oxford University Press, 1957.

Gordon, David M. "A Community of Suffering: Narratives of War and Exile in the Zambian Lumpa Church." In Peterson and Macola, *Recasting the Past,* 191–208.

———. "History on the Luapula Retold: Landscape, Memory and Identity in the Kazembe Kingdom." *Journal of African History* 47, no. 1 (2006): 21–42.

———. *Nachituti's Gift: Economy, Society, and Environment in Central Africa.* Madison: University of Wisconsin Press, 2006.

———. "Rebellion or Massacre: The UNIP-Lumpa Conflict Revisited." In Gewald, Hinfelaar, and Macola, *One Zambia, Many Histories,* 45–76.

———. "Rites of Rebellion: Recent Anthropology from Zambia." *African Studies* 62, no. 1 (2003): 125–39.

Gouldsbury, Cullen, and Hubert Sheane. *The Great Plateau of Northern Rhodesia: Being Some Impressions of the Tanganyika Plateau.* New York: Negro University Press, 1968.

Gunner, Elizabeth. *The Man of Heaven and the Beautiful Ones of God: Umuntu wasezulwini nabantu abahle bakankulunkulu; Writings from Ibandla Lamanazaretha, a South African Church.* Leiden: Brill, 2002.

Haar, Gerrie ter. *How God Became African: African Spirituality and Western Secular Thought.* Philadelphia: University of Pennsylvania Press, 2009.

———, ed. *Imagining Evil: Witchcraft Beliefs and Accusations in Contemporary Africa.* Trenton, NJ: Africa World Press, 2007.

———. *Spirit of Africa: The Healing Ministry of Archbishop Milingo of Zambia.* Trenton, NJ: Africa World Press, 1992.

Hansen, Karen Tranberg. *Keeping House in Lusaka.* New York: Columbia University Press, 1997.

———. *Salaula: The World of Secondhand Clothing and Zambia.* Chicago: University of Chicago Press, 2000.

Harris, Ruth. *Lourdes: Body and Spirit in the Secular Age.* New York: Penguin, 1999.

Heath, F. M. N. "The Growth of African Councils on the Copperbelt of Northern Rhodesia." *Journal of African Administration* 5, no. 3 (1953): 123–32.

Heusch, Luc de. *The Drunken King; or, The Origin of the State.* Translated by Roy Willis. Bloomington: Indiana University Press, 1982.

Higginson, John. "Liberating the Captives: Independent Watchtower as an Avatar of Colonial Revolt in Southern Africa and Katanga, 1908–1941." *Journal of Social History* 26, no. 1 (1992): 55–80.

———. *A Working Class in the Making: Belgian Colonial Labor Policy, Private Enterprise, and the African Mineworker, 1907–1951.* Madison: University of Wisconsin Press, 1989.

Hinfelaar, Hugo F. *Bemba-Speaking Women of Zambia in a Century of Religious Change (1892–1992)*. Leiden: Brill, 1994.

———. "Witch-Hunting in Zambia and International Illegal Trade." In *Imagining Evil: Witchcraft Beliefs and Accusations in Contemporary Africa*, edited by Gerrie ter Haar, 229–46. Trenton, NJ: Africa World Press, 2007.

———. "Women's Revolt: The Lumpa Church of Lenshina Mulenga in the 1950s." *Journal of Religion in Africa* 21 (1991): 99–129.

Hinfelaar, Marja. "Legitimizing Powers: The Political Role of the Roman Catholic Church, 1972–1991." In Gewald, Hinfelaar, and Macola, *One Zambia, Many Histories*, 129–43.

Hodgson, Dorothy L. *The Church of Women: Gendered Encounters between Maasai and Missionaries*. Bloomington: Indiana University Press, 2005.

Hoehler-Fatton, Cynthia. *Women of Fire and Spirit: History, Faith, and Gender in Roho Religion in Western Kenya*. New York: Oxford University Press, 1996.

Hofmeyr, Isabel. *The Portable Bunyan: A Transnational History of "The Pilgrim's Progress."* Princeton, NJ: Princeton University Press, 2004.

Holt, John C. *Spirits of the Place: Buddhism and Lao Religious Culture*. Honolulu: University of Hawaii Press, 2009.

Hooker, J. R. "Witnesses and Watchtower in the Rhodesias and Nyasaland." *Journal of African History* 6, no. 1 (1965): 91–106.

Horton, Robin. "Judaeo-Christian Spectacles: Boon or Bane to the Study of African Religions?" *Cahiers d'Etudes africaines* 24, no. 96 (1984): 391–436.

———. *Patterns of Thought in Africa and the West: Essays on Magic, Religion and Science*. Cambridge: Cambridge University Press, 1993.

Hudson, John. *A Time to Mourn: A Personal Account of the 1964 Church Revolt in Zambia*. Lusaka: Bookworld, 1999.

IJzermans, Jan J. "Music and Theory of the Possession Cult Leaders in Chibale, Serenje District, Zambia." *Ethnomusicology* 39, no. 2 (1995): 245–74.

Ipenburg, At. *"All Good Men": The Development of Lubwa Mission, Chinsali, Zambia, 1905–1967*. Frankfurt: Peter Lang, 1992.

Jenkins, Philip. *The New Faces of Christianity: Believing the Bible in the Global South*. New York: Oxford University Press, 2006.

Johnstone, Patrick, and Jason Mandryk. *Operation World*. Carlisle, UK: Paternoster Lifestyle, 2001.

Kalu, Ogbu. *African Pentecostalism: An Introduction*. Oxford: Oxford University Press, 2008.

Kalusa, Walima T. "Death, Christianity, and African Miners: Contesting Indirect Rule in the Zambian Copperbelt, 1935–1962." *International Journal of African Historical Studies* 44, no. 1 (2011): 89–112.

Kandeke, Timothy K. *Fundamentals of Zambian Humanism*. Lusaka: National Educational Company of Zambia, 1977.

Kaunda, Kenneth D. *Humanism in Zambia and a Guide to Its Implementation*. Parts 1 and 2. Lusaka: Division of National Guidance, 1974.

——. *A Humanist in Africa: Letters to Colin M. Morris from Kenneth D. Kaunda, President of Zambia.* Nashville: Abingdon Press, 1966.

——. *Zambia Shall Be Free: An Autobiography.* London: Heinemann, 1962.

Kirsch, Thomas G. *Spirits and Letters: Reading, Writing and Charisma in African Christianity.* New York: Berghahn Books, 2008.

Klieman, Kairn A. *"The Pygmies Were Our Compass": Bantu and Batwa in the History of West Central Africa, Early Times to c. 1900 C.E.* Portsmouth, NH: Heinemann, 2003.

Kodesh, Neil. *Beyond the Royal Gaze: Clanship and Public Healing in Buganda.* Charlottesville: University of Virginia Press, 2010.

Kynoch, Gary. "Living with Witches in South Africa: Review of Adam Ashforth." H-SAFRICA, H-Net Reviews (June 2005), http://www.h-net.org/reviews/show-rev.php?id=10591.

Labrecque, Edouard. *Beliefs and Religious Practices of the Bemba and Neighbouring Tribes.* Translated by Patrick Boyd. Chinsali, Zambia: Ilondola Language Center, 1982.

——. "La sorcellerie chez les Babemba." *Anthropos* 33 (1938): 260–65.

——. "La tribu des Babemba, 1: Les origines des Babemba." *Anthropos* 28 (1933): 633–48.

Lan, David. *Guns and Rain: Guerrillas and Spirit Mediums in Zimbabwe.* Berkeley: University of California Press, 1985.

Landau, Paul S. *Popular Politics in the History of South Africa, 1400–1948.* Cambridge: Cambridge University Press, 2010.

——. *The Realm of the Word: Language, Gender, and Christianity in a Southern African Kingdom.* Portsmouth, NH: Heinemann, 1993.

Larmer, Miles. "Enemies Within?: Opposition to the Zambian One-Party State, 1972–1980." In Gewald, Hinfelaar, and Macola, *One Zambia, Many Histories,* 98–128.

——. "'A Little Bit Like a Volcano': The United Progressive Party and Resistance to One-Party Rule in Zambia, 1964–1980." *International Journal of African Historical Studies* 39, no. 1 (2006): 49–83.

——. *Mineworkers in Zambia: Labour and Political Change in Post-Colonial Africa.* London: Taurus, 2007.

Lewin, Julius. *The Colour Bar in the Copper Belt.* Johannesburg: Pub. for the Southern African Committee on Industrial Relations by the South African Institute of Race Relations, 1941.

Livingstone, David. *The Last Journals of David Livingstone, in Central Africa: From 1865 to His Death.* New York: Harper and Brothers, 1875.

Lonsdale, John. "The Moral Economy of Mau Mau: Wealth, Poverty and Civic Virtue in Kikuyu Political Thought." In *Unhappy Valley: Conflict in Kenya and Africa; Book Two: Violence and Ethnicity,* edited by Bruce Berman and John Lonsdale, 315–504. Athens: Ohio University Press, 1992.

Luna, Kathryn M. de. "Fame as Fortune: Emotion and the Politics of Knowledge in Central Africa." Paper presented to African Studies Association Meeting, New Orleans, 16–19 November 2009.

Lungu, Gatian F. "The Church, Labour and the Press in Zambia: The Role of Critical Observers in a One-Party State." *African Affairs* 85, no. 340 (1986): 385–410.

MacDonald, Roderick J. "Religious Independency as a Means of Social Advance in Northern Nyasaland in the 1930s." *Journal of Religion in Africa* 3, no. 1 (1970): 106–29.

MacGaffey, Wyatt. *Astonishment and Power: The Eyes of Understanding Kongo Minkisi.* Washington: Smithsonian Institution Press, 1993.

———. "Dialogues of the Deaf: Europeans on the Atlantic Coast of Africa." In *Implicit Understandings: Observing, Reporting, and Reflecting on the Encounters Between Europeans and Other Peoples in the Early Modern Era*, edited by Stuart B. Schwartz, 249–67. Cambridge: Cambridge University Press, 1994.

———. *Kongo Political Culture: The Conceptual Challenge of the Particular.* Bloomington: Indiana University Press, 2000.

———. *Modern Kongo Prophets: Religion in a Plural Society.* Bloomington: Indiana University Press, 1983.

———. *Religion and Society in Central Africa: The BaKongo of Lower Zaire.* Chicago: Chicago University Press, 1986.

Macola, Giacomo. "Harry Mwaanga Nkumbula, UNIP and the Roots of Authoritarianism in Nationalist Zambia." In Gewald, Hinfelaar, and Macola, *One Zambia, Many Histories*, 17–44.

———. "Historical and Ethnographical Publications in the Vernaculars of Colonial Zambia: Missionary Contribution to the 'Creation of Tribalism.'" *Journal of Religion in Africa* 33, no. 4 (2003): 343–64.

———. "'It Means as If We Are Excluded from the Good Freedom': Thwarted Expectations of Independence in the Luapula Province of Zambia, 1964–1966." *Journal of African History* 47, no. 1 (2006): 43–56.

———. *Liberal Nationalism in Central Africa: A Biography of Harry Mwaanga Nkumbula.* New York: Palgrave Macmillan, 2010.

———. "Literate Ethnohistory in Colonial Zambia: The Case of 'Ifikolwe Fyandi na Bantu Bandi.'" *History in Africa* 28 (2001): 187–201.

Macpherson, Fergus. *North of the Zambezi: A Modern Missionary Memoir.* Edinburgh: Handsel Press, 1998.

Magaziner, Daniel R. *The Law and the Prophets: Black Consciousness in South Africa, 1968–1977.* Athens: Ohio University Press, 2010.

Makasa, Kapasa. *Zambia's March to Political Freedom.* Nairobi: Heinemann, 1981.

Makupo, Titus B., ed. *Kaunda's Guidelines.* Lusaka: TMC Publicity, 1970.

Mamdani, Mahmood. *Citizen and Subject: Contemporary Africa and the Legacy of Late Colonialism.* Princeton, NJ: Princeton University Press, 1996.

Marks, Stuart A. *Large Mammals and a Brave People: Subsistence Hunters in Zambia.* New Brunswick, NJ: Transaction Publishers, 2005.

Marshall, Ruth. *Political Spiritualities: The Pentecostal Revolution in Nigeria.* Chicago: University of Chicago Press, 2009.

Martin, Phyllis M. *Catholic Women of Congo-Brazzaville: Mothers and Sisters in Troubled Times.* Bloomington: Indiana University Press, 2009.

Masiye, Andreya S. *Singing for Freedom: Zambia's Struggle for African Govern-ment.* Lusaka: Oxford University Press, 1977.

Masquelier, Adeline. *Prayer Has Spoiled Everything: Possession, Power, and Iden-tity in an Islamic Town of Niger.* Durham, NC: Duke University Press, 2001.

Maxwell, David. *African Gifts of the Spirit: Pentecostalism and the Rise of a Zimba-bwean Transnational Religious Movement.* Oxford: James Currey, 2006.

Maxwell, Kevin B. *Bemba Myth and Ritual: The Impact of Literacy on an Oral Culture.* New York: Peter Lang, 1983.

Mbembe, Achille. *On the Post-Colony.* Berkeley: University of California Press, 2001.

Mbiti, John S. *African Religions and Philosophy.* London: Heinemann, 1969.

McKittrick, Meredith. *To Dwell Secure: Generation, Christianity, and Colonial-ism in Ovamboland, Northern Namibia.* Portsmouth, NH: Heinemann, 2002.

Meebelo, Henry S. *African Proletarians and Colonial Capitalism: The Origins, Growth and Struggles of the Zambian Labour Movement to 1964.* Lusaka: Ken-neth Kaunda Foundation, 1986.

———. *Main Currents of Zambian Humanist Thought.* Lusaka: Oxford University Press, 1973.

———. *Reaction to Colonialism: A Prelude to the Politics of Independence in North-ern Zambia, 1893-1939.* Manchester: Manchester University Press, 1971.

———. *Zambian Humanism and Scientific Socialism: A Comparative Study.* Lu-saka: Government Printer, 1987.

Meyer, Birgit. *Translating the Devil: Religion and Modernity among the Ewe in Ghana.* Edinburgh: Edinburgh University Press, 1999.

Meyer, Birgit, and Peter Pels. *Magic and Modernity: Interfaces of Revelation and Concealment.* Stanford, CA: Stanford University Press, 2003.

Milingo, Emmanuel. *The World in Between: Christian Healing and the Struggle for Spiritual Survival.* Edited by Mona Macmillan. London: Hurst, 1984.

Mitchell, J. Clyde. *African Urbanization in Ndola and Luanshya.* Lusaka: Rhodes-Livingstone Institute, 1954.

———. *The Kalela Dance: Aspects of Social Relationships among Urban Africans in Northern Rhodesia.* Manchester: Manchester University Press, 1956.

Moore, Henrietta L., and Megan Vaughn. *Cutting Down Trees: Gender, Nutri-tion, and Agricultural Change in the Northern Province of Zambia, 1890-1990.* London: James Currey, 1994.

Moore, Reginald J. B. "'Bwanga' among the Bemba." *Africa: Journal of the Inter-national African Institute* 13, no. 3 (July 1940): 211–34.

———. "'Bwanga' among the Bemba, Part 2." *Bantu Studies* 15, no. 1 (1941): 37–41.

———. "The Development of the Conception of God." *International Review of Missions* 31, no. 124 (1942): 412–20.

———. *These African Copper Miners: A Study of the Industrial Revolution in North-ern Rhodesia, with Principal Reference to the Copper Mining Industry.* London: Livingston Press, 1948.

Morrow, Sean. "'On the Side of the Robbed': R. J. B. Moore, Missionary on the Copperbelt, 1933–1941. *Journal of Religion in Africa* 19, no. 3 (1989): 244–63.

Mudimbe, V. Y. *The Invention of Africa: Gnosis, Philosophy, and the Order of Knowledge.* Bloomington: Indiana University Press, 1988.
———. *Parables and Fables: Exegesis, Textuality, and Politics in Central Africa.* Madison: University of Wisconsin Press, 1988.
Mulenga, Kampamba. *Blood on Their Hands.* Lusaka: Zambia Educational Publishing House, 1998.
Mulford, David C. *Zambia: The Politics of Independence, 1957–1964.* Oxford: Oxford University Press, 1967.
Mumba, Nevers. *Integrity with Fire: A Strategy for Revival.* Tulsa, OK: Vincom, 1994.
Musambachime, Mwelwa C. "The Impact of Rumour: The Case of the Banyama (Vampire Men) Scare in Northern Rhodesia, 1930–1964." *International Journal of African Historical Studies* 21, no. 2 (1998): 201–15.
Mushindo, Paul B. *The Life of a Zambian Evangelist: The Reminiscences of the Reverend Paul Bwembya Mushindo.* Lusaka: Institute for African Studies, 1973.
———. *A Short History of the Bemba (As Narrated by a Bemba).* Lusaka: National Educational Company of Zambia, 1977.
Mutambwa, Mulumbwa, and Leon Verbeek. *Bulumbu: Un mouvement extatique au sud-est du Zaire à travers la chanson traditionelle.* Tervuren, Belgium: Musée royal de l'Afrique centrale, 1997.
Mwangilwa, Goodwin B. *The Kapwepwe Diaries.* Lusaka: Multimedia Publishers, 1986.
Niehaus, Isak A. "The ANC's Dilemma: The Symbolic Politics of Three Witch-Hunts in the South African Lowveld, 1990–1995." *African Studies Review* 41, no. 3 (1998): 93–118.
———. "Witches of the Transvaal Lowveld and Their Familiars: Conceptions of Duality, Power and Desire." *Cahiers d'Études africaines* 35 (1995): 513–40.
Nordlund, Per. *Organising the Political Agora: Domination and Democratisation in Zambia and Zimbabwe.* Uppsala: Uppsala University, 1996.
O'Brien, Donal B. Cruise. *Symbolic Confrontations: Muslims Imagining the State in Africa.* London: Hurst, 2003.
O'Ferrall, R. "An Old War Song of the Babemba." *Bulletin of the School of Oriental Studies* 4, no. 4 (1928): 839–44.
Oger, Louis. *Forget Me Not: Saved from Slavery; He Became a Missionary to Zambia.* Ndola, Zambia: Mission Press, 1992.
Olupona, Jacob K., ed. *African Traditional Religions in Contemporary Society.* New York: Paragon House, 1991.
O'Shea, Michael. *Missionaries and Miners: A History of the Beginnings of the Catholic Church in Zambia with Particular Reference to the Copperbelt.* Ndola, Zambia: Mission Press, 1986.
Palmer, Robin, and Neil Parsons, eds. *The Roots of Rural Poverty in Central and Southern Africa.* Berkeley: University of California Press, 1977.
Palmié, Stephan. *Wizards and Scientists: Explorations in Afro-Cuban Modernity and Tradition.* Durham, NC: Duke University Press, 2002.

Parés, Luis Nicolau, and Roger Sansi, eds. *Sorcery in the Black Atlantic.* Chicago: University of Chicago Press, 2011.

Parpart, Jane L. *Labor and Capital on the African Copperbelt.* Philadelphia: Temple University Press, 1983.

Pedridas, Constantine. *Art and Power in the Central African Savanna: Luba, Songye, Chokwe, Luluwa.* Cleveland: Cleveland Museum of Art, 2008.

Peel, J. D. Y. *Religious Encounter and the Making of the Yoruba.* Bloomington: Indiana University Press, 2000.

Pemberton, John. *On the Subject of "Java."* Ithaca, NY: Cornell University Press, 1994.

Perrings, Charles. *Black Mineworkers in Central Africa: Industrial Strategies and the Evolution of an African Proletariat in the Copperbelt, 1911–1941.* London: Heinemann, 1979.

Peterson, Derek R. *Creative Writing: Translation, Bookkeeping, and the Work of Imagination in Colonial Kenya.* Portsmouth, NH: Heinemann, 2004.

Peterson, Derek R., and Giacomo Macola, eds. *Recasting the Past: History Writing and Political Work in Modern Africa.* Athens: Ohio University Press, 2009.

Pew Forum on Religion and Public Life. *Islam and Christianity in Sub-Saharan Africa.* Washington, DC: Pew Research Center, 2010.

Phiri, Bizeck J. *A Political History of Zambia: From the Colonial Period to the Third Republic.* Trenton, NJ: Africa World Press, 2006.

Phiri, Isaac. *Proclaiming Political Pluralism: Churches and Political Transitions in Africa.* Westport, CT: Praeger, 2001.

———. "Why African Churches Preach Politics: The Case of Zambia." *Journal of Church and State* 41, no. 2 (1999): 323–47.

Phiri, Isabel Apawo. "President Frederick Chiluba and Zambia: Evangelicals and Democracy in a 'Christian Nation.'" In Ranger, *Evangelical Christianity and Democracy in Africa*, 95–129.

———. "President Frederick J. T. Chiluba of Zambia: The Christian Nation and Democracy." *Journal of Religion in Africa* 33, no. 4 (2003): 401–28.

Porter, Andrew N. *Religion versus Empire?: British Protestant Missionaries and Overseas Expansion, 1700–1914.* New York: Manchester University Press, 2004.

Pritchett, James A. *Friends for Life, Friends for Death: Cohorts and Consciousness among the Lunda-Ndembu.* Charlottesville: University of Virginia Press, 2007.

———. *The Lunda-Ndembu: Style, Change, and Social Transformation in South Central Africa.* Madison: University of Wisconsin Press, 2001.

Quick, Griffith. "Some Aspects of the African Watch Tower Movement in Northern Rhodesia." *International Review of Missions* 29 (1940): 216–26.

Ranganathan, M. A. *The Political Philosophy of President Kenneth D. Kaunda of Zambia.* Lusaka: Kenneth Kaunda Foundation, 1986.

Ranger, Terence O. "African Traditional Religion." In *The Study of Religion, Traditional and New Religions*, edited by Stewart Sutherland and Peter Clarke, 106–14. London: Routledge, 1991.

———. "Connexions Between 'Primary Resistance' Movements and Modern Mass Nationalism in East and Central Africa: Parts 1 and 2." *Journal of African History* 9, nos. 3–4 (1968): 437–53, 631–41.

———, ed. *Evangelical Christianity and Democracy in Africa*. Oxford: Oxford University Press, 2008.

———. "The Mwana Lesa Movement of 1925." In Ranger and Weller, *Themes in the Christian History of Central Africa*, 45–75.

———. "Nationalist Historiography, Patriotic History and the History of the Nation: The Struggle over the Past in Zimbabwe." *Journal of Southern African Studies* 30, no. 2 (June 2004): 215–34.

———. "Religious Movements and Politics in Sub-Saharan Africa." *African Studies Review* 29, no. 2 (1986): 1–69.

———. "Scotland Yard in the Bush: Medicine Murders, Child Witches and the Construction of the Occult: A Literature Review." *Africa* 77, no. 2 (2007): 272–83.

Ranger, Terence O., and Isaria N. Kimambo. *The Historical Study of African Religion*. Berkeley: University of California Press, 1972.

Ranger, Terence O., and John Weller, eds. *Themes in the Christian History of Central Africa*. Berkeley: University of California Press, 1975.

Rea, W. F. *The Bemba's White Chief*. Salisbury, Rhodesia: Historical Association of Rhodesia and Nyasaland, 1964.

Redding, Sean. *Sorcery and Sovereignty: Taxation, Power, and Rebellion in South Africa, 1880–1963*. Athens: Ohio University Press, 2006.

Reefe, Thomas Q. *The Rainbow and the Kings: A History of the Luba Empire to 1891*. Berkeley: University of California Press, 1981.

Richards, Audrey I. *Chisungu: A Girl's Initiation Ceremony among the Bemba of Zambia*. London: Routledge, 1995.

———. "Keeping the King Divine." *Proceedings of the Royal Anthropological Institute of Great Britain and Ireland* (1968): 23–35.

———. *Land, Labour and Diet in Northern Rhodesia: An Economic Study of the Bemba Tribe*. Oxford: Oxford University Press, 1939.

———."A Modern Movement of Witch-Finders." *Africa: Journal of the International African Institute* 8, no. 4 (1935): 448–61.

———. "Tribal Government in Transition: The Babemba of Northeastern Zambia." *Supplement to Journal of the Royal African Society* 34, no. 137 (1935): 1–27.

Roberts, Allen. "Female Figures." In *Treasures from the Africa-Museum, Tervuren*, edited by Gustaaf Verswijver, Roger Asselberghs, and Els De Parmenaer, 65–369. Tervuren, Belgium: Royal Museum for Central Africa, 1995.

———. "Standing Figures." In *African Art from the Menil Collection*, edited by Kristina Van Dyke, 224. New Haven, CT: Yale University Press, 2008.

Roberts, Andrew. *A History of the Bemba: Political Growth and Change in North-Eastern Zambia before 1900*. London: Longman, 1973.

———. *A History of Zambia*. New York: Africana Publishing, 1976.

———. "The Lumpa Church of Alice Lenshina." In *Protest and Power in Black Africa*, edited by Robert I. Rotberg and Ali A. Mazrui, 513–68. New York: Oxford University Press, 1970.

———. *The Lumpa Church of Alice Lenshina*. Lusaka: Oxford University Press, 1972.

Roberts, Mary Nooter, and Allen F. Roberts, eds. *Memory: Luba Art and the Making of History*. New York: Museum for African Art, 1996.

Rotberg, Robert I. *Christian Missionaries and the Creation of Northern Rhodesia, 1880–1924*. Cambridge, MA: Harvard University Press, 1965.

———. "The Lenshina Movement of Northern Rhodesia." *Rhodes-Livingstone Journal* 29 (1961): 63–78.

———. *The Rise of Nationalism in Central Africa: The Making of Malawi and Zambia, 1873–1964*. Cambridge, MA: Harvard University Press, 1972.

Rutherford, J. F. *Preparation: The revelation of the Prophecy by Zechariah showing Jehovah and his enemies preparing for the final war, and describing the great battle and the conclusion thereof in a glorious victory and the establishment of peace on earth and good will toward men, and the everlasting vindication of Jehovah's name*. Brooklyn: Watch Tower Bible and Tract Society, 1933.

Saidi, Christine. *Women's Authority and Society in Early East-Central Africa*. Rochester, NY: University of Rochester Press, 2010.

Sanders, Todd. *Beyond Bodies: Rain-Making and Sense-Making in Tanzania*. Toronto: University of Toronto Press, 2008.

Sanneh, Lamin O. *Whose Religion Is Christianity?: The Gospel Beyond the West*. Grand Rapids, MI: Eerdmans, 2003.

Schatzberg, Michael G. *The Dialectics of Oppression in Zaire*. Bloomington: Indiana University Press, 1988.

———. "La sorcellerie comme mode de causalité politique." *Politique africaine* 79 (October 2000): 33–47.

———. *Political Legitimacy in Middle Africa: Father, Family, Food*. Bloomington: Indiana University Press, 2001.

Scheub, Harold. *Story*. Madison: University of Wisconsin Press, 1998.

Schoffeleers, J. Matthew. *River of Blood: The Genesis of a Martyr Cult in Southern Malawi, c. A.D. 1600*. Madison: University of Wisconsin Press, 1992.

Schumaker, Lyn. *Africanizing Anthropology: Fieldwork, Networks, and the Making of Cultural Knowledge in Central Africa*. Durham, NC: Duke University Press, 2001.

Shah, Timothy Samuel. Preface to Ranger, *Evangelical Christianity and Democracy in Africa*, vii–xix.

Sheane, J. H. West. "Some Aspects of the Awemba Religion and Superstitious Observances." *Journal of the Anthropological Institute of Great Britain and Ireland* 36 (January–June 1906): 150–58.

———. "Wemba Warpaths." *Journal of the Royal African Society* 11, no. 41 (1911): 21–34.

Sichone, Owen. "The Sacred and the Obscene: Personal Notes on Political Ritual, Poverty and Democracy in Zambia." In *African Democracy in the Era* of *Globalisation*, edited by Jonathan Hyslop, 152–66. Johannesburg: Witwatersrand University Press, 1999.

Snelson, Peter D. *Educational Development in Northern Rhodesia, 1883–1945*. Lusaka, Zambia: National Educational Company of Zambia, 1974.

Soothill, Jane E. *Gender, Social Change, and Spiritual Power: Charismatic Christianity in Ghana*. Leiden: Brill, 2007.

Spear, Thomas, and Isaria N. Kimambo. *East African Expressions of Christianity*. Oxford: James Currey, 1999.

Steedly, Mary Margaret. *Hanging without a Rope: Narrative Experience in Colonial and Postcolonial Karoland*. Princeton, NJ: Princeton University Press, 1993.

Stone, W. V. "The Livingstonia Mission and the Bemba." *Bulletin of the Society for African Church History* 2 (1965–1968): 311–22.

Sundkler, Bengt G. M. *Bantu Prophets in South Africa*. Oxford: Oxford University Press, 1961.

Tanguy, Francois. *Imilandu ya BaBemba*. Lusaka: African Literature Committee, 1948.

———. "Kayambi: The First White Father Mission in Northern Rhodesia." *Northern Rhodesia Journal* 2, no. 4 (1954): 73–78.

Taylor, John V., and Dorothea A. Lehmann. *Christians of the Copperbelt: The Growth of the Church in Northern Rhodesia*. London: SCM Press, 1961.

Thomas, F. M. *Historical Notes on the Bisa Tribe of Northern Rhodesia*. Lusaka: Rhodes-Livingstone Institute, 1958.

Thornton, John K. *The Kongolese Saint Anthony: Dona Beatriz Kimpa Vita and the Antonian Movement, 1684–1706*. Cambridge: Cambridge University Press, 1998.

Tordoff, William, and Robert Molteno. "Government and Administration." In *Politics in Zambia*, edited by William Tordoff, 242–87. Manchester: Manchester University Press, 1974.

Turner, Victor. *The Forest of Symbols: Aspects of Ndembu Ritual*. Ithaca, NY: Cornell University Press, 1970.

van Binsbergen, Wim M. J. *Religious Change in Zambia: Exploratory Studies*. London: Kegan Paul, 1981.

Vansina, Jan. *How Societies Are Born: Governance in West Central Africa Before 1600*. Charlottesville: University of Virginia Press, 2004.

———. *Kingdoms of the Savanna: A History of Central African States until European Occupation*. Madison: University of Wisconsin Press, 1968.

———. *Paths in the Rainforests: Toward a History of Political Tradition in Equatorial Africa*. Madison: University of Wisconsin Press, 1990.

Vaughan, Megan. "'Divine Kings': Sex, Death and Anthropology in Inter-War East/Central Africa." *Journal of African History* 49, no. 3 (2008): 383–401.

———. "Exploitation and Neglect: Rural Producers and the State in Malawi and Zambia." In *History of Central Africa: The Contemporary Years Since 1960*, edited by David Birmingham and Phyllis M. Martin, 167–202. London: Longman, 1998.

Verbeek, Leon. *Filiation et usurpation: Histoire socio-politique de la region entre Luapula et Copperbelt.* Tervuren, Belgium: Musée royal de l'Afrique centrale, 1987.

———. *Initiation et marriage dans la chanson populaire des Bemba du Zaire.* Tervuren, Belgium: Musée royal de l'Afrique centrale, 1993.

———. *Le monde des esprits au sud-est du Shaba et au nord de la Zambie.* Rome: Libreria Ateneo Salesiano, 1990.

Villalón, Leonardo A. *Islamic Society and State Power in Senegal: Disciples and Citizens in Fatick.* Cambridge: Cambridge University Press, 1995.

Wacker, Grant. *Heaven Below: Early Pentecostals and American Culture.* Cambridge, MA: Harvard University Press, 2001.

Ward, Kevin, and Brian Stanley, eds. *The Church Mission Society and World Christianity, 1799–1999.* Grand Rapids, MI: Eerdmans, 2000.

Werbner, Richard P. "Federal Administration, Rank, and Civil Strife among Bemba Royals and Nobles." *Africa: Journal of the International African Institute* 37, no. 1 (January 1967): 22–49.

Werner, Douglas. "Miao Spirit Shrines in the Religious History of the Southern Lake Tanganyika Region: The Case of Kapembwa." In *Guardians of the Land: Essays on Central African Territorial Cults*, edited by J. Matthew Schoffeleers, 89–130. Gwelo, Zimbabwe: Mambo Press, 1978.

———. "Some Developments in Bemba Religious History." *Journal of Religion in Africa* 4, no. 1 (1971): 1–24.

West, Harry G. *Kupilikula: Governance and the Invisible Realm in Mozambique.* Chicago: University of Chicago Press, 2005.

White, Luise. *Speaking with Vampires: Rumor and History in Colonial Africa.* Berkeley: University of California Press, 2000.

White Fathers. *The White Fathers' Bemba English Dictionary.* Ndola, Zambia: Mission Press, 1991.

Wilson, Godfrey. *An Essay on the Economics of Detribalization in Northern Rhodesia.* Livingstone, Northern Rhodesia: Rhodes-Livingstone Institute, 1941–1942.

Wilson, Monica H. *Communal Rituals of the Nyakyusa.* London: Oxford University Press, 1959.

Young, Crawford M. *The African Colonial State in Comparative Perspective.* New Haven, CT: Yale University Press, 1995.

Young, Crawford M., and Thomas Turner. *The Rise and Decline of the Zairian State.* Madison: University of Wisconsin Press, 1985.

Zambia Episcopal Conference, Christian Council in Zambia, and Zambia Evangelical Fellowship. *Marxism, Humanism and Christianity: A Letter from the Leaders of the Christian Churches in Zambia to Their Members about Scientific Socialism.* Lusaka: Teresianum Press, 1979.

Zulu, Justin B. *Zambian Humanism: Some Major Spiritual and Economic Challenges.* Lusaka: National Educational Company of Zambia, 1970.

GOVERNMENT REPORTS

Northern Rhodesia. *An Account of the Disturbances in Northern Rhodesia*. Lusaka, 1961.
Northern Rhodesia. *Evidence Taken by the Commission Appointed to Inquire into the Disturbances in the Copperbelt, Northern Rhodesia, July–September, 1935*. Lusaka, 1935.
Northern Rhodesia. *Report of Commission to Inquire into Disturbances in the Copperbelt, Northern Rhodesia, October, 1935*. Lusaka, 1935.
Northern Rhodesia. *Report of the Commission Appointed to Inquire into the Disturbances in the Copperbelt, Northern Rhodesia, July 1940*. Lusaka, 1940.
Zambia. *Report of the Commission of Enquiry into the Lumpa Church*. Lusaka, 1965.
Zambia. *Report of the National Commission on the Establishment of a One-Party Participatory Democracy in Zambia*. Lusaka, 1972.
Zambia. *Zambia Law Report 1965*. Lusaka, 1972.

NEWSPAPERS

Northern News
Times of Zambia
National Mirror
The Post
Voice of UNIP
The Aurora: A Journal of Missionary News and Christian Work
Livingstonia News
Rhodesia Herald

PUBLIC ARCHIVES

General series indicated below. File numbers are found in the notes.

National Archives of Zambia (NAZ), Lusaka, Zambia

Northern Rhodesia Files (to 1964)
EP   Eastern Province
NP   Northern Province
SEC   Native Secretariat
WP   Western Province

Personal Papers
HM   Personal Papers

District Notebooks
KST   Lundazi District Notebooks, 3 vols.
KTQ   Chinsali District Notebooks, 3 vols.

Zambia Files (after 1964)
CO   Cabinet Office
FA   Foreign Affairs
MHA   Ministry of Home Affairs

British South Africa Company Files (to 1923)
A 1-1-1   Ikawa Collector
A 3-10-7 United Free Church Scotland, Livingstone Mission
BS 1-132 Slave Trade and Pacification of Awemba, NE Rhodesia

Assorted Publications
Box 85 A Independence Celebrations
Box 110 ABC National Guidance
Box 112 National Museums, Notional Monuments Commission
Box 116 Natural and Historical Monuments and Relics
Box 172 A & B Zambia Cultural Services
Box 178 National Museums of Zambia

UNIP Archives, Lusaka (UNIPA), Lusaka, Zambia

ANC African National Congress Papers
UNIP United National Independence Party Papers

White Fathers Archives (WFA), Lusaka, Zambia

Bemba Cultural and Historical Manuscripts
Bemba Dioceses
Bemba Publications
Mission Diaries
Personal Papers

United Church of Zambia Archives (UCZA), Mindolo, Kitwe, Zambia

CCAR   Church of Central Africa in Rhodesia Papers
CS   Church of Scotland Papers
UCCAR United Church of Central Africa in Rhodesia Papers
UCZ   United Church of Zambia Papers
UMCB   United Missions of the Copperbelt Papers

National Archives of the United Kingdom (NAUK), Kew, UK

CO 795 Colonial Office, Northern Rhodesia: Original Correspondence, 1924–1951.
CO 1015 Colonial Office, Central Africa and Aden: Original Correspondence, 1950–1962.
DO 183 Central African Office and Commonwealth Relations Office, 1962–1966.
DO 209 Commonwealth Relations Office: Malawi and Zambia, 1965–1966.

FCO 29 Commonwealth Office and Foreign and Commonwealth Office: Central Africa, 1967–1969.

National Library of Scotland (NLS), Edinburgh, UK

Church of Scotland, Foreign Mission Papers
Livingstonia Mission Papers

London School of Economics (LSE), London, UK

Audrey Richards Collection

Center for the Study of Christianity in the Non-Western World (CSCNWW), Edinburgh, UK

49 Fergus Macpherson Collection.

University of Edinburgh Special Collections

Kenneth Mackenzie Papers

School of Oriental and African Studies (SOAS), London, UK

CWM United Church of Northern Rhodesia Papers
MS 380399 Moore Collection

University of Cape Town Manuscripts and Archives (UCTMA), Cape Town, South Africa

BC 880 Wilson Collection
BC 1081 Simons Collection

PRIVATE COLLECTIONS

Chiponya New Jerusalem Congregation

Chiponya Manuscript of Church History and Prayers

John Hudson Papers

Assorted papers dealing with operations against the Lumpa

Andrew Roberts Papers

Assorted papers dealing with the Lumpa movement

Austin Cheyeka

Student interview with Nevers Mumba Lusaka, n.d. (2006?)

All interviews were conducted by the author. Transcriptions are in his possession. The date of birth of the interviewee is given if it was known and if the interviewee gave consent for it to be published.

Lenshina and UNIP Interviews

Bowa, Kristine. Kapiri Mposhi, 20 July 2005. b. 1947.

Bwali, Jolson. Lubwa, Chinsali, 12 July 2005. b. 1918.

Bwalya, John. Mfuyla, Bright Village, Chinsali, 9 July 2005. b. 1929.

Bwalya, Roda. Kaunda Square, Lusaka, 12 March 2005. b. 1957.

Bwalya, Theresa Nkula, Nkula Village, Chinsali, 13 July 2005. b. 1945.

Chabula, John. Kasomo Village, Chinsali, 9 July 2005. b. 1932.

Chakaniko, James. Choshi Village, Chinsali 10 July 2005. b. 1943.

Chanda, Agnes. Choshi Village, Chinsali, 14 July 2005. b. 1950.

Chewe, Agre. Choshi Village, Chinsali, 4 July 2005. b. 1935.

Chewe, Lazerus. Kasomo Village, Chinsali, 5 July 2005. b. 1942.

Chilufya, Denise. Choshi Village, Chinsali, 10 July 2005. b. 1940.

Chimfwembe, Gabriel. Kapiri Mposhi, 20 July 2005. b. 1933.

Chisanga, Gabriel. Choshi Village, Chinsali, 10 July 2005. b. 1934.

Chofwe, Alex Bwalya. Nkula Village, Chinsali, 12 July 2005. b. 1939.

Filamba, Sebastion Chewe. Mutambo Village, 18 July 2005. b. (1948?)

Hudson, John. Lusaka, 11 March 2005.

Kambala, Ninkamona. Kasomo Village, Chinsali, 5 July 2005. b. 1942.

Kangwe, Jonda. Nkula Village, Chinsali, 12 July 2005. b. 1918.

Kapoma, Wellington. Kasomo Village, Chinsali, 5 July 2005. b. 1941.

Lukonde, Aida. Choshi Village, Chinsali, 10 July 2005. b. (1950?)

Lumumboa, Jena. Makoba Village, Chinsali, 7 July 2005. b. (1925?)

Lutanda [Ngandu], Elizabeth. Chipata Compund, Lusaka, 25 March 2005, b. 1946.

Mafupa, Agnes. Lubwa, Chinsali, 12 July 2005. b.1929.

Makasa, Robert Kapasa. Lubu River Home, Chinsali, 15 July 2005.

Mfula, Foster Mubanga. Chiponya Village, Mpika, 19 July 2005. b. 1948.

Mfula, James. Kaunda Square, Lusaka, 19 March 2005. b. 1955.

Mfula, Mercy. Choshi Village, Chinsali, 10 July 2005. b. 1945.

Mkuka, Sinent. Mutale Village, Chinsali, 9 July 2005. b. 1931.

Mpoyam Jameson Nkonde, Nkula Village, 13 July 2005. b. 1927.

Mpuku, David. Choshi Village, Chinsali, 6 July 2005. b. 1949.

Mulenga, Dixon. Choshi Village, Chinsali, 7 and 15 July 2005. b. 1932.

Mulenga, Helena. Kaunda Square, Lusaka, 19 March 2005. b. 1929.

Mulenga, Jackson. Bright Village, Chinsali, 9 July 2005. b. (1945–1948?).

Mulenga, Shame. Bright Village, Chinsali, 9 July 2005 b. 1927.

Mulenga, Theresa. Choshi Village, Chinsali, 7 July 2005. b. 1943.

Mumba, Felix Chimfwembe. Choshi Village, Chinsali, 10 July 2005. b. 1948–1950?).

Mumba, Lewis. Chiponya Village, Mpika, 19 July 2005. b. 1949.

Mumba, Maria. Nkula Village, Chinsali, 12 July 2005. b. 1927.
Mutapa, Bellita. Kasomo Village, Chinsali, 5 July 2005. b. (1940?).
Mutonga, Leonard. Kaunda Square, Lusaka, 19 March 2005. b. 1938.
Mutonga, London. Kaunda Square, Lusaka, 19 March 2005.
Mwansa, Kachankwa. Kapiri Mposhi, 20 July 2005.
Mwansabama, Rodwell. Chandamali Village, Chinsali, 9 July 2005. b. 1930.
Ngandu, Jennifer. Chipata Compund, Lusaka, 25 March 2005. b. 1949.
Nguni, Stephenia. Chiponya Village, Mpika, 19 July 2005. b. 1946.
Nkamba, Monica. Chiponya Village, Mpika, 19 July 2005.
Nkamba, Rebecca. Choshi Village, Chinsali, 6 July 2005. b. 1935.
Nkonde, Maggie. Chandamali Village, Chinsali, 9 July 2005.
Nkonde, Paison. Kapiri Mposhi, 20 July 2005. b. 1916.
Sinfunkwe, Daniel. Chiponya Village, Mpika, 19 July 2005.
William "Kalomba muli Lesa." Chiponya Village, Mpika, 29 July 2005. b. 1918.

Barak Ministries Interviews

Mhusambazi, Prophetess Elwida. Lusaka, 11 September 2008.
Mumba, Pastor Viness. Lusaka, Barak Ministries, 16 September 2008. b.1955.
Mwale, Pastor Josephine. Lusaka, Barak Ministries, 16 September 2008.

Gospel Outreach Center Interviews

Bwali, Bines. Northmead, Lusaka, 21 September 2008.
Chaaba, Doreen. Lusaka, 19 September 2008. b. 1954.
Chola, Chongo Jonas. Lusaka, 19 September 2008. b. 1975.
Mbindawina, Richard M. Lusaka, 19 September 2008. b. 1953.
Miti, Fatima Chibamba. Lusaka, 19 September 2008. b. 1972.
Reutter, Pastor Helmet. Lusaka, 16 September 2008.

Northmead Assemblies of God Interviews

Banda, Bishop Joshua. Northmead, Lusaka, 10 September 2008 b. 1963.
Kasamanda, Jennifer. Northmead, Lusaka, 21 September 2008.
Makangila, Elder Gibstar. Lusaka, Northmead, 16 September 2008. b. 1967.
Zulu, Josephine. Northmead, Lusaka, 21 September 2008.

Miscellaneous Charismatic and Pentecostal Interviews

Kamfwa, Teddy. Lusaka, 16 September 2008.
Musondo, David. Masupa, Lusaka, 18 September 2008.
Mususu, Bishop Paul. Lusaka, 15 September 2008. b. 1958.
Tembo, Rev. S. Apostolic Faith Mission, Lusaka, 17 September 2008.

Other Interviews

Kalumba, Simon Shindiliya. Kazembe, Luapula, 24 July 2002.
Kanyembo, Peter Chikoko. Kanaya, Luapula, 16 July 2002.

Index

Aaron, 123
abortion, 173, 179
adultery, 34, 43, 56, 57
African Mineworkers Union (AMU), 84,
    85, 118–19
African National Congress (ANC),
    110; activists within, 94; against
    federation, 118, 119–23; Israel
    and, 195; Lumpa within, 101, 110;
    organization of, 84–85, 114–15;
    membership cards, 121, 122; as UNIP
    rival, 134, 137; women's branches of,
    121
African Railway Workers Union, 85
African Representative Council (ARC), 84
"Africa Shall Be Saved" programs, 196
afterlife: God in control of, 155; Christian
    promises of/hope for, 11, 12, 80,
    95–96, 181, 190; Islam focus on, 15;
    rejected by Lenshina vision, 90, 112;
    spirits in, 2, 12, 99, 201
agriculture/crops, 41, 44, 48, 133, 213n16;
    rites of, 36, 45, 47, 65; seeds for, 31,
    32, 36, 45, 65, 99; slash-and-burn,
    21, 97–98, 121. See also chibyalilo;
    fertility
aid organizations, 186
AIDS, 186, 189, 190

air force, Zambian, 157
alcohol, 99, 184. See also beer
AMU. See African Mineworkers Union
ANC. See African National Congress
ancestors: beliefs of, 2; genealogies of, 44;
    names of as titles, 37
ancestral spirits, 9, 27, 32–34, 115, 188, 201;
    appeal to, 43; authority/power of, 22,
    41, 51, 70, 95, 109–13; ceded to God,
    11, 12, 22, 169; chief of, 54; conversion
    into, 44; dissatisfied/angry, 34, 41,
    51, 56, 59, 70, 96; grief and joy as
    agency of, 10; nature spirits and, 35,
    41, 47–48; roaming, 38; "shades," 2, 7,
    15, 48, 56
Anderson, David, 132
angels, 12, 89–90, 189, 197
anger: 10, 34, 39, 48; of spirits, 7, 12, 13, 22,
    28–29, 38, 43, 47, 48
Anglican Church, 195
animals: dancing, 128–29; ngulu spirits in,
    35, 47, 260; on Lenshina, 110; parts
    of as bwanga, 36; slaughter of cattle,
    124–25; threat of, 43, 48–49, 61
animism, industrial, 77
anthropologists, 7–8, 18, 19; on chiefly rule,
    51; religion and, 27–28; repression by,

Bible camps, 182
Bible colleges, 179, 183, 184, 189
"big men"/"big women," 14; Pentecostal,
    182, 184, 185, 196, 197
Billy Graham Foundation, 196
birth: childbirth, 38, 39–40; of crops, 38;
    rebirth, 133, 181, 196; spirit and body
    in, 10
Bisa peoples, 28, 44–47, 67, 111, 219n90
blood, 47
Boma, 40, 52, 107, 136, 137; Chinsala, 107,
    140, 142, 146, 150; Lundazi, 147, 148
Bonnke, Reinhard, 178–79, 182; "Africa
    Shall Be Saved" programs, 196
books: Kaunda's black book, 128;
    Lenshina's, 90–91, 96, 107, 135;
    Lenshina's use of, 94, 95, 112;
    Protestant, 51, 56, 57, 67; spiritual
    power/resource of, 59, 66, 67, 68,
    74, 190; Watchtower, 77, 81; White
    Father, 57–58, 65
bows and arrows, 27, 42, 66, 111, 145, 146
bracelet, 39–40
bravery: of hunters/fighters, 23, 28–29, 36,
    45; of Lenshina/Lumpa, 94, 146
Brazil, 15
Bread of Life Ministries, 179
breasts, of Chilimbulu, 25
Brelsford, W. Vernon, 18, 64–65, 66, 213n21,
    218n80, 223n59
bridges, 151: destruction of, 124, 125, 133, 144
British South Africa Company (BSAC), 18,
    53, 64, 218n80, 220n5
Brown, David, 58
BSAC. See British South Africa Company
Buganda, Uganda, 8
Bulanda, 25
bullets, 23, 132, 141, 144, 145, 146, 148, 155
buloshi, 61, 64, 259
Bulumbu, 45
bupondo, 57
burial grounds, 22, 32, 33, 35, 41;
    desecration of, 112. See also Mwalule
burning: of bodies/bones 32, 38, 47; of
    colonial property, 116, 122, 123, 124;
    of food supplies, 125, 133; of homes,

60, 122, 133, 135, 148, 162; of identify
    documents, 116, 124, 135–36; of
    Lumpa churches, 111, 135, 141, 153,
    237n107, 243n24; of missionary
    property, 124, 125–26; of shrines, 63;
    of villages, 125, 142, 162; of witches,
    39, 59. See also agriculture: slash-
    and-burn; arson
burning bush, the, 97–98
bush: danger of the, 45; father of the, 38;
    fleeing to the, 125, 131, 139, 141, 147–
    51; spirits/cults of the, 37–38, 39
Bush, Laura, 186
butungwa, 116
Butwa peoples, 45, 71, 190, 259; figurine of,
    46 fig. 1.3
Bwanas, 62, 64, 67
bwanga, 36–37, 38, 48, 63, 99, 259, 260;
    associated with sin/witchcraft, 57,
    61, 95, 96, 97 fig. 4.1, 98 fig. 4.2; of
    Bamuchape, 61; burning/destruction
    of, 105, 124, 125; of Catholics, 104–5;
    of chiefs, 63; personal, 40; warfare,
    47, 49
Bwembya, 42, 43

CAF. See Central African Federation
Calmettes, Jean Loup, 93, 102, 166
Cameroon, 9
cannibalism, 5–6
Cape Town, South Africa, 72, 75, 78, 79, 81
capitalism, 57, 94, 173, 180, 181, 186, 198
Capricorn Africa Society, 117, 119, 126
"Captain Solo," 197
captives: blood of, 47; body parts of, 67
catechism, 54–55, 56
Catéchisme en Kibemba (Dupont), 55
caterpillars, 102
Catholics/Catholicism: baptism, 55, 67, 95;
    barrier against, 54; and burning of
    bush, 97; "Catholic Action" cells, 58,
    105–6; charismatic renewal within,
    168–69, 183; conversion, 55; focus
    on afterlife, 11, 68; Lenshina's claims
    against, 104–8; nonspiritual religion
    of, 2, 11, 169, 177; numbers of, 55,

confession: Christian ritual of, 12, 54, 55, 95, 107–8, 201; as a witch, 57, 61
Congo River, 9
consciousness, collective, 7
constitutions, 27; amending of, 196, 197; church, 185
conversions: 2, 14, 52–53, 54–55, 63, 68; backsliding and, 55; to Lumpa Church, 95, 99, 105, 106, 107, 114; mass, 178
copper: figurine eyes, 45; prices of, 170; rulers' wearing of, 42. *See also* mining industry
Copperbelt: employment on, 51 (*see also* mine workers); social transformation on, 73–74; studies of church and missions on, 71; urbanization of, 70–71; vampire rumors on, 6, 71, 119
Corpus Christi processions, 106
cosmology, Bemba, 33, 34
Council of Churches in Zambia (CCZ), 168
councilors, chiefly, 37, 44, 66, 67
councils, urban advisory, 84
Crais, Clifton, 118, 129
crimes: "against progress," 164; compensation for, 43
Crisis, 85
Crocker, Chester, 174–75
Crocodile Clan: ancestral/spiritual authority of, 44, 45, 63, 64, 95, 109, 112–13; celestial connections of, 29, 30, 32, 33–34, 41, 48, 95; conquests, 25, 42, 45, 64; diagram of, 30 fig. 1.2; divine/celestial origins of, 29, 47; expectations of government, 27; indirect rule and, 51, 68; lords of, 26 fig. 1.1, 42, 47, 51; migration of, 17, 22, 31, 33, 41, 48; oral tradition of, 22, 25–49; powers of, 25–29, 39, 40, 47, 48–49; social hierarchy of, 37, 42. *See also* Bemba
crocodiles, 40, 43, 47
Cross, Sholto, 78, 85
crosses, Catholic, 104, 105

crusades, Christian, 178–79, 182–83, 184, 191, 193, 196
Cuba, 15
cults: ancestral, 44–45; cleansing, 92; communal, 45; David Universal Temple, 193–94, 195; Lenshina, 136, 151; possession, 169; territorial, 45, 47, 71, 190, 213n24
curses, 8, 105, 186
cursing, 99

dances/dancing, 40, 43–44, 54, 66–67, 157, 213n18; inspired by nature spirits, 35, 39, 190; Kaunda's "real dancing," 128–29; societies, 70
David Universal Temple, 193–94, 195
dawn, 33, 94–95; prophet of, 31, 41, 49, 114; political idiom of, 114, 116, 121, 129–30, 157
DC. *See* district commissioner
deacons, 99, 101, 141; Lumpa, 96, 133, 145, 151
dead, the: approaches to, 71, 82; bones of, 38; incarnation of, 1; land of, 94, 95, 177, 200; living, 38; relationships with people, 25, 27; salvation for, 52; worship of, 188. *See also* ancestral spirits
death: 36, 37; of Bemba ancestors, 22, 29–31, 33–34, 41, 108; jealousy and anger as cause of, 10, 34; of marriage partner, 35; mortuary rites, 34, 48; in oral tradition, 28, 48; in ritual battles, 44; as separation of spirit and body, 10; spirits as cause of, 11, 38
Democratic Republic of Congo (DRC), 26; Lumpa members' march to, 151–52; Mobutu's Authenticité in, 12–13; refugee camps of, 131–32. *See also* Belgian Congo; Zaire
demons, 11, 12, 14–15, 56, 172; exorcism of, 12, 14, 23, 168–71, 176, 178, 191–92, 196
Department of Culture, 159
detention centers, 151–52, 154. *See also* refugee camps
detribalization, 19

devil, 127, 128, 166, 185; "Devil's organization," 80; colonial state as, 117; enemies as/fighting, 14, 23, 132, 152, 169; Christian, 12, 51, 59; Kaunda allied with, 193–94; Lenshina as, 106, 149; non-UNIP members as, 126; power from, 169. *See also* Satan

diaspora, African, 15

Dillon-Malone, Clive M., 175

discourses: Christian/spiritual, 4–6, 8, 13; historical also religious, 27, 28; political, 5, 197

disciples: of devil, 166; of God, 123, 176; of Lenshina, 101; of trade unionism, 83–84

disease. *See* illness

district commissioners (DCs), 22, 60, 67, 77–78, 85, 134; injuring of, 111; offerings of food and payment to, 121; sovereignty of, 86; tour reports of, 127; UNIP letter to, 134

divorce, 66, 154

doctors, 59–60, 61, 170

Doctrine of Regeneration, 183

DRC. *See* Democratic Republic of Congo

dreams, 10, 47, 60, 99, 189, 190

drums, 31, 39, 47, 79, 105

Dunamis Ministries, 182

Dupont, Joseph, 50, 52–53; biography of, 67; catechism by, 55; as Mwamba, 50, 53; named *Moto Moto* ("the Fire"), 52, 67

Durkheim, Emile, 7, 28

eagle, 159

earth: chief of, 38; Christ's return to, 1, 77; heaven on, 14, 23, 33, 41, 68, 73, 95–96, 114, 116, 129, 158, 163, 193–94; inheritance of, 75, 79; magic of, 32; sky and, 29, 33, 114; slogan "God in heaven, Kaunda on earth," 155, 159, 167, 177; "mother-earth," 38; priest, 32, 213n22; salvation on, 91, 96; Satan on, 72, 86; spirits/cults and, 34, 37–38, 39, 44, 159; sun and, 33

economy: booming, 19–20; colonial, 5–6; declining/strained, 83, 94, 164, 167,

170–74, 202; global, 28; neoliberal, 197; rural/village, 102, 98–99; spiritual history and, 51; urban, 70

Eden, 38

education: basic, 186; lack of, 82; in missions, 50, 54–57, 80, 167; spread of, 106; Watchtower, 77, 81

EFZ. *See* Evangelical Fellowship of Zambia

Ehret, Christopher, 9

Elbourne, Elizabeth, 5

elders, 79, 91, 185; Lumpa Church, 101; tribal, 82–83

elections: church, 185; political, 125, 127, 129, 137, 139, 171, 192, 194, 198; prayer response to, 197

Elizabeth, Queen, 94, 120, 122, 127, 128–29

Ellis, Stephen, 2–3, 6, 117

embalmers, 44

emotions: in Bemba oral tradition, 28–29, 31; destructive, 10, 22, 25, 34, 48, 142, 147; invisible forces and, 1, 4, 9–10; managing, 10, 22, 25, 28–29, 35–36, 40, 44, 47; power of, x, 32–34; in warfare, 47; of women, 48

employment. *See* workers

enemies, 23, 43, 47, 141; bravery to defeat, 28–29; of the church, 76, 106; invisible, 192; missionaries as, 59, 105; Satan/devil as enemy, 57, 169

Enlightenment, 3, 202, 203–4n8

eternal life, 38, 63. *See also* afterlife

ethnicity, 180

ethnographers, 19, 51, 64

Etienne, Louis, 17–18, 57

Evangelical Church of Zambia, 185

Evangelical Fellowship of Zambia (EFZ), 168, 179, 185, 193, 194, 196–97

evangelists, 53, 54, 184, 185, 189. *See also* missionaries

Evans-Pritchard, Edward E., 7

evil: afflictions, 41–48; call to end, 68; of heart, 189; false Christian doctrines as, 67; incarnations of, 14; new concept of, 48–49; spiritual, 12, 88, 169, 171, 175, 177, 200

exorcism, 12, 14, 23, 168–71, 176, 178, 191–92, 196
Exorcist, The, 169
eyes: of Chilimbulu, 25; of figurine, 45, 46 fig. 1.3; scripture reference to, 174

faces, whitening of, 39
faith gospel. *See* prosperity gospel
family, 128, 151, 165, 188; emotions within, 10, 30–38, 188; head of, 35; stability of, 99; ties between sisters and brothers, 29, 31; strife between sons and fathers, 29; women's role in, 99. *See also* mothers
fathers: strife between sons and, 29
fear: of death, 69; in Lumpa-UNIP conflict, 131, 142, 152; men's, 28; overcoming, 114, 116; as source of witchcraft accusations, 60
feathers, 36, 40, 45
federation, 118–26
Federation of African Societies, 84. *See also* African National Congress (ANC)
feet, 45, 46 fig. 1.3
Ferguson, James, 19, 71, 160, 166, 195–96
fertility, 1, 9, 10, 22, 25, 64, 200; objects/ relics, 5, 26 fig. 1.1, 34, 36, 48, 51, 65, 97 fig. 4.1, 98 fig. 4.2; medicines for, 96; spiritual center of, 32
fibanda, 259
field notes, 16–17, 19
Fields, Karen E., 5, 51, 71–72, 93
Fife District, 75
"Fifty Reasons Why I Have Not Joined the Church of Rome," 58
figurines, 25, 26 fig. 1.1, 39–40, 45, 46 fig. 1.3
fitupa, 116, 124, 127, 135–36
fiwa, 259
flag, Zambian, 157, 159
flour, anointing with, 39
food, 99, 121, 135, 137, 142–43, 152; choice between eternal life and, 38; destruction of, 125, 133
Fortes, Meyer, 7
Fox-Pitt, Thomas, 19
freedom, 1, 121, 123, 126–27, 175–76; concept

of, 116, 121; from colonialism, 73, 116, 125, 132; from evil, 87, 96; religious, 80, 173
functionalism, 7–8, 19
fyabubi, 96–97, 124

Gann, Lewis H., 19
genitalia, 25, 46 fig. 1.3
George, King, 75, 76
Geschiere, Pete, 10
Ghana, 15, 160
Gifford, Paul, 180, 185, 186, 187
Giraud, Victor, 42
glossolalia, 5, 10, 35, 93, 189, 190, 260
Gluckman, Max, 19
goats, 37, 43, 111, 146
God: ancestors giving way to, 11, 12, 22, 169; chosen people of, 152; denial of, 173, 176, 177, 194, 198; killing by, 33–34; Lesa/Reza as, 17, 33–34, 37, 38, 56, 62, 65, 95, 96; relationship with, 5, 182, 185, 187, 189, 191, 192; spirit/agent of invisible world, 2, 51, 93; voice of, 89, 106, 189; wrath of, 79
Gondwe, Jeremiah, 72
good works/actions, 175, 189–91
good fortune, 15, 39, 44, 45, 64, 213n17
Gore-Brown, Stewart, 19
Gospel Outreach (GO) center, 179, 186, 187
government: African representation in, 84, 86; ancestral/clan, 1, 27, 40, 41, 48, 112; banning of opposition parties, 165; clergy in 175; colonial, 57, 60, 66, 80–81, 133, 138; corruption and authoritarianism in, 130, 170, 180, 181, 196, 197; decentralization of, 171, 174; failed coup of, 197; Lenshina/Lumpa and, 110, 116, 131–57; philosophies of, 12, 160; Satan in, 75
Grace Ministries, 183
Graham, Billy, 182
graveyards. *See* burial grounds; Mwalule
Great Britain, 75
Great Depression, 78

greed, 43, 161, 167, 200
grief, 10, 28
grudge, 38
guilt, 56, 57
guitar, 128
guns, 42, 43, 45, 138, 140, 143–47

Haar, Gerrie ter, 2–3
Haarhoff, Josephine, 54
Haiti, 15
Ham, 75–76
Hannah, John, 145, 146
Hansen, Karen Tranberg, 21
Harris, Ruth, 4
headdress, 40
healing, 8, 178, 183, 186, 188–89, 196, 202;
    ministry of Bonnke, 178–79; ministry
    of Milingo, 159, 167–71, 173, 176–77,
    183
health, 2, 34, 96, 186, 189, 192, 200
heaven: afterlife in, 2, 12, 63, 90, 152, 175;
    on earth, 14, 23, 33, 41, 68, 73, 95–96,
    114, 116, 129, 158, 163, 193–94; denial
    of, 63; names from, 92, 135; "passports
    to," 90, 107, 117, 135; promise of, 107;
    slogan "God in heaven, Kaunda on
    earth," 155, 159, 167, 177
hell: afterlife in, 2, 12, 200; threat of, 105,
    107, 194
heroes: Christian, 23; solar, 31, 33, 49,
    94–95, 114
heroines, 25, 31, 94, 259
Heusch, Luc de, 31, 33
Higginson, John, 73
Hillcrest School, 182
Hinfelaar, Hugo F., 17, 28, 40, 93, 102, 169
Hinfelaar, Marja, 21–22, 158, 192
history: Bemba reader version of,
    58; interpretation of historical
    documents, 16–17; religion and,
    27–28; writing of Zambian, 17, 18
HIV, 186, 189, 190
hoes, 43, 97
Holy Spirit, 2, 12,189, 192; ancestral shades
    as, 56; blessings by, 23–24, 181; call
    to, 15; chasing of, 190; empowerment

by, 178, 181, 197, 198; Lenshina's
    receiving of, 137; possession by, 177,
    190; protection of Lumpa by, 132,
    140, 142
homosexuality, 179
Hone, Evelyn, 131, 145, 148
horns, 38, 47, 63, 97
Horton, Robin, 205n20, 221n24
humanism, 12, 13, 23; Christian element
    of, 164, 167–68, 175, 190; creation
    of, 20; disenchantment with/
    failure of, 167, 170, 172, 177, 193;
    first published record of, 163;
    moral vision of, 163; as national
    philosophy, 160, 163, 193; as
    religion, 165; scientific socialism
    influence of, 176–77; slogan
    "One Zambia, One Nation," 126,
    159, 195
Humanist in Africa, A (Kaunda), 163
Humanist Moral Code, 166
humankind, origins of, 17
hunger. *See* starvation/hunger
hunters/hunting, 28–33, 36–37, 45, 47, 112;
    restrictions on, 121
husband, 32–34, 39–40, 48. *See also*
    marriage
huts: *chisungu*, 40; marital, 37, 96; shrine,
    35, 37
hymns, 54, 90, 92, 93, 99, 101–2, 105–8,
    110–11, 150–54; political, 117, 129. *See
    also* songs/singing

ibuku lya Mweo, 90
Ichinga, 42, 43, 44
ICOZ. *See* Independent Church
    Organization of Zambia
identity cards: Christian, 82; colonial, 116,
    117, 124, 127; UNIP cards, 129, 134–36,
    174
idolatry, 63, 64, 188, 199, 201
Ifyabukaya, 57–58, 212n14
ilamfya, 47, 259
illness, 10, 11, 13, 36, 38, 39, 59–60;
    smallpox, 94
Ilondokelo, 152

Ilondola Mission, 16, 58, 65–66, 67, 102–3; burning of, 124; spies from, 106; survival of, 156
Imakando, Joseph, 179, 193, 194, 195, 196
imperialism/imperialists, 80, 118, 125, 136, 167
independence, concept of, 116
Independence Day, 157
Independent Church Organization of Zambia (ICOZ), 185
indirect rule: disempowerment by, 22, 51, 61, 63–68, 70, 71, 109, 200; introduction of, 18
Industrial and Commercial Workers Union, 74
injustice, 48, 75, 79, 86, 174, 192, 199, 200
International Missionary Society, 71
Ireland, 58
ishina lya mulu, 92
Islam, 2, 15, 54
Isoka District, 134, 150
Israel, 195
ivory trade, 10, 15, 42

Jager, Petrus Johannes de, 78, 80–81
jealousy, 10, 28, 30, 31, 38, 39, 43, 48; witchcraft link to, 34, 189
Jehovah's Witnesses. *See* Watchtower
Jesuits, 65
Jesus Christ: in afterlife and everyday life, 201; ancestors giving way to, 12, 23, 69; armies of, 75; church of, 106; death/crucifixion of, 34, 104, 152, 176; expectation of at Kamutola Church, 103, 104; faith in vs. belief in evil spirits, 169; gospel/teachings of, 74–75, 79, 123, 137, 174, 178, 189, 191, 196; the Great Physician, 53; return of, 1, 77
Joint Publications Bureau of Zambia, 165
Jordan (inspector), 144
joy, 10
Judas, 123, 154
justice, 86, 120, 174, 199

Kabotwe, 30, 32, 37
Kabwe, Zambia, 74, 75, 76, 79

Kadalie, Clements, 74
Kakokota, Pascal, 107
Kalela dance, 70
Kalikiti, Zambia, 138, 142–43
Kaluba, Austin, 193–94
Kalusa, Walima T., 71
Kamateshi, 66
Kameko Village, 139–41
Kamutola Church, 102–4, 103 fig. 4.4, 104 fig. 4.5, 111
Kamwana, Elliot, 72
Kamwende, 61
Kanama, 38
Kandeke, Timothy, 164, 166
kapasu, 111
Kapele, Alfred, 151
Kapesa, 76
Kapimpi Village, 135
Kapwepwe, Simon, 119, 122, 134, 135, 137, 149, 159, 166, 170; "Cultural Revolution" of, 165; death of, 167
Kasai, DRC, 45
Kasama District, 134, 149–50
Kasomo, Leah, 90
Kasomo Village, 91, 102, 106, 111, 127
Kasutu, 128
Katanga, DRC, 26, 72, 73, 136
Katilungu, Lawrence, 84, 126
Katongo, 29, 30, 31
Kaunda, David, 52, 53–54, 56, 66, 84, 101, 121, 156
Kaunda, Helen Nyirenda, 53, 54, 120, 121, 156
Kaunda, Kenneth, 66, 84, 94, 119, 122, 124, 138–39, 141–42, 157, 174–75, 199–200; arrest of, 122, 123; black book of, 128; denial of spiritual forces, 167; disappointment in/downfall of, 20, 23–24, 163, 192, 194–95, 196, 197; evil embodied in, 193–94; messianic image of, 123, 127–28, 137, 162–63; as prophet, 129, 165; refusal to accept life presidency, 161; as skilled musician, 128; slogan "God in heaven, Kaunda on earth," 155, 159, 167, 177; and UNIP–Lumpa Church

medals, Catholic, 104, 105
media: Christian radio and TV, 196, 198;
    political vs. spiritual broadcasts, 176;
    proscribed/banned, 165–66, 195
medical resources, 50, 186
medicine: to combat spirits/witchcraft,
    60, 61, 63, 260; for growing gardens/
    guarding people, 106; HIV, 186, 189;
    of Jesus, 53; pouches, 97; to protect
    against bullets, 141
Meebelo, Henry S., 20, 165, 173, 175
Merik, 76
meteorite, 45
mfuba, 35, 56, 63, 66, 260
Mfula, Mercy, 145–46
mfumu, 33, 213n23, 260
Mfumu, Mushili, 38
mfumu sha kale, 47, 260
mfumu ya mipashi, 260
Mhusambazi, Elfrida, 184, 186, 188, 189
mikishi, 45, 260
mikowa, 67
milemba trees, 112
Milingo, Emmanuel, 23, 159, 175, 183, 200;
    exorcisms/healing ministry of, 167–71,
    173, 178; recall of, 176, 177; spiritual
    vocabulary of, 169
military: compulsory service, 182;
    operations in Lumpa-UNIP conflict,
    145–51, 161
millenarianism, 73, 79, 85–88, 117, 139, 196
millet, 44, 213n16
mine workers. *See* workers
Mineworkers Union of Zambi (MUZ),
    171, 172
mining industry, 19–20, 22, 69, 73–74;
    companies as agents of Satan, 23;
    European exploitation of, 69–70;
    growth in Zambia, 74, 226n17; towns,
    22–23, 73, 85, 109. *See also* workers
Ministry of Development Planning and
    National Guidance, 165
minkisi, 34
mipashi, 33, 34, 260; as Holy Spirit, 56;
    conversion into, 44; nature spirits
    and, 35

miracles, 8, 152, 178, 189, 200
misfortune, 11, 13, 36, 39, 48, 96–97
missionaries, 4, 17, 52–59; as agents of
    colonialism, 14; Christian ideas
    of, 4, 5, 11, 57, 108; Christianity of
    challenged, 23; claims of spiritual
    powers by, 5; competition/rivalries
    among, 51, 58–59, 104–8; and
    construction of moral civil society, 12;
    denial of spirits/witches, 59, 200; and
    knowledge of tribal customs, 17–18;
    as vampires/witches, 59
misumba, 137, 151, 152
Miyanda, Godfrey, 195
MMD. *See* Movement for Multiparty
    Democracy
Modern Industry and the African (Davis),
    71, 81–82
modernity, 21, 74, 78, 167; Christian, 107;
    expectations of, 2–3, 13, 19, 179;
    Western, 10
Mokambo, 151
monotheism, 56
moon, 188
Moore, Henrietta L., 21
Moore, Reginald J. B., 83
morality: Christian, 12, 56, 57, 95, 104,
    117–18, 123, 174, 182, 190, 191, 198;
    personal, 180, 192; public, 13, 99, 157,
    162, 165–66, 167, 172
Morris, Colin, 160, 163
mortality, human, 38
Moses, 12, 123, 151, 152
mothers: celestial, 29, 41, 95; Lumpa
    Church support of, 99; of *mbusa*
    relics, 40; ties with sons, 31
"mother-earth" spirit, 38
Moto Moto. *See* Dupont, Joseph
Movement for Multiparty Democracy
    (MMD), 171, 194–96
movements: division of into political and
    religious, 117; prophetic, 20, 52,
    93–94, 109; political, 3–4, 199, 201;
    religious/spiritual, 3–4, 9, 14, 20, 23,
    71, 85. *See also specific movements*
mpanga, 39

Mpezeni, 42
Mpika District, 134, 149
Mubanga (chief), 140
Muchapi, 62
Muchime, 43
Mudimbe, V. Y., 27
Mufilira, 192
Mufukwa, Peter, 76, 77
Mufulira, Zambia, 69, 101
muka benya, 36
Mukasa, Mumbi, 29, 30
mukishiI, 260
Mukulumpe, 29–31, 95
Mukungule (chief), 109
Mukuni Village, 97–98
Mulanga Mission, 58, 136, 138, 142, 149
Mulenga, Dixon "Moses," 151–52
Mulenga, Geoffrey, 124
Mulenga, Shame, 127
Mulilansolo Mission, 58, 124
Mulimine, Malekeni, 170
Mulobola Mission, 58
mulopwe, 32, 33, 94–95, 260
muloshi, 259
mulumbi, 45
Mulungushi, Zambia: conference, 127, 128, 161, 162–63
Mulungushi Rock, 161
mulwani, 57, 105, 149
Mumba, Joseph, 107
Mumba, Nevers, 178–79, 182, 184, 185, 189, 196, 197
Mumba, Stephen, 175, 195
Mumbwa, 151
Mundia, Nalimuno, 175
muntu, 149
munyama, 259
mupashi, 260
murder, 31, 38, 43, 47, 57
Musase, Ernest, 192
Mushindo, Paul B., 18–19, 56, 91, 107, 156
Muslims, 179, 195
Musole, Joseph, 166, 174
Musonda, P., 192
musumba, 90, 137, 138, 140, 243n23, 260
Mususu, Bishop, 196–97

Mutale, Elias, 168
Mutende, 81
muti, 60, 63, 260
Muwamba, Ernest, 74
Muwamba, Isaac, 74, 76, 77, 78
Muyombe (chief), 150
MUZ. See Mineworkers Union of Zambia
Mwalule, 32, 37, 42, 48, 64, 65, 260; desecration of, 112; funeral procession to, 44
Mwalwanda, Clive, 192
Mwamba, 26, 41, 44, 45, 47; Joseph Dupont as, 50, 53
Mwambula, Lefati, 76, 78–79
Mwana Lesa, 64, 71, 72, 77, 79, 153
Mwanawasa, Levy, 197
Mwansakabinga, 38
Mwape, Ronald, 194
Mwase, 30 fig. 1.2, 31–32, 34, 39, 47, 48, 64
mwavi poison ordeal, 38–39, 61, 62, 64, 260
Mwenzo Mission, 53, 54
Mwenzo Welfare Association, 75, 84
Mwinilunga, 141
myths: and history, 8, 20, 27, 89; vampire, 119

nachimbusa, 40, 99
Nachituti, 25
narratives: Christian, 12, 17, 114, 117, 123, 151–52, 201; burning bush, 97–98; historical, 17, 18, 22, 28–29
National AIDS Council, 190
national anthems: South African, 15; Zambian, 159
National Archives of Zambia (NAZ), 18
National Christian Coalition, 196
National Citizens Coalition, 196
nationalism/nationalists, 15, 20, 23, 110, 201; African organized movement, 84–85, 87; as Christian movement, 117, 130; exclusionary nature of, 21; history of movement, 114–18; as "Kaunda's people," 128; Lumpa movement and, 93–94, 112; and mobilization of the masses, 124; moralities and ideologies of, 115; rallying cry of, 114;

as representatives of God's will, 128, 129, 155; similarities between Lumpa movement, Watchtower, and, 117, 129–30; Watchtower and, 73; welfare societies seeds of, 87

National Mirror, 22, 168, 173–74, 178, 193–94

National Monuments Commission, 159

Native Authority court, 107

Native Literature Committee, 81

Native Schools Ordinance, 77

Native Treasury, 65

Native Welfare Society, 74, 78

nature spirits, 2, 7, 15, 27, 35–41, 45, 47, 56, 60, 70, 115: reference to sky, 34; shrines to, 42, 45. *See also* Lesa; ngulu

navel, 25, 46 fig. 1.3

NAZ (National Archives of Zambia), 18

Nchanga mine, 84

Ndola, Zambia, 74, 101, 174

Ndola Welfare Society, 82

necklacing, 118

New Jerusalem, 12, 96, 103–4, 111, 158, 163; biblical message of, 167

New Jerusalem Church, 154

Ngandu, Elizabeth, 151

Ngandu, Mulenga Lubusha, 89–90. *See also* Lenshina, Alice

Ngandu, Victor, 149

nganga, 61. *See also* Luchele Ng'anga

Ngoni peoples, 28, 42, 43, 44, 70

ngulu, 34, 35, 37, 47, 66, 214n31, 260; benevolent, 39; hunting and, 45; name of, 39; possession by, 39, 59, 60, 190; and protection from witches, 60; shrines of, 42, 45. *See also* nature spirits

Nigeria, 5, 15

Nimrod, 75–76

Nkana mine, 69, 83, 84

Nkhoma, Francis, 173–74

Nkhweto (chief), 44, 64–65, 112; insobriety of, 65

Nkole, 29, 30, 31, 32, 34, 40, 41, 44, 47, 64

Nkolemfu (chief), 109

Nkonde, Paison, 139–40

Nkongolo, 33

"Nkosi Sikilel' iAfrica," 15

Nkula, 41, 42, 44, 66–67, 107, 111; chieftancy as Lumpa Church members, 91; confrontation at Sione, 111; opposition to White Fathers, 50, 65–66; sister of, 120

Nkulukusa, Anna, 79

Nkumbula, Harry, 84, 116, 122, 123, 134

Nkwale, Gipson, 89

North America, 15

Northern News, 148

Northern Rhodesia, 94, 114, 118: governor of, 95; Watchtower in, 75, 79–80; focus on witchcraft accusations, 62; Witchcraft Ordinance of, 11

Northern Rhodesia Legislative Council, 83–84, 85

Northern Rhodesia Regiment (NRR), 69, 146–47, 148, 150, 157

Northmead Assemblies of God, 182, 186

Northwest University, 179

NRR. *See* Northern Rhodesia Regiment

nsengo, 63, 97, 260

ntambalukuta, 128, 165

Nyakyusa peoples, 28

Nyamwezi, 42, 43

Nyasaland, 55, 94, 114, 118

Nyerere, 163; Ujamaa of, 166

Nyirenda, George, 76

Nyirenda, Tom, 64, 71, 72

Oglethorpe, James C., 160

One Zambia, Many Histories (Gewald, Hinfelaar, and Macola), 21

Operation Born Again, 197

Operation Rescue Group for Ministry of Christ, 183, 191

orphanages, 186

Overtoun Institute, 53

Ovimbundu, 43

paganism, 18, 54, 55–56, 66, 188

Paishuko Village, 148

Paison Village, 148

pallbearers, 44
panshi (earth), 34
Papworth, John, 160
passion, 31, 32, 34; individualizes but
  enslaves, 28
Peel, J. D. Y., 5
Pentecostal churches: church services of,
  189–90; cultivating membership
  of, 185–86; in Nigeria, 5; effect on
  Zambian humanism, 13; gender
  dynamics in, 180; loyalty to founding
  figures of, 185; positions within, 185;
  proliferation of in Zambia, 16. *See
  also* Assemblies of God
Pentecostalism, 177, 180, 181–82; focus
  on witchcraft eradication, 188–91;
  growth of, 182–87; political role of,
  192; promoting of democratization,
  180; as "religious right," 179; spirits
  and, 11; youth fellowship groups, 182,
  183–84
Perrings, Charles, 78
Petauke, 151
Peter, Saint, 176
Phelps-Stokes commissioners, 57
Phillips, Llewen V., 81
Phiri, Bizeck J., 118
Phiri, Isabel Apawo, 181
physicians: theories of emotion, 10
Pig Clan, 45
Pilgrim's Progress, The (Bunyan), 56, 95
Pinto, Father, 37
PLO, 195
poisoning, 38–39, 43, 71
police, 143; attacks involving, 133, 140, 141,
  146–47, 149–50
Polish Communist Party, 172
politicians, 75, 112, 166, 173, 175, 191, 198;
  corrupt, 86, 197; prosperous, 166
politics: anticolonial, 4; dissent in, 21;
  evangelical influence on, 179;
  meaning of, 4; as "mission to heal,"
  196; multiparty, 181, 182, 192, 194, 197,
  198; postcolonial and invisible world,
  2–3; and religion, 25, 191; power of,
  18, 28, 64–65, 155; secularization of,

4, 78–87; spiritual, 4, 9, 50, 59; war as
  continuation of, 154; world, 74
polygamy, 54, 55, 99
Poro societies, 15
possession, spirit, 5, 11, 47; Bulumbu, 45;
  demon, 12, 14, 23, 168–71, 176, 178,
  191–92, 196; gendered, 10; good,
  39; by Holy Spirit, 190; movements
  concerned with, 168–71; by *ngulu*,
  39, 59, 60, 190; sexual component of,
  10, 169–70; women as agents/victims
  of, 39, 168, 169–70
potions, 38, 61
poverty, 20–21, 157–58
Powell, John, 175–76
prayers, 8, 60, 87, 128, 189, 190, 194:
  appropriate response of, 197; in
  battle, 142; before political meetings,
  135; as curses, 105; national, 118–19,
  194; prayer meetings, 101
prayer warriors, 178
preachers: certificates of authorization,
  77–78; Lumpa Church, 101–2;
  number of Jehovah's Witnesses, 85
Presbyterian Church, 50, 53, 54, 56
Preservation of Public Security Act, 145, 150
priests: church, 119, 169; tribal, 32, 65, 67
Princess Royal, 157
Pritchett, James A., 21
promised land, 123, 129, 151, 167
prophecy, 35, 39, 189
prophets, 22, 29, 64, 70; Bisa, 45;
  chiefs forced to work with, 64;
  in Christianity, 11, 52; mediation
  claims of, 47–48; migrant, 31; of
  Watchtower, 77; women as, 39,
  184–89
prosperity: as evidence of goodness, 189;
  evil obstruction to, 187–88, 198;
  individual, 187, 197; national, 197;
  new era of, 195–96; Pentecostal
  focus on, 180–83, 187–90, 195;
  righteousness defined by, 197
prosperity gospel, 1, 180, 187
prostitution, 166
Protestant ethic, 7, 180, 181

Protestants: Christian ideas of, 11, 13; and education key, 55; nonspiritual religion of, 2; publications, 51, 56, 57, 67; rivalry with Catholics, 50, 53–54, 58, 60, 61, 104–8; success measure of, 55
Provincial Operations Committee, 146–47
psychologists, 10
Pule, Dan, 182
Purpose-Driven Life, The (Warren), 187
pythons, 47

Queen: British, 127, 129 (*see also* Elizabeth, Queen); term, 23

railway, 74, 76, 77; workers' strike, 85
rain, 3, 15, 36, 67
Rain, D. S., 82
Rain, Sandy, 101, 110, 119
Ranganathan, M. A., 193–94
Ranger, Terence O., 3–4, 71, 115, 179–80
rape, 14, 60, 148
recordings, gramophone, 81
refugees, 131–32, 149, 150. *See also* detention camps
Regina, term, 23
relics, royal, 31, 37, 43, 66; capturing of, 37, 42, 65, 223n59; mother of the relics, 40; purification of, 63; replacement of with Lesa, 65; wives of the relics, 36, 37. *See also* babenye
religion: "African traditional," 2; Bemba, 27; defined, 1–2, 4, 164; false doctrines of, 51; millenarian, and anticolonial nationalism, 3; modernity and, 2; nonspiritual, 2; as politics, 25; and history, 27–28; as "social fact," 7; spiritual component of, 4–5; as superstition, 4, 27; symbolic study of, 5. *See also specific religions*
religious right, 179
Report of the Commission of Enquiry into the Lumpa Church, 20
Republican Party, 179
Reutter, Helmut, 179, 186, 187, 189, 192, 195
Reza. *See* Lesa

Rhodes, Cecil John, 18, 122
Rhodes-Livingstone Institute (RLI), 19, 70–71
Richards, Audrey I.: pioneer of colonial anthropology, 18; on Lenshina, 99; on religion, 27–28; study of Bemba peoples, 18–19; on chiefly rule, 51; on witches, 59, 60, 62, 63, 66
rituals/ceremonies: in burial of chiefs, 44; in burning witches, 39; chief's installation, 66–67; Christian, 5, 12, 51, 54, 67, 190, 201; fertility, 34, 36, 37, 47, 65; healing, 168; of Humanism, 160; hunting, 47; of Lenshina, 94, 95, 99, 141; focus on, 19; marriage, 96; national, 159, 165; purification, 64; of relic succession, 65; tribal, 10, 29, 34, 47, 65, 70, 81; womanhood initiation, 39–40, 99
rivers, 47
RLI. *See* Rhodes-Livingstone Institute
Roan Antelope mine, 85
Roberts, Andrew, 20, 33, 42, 92
Roman Catholic Church. *See* Catholics/Catholicism; White Fathers
Romans, 104, 105
Rosa Mission, 57
rosaries, 104, 105
Rosary Campaigns, 105
Rotberg, Robert I., 20, 115
Run to Win, 187
Russell Commission of Inquiry, 78, 79, 80, 83
Rutherford, Judge, 75, 81

safe houses, 151
Sahel, African, 15
Sakala, Willie, 174
salvation, 59, 107–8,195; on earth, 91, 96, 155, 191, 200; freedom and independence as, 116, 129; individual, 171, 187, 197–98; promised, 52, 62–63, 116, 121; separation of saving from, 181; from witchcraft, 62–63
Satan, 1, 2, 15, 51, 66, 67, 177; authorities/politicians associated with, 23, 86;

transition from socialist to capitalist, 181; tribal, 19, 21; working class of, 3, 73, 87, 184

Sokoni, John, 119, 122, 127

soldiers: bravery of, 28–29; child, 125–26, 142–43; manipulated by "big men," 14

Solidarity, 172

songs/singing: of Bemba, 106; beer-drinking, 127; of Lumpa choir, 102; political, 117, 124, 126–27, 130; spirit-inspired, 39; of husband and wife, 40. *See also* choirs; hymns

son of God, 64, 71, 153, 163, 169. *See also* Jesus Christ

Sontonga, Enoch, 159

sorghum, 213n16

Sorghum Clan, 32

South African Industrial and Commercial Workers Union, 74

Southern Rhodesia, 72, 94, 114, 118

Soweto, South Africa, 13

speaking in tongues. *See* glossolalia

spears, 138, 141, 142, 145, 146, 149–50

spiritual gifts, 106, 185, 189, 190, 198, 259

stabbers, the (*Muchime*), 43

staff of rule, 25, 26 fig. 1.1, 27, 32, 43

starvation/hunger, 131, 133, 149, 163–64

State House, 157, 193, 195

Stone, Vernon, 106, 108

stools, 27, 66

suicide, 37, 38

sun, 33, 41, 188, 213n17

Sunday schools, 54

superstition, 2, 4, 27, 71, 200

Swahili: land, 43; peoples, 42, 45, 53, 75

symbols, 8, 19, 93; of empire/authority, 120, 122; Lumpa, 93; national, 159–60, 165; social, 8; spirits as, 5, 6; Watchtower, 77

Tabwa peoples, 46

Tanganyika, 51, 125–26

Tanganyika, Lake, 45

Tanzania, 62, 160

taxation, 15, 18, 69, 75–78, 86, 88, 111, 116, 124

Taylor, John V., 86, 92

tear gas, 147, 247n91

teachers: in ANC, 119, 121; in church structure, 185; dismissal of, 119–20; killing of, 148; in Lumpa Church, 101; mission, 53–60, 91; nonpayment of, 101; schooled, 59, 106, 121, 133; underground movement of, 119–22, 129–30, 155, 159

technology, modern, 74; imbued with spirits, 77

têkele, 116

televangelism, 193

temple, Lumpa, 96–97, 97 fig. 4.1, 260

Termination of Pregnancy Act, 173

termite mound, 32, 35, 36, 40; "church of the ancestors," 35

thunder, 38

Times of Zambia, 166, 172, 174, 176

Tonga peoples, 19

Tongnaab deity, 15

trade unions, 21, 69, 73, 74, 83–85, 87–88, 126, 158; against federation, 118–19; autonomy from UNIP, 171–72; incorporation of, 171; Polish, 172. *See also* workers: opposition/strikes of

trances, 10, 39, 45

Trans-Africa Theological Bible College, 179, 189

translation: of Bible and Christian terms and texts, 38, 56, 57, 92, 106, 116; transformative power of, 4

trees: ancestral spirits found in, 47; bark of, 36; figurines of, 39–40; *milemba*, 112; *museshi*, 96, 97 fig. 4.1; planted for coronation, 120; at White Fathers mission, 59

tribalism, cleansing of, 130, 158

Trinity Broadcasting Network, 182

Tshombe, Moïse, 151

Tswana people, 55

tulonde (hoes), 97

tulubi, 45

tumpa, 162

Turner, Victor, 19

of, 75, 78–79; literature/pamphlets of, 70, 75, 76, 77, 79, 80, 81, 82, 85, 198
water, 99
waterfalls, 37, 47
water monitor, 34
wealth, 2, 13, 27, 34, 41, 48, 181–87, 192, 197, 200; promises of, 23–24, 43–44
"We Are the Stone-Throwers!" (song), 126
Weber, Max, 7
Welensky, Roy, 129, 136, 137
welfare associations, 73, 74, 75, 76, 77, 78, 80, 82–83, 115; seeds of democratic nationalism, 87
whimpers, rhymthic, 35
White, Luise, 5–6, 7, 71
White Fathers: 52–53, 59, 156; crusade against Lenshina, 105–6, 110; lack of concern with "civilizing mission," 55; number of schools, 55, 57; opening of missions, 50; prohibition against witchcraft cleansing, 63; scholars of, 102; surveys taken by, 17; translation and publishing by, 57–58; as witches and vampires, 66, 67. See also Catholics
widows, 99
Wilson, Godfrey, 8, 19; on Nyakyusa, 28
Wilson, Monica H., 19
wind, evil, 38
witchcraft: accusations of, 60, 61, 62; cleansers, 22, 59–63, 70 (see also Bamuchape); compensation for, 43; conquerors of, 10; conversion from, 63; eradicating influence of, 23; within family and community, 10, 188; jealousy and anger link to, 34, 189; Lenshina's/Lumpa Church's quest to abolish, 90, 95, 96, 104; modernity and, 3; of Mwase, 34; Pentecostal focus on eradication of, 188–91; sin identified with, 49, 52, 56–57, 67, 94–99, 103, 112, 187, 201; women as agents of, 39–40. See also witches
Witchcraft Ordinance (1914): 11, 59, 61, 66, 107

witchdoctors, 170
witches, 115: apartheid-era, 15; associations of, 38, 39; "boiling water test" for, 60; burning of, 59; in Christianity, 11; Christians as, 50–68; confession as, 57, 61; drowning of, 71, 72; eradication of, 52 (see also Bamuchape); identifying, 61; killing of, 39, 59; manipulation of evil by, 9; missionaries as, 59; refusal to acknowledge, 59. See also witchcraft
wives: head, 36, 44, 213n18; husbands and, 40; of the land, 36; of Mwamba, 45; of the relic, 36, 37; submissive, 40
women: as agents/victims of possession, 39–40, 168; branches of ANC, 121; church leadership roles of, 180; desires inspired by, 32; as heroines, 25, 31, 94, 259; engagement of with Christianity, 4, 17; as ignorant, 109; Lumpa movement as advocate for, 99; magical/spiritual powers/emotions of, 25, 39–40, 48; as marginalized/vulnerable group of society, 21, 23, 94; as prophets, 39; puberty ceremony of, 39–40, 99; as targets of violence, 14, 165
Word of God, 192. See also Bible
workers, 6, 22, 51, 55, 70, 74; mission, 50, 54 (see also teachers); numbers of, 74; opposition/strikes of, 23, 69, 76, 78–85, 119, 166, 171–73; recruitment of, 18, 54, 74; representation of, 82–94; self-employed, 84; sex, 166, 190; unions of, 74, 83–85, 87–88, 118–19, 171–72; wages of, 69, 79, 86, 88, 102, 171, 172; Watchtower movement of, 72
World War I, 75, 89
World War II, 81, 84, 115
writing, invisible powers of, 77–78

Yogi, Maharashi Mahesh, 194
Young, Robert, 64

Zaire. See also Democratic Republic of Congo, 13, 20, 165, 195

Zambia, 9: bankrupt, 186; British withdrawal from, 157; celebration of independence, 157; as Christian nation, 192–93, 195; creation of, 122–29; dress code of, 165; major church bodies of, 168, 173; map of, xii; military attack of, 170; symbols of, 159–60, 165; war of independence, 132; written history of, 17, 18
Zambia African National Congress (ZANC), 94, 114–15, 122–23
Zambia Congress of Trade Unions (ZCTU), 171
Zambia Elections Monitoring Coordinating Committee, 194
Zambia Episcopal Conference (ZEC), 168, 176

Zambia Evangelical Association, 170
Zambia Fellowship of Evangelical Students, 185–86
Zambian Apostolic Faith Mission, 179
Zambian Humanism: Some Major Spiritual and Economic Challenges (Zulu), 164
Zambia Shall Be Saved, 196
ZANC. See Zambia African National Congress
ZCTU. See Zambia Congress of Trade Unions
ZEC. See Zambia Episcopal Conference
Zimbabwe, 18, 169
Zion. See Sione
Zulu, A. G. (Grey), 138, 166